AF361580

Love Seeking Understanding

Love Seeking Understanding

Aquinas, Balthasar, and the Renewal of Sapiential Theology

Edited by Michael Altenburger
and Jacob W. Wood

Foreword by Matthew Levering

Afterword by Michael Waldstein

The Catholic University of America Press
Washington, D.C.

Chapter 7 is was previously published in French in Emmanuel Durand, OP,
Dieu Trinité: Communion et transformation (Paris: Éditions du Cerf, 2016),
as "Où et comment le Dieu Trinité est-il révélé dans la vie de Jésus?"
and is used with permission.

The paper used in this publication meets the requirements of American National
Standards for Information Science—Permanence of Paper for
Printed Library materials, ANSI Z39.48–1992.

∞

Cataloging-in-Publication Data is available from the Library of Congress
ISBN: 978-0-8132-3830-2
eISBN: 978-0-8132-3831-9

Contents

Abbreviations

Albert the Great

Editions

Borgnet | Albert the Great. *Opera Omnia.* 38 vols. Edited by Auguste Borgnet, Jacques Echard, and Jacques Quétif. 38 vols. Paris: Vivès, 1890–99.

Col. | Albert the Great. *Opera Omnia. Editio Coloniensis.* Edited by Bernhard Geyer et al. 41 vols. Münster: Aschendorff, 1951–.

Works

Super de div. nom. | *Super Dionysium De divinis nominibus. Col.* 37.1.

Super Sent. | *Commentarium in IV libros Sententiarum.* Borgnet 25–30.

Augustine

Abbreviations for the works of the Augustine will follow the conventions of the *Augustinus-Lexikon,* ed. Cornelius Mayer et al. Basel: Schwabe, 1986–Present.

Bonaventure

Editions

Quaracchi | Bonaventure. *Opera Omnia.* 10 vols. Rome: Quaracchi, Collegium S. Bonaventurae, 1882–1902.

Works

Super Sent. | *Commentaria in quatuor libros sententiarum.* Quaracchi 1–4.

Hans Urs von Balthasar

Other works of von Balthasar will be cited individually by the contributors.

A | *Apokalypse der deutschen Seele: Studien zu einer Lehre von letzen Haltunge.* 3 vols. Salzburg: Anton Pustet, 1937–39.

C | *Convergences: To the Source of Christian Mystery.* San Francisco: Ignatius Press, 1993. Original: *Einfaltungen.* Koesel, Munich, 1969.

CL	*Cosmic Liturgy: The Universe According to Maximus the Confessor.* San Francisco: Ignatius Press, 2003. Origïnal: *Kosmische Liturgie; Maximus der Bekenner.* Herder: Freiburg im Breisgau, 1941.
CS	*The Christian State of Life.* San Francisco: Ignatius Press, 1983. Original: *Christlicher Stand.* Einsiedeln: Johannes Verlag, 1956.
DWH	*Dare We Hope "That All Men be Saved?" With a Short Discourse on Hell.* 2nd ed. San Francisco: Ignatius Press, 2014. Original: *Was dürfen wir hoffen; Kleiner Diskurs über die Hölle; Apokatastasis: Gastvorlesung an der Theologischen Fakultät Trier am 18 April 1988.* Einsiedeln: Johannes Verlag, 1989.
EG	*Engagement with God: The Drama of Christian Discipleship.* San Francisco: Ignatius Press, 2008. Original: *Dans l'engagement de Dieu.* Paris: Apostolat des Editions, 1972.
ET (I-V)	*Explorations in Theology.* 5 vols. San Francisco: Ignatius Press, 1989–2014. Original: *Skizzen zur Theologie.* 5 vols. Einsiedeln: Johannes Verlag, 1960–1986.
EP	*Epilogue.* San Francisco: Ignatius Press, 2004. Original: *Epilog.* Einsiedeln: Johannes Verlag, 1987.
GL (I-VII)	*The Glory of the Lord: A Theological Aesthetics.* 7 vols. San Francisco: Ignatius Press, 1983–1991. Original: *Herrlichkeit: eine theologische Ästhetik.* 7 vols. Einsiedeln: Johannes Verlag, 1961–1969.
HW	*Heart of the World.* San Francisco: Ignatius Press, 1987. Original: Das Herz der Welt. Zürich: Im Verlag der Arche, 1945.
KB	*The Theology of Karl Barth: Exposition and Interpretation.* San Francisco: Ignatius Press, 1992. Original: *Karl Barth. Darstellung und Deutung seiner Theologie.* Hegner, Köln 1951.
LAC	*Love Alone Is Credible.* San Francisco: Ignatius Press, 2004. Original: *Glaubhaft ist nur Liebe.* Einsiedeln: Johannes Verlag, 1963.
MCW	*The Moment of Christian Witness.* San Francisco: Ignatius Press, 1994. Original: *Cordula oder der Ernstfall.* Einsiedeln: Johannes Verlag, 1987.
MP	*Mysterium Paschale: The Mystery of Easter.* Grand Rapids, MI: Eerdmans, 1990. Original: "Mysterium Paschale." In *Mysterium Salutis,* vol. 3, *Das Christusereignis,* 133–326. Einsiedeln: Johannes Verlag, 1969.
MW	*My Work: In Retrospect.* San Francisco: Ignatius Press, 1993. Original: *Mein Werke—Durchblicke.* Einsiedeln: Johannes Verlag, 1990.
OP	*The Office of Peter and the Structure of the Church.* San Francisco: Ignatius Press, 1986. Original: *Der antirömische Affekt.* Freiburg im Breisgau: Herder, 1974.

OSF *Origen: Spirit and Fire: A Thematic Anthology of His Writings.* Washington, DsC: The Catholic University of America Press, 1984. Original: *Origenes—Geist und Feuer: ein Aufbau aus seinen Schriften.* Salzburg: Otto Müller Verlag, 1938.

PM *Parole et Mystère chez Origène.* Paris: Cerf, 1957.

PR *Prayer.* San Francisco: Ignatius Press, 1986. Original: *Das betrachtende Gebet.* Einsiedeln: Johannes Verlag, 1955.

PT *Presence and Thought: Essay on the Religious Philosophy of Gregory of Nyssa.* San Francisco: Ignatius Press, 1995. Original: *Présence et pensée; essai sur la philosophie religieuse de Grégoire de Nysse.* Paris: G. Beauchesne et ses fils, 1942.

RB *Razing the Bastions: On the Church in This Age.* San Francisco: Ignatius Press, 1993. Original: *Schleifung der Bastionen: von der Kirche in dieser Zeit.* Einsiedeln: Johannes Verlag, 1954.

RG *Romano Guardini: Reform from the Source.* San Francisco: Ignatius Press, 2010. Original: *Romano Guardini: Reform aus dem Ursprung.* Einsiedeln: Johannes Verlag, 1995.

TA *A Theological Anthropology.* New York: Sheed and Ward, 1967. Original: *Das Ganze im Fragment; Aspekte der Geschichtstheologie.* Einsiedeln: Benzinger, 1963.

TD (I-V) *Theo-Drama: Theological Dramatic Theory.* 5 vols. San Francisco: Ignatius Press, 1988–1998. Original: *Theodramatik.* 5 vols. Einsiedeln: Johannes Verlag, 1973–1983.

TH *A Theology of History.* San Francisco: Ignatius Press, 1994. Original: *Theologie der Geschichte: ein Grundriss: neue Fassung.* Einsiedeln: Johannes Verlag, 1959.

THL *The Theology of Henri de Lubac: An Overview.* San Francisco: Ignatius Press, 1991. Original: *Henri de Lubac: sein organisches Lebenswerk.* Einsiedeln: Johannes Verlag, 1976.

TL (I-III) *Theo-Logic: Theological Logical Theory.* 3 vols. San Francisco: Ignatius Press, 2001–2013. Original: *Theologik.* 3 vols. Einsiedeln: Johannes Verlag, 1985–1987.

TS *Truth Is Symphonic: Aspects of Christian Pluralism.* San Francisco: Ignatius Press, 1987. Original: *Die Wahrheit ist symphonisch.* Einsiedeln: Johnnes Verlag, 1972.

TSiS *Two Sisters in the Spirit: Therese of Lisieux and Elizabeth of the Trinity.* San Francisco: Ignatius Press, 1992. Original: *Schwestern im Geist: Thesere von Lisieux und Elisabeth von Dijon.* Einsiedeln: Johannes Verlag, 1970.

Thomas Aquinas

English translations vary widely; those used are indicated by the contributors. Below are the Latin editions of reference.

Editions

Leon.	*Opera Omnia.* 50 vols. Rome/Paris: Commissio Leonina, 1882–.

Works

Comp. Theol.	*Compendium theologiae. Leon.* 42:5–205.
De an.	*Quaestiones disputatae de anima. Leon.* 24.1.
De ent.	*De ente et essentia. Leon.* 43:315–81.
De malo	*Quaestiones disputatae de malo. Leon.* 23.
De pot.	*Quaestiones disputatae de potentia.* In *Quaestiones disputatae.* Vol. 2, 1–276. 10th ed. Edited by P. M. Pession. Turin: Marietti, 1965.
De un. Verb.	*Quaestio disputata de unione verbi incarnati. Quaestio disputata 'De unione verbi incarnati'*, 18–102. Edited by W. Senner et al. Stuttgart: Fromann-Holzboog, 2011.
De ver.	*Quasetiones disputatae de Veritate. Leon.* 22.
In Symb. Ap.	*In Symbolum Apostolorum.* In *Opuscula theologica.* Vol. 2, 191–217. 2nd ed. Edited by R. M. Spiazzi. Turin: Marietti, 1953.
Resp. 108	*Responsio ad magistrum Ioannem de Vercellis de 108 articulis. Leon.* 42:259–94.
SCG	*Summa contra Gentiles. Editio Leonina Manualis.* Rome: Apud Sedem Commissionis Leoninae, 1934.
Sent. De an	*Sentencia libri De anima. Leon.* 45.1.
ST	*Summa theologiae. Leon.* 4–12.
Super I Cor.	*Super Primam epistolam ad Corinthios lectura.* In *Super Epistolas S. Pauli lectura.* Vol. 1, 233–429. Edited by R. Cai. 8th ed. Turin: Marietti, 1953.
Super II Cor.	*Super Secundam epistolam ad Corinthios lectura.* In *Super Epistolas S. Pauli lectura.* Vol. 1, 437–561. Edited by R. Cai. 8th ed. Turin: Marietti, 1953.
Super De div. nom.	*In librum Beati Dionysii De divinis nominibus expositio.* Edited by C. Pera, P. Caramello, and C. Mazzantini. Turin: Marietti, 1950.
Super Eph.	*Super Epistolam ad Ephesios lectura.* In *Super Epistolas S. Pauli lectura.* Vol. 2, 1–87. Edited by R. Cai. 8th ed. Turin: Marietti, 1953.

Super Ethic.	*Sententia libri Ethicorum. Leon.* 47.
Super Heb.	*Super Epistolam ad Hebraeos lectura.* In *Super Epistolas S. Pauli lectura.* Vol. 2, 335–506. Edited by R. Cai. 8th ed. Turin: Marietti, 1953.
Super Ioh.	*Super Evangelium S. Ioannis lectura.* 6th ed. Edited by R. Cai. Turin: Marietti, 1972.
Super Meta.	*In duodecim libros Metaphysicorum Aristotelis expositio.* 2nd ed. Edited by M. R. Cathala and R. M. Spiazzi. Turin: Marietti, 1971.
Super Rom.	*Super Epistolam ad Romanos lectura.* In *Super Epistolas S. Pauli lectura.* Vol. 1, 1–230. Edited by R. Cai. 8th ed. Turin: Marietti, 1953.
Super Sent.	Books 1–2: *Scriptum Super libros Sententiarum.* Vols. 1–2. Edited by Pierre Mandonnet. Paris: Lethielleux, 1929. Books 3 and 4, Distinctions 1–22: *Scriptum Super libros Sententiarum.* Vols. 3–4. Edited by M. F. Moos. Paris: Lethielleux, 1947–1956. Book 4, Distinctions 23–50: *Opera Omnia*, vol. 7, pt. 2, 872–1259. Parma: Typis Petri Fiaccadori, 1858.
Super de Trin.	*Super Boetium De Trinitate. Leon.* 50:1–230.

Other Abbreviations

CCCM	*Corpus Christianorum Continuatio Mediaevalis*
DH	*Enchiridion Symbolorum: A Compendium of Creeds, Definitions, and Declarations of the Catholic Church.* 43rd ed. Edited by Peter Hünermann. Translated by Robert Fastiggi and Anne Englund Nash. San Francisco: Ignatius Press, 2012.
PL	*Patrologia Latina*

Healing a Family Quarrel

MATTHEW LEVERING

THIS VOLUME'S ENGAGEMENT between Thomists and Balthasarians comes at a much-needed time. Thomists today have become inheritors of neoscholastic theology, while Balthasarians are the main inheritors of the original *Ressourcement* movement (or *nouvelle théologie*).[1] By framing things in this way, I have in mind a twofold problem, which this excellent volume will go some way toward solving, God willing. First, Thomists and Balthasarians, as described above, have trouble agreeing that the other is doing real theology, an unresolved issue stemming from debates that occurred in the 1940s and 1950s. Second, Thomists and Balthasarians tend to see few deficiencies in their own school of theology, and they take offense to any dissenting notes posed by the other side. The result is that some Thomists and Balthasarians are led to think that if the other side were wiped from the face of the earth, this would be a good thing. While the two sides fight, the Rahnerian-liberationist camp of progressive theologians has enjoyed a resurgence and now sometimes seems to be the most likely way for the church to achieve doctrinal "unity," via a new understanding of dogma and Magisterial teaching that both Thomists and Balthasarians rightly oppose.[2]

---

1. For the view that the *nouvelle théologie* was Modernist (though in a new context and in a new way, avoiding some weaknesses of the original Modernism), see Gerard Loughlin, "*Nouvelle Théologie*: A Return to Modernism," in *Ressourcement: A Movement for Renewal in Twentieth-Century Catholic Theology*, ed. Gabriel Flynn and Paul D. Murray (Oxford: Oxford University Press, 2012), 36–50. For Loughlin, "Modernism" in its *nouvelle théologie* form is simply a salutary response to "neo-scholastic rationalism" (*Ressourcement*, 50). To my mind, this is mistaken both with respect to neoscholastic theology and with respect to the *nouvelle théologie*.

2. I have discussed this elsewhere, for example, in *Engaging the Doctrine of Revelation: The Mediation of the Gospel through Church and Scripture* (Grand Rapids, MI: Baker Academic, 2013). The key moves are made by Karl Rahner, SJ, and Edward Schillebeeckx, OP, in their reformulations of the meaning of dogma. See also Thomas Joseph White, OP's discussion of Schillebeeckx in his *The Incarnate Lord: A Thomistic Study in Christology* (Washington, DC: The Catholic University of America Press, 2015).

To put it this way is to risk confusing matters, because many nuances will need to be added. After all, one can perceive significant overlap today between Thomists and Balthasarians. I have always considered myself to be a *Ressourcement* Thomist since I draw amply from both wells, having read Balthasar as a master's student and Aquinas in my doctoral study. Many other contemporary theologians likewise draw upon both Thomism and *Ressourcement*, and, indeed, Balthasar drew in notable ways upon Aquinas[3]—as did numerous other *Ressourcement* theologians. Furthermore, Balthasar's relationship to the *nouvelle théologie* can be contested.[4] Yet, it seems to me that the ongoing relationship between Thomists and Balthasarians will perhaps benefit from reflecting on the problem in sharpened terms.[5]

In order to get at the problem, therefore, let me begin with an emblematic and well-known writing from the 1940s debate over the nature of theology, namely, Réginald Garrigou-Lagrange's 1946 *Angelicum* article "La nouvelle théologie où va-t-elle?" By way of context, the Dominicans who oversaw the journal of what would become the Pontifical University of St. Thomas Aquinas, *Angelicum*, differed from those who oversaw the journal of the Toulouse Dominicans, *Revue Thomiste*, with the former advocating a sharper tone toward the nascent *Ressourcement* movement.[6] Both periodicals, however, warned consistently that the "new" way of thinking about dogmatic formulations was a mistake, with the *Revue Thomiste* articles voicing particular concerns that the opposition to neoscholastic theology apparent in the texts of the Fourvière Jesuits overseeing the series *Sources Chrétienne* and *Théologie* (notably Jean Daniélou and Henri de Lubac) would place the scientific status of theology in danger. Although it is not reflected in the texts themselves, some conservative Thomists also had political concerns, believing that *Ressourcement* theologians' tendency to embrace the European center-left was

---

3. See James J. Buckley, "Balthasar's Use of the Theology of Aquinas," *The Thomist* 59 (1995): 517–45; see also the efforts of Michele M. Schumacher, *A Trinitarian Anthropology: Adrienne von Speyr and Hans Urs von Balthasar in Dialogue with Thomas Aquinas* (Washington, DC: The Catholic University of America Press, 2014).

4. See Edward T. Oakes, SJ, "Balthasar and *Ressourcement*: An Ambiguous Relationship," in *Ressourcement*, 278–88.

5. For noteworthy irenic studies, see Christopher Ruddy, "*Ressourcement* and the *Enduring* Legacy of Post-Tridentine Theology," in *Ressourcement*, 185–201; Aidan Nichols, OP, "Thomism and the Nouvelle Théologie," *The Thomist* 64 (2000): 1–19.

6. The core texts written by the Dominicans at the *Revue Thomiste*, along with the text of the response written by the Jesuits of Fourvière, can be found in Raymond-Léopold Bruckberger, OP, Michel Labourdette, OP, and Marie-Joseph Nicolas, OP, *Dialogue théologique: Pièeces du débat entre "La Revue Thomiste" d'une part et les R. R. P. P. de Lubac, Daniélou, Bouillard, Fessard, von Balthasar, SJ, d'autre part* (Saint-Maximin: Les Arcades, 1947).

unwise and bound to cause trouble for the church.[7] At the same time, the embrace of the political right also had much to answer for due to Vichy, which at least in part can be understood in the context of the politics of the Third Republic, including the history of anti-clericalism and the Dreyfus Case.[8]

In "La nouvelle théologie où va-t-elle?," Garrigou-Lagrange focuses on challenging some statements made by Henri Bouillard, Maurice Blondel, Gaston Fessard, de Lubac, and some unpublished anonymous manuscripts that appear to come from the perspective of Pierre Teilhard de Chardin.[9] While I think his concerns about the statements that he quotes are often justified, his conclusions are much too sharply drawn.[10] For example, he takes strong issue with the fact that leading representatives of the *nouvelle théologie* stated "that neo-Thomism and the decisions of the Biblical Commission are 'a guardrail but not an answer.'"[11] In response, defending Thomism, Gar-

---

7. For the political dimension of the *nouvelle théologie*, see Jon Kirwan, *An Avant-Garde Theological Generation: The* Nouvelle Théologie *and the French Crisis of Modernity* (Oxford: Oxford University Press, 2018); Peter J. Bernardi, SJ, *Maurice Blondel, Social Catholicism, and Action Française: The Clash over the Church's Role in Society during the Modernist Era* (Washington, DC: The Catholic University of America Press, 2008).

8. In Germany, some Thomists and some *Ressourcement* theologians had supported the Nazis, with Vichy being supported by some French Thomists (and many French bishops) and generally opposed by French *Ressourcement* theologians. Quick schematization should be avoided, however. For example, a conservative Thomist was the chaplain general for the French Resistance. I note that prior to 1946, almost all Catholic theologians, on both sides, held views about the Jewish people that the Catholic Church since Vatican II has repudiated. For more discussion of this point, see my *Engaging the Doctrine of Israel: A Christian Israelology in Dialogue with Ongoing Judaism* (Eugene, OR: Cascade, forthcoming).

9. For further background, see the essays in *Surnaturel: A Controversy at the Heart of Twentieth-Century Thomistic Thought*, ed. Serge-Thomas Bonino, OP, trans. Robert Williams, trans. revised by Matthew Levering (Ave Maria, FL: Sapientia Press, 2009).

10. For a helpful exposition and defense of Bouillard's overall project, see James Hanvey, SJ, "Henri Bouillard: The Freedom of Faith," in *Ressourcement*, 263–77. For Blondel, see Robert C. Koerpel, *Maurice Blondel: Transforming Catholic Tradition* (Notre Dame, IN: University of Notre Dame Press, 2018). Balthasar felt free to criticize both Blondel and, especially, Teilhard de Chardin.

11. Réginald Garrigou-Lagrange, OP, "Where Is the New Theology Leading Us?" trans. Suzanne M. Rini, *Josephinum Journal of Theology* 18 (2011): 63–78, at 69. The Biblical Commission's decisions had to do, for instance, with whether Moses authored the Pentateuch, whether the devil actually took the form of a serpent in tempting Eve, whether the matter from which Eve was made was literally taken from the side of Adam, and so on. Since his focus is on Thomism, Garrigou-Lagrange does not make an explicit judgment regarding the Biblical Commission's determinations. Many of the early works of the *nouvelle théologie*—one thinks of Maurice Blondel's *Letter on Apologetics* and Henri de Lubac's inaugural lecture, as well as the motivating concerns of Yves Congar and Hans Urs Balthasar

rigou-Lagrange asks rhetorically: "And, where is this 'new theology' going, with the new teachers it has inspired? Where but onto the road of skepticism, fantasy and heresy?"[12] After cataloguing certain dogmatic positions expressed in the anonymous manuscripts mentioned above, he draws a conclusion: "This then is the way of the rationalists, the school most desired by the enemies of the faith, which reduces all to mere and changeable opinion so that there is no value retained in them. What remains of the word of God given to the world for the salvation of souls?"[13]

In the wake of "La nouvelle théologie où va-t-elle" and the controversy it stirred up, Garrigou-Lagrange published article after article concerned with the immutability of truth, in particular, those related to dogmatic declarations.[14] And in some sense, his concern that rationalistic undermining of dogma was a real danger was justified, as events later proved. After the Council, Hans Urs Balthasar and de Lubac frequently and powerfully inveighed against just such rationalism. Yet, Garrigou-Lagrange's critique is too sweeping and undifferentiated. Although his article is limited in its specific critiques (focusing on Bouillard, Blondel, Fessard, and de Lubac), he nonetheless names the "nouvelle théologie" *en bloc*, thus implicitly invoking the entire movement that in 1946 was well known and led by de Lubac, Fessard, and Daniélou. Garrigou-Lagrange answers his question, "Whither the New Theology [*nouvelle théologie*]?" in a far-too-sweeping fashion: "It leads back to modernism."[15] He urges theologians to renounce this movement and turn instead to "true doctrinal renewal, achieved through a more profound study of the works of St. Thomas."[16]

(as appears in the first volume of his *Theological Aesthetics*, summarized in the short book *Love Alone Is Credible*)—were rooted in a desire to strengthen and enrich with greater nuance the work of high-level Catholic apologetics. See Karl H. Neufeld, SJ, "La théologie fondamentale dans un monde transformé," in Henri Bouillard, SJ, *Vérité du Christianisme*, ed. Karl Neufeld, SJ (Paris: Desclée, 1989), 359–90.

12. Garrigou-Lagrange, "Where Is the New Theology Leading Us?" 69.

13. Garrigou-Lagrange, "Where Is the New Theology Leading Us?" 71.

14. See the instructive essays by Guy Mansini, OSB: "The Historicity of Dogma and Common Sense: Ambroise Gardeil, Reginald Garrigou-Lagrange, Yves Congar, and the Modern Magisterium," *Nova et Vetera* 18 (2020): 111–38; "Experience and Discourse, Revelation and Dogma in Catholic Modernism," *Nova et Vetera* 17 (2019): 1119–43.

15. Garrigou-Lagrange, "Where Is the New Theology Leading Us?" 76; translation altered ("Elle revient au modernisme").

16. Garrigou-Lagrange, "Where Is the New Theology Leading Us?" 78. For a helpful treatment of Réginald Garrigou-Lagrange's theology written by an adherent of *Ressourcement* who has published numerous instructive books on Hans Urs Balthasar's theology, see Aidan Nichols, OP, *Reason with Piety: Garrigou-Lagrange in the Service of Catholic Thought* (Ave Maria, FL: Sapientia Press, 2008). See his most recent book on Balthasar, *Balthasar for Thomists* (San Francisco: Ignatius Press, 2020).

At the same time, the leaders of the *nouvelle théologie*—both before and after suffering ecclesiastical reprisals in the 1950s—were also much too sweeping and undifferentiated in criticizing the positions of their opponents. For example, writing after the Second Vatican Council, Balthasar bemoans "the shortcomings of the theology that has come down to us through the centuries" and agrees with those who "see theology stuck fast on the sandbank of rationalist abstraction and want to get it moving again."[17] Maurice Blondel, M.-D. Chenu, Étienne Gilson, and others suggested that the Thomists were Wolffian rationalists. Yves Congar and Daniélou called for the liquidation of Baroque scholasticism. In some ways, at least, de Lubac deemed the period from Cardinal Cajetan onward to have falsified Aquinas and the patristic heritage.[18] Almost forty years after first reading de Lubac's *Catholicism* (published in 1938), Joseph Ratzinger recalled that de Lubac's book was "a turning point" for him and for many others, recalling "the narrow-minded individualistic Christianity against which he [de Lubac] strove."[19] Whether or not Ratzinger means to pin the blame on neoscholasticism, the commonplace charges of narrow-minded, individualistic rationalist abstraction, among other deficits, had to hurt—and, indeed, did greatly hurt—the reputation and reception, and no doubt also the feelings, of Garrigou-Lagrange's generation of neoscholastic Catholic theologians.

In *True and False Reform in the Church*, originally published (after some delays caused by the Vatican) in 1950—prior to the condemnations of that year that resulted in the removal of a number of key figures from their teaching positions and that would eventually strike at Congar himself—Yves Congar looked back to 1946 as a banner year for renewal in the church in the wake of the dreadful experiences of Vichy and, in general, the horrors of World War II and Nazism. In a tone that contrasts sharply with Garrigou-Lagrange's article from 1946, Congar makes clear his view that neoscholastic theology and philosophy had been a pastoral failure, commenting that in 1946 the main desiderata were "a real, less artificial preaching; catechetics more apt to prepare Christians for real life; less routine and mechanical liturgy, one which really expresses the living worship of the community; forms of parish life that are less legalistic, more dynamic, truer to the real needs of

---

17. *TD* 1, *Prolegomena*, 25.

18. For a particularly nuanced presentation of the background to de Lubac's *Surnaturel*, see Jacob W. Wood, *To Stir a Restless Heart: Thomas Aquinas and Henri de Lubac on Nature, Grace, and the Desire for God* (Washington, DC: The Catholic University of America Press, 2019).

19. Joseph Ratzinger, foreword, in Henri de Lubac, SJ, *Catholicism: Christ and the Common Destiny of Man*, trans. Lancelot C. Sheppard and Elizabeth Englund, OCD (San Francisco: Ignatius Press, 1988), 11–12, at 12.

the people, etc."[20] Later, Congar adds to this list of needed reforms the encouragement of "authentic self-expression," especially in the liturgy, but also obviously among theologians and churchmen.[21] Catechetically, he calls for presenting the Church's doctrine in a way that "it doesn't just remain a truth *in itself*, but a truth with living roots in the minds of real persons, able to enrich them in the way they actually live."[22] Even more pointedly, he suggests that the present-day church is carrying a lot of baggage that does not pertain to Christianity's "essential reality" but pertains instead to "the history it [Catholicism] has passed through . . . affected by all kinds of human circumstances," and he calls for "rediscover[ing], as far as possible, pure evangelical attitudes and the authenticity of Christian teaching—and this in all domains."[23]

Imagine how hurtful all this was to neoscholastic theologians who gave their lives to teaching doctrine in a way that enriched real Catholics "in the way they actually live!" Congar's statements are, indeed, too sweeping and exaggerated. Consider Garrigou-Lagrange's brilliant and inspiring *The Three Ages of the Interior Life* or his easily readable *Our Saviour and His Love for Us*, published around the same time as Congar's book, or his instructive commentaries on the *Summa theologiae*. Likewise, consider the extraordinary volumes of Ambroise Gardeil, Jacques Maritain, and so many other neoscholastics. Even the much-maligned doctrinal and moral manuals (or textbooks) turn out upon closer inspection to be filled with a good deal of wisdom and pastoral relevance. Add to this Congar's call for "the synthesis of Christianity and [economic and political] liberalism (inescapable and already begun), an updated conception of the role of humanity in the universe and in evolution, and (on a more practical level) the search for a meaningful religious life,"[24] and the author of such profound and dogmatically instructive works as *Tradition and Traditions* and *I Believe in the Holy Spirit* may seem to some to be almost a revolutionary. No doubt he passionately sought theological and administrative reform, but he believed in enduringly true dogma, as did his opponents.[25]

Congar was wounded, of course, by his experience at the hands of Vatican authorities from the late 1930s onward. It is possible to read Congar, like

---

20. Yves Congar, OP, *True and False Reform in the Church*, trans. Paul Philibert, OP (Collegeville, MN: Liturgical Press, 2011), 25–26. See also Henri de Lubac's "Internal Causes of the Weakening and Disappearance of the Sense of the Sacred," in de Lubac, *Theology in History*, trans. Anne Englund Nash (San Francisco: Ignatius Press, 1996), 223–40.

21. Congar, *True and False Reform in the Church*, 45.

22. Congar, *True and False Reform in the Church*, 47.

23. Congar, *True and False Reform in the Church*, 47.

24. Congar, *True and False Reform in the Church*, 298.

25. See the helpful study by Andrew Meszaros, *The Prophetic Church: History and Doctrinal Development in John Henry Newman and Yves Congar* (Oxford: Oxford University Press, 2016); see also Mansini, "The Historicity of Dogma and Common Sense."

other theologians of the *nouvelle théologie*, in an unflattering way. It is also possible to read Garrigou-Lagrange in a similarly unflattering way. Admirers on both sides will call attention to their great contributions and be dumbfounded and hurt when critics see only negative things. Reading for the umpteenth time that the neoscholastic period or even the whole post-Tridentine period was "abstract" and "rationalistic" is enough to make Thomists throw up their arms in dismay over the ignorance of such claims. Likewise, reading that the *nouvelle théologie* was Modernist or somehow lacking in profound dogmatic commitment to Christ and his church is enough to make Balthasarians throw up *their* arms in dismay.

All these tensions have exacted a cost. For example, in a moment of frustration, Balthasar dismissed Bertrand de Margerie, a scholarly Jesuit who made significant contributions in patristics while sharply criticizing Balthasar on cross and Trinity, as merely "an old school-Thomist." Thomists returned the favor, deeming Balthasar to be a mere Hegelian. These attitudes persist today. In conversation, Balthasarians often deplore Thomists as engineer-like minds temperamentally attracted to arid rationalism. Likewise, in their conversation, Thomists deplore Balthasarians as poets in search of aesthetic beauty but careless of solid truth. You get the picture. Areas of convergence, such as Balthasar's trenchant critiques of Pierre Teilhard de Chardin, Jürgen Moltmann, and Karl Rahner—or Balthasar's powerful witness to the inbreaking of the divine Word, to the magisterial teaching of the church, and to Christ-centered self-surrendering love as the heart of all reality—merit renewed highlighting. So does the fact that Balthasar's theology was often deliberately bold and experimental, to the point that he would not have expected to have gotten everything right. The present volume goes a long way toward showing his rich insights.

I have recounted all these tensions not to further inflame them. God forbid! Rather, it seems to me that the church has suffered from a painful family quarrel, one that still needs to be brought a resolution through mutual forgiveness. In the past two decades, as Thomism has begun to recover from its postconciliar desuetude, the quarrel has reemerged and again threatens to divide Catholic theologians who agree with each other about the core dogmatic and moral commitments of Catholic life. Normally, the church lives with such competing schools of thought, but today, the church needs a relatively unified theological witness to dogmatic and moral truth given the resurgent liberal challenge. Leaders of the *nouvelle théologie*, such as Daniélou and de Lubac, as well as Balthasar, Ratzinger, Louis Bouyer, and others, spent much energy in the postconciliar years combatting this liberal movement (one thinks of Balthasar's *Cordula* and many other passages from his writings). It is high time, then, to overcome the family quarrel from the 1940s and 1950s. Besides, both sides have much to learn from each other's writings, and the present volume contributes to such healing.

In order to foster a fruitful conversation, both sides need to allow for criticism without coming down on it like a load of bricks. Through accepting the validity of the other, both sides need to let go of the grievances of the past and move forward with awareness of shared faith, hope, and charity. Healthy debate between the two schools of thought over how best to articulate dogmatic realities will continue. Fortunately, many theologians today exemplify such salutary practice, and the present volume will enhance it. Aquinas and Balthasar represent significantly different theological and philosophical schools within Catholicism, yet as the present volume shows, their main affirmations—allowing for difference of theological approach—cohere and can be fruitfully brought into conversation. Today, an important task that all Catholic theologians must share consists in faithfully exposing and developing the teachings of Vatican II against the mistaken reading of the Council's "spirit" that so concerned Balthasar after the Council, and now without the note of triumphalism (vis-à-vis neoscholasticism) that is off-putting. When one recalls the criticisms made by Congar in 1950 against the liturgy, catechesis, the state of Catholicism in Europe, the general condition of theology, and so on, it is clear that these criticisms can be shown to apply to the postconciliar church as well. Let both sides enrich each other and enrich the whole church!

I foresee that in the years to come, Thomists and Balthasarians will focus their zeal upon teaching the faith with conviction and charity while allowing the other to teach the faith from the perspective of its school of thought, encouraging intersections and mutual enrichment whenever possible. The goal is to invite Catholics and, indeed, the whole world to live the faith revealed by God to Israel, made manifest in a supreme and wondrous way in Christ Jesus, and handed down in the church's scripture and tradition. May this notable book contribute amply to that task.

BIBLIOGRAPHY

Bernardi, Peter J. *Maurice Blondel, Social Catholicism, and Action Française: The Clash over the Church's Role in Society during the Modernist Era.* Washington, DC: The Catholic University of America Press, 2008.

Bonino, Serge-Thomas, ed. *Surnaturel: A Controversy at the Heart of Twentieth-Century Thomistic Thought.* Translated by Robert Williams. Translation revised by Matthew Levering. Ave Maria, FL: Sapientia Press, 2009.

Bruckberger, Raymond-Léopold, Michel Labourdette, and Marie-Joseph Nicolas. *Dialogue théologique: Pièces du débat entre "La Revue Thomiste" d'une part et les R. R. P. P. de Lubac, Daniélou, Bouillard, Fessard, von Balthasar, SJ, d'autre part.* Saint-Maximin: Les Arcades, 1947.

Buckley, James J. "Balthasar's Use of the Theology of Aquinas." *The Thomist* 59 (1995): 517–45.

Congar, Yves. *True and False Reform in the Church*. Translated by P. Philibert. Collegeville, MN: Liturgical Press, 2011.

De Lubac, Henri. "Internal Causes of the Weakening and Disappearance of the Sense of the Sacred." In *Theology in History*, translated by A. Englund Nash, 223–40. San Francisco: Ignatius Press, 1996.

Garrigou-Lagrange, Réginald. "Where Is the New Theology Leading Us?" Translated by S. M. Rini. *Josephinum Journal of Theology* 18 (2011): 63–78.

Hanvey, James. "Henri Bouillard: The Freedom of Faith." In *Ressourcement*, edited by G. Flynn and P. D. Murray, 263–77. New York: Oxford University Press, 2012.

Kirwan, Jon. *An Avant-Garde Theological Generation: The* Nouvelle Théologie *and the French Crisis of Modernity*. Oxford: Oxford University Press, 2018.

Koerpel, Robert C. *Maurice Blondel: Transforming Catholic Tradition*. Notre Dame, IN: University of Notre Dame Press, 2018.

Levering, Matthew. *Engaging the Doctrine of Israel: A Christian Israelology in Dialogue with Ongoing Judaism*. Eugene, OR: Cascade, 2021.

———. *Engaging the Doctrine of Revelation: The Mediation of the Gospel through Church and Scripture*. Grand Rapids, MN: Baker Academic, 2013.

Loughlin, Gerard. "Nouvelle Théologie: A Return to Modernism." In *Ressourcement: A Movement for Renewal in Twentieth-Century Catholic Theology*, edited by G. Flynn and P. Murray, 36–50. Oxford: Oxford University Press, 2012.

Mansini, Guy. "Experience and Discourse, Revelation and Dogma in Catholic Modernism." *Nova et Vetera* 17 (2019): 1119–43.

———. "The Historicity of Dogma and Common Sense: Ambroise Gardeil, Reginald Garrigou-Lagrange, Yves Congar, and the Modern Magisterium." *Nova et Vetera* 18 (2020): 111–38.

Meszaros, Andrew. *The Prophetic Church: History and Doctrinal Development in John Henry Newman and Yves Congar*. Oxford: Oxford University Press, 2016.

Neufeld, Karl H. "La théologie fondamentale dans un monde transformé." In *Vérité du Christianisme*, edited by K. Neufeld, 359–90. Paris: Desclée, 1989.

Nichols, Aidan. "Thomism and the Nouvelle Théologie." *The Thomist* 64 (2000): 1–19.

———. *Reason with Piety: Garrigou-Lagrange in the Service of Catholic Thought*. Ave Maria, FL: Sapientia Press, 2008.

Oakes, Edward T. "Balthasar and *Ressourcement*: An Ambiguous Relationship." In *Ressourcement*, edited by G. Flynn and P. D. Murray, 278–88. New York: Oxford University Press, 2012.

Ratzinger, Joseph. Foreword. In Henri de Lubac, SJ, *Catholicism: Christ and the Common Destiny of Man*, translated by L. C. Sheppard and E. Englund, 11–12. San Francisco: Ignatius Press, 1988.

Ruddy, Christopher. "*Ressourcement* and the Enduring Legacy of Post-Tridentine Theology." In *Ressourcement*, edited by G. Flynn and P. D. Murray, 185–201. New York: Oxford University Press, 2012.

Schumacher, Michele M. *A Trinitarian Anthropology: Adrienne von Speyr and Hans Urs von Balthasar in Dialogue with Thomas Aquinas.* Washington, DC: The Catholic University of America Press, 2014.
White, Thomas J. *The Incarnate Lord: A Thomistic Study in Christology.* Washington, DC: The Catholic University of America Press, 2015.
Wood, Jacob W. *To Stir a Restless Heart: Thomas Aquinas and Henri de Lubac on Nature, Grace, and the Desire for God.* Washington, DC: The Catholic University of America Press, 2019.

PREFACE

MICHAEL ALTENBURGER AND JACOB W. WOOD

IN 1992, *DONUM VERITATIS* IDENTIFIED two sources in the human heart that lay at the center of theological study: the desire to come to a deeper knowledge of the Beloved and the desire to communicate the knowledge and love of the Beloved to the world.[1] In itself, this description may seem self-evident to the believing theologian today, but in context, then-Cardinal Joseph Ratzinger, under whose auspices it was written, suggests that the document was challenging the push toward "practicality" that had progressively begun to weigh on theology throughout the twentieth century: first in a general push toward the "professionalization" of theology as university discipline after the model of the natural sciences in the 1930s,[2] then in the Rahnerian push to reduce the immanent Trinity to the economic Trinity and our own salvific encounter with the Lord to the experiences in which we serve others in the 1960s and 1970s,[3] and finally in some of the more radical forms of liberation

---

1. Congregation for the Doctrine of the Faith, *Instruction* Donum veritatis *on the Ecclesial Vocation of the Theologian*, 7.

2. Joseph Ratzinger, *The Nature and Mission of Theology: Essays to Orient Today's Debates* (San Francisco: Ignatius Press, 1995), 79.

3. Ratzinger, *The Nature and Mission of Theology*, 79–80, avoids identifying any particular interlocutor in this regard but notes on pp. 107–10 the particular importance of the opposition of German theologians to *Donum veritatis*. Rahner died in 1984, but his practical approach to theology had already been translated into more explicitly political terms by his student, Johann Baptist Metz. For a concise account of the relationship between Rahner and Metz, see J. Matthew Ashley, "Johann Baptist Metz," in *The Wiley Blackwell Companion to Political Theology*, ed. William Cavanaugh and Peter Manley Scott (Hoboken, NJ: Wiley Blackwell, 2019), 236–49.
One finds the characteristic expression of Rahner's reduction of the immanent to the economic Trinity and the kerygmatic reduction of theological contemplation in Karl Rahner, *The Trinity* (London: Herder and Herder, 1970). The social consequences of that reduction for the theology of grace—understood through the lens of Rahner's supernatural existential—are expressed in their classic form in Rahner, "Anonymous Christians," in *Theological Investigations* 4, trans. Karl-H. and Boniface Kruger (London: Darton, Longman, and Todd, 1969), 390–98. At the time when Ratzinger was writing, Metz's most influential works in developing the political dimensions of a Rahnerian approach to theology were *Theology of the World* (London: Burns and Oates, 1968); Metz, *Faith and Society: Toward a Foundational Political Theology* (London: Burns and Oates, 1980).

theology that materialized our service to others in the 1970s and 1980s.[4] It was not that all of the goals that a practical approach to theology emphasized were inherently problematic—what Christian would argue against the obvious necessity of contemplating the work of God in the world, or of placing our theological labors at its service?—but that the practical approach to theology offered something fundamentally *incomplete*. Without a direct, prayerful encounter with Jesus Christ, by which we ascend from the knees of humility on earth to the communion of saints in heaven, we lose a sense of the communion of intra-Trinitarian love from which God's action in the world emerges, of the font of grace from which our participation in that action springs forth, and of the supernatural life that imbues our charitable service with its ultimate fecundity.[5]

Those sympathetic to Ratzinger's theological vision—to a theology that is not only practical but above all *sapiential*—can find ample ideal models throughout the tradition. Yet in the postconciliar church, sapiential theologians have looked to two figures above all to give voice to this theological orientation: St. Thomas Aquinas and Hans Urs von Balthasar. One could offer a variety of explanations for why these two were chosen. In the foreword to this volume, Matthew Levering explores the ongoing significance of the early and mid-twentieth century polemics between neoscholastics and *Ressourcement* theologians. This way of framing the history of the relationship between Thomists and Balthasarians helps to explain the adversarial relationship that has often developed between those who place themselves under one or the other theological patronage. It is a polemic whose contemporary existence is impossible to deny, but which it is our goal in this volume to help overcome. Accordingly, here we would like to explore another way of framing the significance of these two figures for sapiential theology today: the fact that they are both theologians of encounter.

Henri de Lubac pointed out that the world of the 1940s—devastated as it was by the ravages of war—had lost this sense of encounter. He described it as a "loss of the sense of the sacred."[6] He was not referring to a bland sense

---

4. Ratzinger, *The Nature and Mission of Theology*, 80, does not identify the object of his criticism here, but it may be Leonardo Boff, *Church: Charism and Power: Liberation Theology and the Institutional Church* (New York: Crossroad, 1985), 98, 122.

5. *Donum veritatis*, 8. Compare this with Ratzinger, *The Nature and Mission of Theology*, 57. "Theology is based upon a new beginning in thought which is not the product of our own reflection but has its origin in the encounter with a Word which always precedes us. We call the act of accepting this new beginning 'conversion.' Because there is no theology without faith, there can be no theology without conversion."

6. Henri de Lubac, "Internal Causes of the Weakening and Disappearance of the Sense of the Sacred," in *Theology in History*, trans. Anne Englund Nash (San Francisco: Ignatius Press, 1996), 223–40.

of awe, much less to the secular categories of anthropology that contrast sacred and profane. He was referring quite simply to the supernatural sense of God's loving presence, an encounter that is the beginning of friendship with the one who became man so that we might become God. To capture the essence of this encounter, he is fond of quoting Paul Claudel's *Magnificat*, in which the poet describes his attitude toward God at the moment of his conversion: "And behold, you are now somebody all of a sudden!"[7] Notwithstanding the many fruits of the *Ressourcement* movement in the study of scripture, liturgy, the fathers, and the medievals, for de Lubac—as indeed for Ratzinger—its most important contribution to the study of theology was not textual but spiritual: the restoration of a personal encounter with Jesus Christ to the heart of theological contemplation.

To be sure, Jesus Christ was never entirely *absent* from theology in the first place. That is one of the misleading presuppositions that a polemical spirit has forced upon the metanarrative of the twentieth century. One has only to turn from the metaphysics to the mystical theology of such a quintessential neoscholastic as Réginald Garrigou-Lagrange to see that it was not by accident that he was sought out as a spiritual director by those longing for deeper union with the Lord.[8] Whether one agrees or disagrees with the finer points of "Thomism of the strict observance," as it is both affectionately and pejoratively called, it is clear that Garrigou-Lagrange and those similarly minded considered every aspect of their intellectual labors as part of their loving service to their Savior and his church. Rather, Christ's "absence" was felt not so much by leaving him out of theological reflection but by disconnecting our contemplative ascent to him at key points in that reflection. In the universities, Ratzinger points out that there was pressure put on theolo-

---

7. Paul Claudel, "Magnificat," *La Nouvelle Revue Française* 3 (1910): 556. "Et voici que vous êtes quelqu'un tout-à-coup!" qtd. in Henri de Lubac, *La foi chrétienne: Essai sur la structure du symbole des apôtres* (Paris: Cerf, 1998), 332n71 [English translation: *The Christian Faith: An Essay on the Structure of the Apostle's Creed* (San Francisco: Ignatius Press, 1998) 284n71]; also qtd. in de Lubac, *Le prière du père Teilhard de Chardin* (Paris: Cerf, 2007), 26 [English translation: *The Faith of Teilhard de Chardin* (London: Burns and Oates, 1965), 14].

8. See, for example, the succession of works in mystical theology that Garrigou-Lagrange published in the 1920 and 1930s: Réginald Garrigou-Lagrange, *Perfection chrétien et contemplation selon S. Thomas d'Aquin et S. Jean de la Croix*, 2 vols. (Saint-Maximin: Éditions de la vie spirituelle, 1923) [English translation: *Christian Perfection and Contemplation according to St. Thomas Aquinas and St. John of the Cross* (St. Louis: Herder, 1937)]; *Les trois conversions et les trois voies* (Paris: Cerf, 1933) [English translation: *Three Ways of the Spiritual Life* (Westminster, MD: Newman Press, 1965)]; and *Les Trois âges de la vie intérieure, prélude de celle du ciel*, 2 vols. (Paris: Cerf, 1938–39) [English translation: *The Three Ages of the Spiritual Life: Prelude to Eternal Life*, 2 vols. (St. Louis: Herder, 1947–48)].

gians to produce literature on the history of theology instead of engaging in the direct contemplation of theological mysteries themselves, the idea being that the achievements of historical research are more readily comparable to the quantifiable products of the natural sciences.[9] In the seminaries, de Lubac observes that there was a similar but more subtle attitude toward doctrine that sought the concrete clarity and encyclopedic organization of the natural sciences, but in so doing risked replacing the humility proper to one standing before the incomprehensible God with the confidence of one who feels that he or she has mastered some aspect of created nature.[10] The result was that it made it intentionally difficult to do theology *in the same way* as the church fathers and doctors: to unite the reading of, reflection upon, and proclamation of the Word of God into a single, prayerful synthesis coming from an encounter with Christ crucified and leading to the vision of Christ glorified. All this came at time when the world, suffering the painful effects of Nazi Socialism, Fascism, and Communism, needed a sense of the presence of Jesus Christ more than ever.

Balthasar, as is well-known, constructed an entire systematic theology out of encounter, one which descends analogously from the encounters among the Trinitarian persons to the encounter between ourselves and our Trinitarian Creator.[11] Both encounters reach their climax for us in the cross, whereon Balthasar argues that the Son encountered the alienation from the Father that our sins entail, so that through his kenotic love we might encounter communion with the Father in the Spirit once again. In this way, the relationship between Christ's encounter with the Father and our encounter with Christ shapes the entirety of Balthasar's trilogy: from seeing the form of Christ, to acting in Christ through theo-drama, to thinking with Christ in theo-logic. Balthasar thus offers a directly Christological reorientation to the scientistic limitations of the early twentieth century: not only does he place Christ at the center of theology topically, such that no "treatise" of theology can now be spoken of apart from Christ, but he also places Christ at the center of theology spiritually, for how can one reflect on a personal encounter that one has never had?[12]

Aquinas also offers a theology that is based in a personal encounter with Jesus Christ, albeit not in an identical way. Instead of beginning with the cross

---

9. See Ratzinger's description of the plight of Romano Guardini in *The Nature and Mission of Theology*, 78.

10. De Lubac, "Disappearance of the Sense of the Sacred," 233.

11. See Michele Schumacher, *A Trinitarian Anthropology: Adrienne von Speyr & Hans Urs von Balthasar in Dialogue with Thomas Aquinas* (Washington, DC: The Catholic University of America Press, 2014).

12. "Theology and Sanctity," *ET* 1.

here below, in the *Summa theologiae*, Aquinas begins with the encounter between the communion of saints and the Triune God above. Gazing upon the face of the Lord in wonder and love, the saints alone enjoy the fullness of knowledge for which on earth we can but long.[13] Our participation in that fullness here below takes place through a cascading series of encounters, which draw us up in mystical ascent until we take our place with the saints in "the peace of God which passes all understanding" (Phil 4:7): encounters between the Lord and his prophets, to whom the mysteries of salvation were first made known;[14] between ourselves and the preachers of his church, who carry across the centuries the good news of the fulfillment of those mysteries through the Incarnation, Life, Death, and Resurrection of Jesus Christ;[15] and between all of us and the Word, for whose birth the prophets longed, on whose words the preachers depend, by whose Passion is poured out upon us the grace to restore to the Father the love that sin had once withheld, and into the glory of whose Resurrection the Holy Spirit draws us forth in faith and hope.[16] Aquinas does speak in the *Summa theologiae* of theology as a science in the classical sense, that is, a habit of wisdom concerning the highest principles,[17] as well as of its necessity in terms of our need to know the heights to which God has called us.[18] But since our only access to the habit whereby those principles are understood is through a grace that calls us to the glory from which they descend,[19] a theologian who did not know Jesus Christ personally might be *aware* of certain truths of divine Revelation, and even draw correct con-

---

13. *ST* 1.1.2 co.

14. Aquinas's understanding of prophecy is based in his reading of 1 Corinthians 12–14, in which Paul lists prophecy among the "charismatic graces" (the scholastic term was *gratiae gratis datae*), which are given by God for the building up of the church. See *Super 1 Cor.* 14.1, para. 812–13. See also *De ver.* 12.1; *ST* 2.2.171.2.

15. Both Aquinas's religious life as a member of the Order of Preachers, as well as his academic life as a medieval theologian, were ordered ultimately toward preaching. For a detailed treatment of his understanding of preaching in relation to Romans 10:14, see *Super Rom.* 10.2.

16. For Aquinas, the object of the virtue of faith is God himself as first truth. Particular doctrines come under the virtue of faith insofar as God reveals them for the purpose of assisting us on the road to union with him in heaven (*ST* 2-2.1.1 co.). Because of that, any scientific inquiry we conduct concerning the "knowledge" of faith has to be seen as coming from God and leading to God: coming from God as a share in his own knowledge and that of the saints (*ST* 1.1.2 co.) and leading to the very vision from which it descends through the Incarnation, Passion, Death, and Resurrection of Jesus Christ (*Super Heb.* 11.1, para. 557).

17. See *ST* 1.1.2, 1.1.6.

18. *ST* 1.1.1.

19. That is, by faith. On the theology of the grace of faith as tending toward beatitude, see Aquinas's discussion of Hebrews 11:1 in *ST* 2-2.4.1 co., as well as *ST* 2-2.4.7.

clusions about them at times, but in no sense could such a one be said to "know" them, let alone to have a sense for what it is that they truly entail.[20]

Aquinas and Balthasar, therefore, may not agree in all respects on where *theology* begins, but they offer us an absolutely united vision as to where a sapiential *theologian* begins—on his or her knees in humility and prayer, faith and love, desire and hope. It is only from within this common starting point that critical inquiry among Thomists and Balthasarians can bear fruit for the church and for the world. For within the bonds of charity, even the most scientific of critical inquiry can serve as an act of Christian charity by which we assist one another in our common ascent to the Lord, and by which we serve the church in the proclamation of the Gospel. Outside those bonds, it is liable to distract us from our ultimate goal, not, indeed, because love somehow *substitutes* for knowledge but because love *propels* it, while an absence of love too often misdirects it.

A will that is inflamed by the love of truth will spur reason on to ever and deeper heights of sapiential contemplation. But because "he who does not love his brother whom he has seen, cannot love God whom he has not seen" (1 Jn 4:20), the loving will longs not only for union with the Beloved but also for Christian friendship with our fellow theological sojourners toward that union. It restrains the intellect from the temptation to pigeonhole people into theological "camps"; it directs the intellect in the painstaking work of separating the wheat from the chaff in each theological argument it encounters. Indeed, it readily accepts both the good in another's argument as well as—and especially—the good in another's criticism. In this way, the amount of love with which we pursue sapiential theology has a direct effect not so much on the rhetorical form of our theological discourse—both narrative and dialectic can be an act of love—but especially on the quality of our critical reflection. Where prejudice flourishes, polemics rage; where love abounds, we ascend together through our critical reflection in the light of the Lord and offer the world through our unity in charity a credible witness to his love. The Lord foresaw this, emphasizing that his disciples would move the hearts of the world more than anything else by their love for one another (Jn 13:35). How much more so must this apply to those who dedicate themselves to a life of intimacy with the Lord and with the mysteries of his Revelation, so as to make both he and they known to the world?

---

20. Since the articles of faith surpass human understanding, only grace can confer upon us the certitude about them proper to knowledge (*ST* 2–2.4.8). Moreover, since the mysteries to which the articles of faith refer surpass the light of human understanding, the human mind requires further grace to have a sense for what they entail: Aquinas points to the Gifts of the Holy Spirit, specifically understanding (see *ST* 2–2.8.2 on its relation to faith), knowledge (see *ST* 2–2.9.1), and wisdom (see *ST* 2–2.45.1).

The goal of the present volume is to encourage and to contribute toward the renewal of sapiential theology in Christian charity. It brings Thomists and Balthasarians together in an irenic discussion of seven topics that are integral to the discipline: Metaphysics, Revelation, Christology, Trinity, Theodicy, Theological Anthropology, and Eschatology. Each topic features a pair of essays, one from a Thomist and one from a Balthasarian, placed in juxtaposition with one another so as to offer the reader the beginnings of a dialogue between Thomists and Balthasarians on that subject. For those who are new to the study of a given topic, the essays offer an introduction to some of the more important themes under consideration by sapiential theologians in that area. For veterans of the longstanding polemics within sapiential theology, the essays propose constructive ways in which the adversarial relationship between Thomists and Balthasarians might be overcome in a love that animates—rather than detracts from—authentic critical inquiry.

METAPHYSICS

Michael Rubin's contribution on Aquinas's metaphysics focuses on the transcendentals. Although Aquinas and Balthasar are typically thought to differ on the number and order of the transcendentals, as well as the question of whether beauty should be considered a transcendental, Rubin draws on the work of Jan Aertsen to show that this opposition is based upon an overly simplistic understanding of Aquinas's metaphysics. In the *De veritate*, Aquinas distinguishes between the transcendentals as modes of being in themselves and as modes of being in relation to the human soul. While Aquinas is strict regarding the number and order of the transcendentals in themselves, he allows for a variety of orderings of the "relational" transcendentals. Drawing upon a variety of Thomistic texts, including Aquinas's commentaries on Aristotle's *De anima* and Nicomachean Ethics, Rubin shows that Aquinas allows for an account of the relational transcendentals in which the delight of the soul in the beautiful leads it to the love of the good, and the love of the good spurs the soul on to the fullness of the knowledge of truth.

Anne Carpenter's contribution on Balthasar's metaphysics focuses on his understanding of the distance between the Trinitarian persons by examining its dependence on the idea that there are "areas of freedom" in God. Carpenter offers an important contribution to the current literature in English by examining Balthasar's incorporation of key insights from Gustav Siewerth, who engaged extensively with both Aquinas and Martin Heidegger, deploying Aquinas's metaphysics of participation and Heidegger's historicity in an effort to balance the integrity of human knowing and willing as it strives toward the infinite. While Aquinas provides the controlling metaphysical discourse, Balthasar still follows Siewerth in allowing Heidegger's insight that all being requires an attitude of "letting be." This synthesis creates the foundation for an analogy that renders human freedom intelligible as a distant echo of the Trinitarian "letting be" of the divine persons.

Revelation

Roger Nutt examines Aquinas's understanding of Revelation in relation to that of Balthasar, using this juxtaposition to highlight the relationship between personal and propositional Revelation in Aquinas. Nutt argues that propositional Revelation, of itself, is for Aquinas not only the means by which we arrive by faith at the knowledge of truths necessary for salvation, which we could not otherwise know, but also the means by which we are brought—by the gifts of knowledge, wisdom, and understanding—into a participation in the mysteries of faith themselves. For Aquinas, Revelation thus begins in the personal mission of the Spirit by which the grace of prophecy is conferred gradually upon human mediators and offers through the words of those mediators a participation in the New Law, which *is* that same Spirit, dwelling in the hearts of the faithful in love. The culmination of Revelation is found between the Spirit's work of prophecy, on the one hand, and the Spirit's work of sanctification, on the other. It is the cross of Jesus Christ, which the former anticipated and by which the latter is made possible. In the cross is contained the culmination of the Son's mission and the fullness of Revelation of his union with the Father, a union into which the Spirit's prophetic and sanctifying mission gathers the faithful.

Jonathan Ciraulo takes us through what he calls Balthasar's "monastic" theology of Revelation. Ciraulo begins by working out the intricate distinctions of philosophy, myth, and theology. The post-Christian constantly seeks to expunge the mythic (which can loosely be understood as "that which is so locally true that it stubbornly resists the universal and transcendental"), but Aquinas, as Balthasar reads him, is the paradigm of the proper integration of theology, philosophy, and the mythic. Indeed, Balthasar leans into Thomas's *compassio sive connaturalitas* to amplify the often-overlooked "monastic" dimension of Thomas's theology. What emerges is an account of Balthasar's theology of Revelation that has the same basic components as that which Nutt identifies in Aquinas, uniting a propositional component, which Balthasar describes as "exoteric," with a relational component, which Balthasar describes as "esoteric." Differences may remain (e.g., in Balthasar's use of Blondel's anthropology to describe the human longing that the exoteric component of Revelation fulfills and the esoteric empowers), but Ciraulo's discussion of Balthasar's re-integration of theology, philosophy, and mythos through a deepened understanding and practice of the "open secret" of Christian faith opens up several avenues toward rapprochement in the central aspects of the theology of Revelation.

CHRISTOLOGY

Andrew Liaugminas offers a tour of Aquinas's Christology through the lens of Christ as mediator, which ultimately suggests an important avenue for rapprochement between Thomists and Balthasarians on the much-vexed question of Holy Saturday. Focusing on Aquinas's Chalcedonian understanding of Christ's humanity, which is at once subject to the fragility of human nature and perfected by grace and union with his divine nature, Liaugminas illustrates how at each juncture of Aquinas's Christology, Christ *as man*, albeit hypostasized by the Word, mediates salvation to the human race: as the exemplar of the moral life, as the fount of grace, as the light of wisdom and knowledge, and ultimately as the suffering servant who ascends to the cross in love and obedience to free us "*from* guilt" and "*for* union with God." This understanding of Christ's mediation offers an important development in the Thomistic understanding of Holy Saturday. Although Aquinas does not share Balthasar's precise view of the harrowing of Hell, Aquinas does think that Holy Saturday is the day on which Christ the mediator begins to apply the benefits of his Passion to the human race. In that sense, a Thomist can see the church's entire sacramental work in ministering the effects of Christ's Passion as a participation in the work of Christ the mediator on Holy Saturday.

Francesca Murphy takes up a different area of Thomist-Balthasarian debate: the origin of the dramatic character of human existence. Questioning the idea that it results merely from the finite span of chronological time that fallen human persons have to make their moral choices, Murphy grounds the drama of human life outside of time in the Father's infinite gift of freedom to the Son and in the finite participation of that freedom, which is bestowed upon each person made in the image of God. Within this context, the dramatic character of human life originates formally in the "lifelong contest to connect interior freedom with illuminating, infinite freedom" so to fulfill the unique and unrepeatable dramatic role to which God has called each one of us upon the stage of human existence. The entry of sin into the world disrupts this drama: it closes the stage in upon itself and subjects the actors to an unending monotony in which the failures of life's tragedies become fatalistic "disasters" without purpose, the joys of life's successes become "escapist entertainment" without permanence, and our finite wills thus become unable to fulfill the transcendent calling that God has given them. Only in Christ, who so perfectly joins finite and infinite freedom together that we can say that he *is* his calling, particularly in the "'super-drama' of [his] Cross and Resurrection," are the climax and dénoument of human existence restored. For the love with which Christ embraces the experience of separation from the Father on the cross paradoxically restores to suffering its tragic character by simultaneously enveloping it within the comedy of human redemption. By restoring the tragic and comedic dimensions of human life in this way, Christ's kenosis creates an "acting area" within his Body, the church, in which his grace restores the image of God in us, sets us free to embrace our transcendent vocation, and empowers us to advance by degrees toward the perfect freedom of the children of God. Seen in this light, the success or failure of our performance is ultimately judged not in terms of the conclusion of a chronological process but in terms of its supratemporal conformity to its model in the person and mission of Jesus Christ.

TRINITY

Emmanuel Durand approaches Aquinas's Trinitarian theology through the lens of a comparison between Augustine and Balthasar on the relationship between Revelation and manifestation. Augustine moves from the rule of faith concerning the eternal acts and properties of the persons within God, which he illustrates with the psychological model of the Trinity, to God's manifestation in the world. Approaching the life of Christ in this way, he does not see any one event from the Nativity to Pentecost as privileged above another in the manifestation of the Trinitarian persons. Balthasar, by contrast, begins with the manifestation of the kenotic love of the Son on the cross and from there derives a model of the Trinity founded in kenotic love. Approaching the life of Christ in this way, he sees the cross as the privileged manifestation of Trinitarian witness. Comparing both approaches to scripture, Durand sees room for Balthasar's framing of our Trinitarian theology in terms of love, as well as a kenotic Christology, but raises questions about the extension of a similar kenosis to the other Trinitarian persons. Durand concludes by highlighting the importance of Aquinas's understanding of the *lumen fidei* as the means by which we receive rule of faith in Trinitarian theology.

Michelle Schumacher offers a comparative exegesis of both St. Thomas's and Balthasar's Trinitarian theology with the goal of seeing how the followers of each figure may learn from one another. She begins by exploring how Aquinas's use of Augustine's psychological analogy allows Aquinas both to preserve divine unity (against Arianism) and also offer a meditation on the communion of the intra-Trinitarian persons that is consistent with his explanation of how humanity comes to participate in that very communion. Schumacher then takes up Durand's concession to Balthasar's biblical emphasis on the role of love in the procession of the Son and explores how the central role played by ecstatic love allows Balthasar to offer an equally consistent—but very different—meditation on intra-Trinitarian communion and our participation therein. Schumacher concludes by showing how Aquinas's use of Augustine's psychological model could benefit from Balthasar's rehabilitation of the ecstatic, Christological dimensions of Trinitarian Revelation and how Balthasar, in turn, could benefit from Aquinas's precision regarding essential analogies.

THEODICY

Brian Carl looks into one of the foundational influences of Balthasar's own theodicy, Jacques Maritain, and revisits the question of whether we should identify an "unnamable suffering" in God as an attribute that corresponds analogically with human suffering. Although Carl finds with Gilles Emery that Maritain's unnamable suffering, as Maritain expressed it, can be reduced simply to love, Carl mines Aquinas's attribution of pity to God in the *Summa theologiae* to identify two possible avenues for discussing divine sorrow. On the one hand, Aquinas sometimes uses "pity" as a metaphorical name, attributing to God the greatest of the virtues on the basis of the effects of mercy that he manifests among us. On the other hand, Aquinas also seems to use "pity" as a proper name designating "the loving act of will by which God pours out goods upon others and alleviates their defects." Either way, the attribution of pity to God helps us to speak of divine "sorrow," for although God possesses none of the defects that are associated with sorrow, our own participation in the greatest of divine virtues is always accompanied by such a sorrow over the sufferings that are faced here below.

Kristen Drahos focuses on the question of how the cross of Christ overcomes evil, whether by negating it or by transfiguring it. For Balthasar, the answer is found in the distinguishing feature of drama as a theological category. Drama walks the edge between tragedy and epic, both of which are defined by a predetermined end. Balthasar frees the category of drama from the oversimplification to which these genres are liable by opening up a space for mystery and in the process provides a more robust explanation of the presence, power, and mystery of evil. Drahos identifies the "solution" to the problem of evil in Balthasar's understanding of the cross, which "transfigures" evil by entering into it with kenotic love rather than "negating" as Thomistic theodicy tends to do. This approach also allows Drahos to focus on what it means for Balthasar to talk about participation in the Lamb slain through the mission of the church, in which we find the extension of the drama of the cross played out in the hearts of the faithful, which are consumed in the "fire" of divine love and in the church as a whole, which "marches" through history, enveloping all times with the kenotic love of the cross. Such an approach to theodicy cannot be considered an epic or a tragic solution. Drahos is careful to balance the fact that the Revelation of Christ not only pours kenotic love into the world (and so overcomes the limits of tragedy) but also provokes greater resistance through time (and so overcomes the limits of epic).

THEOLOGICAL ANTHROPOLOGY

Jacob Wood examines the contemporary debate between Thomists and Balthasarians over Balthasar's idea of nature as a "limit concept." Noting that the question of human nature has been subsumed in contemporary literature under the wider question of the *analogia entis* between creation and God, and that any irenic debate on this question must take place on the basis of shared assumptions, Wood proposes that Thomists and Balthasarians can seek a path towards reconciliation by inquiring after the theological role of the *analogia entis* from within the Doctrine of Creation: "Does Aquinas have any *theological* reasons from within the Doctrine of Creation as to why it would be important for natural reason to be able to know created natures and to know God through them outside the sphere of Revelation and faith?" By retrieving both the Victorine and Lombardian context to the thirteenth-century understanding of the *ratio creationis* (God's purpose for creation), Wood shows that, for Aquinas, our natural knowledge of creation and of God through it is the means by which the human intellect confers a series of gifts upon the universe that God intends for the universe to receive through humanity: first, it confers the gifts of immateriality and intelligibility through abstraction, then it confers the gift of order through judgment, and then it confers the gift of participation in the knowledge of God's unity through analogical reasoning and attribution. Ultimately—under the influence of grace—it confers the gift of participation in Trinitarian contemplation through appropriation. In this way, our natural knowledge of creation and of God forms an important part not only of our own ascent to God but also and especially on how we fulfill God's purpose for creation by drawing the whole of the cosmos up into a participation in that ascent.

Michael Altenburger argues that Balthasar resists offering us an explicit, extended treatment on anthropology in se with clearly delineated features, instead offering an approach that understands human persons within the sphere of the *analogia entis* so as to open up new avenues of anthropological reflection. Above all, the *analogia entis* places two questions at the center of anthropology: 1) the distinction between divine freedom and human freedom, and 2) the challenge of showing how divine freedom "overcomes human rebellion from within actual human freedom." Balthasar answers these questions from within the Trinity, pointing to the poles of "self-possession" and "letting-be" at the heart of the Trinitarian relations, and argues that humanity, made in the *imago dei*, is constituted by a similar polarity of self-possession and self-gift, which expresses itself in four analogical distinctions: the cosmos and its ordered relation, spirit and body, man and woman, and individual and community. Rather than finding resolution, these tensions are "heightened" in Christ, who offers "myriad forms of new correlating and harmonizing in grace to achieve expressions of the ever-greater love which is their source." The core of Balthasar's anthropology thus returns to the analogical font from which his four anthropological tensions emerge: the relationship between divine and human freedom and the primal question addressed to each human person: Who are you? Who do you choose to be and become?

ESCHATOLOGY

Bryan Kromholtz takes up the role of eschatology in Aquinas's theology. Pushing beyond the dichotomy that frames Aquinas's theology as "abstract/systematic" and Balthasar's as "concrete/historical," Kromholtz identifies not only the Aristotelian but also the Dionysian elements of Aquinas's view of final causality, showing how Aquinas considers the "end" of the human person within the intentional arrangement which God freely bestowed upon the universe at creation. This more nuanced framing of Aquinas's teleology allows Kromholtz to place aspects of Aquinas's theology that combine the abstract with the concrete, such as the Resurrection of the body and the actions of the saints after the Final Resurrection, at the forefront of Aquinas's teleological approach to nature, uncovering some of the Christological and Trinitarian dimensions not only of Aquinas's approach to salvation history but also to creation and anthropology.

Patrick Gardner explores how Balthasar exegetes what he calls the "Scholastic axiom" of *exitus* and *reditus* in light of his Trinitarian theology. In particular, Balthasar incorporates his *analogia* of distance to reenvision the traditional "four last things" in a way that is Christological, realized, and apocalyptic: seeing death as a positive participation in the Trinitarian "super-death" of kenotic love; judgment as an event realized in Christ's death that takes place in the "super-time" of Trinitarian life; heaven as a state realized in Christ's Resurrection and in which we participate by entering into God here and now; and hell as the possibility of rejecting the reconciliatory judgment already accomplished in Christ's saving work. In so doing, Gardner offers not only a lucid synthesis of Balthasar's eschatological framework but also a map of the similarities and differences between Aquinas and Balthasar on each of the four last things that will prove indispensable to future Thomistic-Balthasarian dialogue on the subject.

No one volume can possibly resolve all the *quaestiones disputatae* that exist among those who have answered the call of the Lord to the contemplation of theological wisdom. The questions are too many and the points of disagreement too disputed. What one volume may hope to accomplish is to show how seeking the truth specifically in love, love both for Christ and for one's fellow theologians, can open new avenues for sapiential contemplation together, where previous scholarship has found only the impasses of polemics.

Our hope is that by pursuing some of these pathways to their ultimate conclusions, and above all by adopting this irenic method of identifying new ones, Thomists and Balthasarians may increasingly enjoy the sapiential fruits of theological friendship in the contemplation of the Lord and the service of the world. For those two tasks of sapiential theology were not of Ratzinger's choosing. In them, we find nothing other than the two great commandments of the Lord applied to our theological vocation. No Christian in any walk of life can afford to shirk from the sacrificial challenge to which those two commandments call us. For on them depend not only the law and the prophets but also our souls and those of the whole world.

MICHAEL ALTENBURGER
JACOB WOOD
Editors
November 26, 2023
The Solemnity of Christ the King

BIBLIOGRAPHY

Ashlez, J. Matthew. "Johann Baptist Metz." In *The Wiley Blackwell Companion to Political Theology*, edited by W. Cavanaugh and P. M. Scott, 236–49. Hoboken, NJ: Wiley Blackwell, 2019.

Balthasar, Hans Urs von. "Theology and Sanctity." In *Explorations in Theology*. Vol. 1, *The Word Made Flesh*. San Francisco: Ignatius Press, 1989.

Boff, Leonardo. *Church: Charism and Power: Liberation Theology and the Institutional Church*. New York: Crossroad, 1985.

Claudel, Paul. *The Christian Faith: An Essay on the Structure of the Apostle's Creed*. San Francisco: Ignatius Press, 1998.

———. *The Faith of Teilhard de Chardin*. London: Burns and Oates, 1965.

Congregation for the Doctrine of the Faith. *Instruction Donum veritatis on the Ecclesial Vocation of the Theologian*. May 24, 1990.

De Lubac, Henri. "Internal Causes of the Weakening and Disappearance of the Sense of the Sacred." In *Theology in History*, translated by A. Englund Nash, 223–40. San Francisco: Ignatius Press, 1996.

Garrigou-Lagrange, Réginald. *Christian Perfection and Contemplation according to St. Thomas Aquinas and St. John of the Cross*. St. Louis: Herder, 1937.

———. *Three Ways of the Spiritual Life*. Westminster, MD: Newman Press, 1965.

———. *The Three Ages of the Spiritual Life: Prelude to Eternal Life*. 2 vols. St. Louis: Herder, 1947–1948.

Metz, Johann B. *Theology of the World*. London: Burns and Oates, 1968.

———. *Faith and Society: Toward a Foundational Political Theology*. London: Burns and Oates, 1980.

Rahner, Karl. *The Trinity*. London: Herder and Herder, 1970.

———. "Anonymous Christians." In *Theological Investigations* 4, translated by K. and B. Kruger, 390–98. London: Darton, Longman, and Todd, 1969.

Ratzinger, Joseph. *The Nature and Mission of Theology: Essays to Orient Today's Debates.* San Francisco: Ignatius Press, 1995.

Schumacher, Michele. *A Trinitarian Anthropology: Adrienne von Speyr & Hans Urs von Balthasar in Dialogue with Thomas Aquinas.* Washington, DC: The Catholic University of America Press, 2014.

Metaphysics

CHAPTER 1

Thomas Aquinas on the Metaphysics of Beauty

MICHAEL J. RUBIN

IT IS NO EXAGGERATION to say that for Thomas Aquinas, metaphysics studies everything.[1] While other sciences examine only a certain kind of being—for example, biology is the science of living being—metaphysics is the study of being in general (*ens commune*) or being insofar as it is being. Moreover, since every science aims to know the causes of its subject, metaphysics ends by studying God as the First Cause of all being.[2] Hence, to give a complete description of Aquinas's metaphysics and how it compares to that of Balthasar is an impossible feat.

A more manageable task would be to compare their treatments of a metaphysical topic that is important to both thinkers: the relational transcendentals. The transcendentals in general have an obvious importance in metaphysics since each of them expresses a distinct attribute of every being insofar as it is a being and therefore reveals something unique about the nature of all reality.

---

1. All translations are my own unless otherwise noted. I have used the following Leonine editions: *Sancti Thomae Aquinatis, Doctoris Angelici, opera omnia, iussu impensaque Leonis XIII P.M. edita*, vols. 4–12; *Summa theologiae*, vol. 22/1–3; *Quaestiones disputatae de Veritate*, vol. 43; *De ente et essentia*, vol. 45/1; *Sentencia libri De anima*, vol. 47/1–2; *Sententia libri Ethicorum*, vol. 50; *Super libros Boethii De Trinitate et De hebdomadibus* (Rome: S.C. de Propaganda Fide, 1882–). Hereafter, Leonine editions will be referred to with the abbreviation "Leonine" and a page number. All other citations of Aquinas come from the following editions: *Scriptum super libros sententiarum magistri Petri Lombardi*, vols. 1–4, ed. P. Mandonnet and M. F. Moos (Paris: Lethielleux, 1929–47); *In librum Beati Dionysii De divinis nominibus expositio*, ed. C. Pera, P. Caramello, and C. Mazzantini (Turin: Marietti, 1950); *Liber De veritate catholicae Fidei contra errores infidelium seu Summa contra Gentiles*, vols. 2–3, ed. P. Marc, C. Pera, and P. Caramello (Marietti: Turin-Rome, 1961); *In duodecim libros Metaphysicorum Aristotelis expositio*, ed. M.-R. Cathala and Raymond M. Spiazzi (Turin: Marietti, 1964). Hereafter, Marietti editions will be referred to with the abbreviation "Marietti" and a page number. Those edited by P. Mandonnet will be referred to with the last name "Mandonnet" and a page number.

2. See Aquinas, *Super Meta.*, 1 proem. (Marietti, 1–2).

3

Moreover, the relational transcendentals—truth, goodness, and beauty—have a special importance among these terms since they express relations of every being to the human soul.

While Aquinas and Balthasar agree on the importance of the relational transcendentals, there appear to be two significant differences between their accounts of these terms. First, although Aquinas never says whether beauty is a transcendental, Balthasar emphatically declares it a transcendental of foundational importance; second, whereas the order of the relational transcendentals for Aquinas is truth, goodness, and (possibly) beauty, the order that Balthasar gives is beauty, goodness, and truth. Since Aquinas and Balthasar apparently disagree on both the number and the order of the transcendentals, they seem to be giving contradictory accounts of these terms.

In this chapter, I will examine the degree to which Balthasar's account of the relational transcendentals can be harmonized with that of Aquinas. I will begin by summarizing Aquinas's views on the transcendentals in general and the relational transcendentals in particular; then, I will analyze the ways in which Balthasar's account of the relational transcendentals diverges from that of Aquinas. Finally, I will show how these differences can be reconciled with statements made by Aquinas himself.

The Relational Transcendentals in Aquinas

The transcendentals are not an original philosophical discovery of Aquinas but rather a tradition he inherits from other thinkers. The roots of this tradition go as far back as Aristotle,[3] and extend to such varied sources as Boethius, pseudo-Dionysius, and Avicenna.[4] Nevertheless, Aquinas's medieval predecessors were the first to explicitly develop the theory of the transcendentals. The earliest formal treatment of the transcendentals is found in the *Summa de bono* of Philip the Chancellor,[5] which was soon followed by similar discussions in the *Summa theologica* attributed to Alexander of Hales,[6] and in the works of Aquinas's own teacher, Albert the Great.[7]

---

3. Aristotle was the first to argue that "one" and "being" are convertible, as he does in the fourth book of his *Metaphysics.* For Aristotle's influence on the theory of the transcendentals, see Jan Aertsen, *Medieval Philosophy as Transcendental Thought: From Philip the Chancellor (ca. 1225) to Francisco Suárez,* Studien und Texte zur Geistesgeschichte des Mittelalters, 107 (Leiden: Brill, 2012), 54–75, hereafter cited as *Transcendental Thought.*

4. Aertsen, *Transcendental Thought,* 35–46, 101–7, and 75–100.

5. Aertsen, *Transcendental Thought,* 109–33.

6. While supervised by Alexander, several other Franciscans contributed to it, such as John of la Rochelle. See Aertsen, *Transcendental Thought,* 135–61.

7. Aertsen, *Transcendental Thought,* 177–207.

There were several motivations behind this development. First, discussions of logic in the twelfth and thirteenth centuries had revealed that certain terms, such as "being," "thing," and "one," had distinctive characteristics because they transcended the categories of being,[8] for which reason they came to be known as the *nomina transcendentia,* or "transcending names."[9] Moreover, the notions signified by these names were seen to have an epistemological priority since they could not be defined in terms of anything prior and therefore must be the first concepts formed by the human mind.[10] At the same time, the transcendentals were of theological interest because they seemed to be divine attributes that all creatures shared.[11] Finally, there was even an evangelical motivation for this theory: the thesis that goodness is convertible with being, which means that every being is good insofar as it exists, was seen as an effective refutation of the Manichean heresy that everything material is intrinsically evil, which was being made popular again by the Cathar and Albigensian movements.[12]

As we will see, Aquinas fulfills these motivations in a masterful way. He does so first by giving an account of the transcendentals that is striking for its completeness, rigor, and even elegance. What is more, he underscores the goodness of not only the universe as a whole but even the special dignity of human beings in particular with his most significant addition to the theory: his anthropocentric explanation of the relational transcendentals.

The Transcendentals in General

For Thomas, a transcendental is a word or name (*nomen*) that expresses a distinct general mode of being.[13] Every word expresses a mode of being (since anything we can think or speak of is a being of some kind),[14] but what

---

8. For instance, medieval logicians observed that putting the word "not" in front of these terms does not produce an indefinite expression, as happens with all other terms. See Aertsen, *Transcendental Thought,* 42–44.

9. In fact, these logical treatises seem to be the origin of the term "transcendental." See Aertsen, *Transcendental Thought,* 31.

10. Aertsen, *Transcendental Thought,* 125–26, 140–42.

11. Aertsen, *Transcendental Thought,* 122–24.

12. Philip the Chancellor explicitly mentions the Manicheans in his prologue to the *Summa de bono;* moreover, he wrote numerous sermons against them. See Aertsen, *Transcendental Thought,* 111–13.

13. See Aquinas, *Super Sent.* 1.8.1.3 (Mandonnet 1:199); *De ver.* 1.1 (Leonine 22/1:4.129–5.61); *De ver.* 21.1 (Leonine 22/3:593.144–52); and *De ver.* 21.3 (Leonine 22/3:598.59v63).

14. One might object that we can and do speak about non-beings, such as blindness (which is merely the absence of something, i.e., the power of sight) or the purely

most words express are special modes of existing (*modi essendi*), that is, certain kinds of being; for example, the word "horse" expresses the specific kind of being that horses have. Each of the transcendentals, however, such as "being," "one," "true," and "good," expresses a unique general mode of being (*modus entis*) that belongs to every being precisely because it is a being.[15] For example, since no being can exist if its parts are divided from one another, every being is necessarily undivided in itself, which is expressed by the transcendental "one."[16] Hence, the essential function of the transcendentals other than "being" is to express attributes that belong to every being but which are not expressed by the word "being," and which therefore reveal the richness of what it means to be a being.[17]

The defining characteristic of the transcendentals is (1) expressing general modes of being, and this characteristic gives rise to six other characteristics of the transcendentals that fall into two distinct classes: three according to reality and three according to meaning.[18] Because the transcendentals express attributes that belong to every being, they refer to the same reality as the term "being." Hence, according to the reality that they signify, the transcendentals are first of all (2) identical, from which it follows that they are also (3) convertible, meaning that "being" and the other transcendentals can be predicated of each other "conversely" or in either direction;[19] for example, it is true to say both that "every true thing is good" and that "every good thing is true," as Thomas himself does.[20] Finally, it follows from the convertibility of the transcendentals that they are (4) coextensive, which means that, like "being," the other transcendentals are found in all the categories of being. It is from this fourth characteristic that the transcendentals receive their name since they "climb across" (*scendere trans*) the divisions of being.[21]

Because the transcendentals express modes that belong to every being but that are not expressed by the word "being," they have distinct meanings (*rationes*) that they add to the notion of "being." Hence, although the transcendentals are identical according to the reality that they signify, they are (5)

---

characters in fantasy novels. But even things that do not exist in reality still have existence in the mind that thinks about them and are therefore "beings of reason." See *ST* 1.16.3 ad 2 (Leonine 4:210).

15. See Aquinas, *De ver.* 1.1 (Leonine 22/1:4.95–5.161).

16. Aquinas, *ST* 1.11.1 (Leonine 4:107).

17. Aertsen makes this point in *Medieval Philosophy and the Transcendentals: The Case of Thomas Aquinas* (Leiden: E. J. Brill, 1996), 97, hereafter cited as *The Transcendentals*.

18. For Thomas's most complete discussion of these characteristics, see *Super Sent.* 1.8.1.3 (Mandonnet 1:199–200).

19. Aquinas, *De ver.* 1.2 obj. 2 (Leonine 22/1:8.15–16).

20. Aquinas, *ST* 2–2.109.2 ad 1 (Leonine 9:417).

21. Aertsen, *The Transcendentals*, 92–93; cf. *Transcendental Thought*, 17–18.

distinct according to the meanings through which they signify that reality.[22] Moreover, while according to reality they can be predicated conversely of each other, that is, in either direction, according to meaning, they (6) have a strict order on the basis of how directly and how much they add to "being"[23]—an order that we will discuss more in the next section. Finally, because the transcendentals add to "being" in a certain order, each one (7) adds to and includes in its meaning not only "being" but all terms preceding it in that order;[24] thus, whereas the transcendentals are coextensive with each other in reality, later transcendentals contain and exceed the earlier ones in meaning. These seven characteristics of the transcendentals according to meaning are thus not merely different from but even the opposites of their characteristics according to reality.

As Aertsen observes, these characteristics of the transcendentals give them a threefold significance in Aquinas's thought.[25] First, because they express attributes of every being insofar as it is a being, the transcendentals are central to ontology or metaphysics, whose very subject is being insofar as it is being (*ens inquantum est ens*). Secondly, since everything that we can think or speak about is a being of some kind, every concept that we have is formed by adding some meaning to "being," which is therefore the first conception of the mind; likewise, since the other transcendentals express attributes that follow directly from being, they would be the first conceptions of the mind after "being." Hence, "being" and the other transcendentals have epistemological significance because they are the first things that the mind knows.[26] Finally, since

---

22. Thomas frequently describes two or more transcendentals as being "identical in reality but distinct in meaning." See, for example, *ST* 1.5.1 (Leonine 4:56).

23. For instance, Thomas states in *Super Sent.* 1.8.1.3 (Mandonnet 1:200) that "one" is the closest to "being" because it only adds a negation, while "true" and "good" both add relations.

24. For example, Aquinas notes that everything is knowable by the intellect insofar as it is one since, as Aristotle says, he who does not understand one thing understands nothing. Hence, Thomas concludes that "true," or "that which is knowable," adds to and contains the meaning of "one" or "that which is undivided." See *De ver.* 21.3 (Leonine 22/3:598.40–63).

25. Jan Aertsen, "The Philosophical Importance of the Doctrine of Transcendentals in Thomas Aquinas," *Revue Internationale de Philosophie* 204, no. 2 (1998): 249–68.

26. See Aquinas, *De ver.* 1.1 (Leonine 22/1:4.95–5.102) and *Super Sent.* 1.8.1.3 (Mandonnet 1:199). It is important to note here that "being" and the other transcendentals are what is first known by the mind, not in the order of time, but rather in the order of resolution or explanation. In other words, they are the concepts in terms of which all our other concepts are defined and explained, and which do not need to be defined or explained by any prior notions. Hence, the transcendentals are not necessarily (and indeed are almost certainly not) the mind's first conceptions in the temporal order, that is, what it happens to think of in its first moments of consciousness. See Aertsen, *The Transcendentals*, 84; cf. *Transcendental Thought*, 213–14.

the transcendentals express attributes that belong to all created being, which participates in the Uncreated Being of God, it follows that the transcendentals are themselves participations in divine perfections, namely the Unity, Truth, and Goodness of God. Hence, the transcendentals have significance in natural theology, that is, the part of metaphysics that studies the existence and attributes of God as the First Cause of being, insofar as they reveal something not only about the nature of reality but also about the nature of God himself.

The Relational Transcendentals in Particular

One of Aquinas's most significant contributions to the doctrine of the transcendentals is his introduction of relational transcendentals, that is, transcendentals that relate to the human soul. As we will see, this innovation has important implications for the dignity of the human being.

While Thomas derives the order of the transcendentals in several places throughout his corpus, his most famous and thorough presentation of this order occurs in the first article of his *Quaestiones disputatae de Veritate*.[27] The first transcendental is "being" (*ens*), which means "that which is"; as Thomas explains elsewhere, "being" is the first conception of the mind because everything is knowable insofar as it is actual.[28]

The other transcendentals express general modes of being, which can follow on being either in itself or in relation to another. A general mode of being in itself can be expressed either affirmatively or negatively; thus, since nothing can be said positively of every being except its essence, the only transcendental that expresses an affirmative general mode of being in itself is "thing" (*res*), which means "that which has an essence." Then comes "one" (*unum*), which means "that which is undivided in itself" and therefore expresses a negative general mode of being in itself, the negation of division. A general mode of being in relation to another can also be said in two ways, either "according to the division of one from another" or "according to the conformity of one being to another." Hence, after "one" comes "something" (*aliquid*), which is the only transcendental to express a general mode of being according to division since its very meaning is "that which is divided from others."[29]

At this point, Thomas introduces what are known today as the relational transcendentals. According to Thomas, a general mode of being in conformity with others "cannot exist unless there is something whose nature is to conform with every being." That something is "the soul," which "as Aristotle

---

27. Aquinas, *De ver.* 1.1 (Leonine 22/1:4.95–5.161).

28. Aquinas, *ST* 1.5.2 (Leonine 4:58).

29. Aquinas, *De ver.* 1.1 (Leonine 22/1:5.124–41).

says . . . 'is in a certain way all things.'" Hence, corresponding to the soul's two powers are two transcendentals that express general modes of being according to conformity with others: "good," which means "that which is lovable" and thus expresses "the conformity of being to the appetite" or will, and "true," which means "that which is knowable" and therefore expresses "the conformity of being to the intellect.[30] Although Thomas presents "goodness" before "truth" in his article, he makes clear elsewhere that truth actually precedes goodness in the order of transcendentals, for the reason that one cannot love a thing without knowing it, and thus a being's desirability presupposes its intelligibility.[31]

As Aertsen observes, Thomas's position that the transcendentals truth and goodness express relations to the human soul is his "most important innovation" in the doctrine of the transcendentals.[32] Previous medieval accounts of truth and goodness either did not mention relations to the human soul or gave them secondary importance;[33] thus, Thomas's thought on the transcendentals possesses a certain "anthropocentrism"[34] that was absent in previous thinkers. Moreover, in declaring that all reality has attributes defined in relation to the human intellect and will, Thomas simultaneously affirms that man is capable of knowing and loving all of reality, and thus "is marked . . . by a 'transcendental' openness."[35] Finally, since truth and goodness are not merely attributes of being but also attributes of God, it follows that the human being

---

30. Aquinas, *De ver.* 1.1 (Leonine 22/1:5.142–61): "Alio modo secundum convenientiam unius entis ad aliud, et hoc quidem non potest esse nisi accipiatur aliquid quod natum sit convenire cum omni ente; hoc autem est anima, quae «quodam modo est omnia», ut dicitur in III De anima: in anima autem est vis cognitiva et appetitiva; convenientiam ergo entis ad appetitum exprimit hoc nomen bonum, ut in principio Ethic. dicitur quod «bonum est quod omnia appetunt», convenientiam vero entis ad intellectum exprimit hoc nomen verum."

31. See Aquinas, *ST* 1.16.4 co. and ad 3 (Leonine 4:211).

32. Aertsen, *Transcendental Thought*, 225; cf. *The Transcendentals*, 257.

33. As Aertsen notes (*Transcendental Thought*, 225–26), "it is true that in the *Summa fratris Alexandri* one of the ordering principles of the first determinations of being is . . . the relation of being to the human soul," but this relation is merely "one of the ways in which the transcendental determinations can be considered and is therefore not distinctive for the 'true' and the 'good' but holds also for the 'one.'" Moreover, for the Franciscans "the basis of the relation of being to the soul is trinitarian": unity, truth, and goodness first relate to the Father, Son, and Holy Spirit, and only because of this do they relate to man, who is "the image of God on account of the (Augustinian) triad of his faculties," that is, memory, intellect, and will. By contrast, for Aquinas, "the ontological basis for the relationality of 'true' and 'good'" is the dignity of the human soul, as expressed in "the Aristotelian thesis 'the soul is in a sense all things.'"

34. Aertsen, *The Transcendentals*, 257.

35. Aertsen, "Philosophical Importance," 262.

is not merely *capax universi*, or capable of knowing and loving the universe,[36] but also *capax Dei*, that is, capable of knowing and loving God himself.[37] The relational transcendentals thus have a privileged place not only within Thomas's account of the transcendentals but within his thought as a whole since they reveal the dignity that the human soul has for Thomas.

Differences between Balthasar's and Aquinas's Accounts

Beauty as a Transcendental

The most obvious way in which Aquinas and Balthasar differ in their accounts of the transcendentals is their treatment of beauty. While Balthasar repeatedly affirms that beauty is a transcendental, Thomas never mentions beauty in his lists of the transcendentals, not even the most complete one given in *De veritate* 1.1. Moreover, Aquinas might have difficulty accepting Balthasar's account of *how* beauty is a transcendental. As we will see, however, these differences are not as great as they appear.

Although Thomas never mentions beauty when discussing the transcendentals in general, he does address beauty when discussing one transcendental in particular: the good. In two texts from his *Summa theologiae*, for example, Thomas states that beauty and goodness are identical in reality but distinct in meaning (*ratione*) because the good relates to the appetite as "that which all desire," whereas the beautiful relates to the cognitive power because it pleases when seen or known.[38] Hence, Thomas concludes in the latter of these texts that "the beautiful adds to the good a certain relation to the cognitive power," because, while the good is said to be "that which pleases the appetite absolutely (*simpliciter*)," the beautiful is said to be "that of which the mere apprehension pleases (*id cuius ipsa apprehensio placet*)."[39]

At first glance, these texts would seem to indicate that Thomas considers beauty to be a transcendental. If beauty is identical in reality with goodness,

---

36. See Aquinas, *De ver.* 2.2 (Leonine 22/1:44.103–33).

37. Aertsen, "Philosophical Importance," 267. See also *ST* 2–2.2.3 (Leonine 8.28–29).

38. Aquinas, *ST* 1–2.27.1 ad 3 (Leonine 6:192): "Pulchrum est idem bono, sola ratione differens. Cum enim bonum sit quod omnia appetunt, de ratione boni est quod in eo quietetur appetitus: sed ad rationem pulchri pertinet quod in eius aspectu seu cognitione quietetur appetitus." See also *ST* 1.5.4 ad 1 (Leonine 4:61).

39. Aquinas, *ST* 1–2.27.1 ad 3: "Et sic patet quod pulchrum addit supra bonum, quendam ordinem ad vim cognoscitivam: ita quod bonum dicatur id quod simpliciter complacet appetitui; pulchrum autem dicatur id cuius ipsa apprehensio placet." For other texts that discuss beauty in the context of the transcendental good, see *Super Sent.* 1.31.2.1, ad 4 (Mandonnet 1:725) and *Super De div. nom.* 4.5.355–56 (Marietti 115).

then it is likewise identical with being and the rest of the transcendentals since to be identical with one transcendental is to be identical with them all; additionally, if beauty is identical with the transcendentals in reality, it must also be convertible and coextensive with them since these relations follow logically from identity.[40] Hence, in these passages, Thomas clearly attributes to beauty the charasteristics of the transcendentals according to reality, as he does elsewhere.[41] Moreover, by speaking of how the "meaning of the beautiful" (*rationem pulchri*) differs from that of the good, Thomas seems to indicate that beauty has its own distinct meaning. If so, beauty possesses not only the defining characteristic of the transcendentals, that is, expressing a unique general mode of being, but also their characteristics according to meaning, that is, distinction, order, and inclusion, and therefore is a transcendental.

Aertsen, however, has argued that these and other texts actually prove that beauty is *not* a distinct transcendental for Aquinas. According to Aertsen, while it is true that beauty adds to the good a relation to the cognitive power, this addition to the good cannot be considered an addition to being because the relation to the cognitive power has already been added to being by truth.[42] Hence, what beauty expresses is not a unique general mode of being but rather simply the combination of truth and goodness, or "the true taken as good."[43]

Aertsen's position is plausible for two reasons. First, Thomas's definition of beauty as "the mere apprehension of which pleases" does seem to contain both knowing and loving, and thus both truth and goodness. Moreover, Aertsen's interpretation of Aquinas explains how beauty can be identical in reality with being and the other transcendentals even if it is not a transcendental itself: by being a mere combination of transcendentals. According to this view, while beauty would indeed be *transcendental*, that is, an attribute of all reality, it would not be *a transcendental*, that is, a *distinct* attribute of all reality.

---

40. If two attributes are identical in reality, they can be truly predicated of each other, of course, and are thus convertible; likewise, they will obviously be found in all the same categories of being and are therefore coextensive.

41. See Aquinas, *Super De div. nom.* 4.5.355 (Marietti 115) and 4.22.590 (Marietti 216).

42. Aertsen, *The Transcendentals*, 344. In making this argument, Aertsen fails to note a significant detail: in *ST* 1–2.27.1 ad 3, what Thomas says beauty adds to goodnesss is not *the* relation to the cognitive power but *a certain* relation (*quendam ordinem*). The *quendam* suggests that there is more than one relation to the cognitive power, in which case the relation that beauty adds to goodness could be distinct from the one added to being by truth and therefore a unique addition to being.

43. Aertsen, *The Transcendentals*, 357–59. See also Leo Elders, *The Metaphysics of Being of St. Thomas Aquinas* (Leiden: E. J. Brill, 1993), 142, and Kevin O'Reilly, *Aesthetic Perception: A Thomistic Perspective* (Dublin: Four Courts Press, 2007), 110.

Nevertheless, although Thomas never explicitly states that beauty is a transcendental, he does seem to lean toward this view. It is true that Thomas does not say what unique general mode of being is expressed by beauty, but there is an early text from his *Sentences* commentary in which he clearly distinguishes beauty from the true taken as good.[44] Moreover, he writes this passage only a few years after hearing his own teacher Albert express the opinion that beauty is the true taken as good.[45] Thus, in this text from his *Sentences* commentary, Thomas appears to have quietly but consciously rejected the view that beauty is merely the combination of truth and goodness—an impression that is strengthened by the fact that, despite hearing this opinion voiced by his own teacher, Thomas never mentions it anywhere in his corpus. Thomas therefore seems to have held that beauty has its own distinct meaning and consequently does express a unique general mode of being, even if he does not state what that mode of being is. Hence, while Thomas never clearly expresses an opinion on beauty's transcendental status, his metaphysics and his writings on beauty imply that for him beauty is indeed a distinct transcendental.[46]

While Thomas thus might agree with Balthasar on the question of *whether* beauty is a transcendental, he would presumably have difficulty accepting Balthasar's account of *how* beauty is a transcendental. For Balthasar, beauty combines two elements: an appearance, which he calls "form" (*Gestalt*) or "figure" (*Gebilde*) and the shining of a higher reality through this appearance, which he calls "splendour." In the experience of beauty, "we are confronted simultaneously with both the figure and that which shines forth from the figure, making it into a worthy, a love-worthy thing."[47] By describing beauty as entailing an

---

44. Aquinas, *Super Sent.* 1.31.2.1 ad 4 (Mandonnet 1:725): "Beauty does not have the meaning of desirability except insofar as it takes on the meaning of the good; for in this way even the true is desirable: but according to its own meaning it has brightness and those things that were said above." ("*Pulchritudo non habet rationem appetibilis nisi inquantum induit rationem boni: sic enim et verum appetibile est: sed secundum rationem propriam habet claritatem et ea quae dicta sunt.*") Thomas says here that desirability does not belong to the meaning (*rationem*) of beauty. Yet if beauty were synonymous with "the true accepted as good," desirability *would* be a part of the meaning of beauty since (as Thomas says in this very text) truth becomes desirable when it takes on the meaning of good. Hence, this passage not only distinguishes beauty from the true and the good but also directly contradicts the view that beauty is "the true accepted as good."

45. Albert expresses the view that beauty is the true taken as good in a passage from his commentary on the *Divine Names*. Since Thomas wrote a *reportatio*, or copy, of this very passage, we can be sure that he was familiar with the views Albert expressed there. See Aertsen, *The Transcendentals*, 358.

46. For a more complete defense of this interpretation of Aquinas on beauty, see Michael J. Rubin, "The Meaning of 'Beauty' and Its Transcendental Status in the Metaphysics of Thomas Aquinas" (PhD diss., Catholic University of America, 2016), chaps. 1, 2.

47. Balthasar, *Seeing the Form*, vol. 1 of *GL*, 19–20.

appearance or figure, Balthasar seems to be saying that beauty relates to the senses, or at least that it relates to man's intellect and will *through* the senses.[48] But if beauty relates to the senses, then beauty is not an attribute of every being since purely spiritual creatures, that is, angels, are entirely unperceivable by the senses and so would only be beautiful metaphorically.[49] What is more, Thomas himself explicitly distinguishes sensible and intelligible beauty and makes clear that it is only the latter that is identical in reality with being.[50] Consequently, if Balthasar, in fact, holds that beauty is being as related to the soul through the senses, then, by Thomas's principles, Balthasar does not even give an account of how beauty is *transcendental*, that is, an attribute of every being, much less that it is *a transcendental*, meaning a *distinct* attribute of every being.

Nevertheless, it may be possible to interpret Balthasar's definition of beauty in a broader way that is not directly tied to the senses, though there is disagreement in the secondary literature on this question. D. C. Schindler, for instance, maintains that beauty has a necessary relation to the senses because "the perception of beauty . . . is the coincidence of the intellect and will" and thus "the act of perception must itself be *concrete* and therefore *sensible*."[51] Likewise, Anne Carpenter states that the "form" (*Gestalt*) required for beauty "implies sensibility."[52] Aidan Nichols, by contrast, argues that the "form" involved in beauty for Balthasar is primarily the "metaphysical form" or nature of the thing and only secondarily its sensible form or appearance; furthermore, Nichols argues that the splendor manifested by a being's substantial or metaphysical form is that of "the inherent possibilities of being at large."[53] A statement from Balthasar himself seems to support Nichols's interpretation:

---

48. In one of his earlier essays, Balthasar even gives a quasidefinition of the beautiful as essentially relating to the senses (as translated by Schindler): "When *truth*, which is thought, is found in matter, it is *beauty*" (emphasis Schindler's). See Hans Urs von Balthasar, *Die Entwicklung der musikalischen Idee: Versuch einer Synthese der Musik (1925), Bekenntnis zu Mozart (1955)* (Freiburg, Johannes Verlag Einsiedeln, 1998), 42, quoted in D. C. Schindler, *Hans Urs von Balthasar and the Dramatic Structure of Truth: A Philosophical Investigation* (New York: Fordham University Press, 2004), 404.

49. In fact, it is precisely on this basis that Horst Seidl argues against beauty being a transcendental, both for Aquinas and in reality. See Horst Seidl, "Sulla questione se il bello sia un trascendentale," *Aquinas: Rivista Internazionale di Filosofia* 53, no. 1 (2010): 259.

50. See Aquinas, *ST* 2–2.145.2 (Leonine 10:147).

51. Schindler, *Hans Urs von Balthasar and the Dramatic Structure of Truth*, 404.

52. It is for this reason, according to Carpenter, that "it would be better not to apply *Gestalt* to God in the strict sense, or it would seem Balthasar makes the mistake of giving God a 'body.'" See Anne Carpenter, "Theo-Poetics: Figure and Metaphysics in the Thought of Hans Urs von Balthasar" (PhD diss., Marquette University, 2012), 76.

53. Aidan Nichols, "Key-Word 'Form': Balthasar and the Beautiful," in *A Key to Balthasar: Hans Urs von Balthasar on Beauty, Goodness, and Truth* (Grand Rapids, MI: Baker Academic, 2011), 1–17.

> Here, where, with greater or lesser clarity, the totality of Being radiates within the individual being, the concept of *Gestalt* suggests itself. It signifies a coherent, limited totality of parts and elements perceived as such, yet which demands for its existence not only "a" context, but "the" context of being in its totality.[54]

Hence, it seems possible to interpret Balthasar's notion of "form" (*Gestalt*) in an analogical sense as referring to any form, whether sensible or intelligible, and the splendor manifested by it as that of the infinity of being in which the form participates, just as Nichols suggests.

Understanding Balthasar's account of beauty in this way removes the Thomistic concern about restricting beauty to the realm of the senses, but it runs the risk of blurring the distinction between beauty and truth. If beauty essentially consists in the manifestation of higher realities to the intellect by means of a thing's form, then it is hard to see how it differs in meaning from truth, which consists in the intelligibility of being and is also founded on a thing's form.[55] Balthasar might respond that beauty differs from truth because it relates not only to knowledge but also to love since it reveals the splendor that makes the being "love-worthy." This move succeeds in distinguishing beauty from truth, but it would also seem to reduce beauty to Aertsen's combination of truth and goodness. In that case, beauty would not constitute a distinct transcendental. Hence, it seems that, even when interpreted in a broader way that is not tied to the senses, Balthasar's account of how beauty is a transcendental is incommensurable with Aquinas's thought.

Nevertheless, a reconciliation between Balthasar and Aquinas may still be possible. For one thing, Aquinas does seem to favor Balthasar's view that beauty is a distinct transcendental. Moreover, while Balthasar does not provide a clear account of how beauty is a distinct transcendental, neither does Aquinas. Hence, there may be an explanation of transcendental beauty on which both thinkers could agree. For one possible account of how beauty expresses a unique general mode of being in Aquinas's thought, one may consult my doctoral dissertation.[56] There, I argue that in Aquinas's metaphysics, the general mode of being that beauty expresses is being's capacity to be possessed (and consequently enjoyed) by the will merely through being apprehended by the intellect, which is distinct from the modes of being expressed by truth and goodness because it is a relation *to* the will but *through* the intellect. While I confine my attention to Aquinas's metaphysics in the dissertation,

---

54. Hans Urs von Balthasar, "Transcendentality and *Gestalt*," *Communio* 11, no. 1 (1984): 5.

55. See Aquinas, *De ent.* 1 (Leonine 43.369–70).

56. Rubin, "The Meaning of Beauty," chaps. 3–6.

I think that this account of transcendental beauty may accord with Balthasar's thought as well.

The Order Among Truth, Goodness, and Beauty

The other way in which Aquinas and Balthasar differ is regarding the order of the relational transcedentals. As we have seen, Thomas argues that the true precedes the good in the order of transcendentals because knowledge causes love. Moreover, although he does not say whether beauty is a transcendental, Thomas does make clear that *if* beauty belongs to the order of transcendentals, it will follow goodness because beauty "adds to the good a certain relation to the cognitive power," which shows that beauty conceptually presupposes and includes goodness.[57] Thus, for Thomas, the order of the relational transcendentals is truth, then goodness, and finally (maybe) beauty.

Balthasar reverses this order. For him, beauty is the "self-showing" or "epiphany" of being and thus precedes both goodness (the "self-giving" of being) and truth (the "self-saying" of being) since a being must first appear to man before it can be loved or known by him.[58] Hence, beauty is not merely counted among the relational transcendentals but is even the first and foundational member of this triad because "without beauty . . . the good also loses its attractiveness" and "the proofs of the truth have lost their cogency."[59] Though goodness follows beauty, it precedes truth because man must first be drawn toward being by love before he can know it fully. Hence, the order of the relational transcendentals for Balthasar is beauty-goodness-truth, as is reflected in the order of the parts of his theological trilogy.

The difference between Aquinas's and Balthasar's orderings of the relational transcendentals is difficult to overcome for two reasons. First, in placing goodness before truth, Balthasar seems to contradict Thomas's firmly held position that knowledge precedes love as its cause, and that consequently a being's knowability or truth precedes its lovability or goodness.[60] D. C. Schindler defends Balthasar here on the grounds that in his account, loving

---

57. Aquinas, *ST* 1–2.27.1 ad 3 (Leonine 6:192). See note 42.

58. *EP*, 83–86.

59. *GL*, 19.

60. See Aquinas, *ST* 1.16.4 (Leonine 4:211) and 1–2.27.2 (Leonine 6:193). It is true, however, that Aquinas changed his mind on precisely *how* knowledge causes love. While his early works state that the intellect's knowledge is the *final* cause of the will's act, Thomas later came to hold that it is merely the *formal* cause. On this point, see Odon Lottin, *Psychologie et morale aux XIIe et XIIIe siècles*, vol. 1 (Louvain-Gembloux: J. Duculot, 1942), 226v43, 252–62. Nevertheless, this development does not change the fact that throughout his career, Thomas consistently held that knowledge precedes love as its cause, whether that causality is formal or final.

the good is still preceded by a type of knowledge: seeing the beautiful. As Schindler puts it, "this view avoids irrationalism—of which it might be suspected to the extent that it places the willing of the good before the knowledge of the object's truth—because the good here is preceded by the *beautiful*, which is an intellectual perception of form even if it is not yet a perception in the mode specifically of comprehended truth."[61] Thomas, however, could not accept this explanation, since for him truth is defined as the knowable, so any kind of knowledge—even if it falls short of full comprehension—is an engagement with truth.[62] Thus, since Thomas holds that one cannot love something without knowing it at least vaguely, truth necessarily precedes goodness for him.

The second obstacle to reconciling Balthasar's and Thomas's orderings of the relational transcendentals is the relationship between goodness and beauty. As mentioned above, Thomas makes clear that the beautiful conceptually presupposes the good when he says that beauty "adds to the good a certain relation to the cognitive power." Thomas's view that goodness is prior to beauty makes more sense when one remembers his definition of beauty as "that the mere apprehension of which pleases." As Thomas says elsewhere, taking pleasure in an object presupposes having love for it since we only take delight in what we love;[63] hence, it naturally follows that a being's beauty, or capacity to cause pleasure when seen, is conceptually preceded by its goodness or capacity to cause love. Hence, in placing beauty before goodness, Balthasar apparently contradicts Thomas's views on the order between love and delight.[64]

---

61. David Schindler, "Beauty and the Analogy of Truth: On the Order of the Transcendentals in Hans Urs von Balthasar's *Trilogy*," *American Catholic Philosophical Quarterly* 85, no. 2 (2011): 312.

62. Schindler might respond that the beautiful relates to the intellect's first act, that is, apprehension, while truth relates to the intellect's second act, that is, judgment, since Thomas says on several occasions that truth as known by the mind is found properly in judgment rather than apprehension (e.g., *De ver.* 1.3 [Leonine 22/1:10–11] and *ST* 1.16.2 [Leonine 4:208]). The problem with arguing this way is that love, to which the good relates, is a motion of the soul toward a thing as it exists in reality (see *De ver.* 1.2 [Leonine 22/1:9.62–71]); consequently, love presupposes judgment, which is the act by which the intellect knows the existence of things in reality (see *Super Sent.* 1.19.5.1 ad 7 [Mandonnet 1:489–90] and *Super de Trin.* 5.3 [Leonine 50:147]). Hence, even if one does say that truth relates to judgment and not apprehension, it would still have to precede the good.

63. See Aquinas, *ST* 1–2.27.4 ad 1 (Leonine 6:196) and 1–2.25.2 (Leonine 6.184–85).

64. Someone might argue that delighting in something as beautiful does not presuppose loving it as good because the pleasure caused by beauty is "disinterested"—it is a pleasure taken not in the object of beauty itself but solely in the act of knowing it. Schindler, for instance, characterizes aesthetic pleasure in this way (Schindler, "Beauty and the Analogy of Truth," 314). This explanation would not work for Aquinas, who makes clear that the pleasure caused by beauty is a delight in the thing seen rather than in the act of seeing it.

A Possible Reconciliation of the Two Accounts

While it seems at first glance that Balthasar and Aquinas are giving contradictory accounts, there are two reasons to think that there is a place within Thomas's thought for Balthasar's order of the relational transcendentals. First, although Aquinas does insist on a strict order among the transcendentals in themselves or according to their meanings, he acknowledges the possibility of other orders of the transcendentals according to different rationales. Secondly, and more importantly, there are places in Thomas's corpus where he writes that, in a certain sense, delighting in beauty precedes loving the good, and loving the good precedes knowing the true. When one examines these statements, one finds a rationale according to which the relational transcendentals could be ordered in the way that Balthasar presents them.

Thomas actually acknowledges an alternate ordering of the transcendentals in one of his earliest discussions of them, in his commentary on the *Sentences*. In this text, "being" is the first of the transcendentals—and consequently of the Divine Names—because it is the first conception of the mind and thus precedes all other terms according to meaning.[65] Nevertheless, Thomas acknowledges at the end of his response that "good"—which comes last in the order according to meaning, as we saw above—is actually first in the order of causality, because "good has the nature of a final cause, but being has the nature of an exemplary and effective cause," and the end or final cause is the first in the order of causality.[66] Thus, even while emphasizing that "being" is the first of the transcendentals and of the Divine Names when they are considered in themselves or according to their meanings, Thomas acknowledges another order in which "good" is first.

Just as he acknowledges an alternate order of the transcendentals in general, so Thomas acknowledges an alternate order between truth and goodness, in particular. In question 21, article 3 of the *De veritate*, Thomas argues that although truth is prior to goodness "in themselves" or "according to meaning," the good is prior to the true when they are considered "on the part of

---

For the evidence that such is indeed Aquinas's position, see Rubin, "The Meaning of 'Beauty,'" chap. 4.

65. Aquinas, *Super Sent.* 1.8.1.3 (Mandonnet 199–200).

66. Aquinas, *ST* 1–2.27.1 ad 3 (Mandonnet 200): "Si autem considerentur secundum rationem causalitatis, sic bonum est prius; quia bonum habet rationem causae finalis, esse autem rationem causae exemplaris et effectivae tantum in Deo: finis autem est prima causa in ratione causalitatis." As Thomas explains elsewhere, the end is the first of the causes because the agent or efficient cause does not act except for the sake of some end, and it is through the activity of an agent that matter is given its form. Thus, the efficient, material, and formal causes all depend for their activity on the final cause or end. See *ST* 1.5.2 ad 1 (Leonine 4:58).

what they perfect."[67] Thomas gives two reasons for this priority: the good perfects more beings than the true, and those beings that are perfected by both truth and goodness are perfected by the good before being perfected by the true.[68] The reason underlying both of these arguments is Thomas's conviction that all beings, even those lacking consciousness, have a natural inclination to preserve and perfect their being and can thus be truly said to love their being as good (though not consciously, of course).[69] Thus, while only certain beings can be perfected by a knowledge of truth (i.e., human beings and angels), all beings are perfected by a love for the good. Moreover, even beings that are capable of knowledge, and thus capable of being perfected by truth, are first perfected by goodness because they must exist before they can know, and they therefore have a natural love for their being before they have knowledge of anything. Hence, in the same work in which Thomas gives his most complete derivation of the transcendentals, he acknowledges an alternate order of the relational transcendentals in which goodness precedes truth.

Since Aquinas is evidently open to alternate orderings of the transcendentals, the question arises of whether his thought is open specifically to Balthasar's ordering of the relational transcendentals: beauty, goodness, and truth. While we have just seen two orderings given by Aquinas in which the good precedes the true, these were not derived from the perspective of the human being, as Balthasar's is, but rather from the order of causality and from the natural desire of all beings for the good. Nevertheless, several texts indicate that Balthasar's order has validity within Aquinas's thought as well.

That there is a sense in which loving the good precedes knowing the true for a human being is explicitly endorsed by Thomas in *Summa theologiae* I-II, q. 27, a. 2. Here, Thomas is arguing that knowledge precedes love as its cause, to which the objection is raised that there are some beings that we love more than we know. For instance, in this life, we can love God as he is in himself but cannot know him as he is himself. Thomas begins his reply to the objection by noting that "something is required for the perfection of knowledge that is not required for the perfection of love." Knowledge is an act of reason, which has the capacity "to distinguish between things that are conjoined according to reality, and in a certain sense to combine those things that

---

67. Aquinas, *De ver.* 21.3 (Leonine 22/3:598.40–599.67): "Considerando ergo verum et bonum secundum se, sic verum est prius bono secundum rationem. . . . Si autem attendatur ordo inter verum et bonum ex parte perfectibilium, sic e converso bonum est naturaliter prius quam verum duplici ratione."

68. Aquinas, *De ver.* 21.3 (Leonine 22/3:599.67–93). See also *De ver.* 21.2 (Leonine 22/3:596.61–597.96) and 22.1 (Leonine 22/3:611.1–616.383).

69. See Aquinas, *De ver.* 21.2 (Leonine 22/3:596.61–597.96) and 22.1 (Leonine 22/3:611.1–616.383).

are diverse, by comparing one with the other"; consequently, "it is required for the perfection of knowledge that a man knows singly whatever is in a thing, such as parts and powers and properties." Love, on the other hand, "is in the appetitive power, which regards a thing as it is in itself," and thus, "for the perfection of love it suffices that a thing is loved insofar as it is apprehended in itself." Hence, it is possible "that something is loved more than it is known, for it can be perfectly loved, even if it is not perfectly known."[70]

These statements show that there is a sense in which Aquinas would agree with Balthasar that loving the good precedes knowing the true. According to Aquinas, perfect love for a thing can precede perfect knowledge of it because knowing something perfectly requires apprehending every aspect of it, while loving it perfectly requires only that one love it "insofar as it is apprehended in itself," that is, to the degree that one knows it. As this qualification indicates, to be perfect does not mean for Aquinas what it usually means for us today, that is, to be as good as possible; rather, for him it simply means to be complete, to have everything that one's nature requires.[71] Hence, even though we cannot love God as intensely in this life as we will when we see him face to face, we can nevertheless love him "perfectly" or completely in this life so long as we love him as much as our current knowledge of him permits.[72] By contrast, we cannot know God completely in this life because that requires apprehending all of his Being, which is not possible until we behold him directly in heaven.[73] Thus, although knowledge precedes love, absolutely

---

70. Aquinas, *ST* 1–2.27.2 ad 2 (Leonine 6:193): "Aliquid requiritur ad perfectionem cognitionis, quod non requiritur ad perfectionem amoris. Cognitio enim ad rationem pertinet, cuius est distinguere inter ea quae secundum rem sunt coniuncta, et componere quodammodo ea quae sunt diversa, unum alteri comparando. Et ideo ad perfectionem cognitionis requiritur quod homo cognoscat singillatim quidquid est in re, sicut partes et virtutes et proprietates. Sed amor est in vi appetitiva, quae respicit rem secundum quod in se est. Unde ad perfectionem amoris sufficit quod res prout in se apprehenditur, ametur. Ob hoc ergo contingit quod aliquid plus amatur quam cognoscatur, quia potest perfecte amari, etiam si non perfecte cognoscatur."

71. As Thomas observes, the original meaning of the word "perfect" (*perfectum*) is "completely made" (*complete factum*), "just as we say that we have walked through [a place] (*perambulasse*) when we have completed the walking." See *Super De div. nom.* 2.1.114 (Marietti 39): "*Perfecta*, non est accipiendum secundum modum significationis vocabuli, quo perfectum dicitur quasi complete factum, sicut perambulasse nos dicimus, quando ambulationem complevimus." See also *SCG* 1.28 (Marietti 2.41); *ST* 1.4.1 arg. 1 and ad 1 (Leonine 4:50).

72. See Aquinas, *ST* 2–2.184.2 (Leonine 10.451–52).

73. Even then, we will still not *comprehend* God in the sense of knowing God as perfectly as he can be known since we will not see him as clearly as he sees himself; nevertheless, there will be no part of God that we do not see, and therefore we will see and know him completely. See *ST* 1.12.7 (Leonine 4.127–28).

speaking, since one cannot love something without knowing it at least vaguely, love nevertheless precedes knowledge in attaining perfection or completeness for the reason that knowledge requires more to be complete than love does.

At this point, the reader might still wonder *why* love requires less for its completeness than knowledge does, especially since the only reason given in this work is the rather cryptic statement that "love is in the appetitive power, which regards a thing as it is in itself." In fact, Thomas is referring here to a difference between knowledge and appetite that he discusses at greater length elsewhere: knowing occurs when something in reality comes to exist inside the soul through the mind's receiving its form immaterially,[74] while acts of the appetite (like loving or desiring) consist in the soul moving and striving toward something as it exists in reality, not simply as it exists in the soul.[75] For instance, seeing a cheeseburger means having the form of the burger inside my mind, but desiring a cheeseburger means wanting to possess the burger itself by eating it. Hence, knowing can only be perfect if the thing outside the soul comes to exist inside the soul as perfectly as it can, that is, through the mind's apprehending every aspect of it, whereas acts of love and desire can be perfect so long as the soul is moving and striving toward the thing as much as it can, that is, to the degree that it apprehends or knows the thing. It is for this reason that knowledge requires more for its perfection than love does, and consequently that love precedes knowledge in becoming complete or perfect.

That delighting in the beautiful likewise precedes loving the good in attaining perfection is indicated by a text in Thomas's commentary on the *Nicomachean Ethics*. In it, Thomas is discussing Aristotle's statement that good will is the beginning of friendship just as delighting in a person's beauty is the beginning of romantic love. Thomas gives the following explanation:

> No man begins to love some woman unless he has first been delighted by her beauty, yet he does not then immediately love her when he rejoices in the sight of the woman's beauty; but the sign of complete love is this, when if she is absent, he desires her, as if hardly bearing her absence, and desiring her presence.[76]

---

74. See Aquinas, *Sent. De an.* 2.24 (Leonine 45/1:168.13–169.56). For a fuller discussion of Thomas's views on the nature of knowing, see Rubin, "The Meaning of 'Beauty,'" 157–69.

75. Aquinas, *De ver.* 1.2 (Leonine 22/1:9.62–71).

76. Aquinas, *Super Ethic.* 9.5.5 (Leonine 47/2:518.64–72): "Dicit ergo primo quod benevolentia videtur esse principium amicitiae, sicut delectari in aspectu alicuius mulieris, est principium amationis eius. Nullus enim incipit amare aliquam mulierem nisi prius fuerit delectatus in eius pulcritudine, nec tamen statim tunc cum gaudet in aspectu formae mulieris amat eam; sed hoc est signum amationis completae, quando si sit absens desiderat eam, quasi graviter ferens eius absentiam, et praesentiam concupiscens."

Thomas then concludes that good will is likewise necessary but not sufficient for friendship: one cannot be friends with someone without wishing for his good, but one does not thereby become his friend until one actively works for his good and grieves over his misfortunes.[77]

Thomas indicates that, just as loving the good precedes knowing the true in attaining completeness, so delighting in the beautiful precedes loving the good. As we saw earlier, Thomas holds that one cannot delight in what one does not love; hence, when a man delights in a woman's beauty, he must already love her to some degree and thus be responding to her goodness. Nevertheless, if the man merely enjoys seeing her beauty and desires nothing further, his love for her is not yet "complete." Love's completeness occurs when he cannot bear to be apart from her and consequently desires a more intimate and permanent union with her. Thomas tells us that this "complete love" presupposes taking pleasure in the woman's beauty, which implies that he thinks delight in beauty attains completeness before love does. This view would be reasonable, because while a man obviously takes greater delight in a woman's beauty after falling in love with her, the pleasure he takes in her beauty can still be complete before that happens so long as it possesses everything that belongs to the nature of delighting in beauty, which is simply that he truly enjoys seeing her. Thomas thus appears to hold that delighting in the beautiful precedes loving the good in the order of attaining completeness.[78]

It therefore seems that Aquinas's thought could provide the following justification for Balthasar's ordering of the relational transcendentals. Although one cannot delight in a thing's beauty without first loving its goodness, and cannot love its goodness without first knowing its truth, one can nevertheless fully delight in a thing's beauty before fully loving its goodness, and can fully love a thing's goodness before fully knowing its truth. Hence, whereas the order of the relational transcendentals in themselves or according to their meanings is truth, goodness, and beauty, the order in which their corresponding activities reach completeness is beauty, goodness, and truth.

There is, however, one major objection to the rationale that I have suggested for Balthasar's ordering of the relational transcendentals. Since Aquinas

---

77. Aquinas, *Super Ethic.* 9.5.5 (Leonine 47/2:518.73–86).

78. One might object that this text is only discussing bodily or sensible beauty, and thus what Thomas says here does not apply to spiritual or intelligible beauty, that is, the kind of beauty that is a transcendental. Yet Thomas confirms elsewhere that what this passage states about sensible beauty is also true of spiritual or intelligible beauty. See *ST* 1–2.27.2 (Leonine 6:193) and *ST* 2–2.145.2 ad 1 (Leonine 10:147). Thus, Thomas apparently holds that just as perfect delight in sensible beauty precedes perfect love for its goodness, so perfect delight in a being's intelligible or transcendental beauty precedes perfect love for its intelligible or transcendental goodness.

defines beauty as that which pleases by being apprehended, it seems that for him one cannot fully delight in a thing's beauty until one fully apprehends that beauty. Such seems to be especially the case with God, whose beauty we will not directly behold until heaven. If so, then complete delight in a thing's beauty would presuppose complete knowledge of its truth, in which case beauty should come *after* truth and goodness in the order of completeness, rather than before.

One can resolve this difficulty in a way similar to Aquinas's explanation of how perfect love can precede perfect knowledge. As we saw, Thomas explains that for love to be perfect, one does not need to love the being as much as it can be loved but simply as much as one knows it, for the reason that love "is in the appetitive power, which regards a thing as it is in itself."[79] Now delight is an act of the appetitive power just as love is and therefore also regards a thing as it is in itself, as confirmed by Thomas's statement that delight is nothing other than the resting of the appetite *in* the beloved object when it is present.[80] Thus, one can say that complete delight in a thing's beauty does not require that one delight in the thing as much as it can be delighted in but rather only that one delights in it *to the degree that one apprehends it*. Thus, for example, while one cannot delight in God's beauty in this life as much as one can when one sees him perfectly, one can nevertheless delight in that beauty to the degree that one apprehends it, that is, insofar as one sees that beauty reflected in the beauty of his creation. Since perfect delight in beauty can thus still precede perfect love and perfect knowledge, beauty still precedes goodness and truth in the order of causing perfect or complete activities.

CONCLUSION

We began this essay with a problem: Balthasar and Aquinas seem to disagree on not only the number but the order of the transcendentals, and therefore to be giving contradictory accounts of the transcendentals. As we have seen, however, both problems are merely apparent. First, although Aquinas never officially declares beauty to be a transcendental, his metaphysics appears to entail it; moreover, while he would probably not accept Balthasar's account of how beauty is a transcendental, he might be open to a different account that would incorporate at least some of Balthasar's views. Secondly, Aquinas is open to alternate orderings of the relational transcendentals, and Balthasar's arrangement of these terms can be justified in Aquinas's metaphysics as proceeding according to the order of causing complete activities. Thus, Aquinas

---

79. See note 70.

80. See Aquinas, *ST* 1–2.2.6 ad 1 (Leonine 6:22).

and Balthasar are not giving contradictory accounts of the transcendentals; rather, they are describing different but compatible relationships among these terms.

Aquinas thus has a nuanced view on how a human being develops in his relationship to the true, the good, and the beautiful. On the one hand, since the absolute ordering of these transcendentals is truth, goodness, and beauty, Aquinas would say that in a person's approach toward some true, good, and beautiful reality—for example, the Christian faith or the virtuous life—the person must to some degree understand its truth before he can love it as good and consequently delight in it as beautiful. On the other hand, since the order of the relational transcendentals with regard to causing perfect activities is beauty, goodness, and truth, Aquinas would also agree with Balthasar that one cannot *fully* know the truth before fully loving it as good, nor *fully* love the good without fully delighting in it as beautiful. A full understanding of the Christian faith or the moral life comes only in the next life, and a full love for these realities comes only as the result of developing virtue. Fully delighting in the beauty of the Christian faith and the moral life (to the degree that one apprehends them), however, is something of which any person is capable in this life. Aquinas could therefore say that in drawing someone closer to the true, the good, and the beautiful, one should present all three aspects, but one should emphasize its beauty since that is the easiest aspect to engage with at first. Hence, regardless of whether Aquinas considered beauty a distinct transcendental, there is no question that he would agree with Balthasar on the importance of beauty for the moral and spiritual development of a person. It thus seems likely that he would also agree with Balthasar's famous statement that anyone who sneers at the name of beauty "can no longer pray, and soon will no longer be able to love."[81]

BIBLIOGRAPHY

Aertsen, Jan. *Medieval Philosophy and the Transcendentals: The Case of Thomas Aquinas.* Leiden: E. J. Brill, 1996.

———. *Medieval Philosophy as Transcendental Thought: From Philip the Chancellor (ca. 1225) to Francisco Suárez.* Leiden: Brill, 2012.

———. "The Philosophical Importance of the Doctrine of Transcendentals in Thomas Aquinas." *Revue Internationale de Philosophie* 204, no. 2 (1998): 249–68.

Balthasar, Hans Urs von. *Die Entwicklung der musikalischen Idee: Versuch einer Synthese der Musik (1925), Bekenntnis zu Mozart (1955).* Freiburg: Johannes Verlag Einsiedeln, 1998.

---

81. Balthasar, *Seeing the Form,* 18.

———. "Transcendentality and *Gestalt*." *Communio* 11, no. 1 (1984): 5.

Carpenter, Anne. "Theo-Poetics: Figure and Metaphysics in the Thought of Hans Urs von Balthasar." PhD diss., Marquette University, 2012.

Elders, Leo. *The Metaphysics of Being of St. Thomas Aquinas*. Leiden: E. J. Brill, 1993.

Lottin, Odon. *Psychologie et morale aux XIIe et XIIIe siècles*. Vol. 1. Louvain-Gembloux: J. Duculot, 1942.

Nichols, Aidan. *A Key to Balthasar: Hans Urs von Balthasar on Beauty, Goodness, and Truth*. Grand Rapids, MI: Baker Academic, 2011.

O'Reilly, Kevin. *Aesthetic Perception: A Thomistic Perspective*. Dublin: Four Courts Press, 2007.

Rubin, Michael J. "The Meaning of 'Beauty' and Its Transcendental Status in the Metaphysics of Thomas Aquinas." PhD diss., Catholic University of America, 2016.

Schindler, D. C. "Beauty and the Analogy of Truth: On the Order of the Transcendentals in Hans Urs von Balthasar's *Trilogy*." *American Catholic Philosophical Quarterly* 85, no. 2 (2011): 312.

———. *Hans Urs von Balthasar and the Dramatic Structure of Truth: A Philosophical Investigation*. New York: Fordham University Press, 2004.

Seidl, Horst. "Sulla questione se il bello sia un trascendentale." *Aquinas: Rivista Internazionale di Filosofia* 53, no. 1 (2010): 259.

CHAPTER 2

The Metaphysics of Freedom and of the Trinity

ANNE MICHELLE CARPENTER

EARLY IN *THEO-DRAMA*, Hans Urs Balthasar proposes that, "If there is to be absolute freedom, it follows that, in what takes place between the divine 'hypostases,' there must be *areas of infinite freedom* that are *already there* and do not allow everything to be compressed into an airless unity and identity."[1] This is an unusual claim, at once highly suggestive and deeply confusing. It sounds at first as if Balthasar is suggesting either some kind of infinite "space" or "spaces" between the hypostases—nonsense in a God who is not material—or is suggesting that there are three pseudo-freedoms in the Triune God, which seems far too close to three divine wills for comfort. Yet if the claim is not a kind of nonsense, what "sense" does it make? We are left at an impasse that requires resolution. After all, this claim, that there are "areas of infinite freedom" in God is one that serves as the fundamental ground for other, later claims regarding the "distances" between the hypostases, particularly the distance between the Father and the Son as it plays out on the drama of the cross.[2] Indeed, for Balthasar, these "areas" are the presupposition of finite, created freedom.[3] There are many possible angles one could take in explaining this idea, from Balthasar's self-evident reliance on Adrienne von Speyr[4] to his adoption of Gregory of Nyssa's schemata.[5] Since much of our possible con-

---

1. *TD* 2, 237.

2. See, for example, "The Descent of the Son," in *TD* 5, 247–68, perhaps the most famous use of the claim. It also receives elaboration in the third and fourth volumes of the dramatics, variously throughout, and I detail certain aspects below.

3. *TD* 2, 259.

4. Adrienne von Speyr's *The World of Prayer* (San Francisco: Ignatius Press, 1985) appears in a citation in the same paragraph as the excerpt quoted (see n. 1).

5. See Christopher Hadley, *A Symphony of Distances: Patristic, Modern, and Gendered Dimensions of Balthasar's Trinitarian Theology* (Washington, DC: The Catholic University of America Press, 2022). This chapter's development of Balthasar's metaphysical claims aligns especially well with the final chapter of Hadley's book, which borrows Gregory of Nyssa for its major constructive elaboration of Balthasar's notion of the Trinity.

fusion resides at the level of metaphysics, involving as it does the unity of God's being, I will take up some of the major *metaphysical* claims that Balthasar makes in his theological dramatics and attempt to understand them in their Heideggerian and Thomistic registers. We will come to see how Balthasar's theo-dramatic Trinitarian thesis about "areas of freedom" in God is based in a metaphysical claim about being as derived from the thought of Thomas Aquinas and Gustav Siewerth, among others, while also borrowing Heidegger's understanding of "letting be."

THE STRUCTURE OF THE CLAIM

I begin with a preliminary review of Balthasar's position, which I will return to and outline in further detail at the end of the chapter. When he speculates that there are "areas of infinite freedom" in the Trinity, Balthasar is in the midst of describing the natures of finite and infinite freedom, respectively, as well as describing the interaction between the two, all of which together forms the structural basis for all theological drama: "All that is human is lifted beyond itself and enabled to participate in the unique, concrete reality of this same theo-drama."[6] Balthasar is quick to clarify that he does not mean anything temporal when he makes his suggestion that there are areas of infinite freedom in God. They are *already there,* for eternity. At the same time, he argues, "Something like infinite 'duration' and infinite 'space' must be attributed to the [Trinitarian] acts of reciprocal love, so that the life of the *communio,* of the fellowship, can develop."[7] In some kind of analogous fashion, then, there has to be eternal "movement" in God, and corresponding realms from which the movement emerges, such that the three Persons are able to—and eternally do—give themselves to one another without reserve.[8]

---

6. *TD* 2, 54.

7. *TD* 2, 237.

8. This framework is not without its controversy even from the outset, especially in early Anglophone scholarship on Balthasar. It has been argued that Balthasar lacks a properly "social" dimension in his dramatics, to the detriment not only of sociality but of social justice, due at least in part to his interest in speculating about the immanent Trinity and his attachment to the analogy of being. It has also been argued that Balthasar's *Theo-Drama* "undermines God's ongoing engagement in history" through its focus on the immanent as well as the economic Trinity. This is so even while the theological dramatics have been, at the same time, explicitly connected to liberation theology, despite Balthasar's critiques of liberation theology and the more general failure to detail matters of liberation in his work. See Thomas G. Dalzell, "Lack of Social Drama in Balthasar's Theological Dramatics," *Theological Studies* 60 (1999): 457–75; Steffen Lösel, "Unapocalyptic Theology: History and Eschatology in Balthasar's Theo-Drama," *Modern Theology* 17 (2001): 202 and "Murder in the Cathedral: Hans Urs von Balthasar's New Dramatization of the Doctrine of the Trinity," *Pro Ecclesia* 5 (1996): 427–39.

Balthasar's interest in having these areas of freedom in God is, on the one hand, a "dramatic" one. The historical fact of the Incarnation, death, and resurrection—the whole Christ-event—is the "single 'point'" where "the sphere of the eternal touches the temporal sphere," giving ultimate meaning to all that is temporal.[9] Balthasar insists that everything eternal that comes into contact with history in Christ is God as he is for all eternity: distinct from the economy yet the same Triune God. This is not without its complexities.[10] Nevertheless, in the theo-drama, "quite explicitly, we are presented with a total meaning which—in spite of its historical, a posteriori character—cannot be surpassed,"[11] and this total meaning, at once historical and transcendent, is an encounter with "God himself, the unique one."[12] That is to say, the theo-drama is, from first to last, a Trinitarian drama.

Balthasar's argument is fundamentally that the Christological drama, the drama that created freedom is asked to participate in, is, while bound inextricably to history, at the same time an experience of the one, eternal "drama" of the Trinity, the drama that *is* irrespective of creation. As such, the Trinity is the ground for all created drama (and thus also the theo-drama). Here, Balthasar bypasses any separation between what we might call, in Thomist terms, the *De deo uno* and the *De deo trino*.[13] This unity (of God as one and three) is radicalized in Balthasar in at least one sense, if not more: for Balthasar, creaturely freedom is grounded in the Son, in the distinction between the Father and the Son.[14] That is to say, for Balthasar, human freedom is best understood not through the one transcendent God "in general," as it were, but specifically through the Trinity. In Trinitarian terms, then, the Father's word of creation is associated with the eternal Word.[15] This theological assertion pushes back against philosophical claims in that it means that philosophy is left unable to entirely answer for created or infinite freedoms, even as it opens up room for theology to go further in its speculations.[16]

---

9. *TD* 2, 115.

10. As in, for example, his "Trinitarian inversion" thesis. See "Trinitarian Inversion" in *TD* 3, 183–91.

11. *TD* 2, 116.

12. *TD* 2, 117.

13. Their unity in Thomas himself is argued for at length in D. Stephen Long's *The Perfectly Simple Triune God: Aquinas and His Legacy* (Minneapolis, MN: Fortress Press, 2016).

14. *TD* 2, 268. "If a world is to come into being containing people endowed with finite freedom, requiring a drama to be played and a stage on which to play it, the Son alone can be its ground and goal."

15. Cf. *Summa theologica* I.45.6, where Thomas argues that the model of the processions of the persons are the model of creation in creatures.

16. Cf. *TD* 2, 272, 285, 290–91, 296. This thesis about human freedom aligns with, notably, Maurice Blondel's argument about human action's inability to immanently "equal

Balthasar's "dramatic" logic for areas of freedom in the Trinity is, at its most fundamental, an effort to relate the drama of human freedom to the eternal drama of the Trinity. There is an analogy—albeit one with infinite difference—between earthly drama and heavenly drama, an analogy made more intense and more present through the Incarnation of the Son (though also *always* "in and beyond," to borrow a phrase from Erich Przywara). Balthasar says,

> If we call the incarnate Son God's primal Idea [*Uridee*] in creating the universe, since all things were created 'for him,' and hence 'in him' and 'through him' (Col 1:16), this all embracing primal Idea contains the (primal) ideas of the individual creatures. In God's view, these individual creatures are and should be as they are envisaged and contained in the primal Idea.[17]

We are presented with a modified version of Thomas's theology of divine ideas as it is found in the *Summa theologica*, a modification that carefully shades in details of God's Triune life, rendering a Trinitarian understanding of the God-creature relationship fundamental to the total picture.[18] This is not to say that Thomas's understanding is non-Trinitarian but rather to indicate that Balthasar's emphasis is decisively Trinitarian in how it amplifies the Trinitarian dimensions of the act of creation itself. The passage above reveals how, for Balthasar, every positive aspect of being a creature finds an analogy in God, a theological law he considers again later and that we will also return to after further exploration.[19] For now, it is sufficient to notice the basic pattern of the theo-drama: it is always, at every turn, Trinitarian.

I have thus far studied the essential structure of Balthasar's claim that there are "areas of freedom" in the Trinity, under the lights of both drama and reason. Balthasar's desire is to render freedom, human and divine, in explicitly Trinitarian terms, and also to provide a theological foundation for the stage and players in the drama. Beyond the demands and logic of the stage, we have to ask what further coherency (if any) we might find in Balthasar's argument. To do that, I will turn to a Thomist interlocutor of both Heidegger and Balthasar: Gustav Siewerth.

---

itself" in *L'Action,* and there the argument is explicitly philosophical and about philosophy rather than theology.

17. *TD* 2, 302.

18. See *ST* I.I.15.

19. See *TD* 5, 61–66 for the most explicit account in the dramatics. A perhaps clearer argument about the Trinity is available in *Theo-Logic* volumes, especially the third, for which there is not the space to detail here.

GUSTAV SIEWERTH:
BETWEEN HEIDEGGER AND THOMAS AQUINAS

Siewerth is one of a handful of Thomistic philosophers that Balthasar engaged with in his lifetime, influencing his appropriation of Thomas in his work.[20] Concretely speaking, Balthasar began direct engagement with Siewerth in the 1950s, which continued until the latter's death in 1963.[21] It is impossible, in any case, to really untangle exactly *who* influenced *what* aspect of Thomas that Balthasar borrows, and to say where he does so, at least outside of direct citations. And this is further complicated by Balthasar's and Siewerth's engagement with Martin Heidegger, which is also difficult to track. The goal, then, is not to offer a historical-critical "what" and "where" between Siewerth, Heidegger, and Balthasar. It is, rather, to better understand aspects of Siewerth's engagement with Thomas and with Heidegger, which remains entirely in German, and then—out of that understanding—to turn again to Balthasar in order to better grasp his claim that there are "areas of freedom" in God.

Siewerth's highest praise of Heidegger arises in the form of the book *Metaphysik der Kindheit* (1957), in which he assembles a metaphysical philosophy around the essential image—dear to Balthasar as well—of a mother and a child.[22] It is at once a lengthy effort to appropriate Heidegger, particularly the *Sorge* that Heidegger attributes to Dasein, and it is a detailed critique of Heidegger's lack of emphasis on interpersonal connection, similar to Edith Stein's critique of the same.[23] Siewerth brackets Heidegger's stance on being in order to focus on the historical situated-ness of human being that Heidegger highlights.[24] In doing so, Siewerth also appropriates elements of the later

---

20. Of these, Erich Przywara and Ferdinand Ulrich loom just as large as Siewerth, indeed, rather much more so in terms of direct influence and length of interaction. Siewerth is important for the purposes of this essay, however, in at least two ways: (1) specific philosophical achievements of his appear in the Balthasarian thesis under question here, and (2) Siewerth has garnered considerably less Anglophone attention, despite his essential contributions to Balthasar's thought. The essay, then, serves as both a clarifying Balthasarian argument and a recovery of Balthasarian sources.

21. See Manfred Lochbrunner's extended considerations: *Hans Urs von Balthasar und seine Philosophenfreunde: Fünf Doppleporträts* (Würzburg: Echter Verlag, 2005), 144–45. Balthasar acknowledges a deep debt to Siewerth with respect to his trilogy, particularly for elements of *Herrlichkeit* (167).

22. Gustav Siewerth, *Metaphysik der Kindheit* (Einsiedeln: Johannes Verlag, 1957).

23. See James Tristan Ward Orr, "Edith Stein's Critique of Sociality in Early Heidegger," *Neue Zeitschrift für systematische Theologie und Religionsphilosophie* 55, no. 3 (2013): 379–96.

24. Siewerth, *Metaphysik der Kindheit*, 12. Cf. Martin Heidegger, "Letter on 'Humanism,'" trans. Frank A. Capuzzi, in *Pathmarks,* ed. William McNeil (New York: Cambridge University Press, 1998), 239–76, esp. 252–54.

Heidegger. This human being, the one presented with a freedom and a history that are inextricably entwined, a freedom that somehow has to become "one's own" despite also being given, is Siewerth's preoccupation in the work.[25] Siewerth employs it for his own interests. *Metaphysik der Kindheit* spends itself describing and understanding the historical situated-ness of a child and the immensity of caring for the child who develops into an adult.[26] Siewerth is eager to remind his reader that this is a communal task, a task that indeed takes a community and the whole person.[27]

One of the essential horizons of being human is nevertheless (as in Balthasar) the experience of a parental love that stands "above" the human being and that demands some kind of corresponding answer. The call for a response is fundamentally a "demand" of love, and so not an effort of coercion from a place of power.[28] The experience of parental love, a love that demands a response, is, as in Balthasar, an interpersonal, human exemplar of the creature's fundamental relationship with its creator. It is here where Siewerth, while working within a broadly Heideggerian framework, begins to break its bonds.[29]

The critique of Heidegger's system as one that lacks transcendence of a certain kind takes a specific shape in Siewerth, as it does (differently) in Balthasar. It appears first in Siewerth's habilitation thesis at Freiburg in 1936, titled *Die Apriorität der Erkenntnis als Einheitsgrund der philosophischen Systematik des Thomas von Aquin* (*The Apriority of Knowledge as the Unified Ground of Thomas Aquinas's Philosophical System*), later published in 1939 as *Der Thomismus als Identitätssystem* (*Thomism as a System of Identity*),[30] which was revised and republished in 1961.[31] Siewerth leaves behind modern options

---

25. Siewerth, *Metaphysik der Kindheit*, 13: "Der vom Sein ermächtigte, zu sich selbst erst auf das Sein hin ,ereignete' Mensch erscheint nunmehr als vernehmender und dichtender, als bekundender und fügender im ,hervorgehen-lassenden' und ,anwesenmachenden' Werk in der Freiheit eines geschichtlichen Waltens aus dem Sein."

26. See Martin Heidegger, "On the Essence of Truth," trans. John Sallis, in *Pathmarks*, ed. William McNeill (New York: Cambridge University Press, 1998), 136–54, esp. 141–45.

27. Siewerth, *Metaphysik der Kindheit*, 15.

28. Siewerth, *Metaphysik der Kindheit*, 22: "So ergibt sich an einer dritten Stelle ein menschheitliches Mysterium daß das, was göttlich begründeter Anspruch, unabdingbar forderndes Recht ist, dennoch nicht als herrische Nötigung, sondern als Ruf an die geneigte Liebe ergeht, die das Gesollte im Überschwang der Erfüllung in die Gabe ihres Lebens verwandelt, das aus Freiheit dem Guten geweiht und aus Liebe ins Opfer gestellt ist."

29. Franz Pöggeler, "Gustav Siewerth—Wirk und Wirken," in *Innerlichkeit und Erziehung: In memoriam Gustav Siewerth*, ed. Franz Pöggeler (Freiburg: Herder, 1964), 4–6.

30. Pöggeler, "Wirk und Wirken," 5.

31. Gustav Siewerth, *Der Thomismus als Identitätssystem* (Frankfurt: Verlag Gerhard Schulte-Bulmke, 1961).

against transcendence and moves to Thomas's position as it is expressed in the *Summa contra gentiles*. Siewerth describes the "unending striving" (*unendliche Streben*) on the part of finite being, which is then the ground of transcendence. "The finite form," he writes, "is originally 'unending striving.' As 'striving,' the 'unfinished' finite being has its end (*Zeil*) beyond itself."[32] He cites book three of the *Summa contra gentiles*: "that toward which a thing tends, while it is beyond the thing, and in which it rests, when it is possessed, is the end (*finis*) for the thing."[33] This model of transcendence explicitly distinguishes between a being and its end, a move that already differs from Heidegger, and in so doing structurally holds open being to its transcendent dimension.[34] Yet it is not simply that Siewerth reintroduces a teleological framework to transcendence; it has much more to do with *how* that teleology is worked out in Thomas. There are three aspects of Thomas's thought that Siewerth highlights in order to harmonize this account of transcendence with the previous emphasis on the historical and existential: the relation of the human intellect to its end, the infinite desire of the human intellect, and the intelligible delight of God in his own willing. In the first place, the relation between a finite form and the infinite God is participatory. What exactly that means for Siewerth is complex. In the *Summa contra gentiles*, which remains Siewerth's focus, Thomas explains that "the end of any intellectual substance . . . is to understand God." This is true even of the human intellect, despite its lowly status. Thomas says, "The human intellect reaches (lit. 'stretches out to' [*pertingit*]) God as its end, through an act of understanding."[35] Though the finite intellect can indirectly know God through (finite) acts of understanding in this way, it is not satisfied by this knowledge, but rather desires "the understanding of substance which is of infinite eminence," that is to say, the finite intellect desires to know the divine substance. The intellect does not simply want to know "about" God but wants to know God *in se*. Siewerth stresses the infinite-ness of this desire: *desiderium infinitum*. It is a shorthand for Thomas's actual argument, as when he says, "nothing finite is able to satisfy intellectual desire" (*nihil finitum desidierium intellectus quietare potest*).[36]

---

32. Siewerth, *Thomismus als Identitätssystem*, 4: "Die endliche Form is ursprünglich, 'unendliches Streben.' Als ,strebende' ist sie 'unvollendetes' endliches Wesen, das sein Zeil außer sich hat."

33. Aquinas, *SCG*, 3.16.

34. A Heideggerian explanation of Heidegger's rejection of God and transcendent telos can be found in Owen T. Cummings, "Divine Refusal: An Aspect of the Internal Link Between God and Truth in Heidegger," *International Journal of Philosophy and Theology* 74 (2013): esp. 183–84.

35. Aquinas, *SCG*, 3.25. Indeed, in *De veritate*, Thomas says that in *every* act of understanding, the intellect implicitly knows God (q. 22, a. 2).

36. Aquinas, *SCG*, 3.50.

It is important to understand that this striving toward God is not a striving across a distance, a movement, as it were, from far to near. Rather, Siewerth clarifies his position by explaining that the ground out of which a finite form seeks perfection and the end through which it is perfected are the same. That is, *being* is the ground and end of a finite form. "Being," here, is understood in the specific sense that Thomas Aquinas means it. It is not Dasein's experience of the immanent unveiling of its own ground, nor the unquestioned, staid, being of the metaphysics that Heidegger derides but "being" as that which only God properly has and is. Siewerth explains: "'Being itself' can be presented as pure universality (*reine Allgemeinheit*)." This is a sense in which Heidegger understood the word "being," and, indeed, that he saw as a problem, since it is simply a generalization. Siewerth continues with an important clarification in this regard: when being is predicated to a particular thing, "it supposes the 'principle of an act' (*Aktgrund*), 'whereby something is' (*wodurch etwas ist*)." In other words, "being" in this second case refers to the "act" through which that being is, and Siewerth insists that this adds nothing to being (understood in the universal sense) but rather is something like "an inward development, 'like an act through its potency.'"[37] This clarification moves Siewerth into firmly Thomist territory, and at the same time—at least for Siewerth—rescues being from Heidegger's critique in that metaphysics is no longer an abstraction but accessible only in and through the act of the particular.[38]

However, if the universal is accessible only through the particular, how do the two not become simply synonymous? One of Siewerth's resources here is Thomas's *De potentia*, specifically q. 9 a. 2, where Thomas asks whether God's essence is the same as his existence. Thomas answers that, yes, in God, these are the same; God is (as Thomas says in the *Summa theologiae*) "pure act." Siewerth points us specifically to where Thomas explains how this can be so if other beings also exist, that is, if other beings also have being. This, after all, suggests a limit or imperfection in God's being, since it seems it is possible to have "more" beings despite God already *being*. Thomas's inter-

---

37. Siewerth, *Thomismus als Identiätssystem*, 9: "'Das Sein selbst' kann als reine Allgemeinheit vorgestellt werden. In der urteilenden 'Prädikation' aber vermeint es den 'Aktgrund,' wodurch etwas ist. Diese Aussage folgt daher der Kontraktion des Aktes zu einer bestimmten Wesenheit. Das allegemeine Sein wird 'determiniert' und 'kontrahiert.' Diese Kontraktion fügt zwar dem Sein nichts äußerlich hinzu, so wie ein aktuales Seiendes zu aktualem Seienden tritt, sondern es ist eine innerliche Entfaltung, 'wie ein Akt durch seine Moglichket.'"

38. A far more detailed review of Siewerth's understanding of being can be found in Emmanuel Tourpe, *Siewerth apres Siewerth: Le lien idéal de amour dans le Thomisme spéculatif de Gustav Siewerth et la visée de réalisme transcendental* (Paris: Louvain, 1998). I follow Tourpe regarding the communal, love-oriented read of Siewerth's Thomism.

vention here is fundamental to Siewerth's understanding of being: "*Being* (esse), as we understand it here," Thomas writes, "signifies the highest perfection of all: and the proof is that act is always more perfect than potentiality. Now no signate form is understood to be in act unless it be supposed to have *being* (*in actu nisi per hoc quod esse ponitur*)."[39] Here as well as elsewhere, Thomas identifies "being" and "act."

This requires some clarification. "The question," writes Rudi te Velde, "is how to explain that things are good in virtue of their being without this resulting in an identity of 'to be' and 'to be good.'"[40] If being and goodness are the same in a creature, then that makes it identical with goodness itself, that is, identical with the first principle. Yet if being and goodness are not the same in created things, then it cannot be said that to exist is good. Where we have to begin, te Velde explains, is with Dionysius: "the first Good produces everything else by making it share in itself, by communicating its goodness to it."[41] This is the *communicatio boni* by which all created things come to be. Within this Neoplatonic framework, Thomas strives to introduce or maintain the intrinsic goodness of creatures, which is an Aristotelian emphasis derived from efficient causality.[42] Thomas's elaboration has two parts, one that refers to the immanent qualities of created being, and one that refers to the nature of being itself. For the first set of concerns, says te Velde: "things are good, formally in virtue of an immanent form given to them as a likeness of the highest good, and furthermore (*ulterius*) in virtue of the first goodness as the exemplary and effective principle of all created goodness."[43] Beings are good according to their immanent form and according to their having-been-caused. In this way, things are good "in themselves," and yet not without reference to goodness itself, both with respect to their own form (as a likeness) and the cause of their existence (the highest good).

Thomas's thought about being (*esse*) is, as te Velde has it, that "God is being *by his essence*, the creature is being *by participation*."[44] So, strictly speaking, only God "has" being such that it is identical with his nature or essence, and this essence is pure actuality. With respect to the creation, "God is in act with regard to every possible being. . . . The proper effect of God, according to which each thing assimilates his nature, is being; and therefore, it is this

---

39. Aquinas, *De potentia*, 7.2.9. Emphasis mine.

40. Rudi te Velde, *Participation and Substantiality in Thomas Aquinas* (New York: Brill, 1995), 17.

41. Te Velde, *Participation and Substantiality*, 21.

42. Te Velde, *Participation and Substantiality*, 23.

43. Te Velde, *Participation and Substantiality*, 26.

44. Te Velde, *Participation and Substantiality*, 100.

45. Te Velde, *Participation and Substantiality*, 106.

'being' in which consists God's nature or substance."[45] So "to be" is identical with God's essence. The degree to which anything also *is*, the degree to which anything can be said *to be*, is participation in God by virtue of that *being*. At the same time, each "being" (in this latter sense) also has being in a specific mode that differentiates it from other beings.[46] Beings have a "double" similitude to God, through the being that they share in and through the way in which they are beings.

This turns the meaning of "being" on its head, at least as far as Heidegger is concerned. Whereas Dasein is thrown in the midst of its own ecstatic being—and thus "being" bears the qualities of event, of unveiling, and of letting-be—for Thomas, the way in which any creature *is*, is a participation in God's being. "Being," in this Thomistic sense, means not only 'to be' but also *how* and *whence* a being 'is,' and this by virtue of the actuality that God is and that the creature receives from God. As Siewerth explains in the book *Das Schicksal der Metaphysik*:

> For Thomas, being is the highest of all names that can designate God. Nevertheless, [Thomas] is primarily concerned with the things of this world. In this first and essential determination, 'being' signifies substance, in such a way that the literal sense of being (*ens*) is taken from the 'act' of beings (*actus essendi*). But as an act, it signifies *that by which something is* (*wodurch etwas ist*).[47]

So Siewerth clarifies how "being" can mean God, where essence and existence are identical (not, it should be said, as *causa sui*), but it can also mean the "substance" of a being, which is not identical with its materiality but rather that by which a being is. Siewerth pushes for a theocentric, metaphysical perspective not so much out of theological concerns but out of concern for explaining finite beings. This helps to clarify why he presses Heidegger so hard when it comes to God and why he can leverage the analogy of childhood to emphasize the received, communal dimension of being itself.

Siewerth is out for a synthesis of Heidegger and Thomas rather than a capitulation to one or the other. If, for him, the root sense of "being" is something like Thomas's, it nevertheless carries with it the further sense of historical happening and experiencing that is so key to Heidegger's use of "being."

---

46. Te Velde, *Participation and Substantiality*, 109.

47. Gustav Siewerth, *Das Schicksal der Metaphysik: von Thomas zu Heidegger* (Einsiedeln: Johannes Verlag, 2003), 478: "Für Thomas ist das Sein der höchste aller Namen, der Gott bezeichnen kann. Dennoch geht er primär auf die seienden Dinge dieser Welt. In dieser ersten und wesenhaften Terminierung bezeichnet es die Substanz, und zwar so, daß der Wortsinn des Seins (ens) vom ‚Akt' des Seienden her (actus essendi) genommen ist. Als Akt aber bezeichnet es dasjenige, *wodurch* etwas ist."

Late in *Thomismus als Identiätssystem*, Siewerth offers a Heideggerian-tinged description of "being" in Thomas:

> Being was exposed as the most common, first, holistic, and grounding proposition, [and] as the center. Therefore, the unfolding of being by its archetypal ground was always also a movement from this center to its ground, and a return to it as the unity of its possible determinations. This 'movement' was not somehow done to determinant beings, it was not made by them or considered as a reasonable possibility, but *it was the manifest sense of being itself*.[48]

We can see the Heideggerian accent on "unfolding" and becoming, even a concern that being "itself" is involved in this unfolding, a narrative that resembles Dasein. We can also see how and why it is that Siewerth insists that this unfolding does not happen "to" being but is a quality of being itself. He does not mean it only in a Heideggerian sense; he means it in a Thomistic one as well, one that relies on participation for its account of how a being can be "itself" and yet also draw nearer to its ground. All the particularity of Heidegger's Dasein is preserved but now opened up to an infinite striving as being desires to participate in the highest good by becoming more itself, what it was eternally willed to be. So it is that Siewerth unites Heidegger's interest in Dasein with Thomistic concerns about the nature of being.[49] As much as Siewerth is willing to give to Heidegger—and he is quite a bit more generous than Balthasar ever is—he is not convinced by Heidegger's definition of "being" and prefers the Thomist one, which can ask about God and difference in the same breath. Without this key, all the doors to thought remain locked.

---

48. Siewerth, *Thomismus als Identitätssystem*, 147: "Das Sein war als allgemeinste, erste, ganzheitliche und gründende Aussage als diese Mitte herausgestellt. Deshalb war die Entfaltung des Seins von seinem urbildlichen Grunde immer auch ursprünglicheine Bewegung aus dieser Mitte auf den Grund him und eine Rückkehr zu ihr als der Einheit seiner möglichen Bestimmungen. Diese ‚Bewegung' wurde den Bestimmungen nicht irgendwie angetan, sie wurde nicht an ihnen vorgenommen oder als vernünftige Möglichkeit hinzugedacht, sondern *sie war der sich manifesterende Seinssinn selbst*."

49. It is important to understand that this unity is at the same time based in a critique of Heidegger, one focused at once on the meaning of being and, in what we will see now, on the problem of "the other" (Siewerth, *Schicksal der Metaphysik*, 581): "Warum hält Heidegger sich statt dessen im Abgrund eines Umfänglichen und Waltenden, das sich zwar in seinem Höchsten, wie wir oben zeigten, auf ein letztes Geheimnis hin, ‚den Hohen selbst, der ist, wer er ist' und der ‚durch die Lichtung' waltet, geheimnisvoll zu öffnen scheint, aber zugleich sich als das Umgreifende erhält, das auch der Gottheit erst ‚Wohnung" gewährt?'" In Siewerth's parlance, Heidegger fails to deeply consider "externality" or "outwardness" (*Äußerlichkeit*), which for Siewerth means the relation of a being to what it is not, to what is "other" or "different" (582).

Returning to Trinitarian Dramatics

After a lengthy study of Siewerth's iteration of Heideggerian-inflected Thomism, it is possible to turn again to Balthasar in an attempt to make sense of his "areas of freedom" in the Trinity. In the broadest sense, Siewerth and Balthasar resemble each other since the grounding meaning of "being" is a Thomist one in both, and their further accents on being are in various respects Heideggerian. In neither case could it be said that Heidegger is a superficial add-on to an already complete system. It bears repeating that, direct citations aside, it is difficult to discern which Thomist mentor Balthasar is borrowing from, and when, in his efforts. This is complicated by the fact that, unless he signals otherwise, Balthasar typically draws from several resources at once; be they biblical, Augustinian, Irenaean, Thomist, and so forth. So, my focus will not be on describing every influence operating in Balthasar's claims but will instead be on the essential puzzle of the essay—areas of freedom in God— and discerning its various Heideggerian and Thomist stresses.

And Balthasar does, quite clearly, borrow from Thomas. If Siewerth says of Thomas that his interest is primarily in describing the created world even when he is describing God, the same can be said of Balthasar. Besides explicitly distinguishing between the eternal "act" of the Trinity and the act of creation, such that we are clearly speaking analogously when we relate the actions of the immanent Trinity to those of the economic Trinity,[50] Balthasar also devotes himself to explaining created freedom even in the midst of describing infinite freedom.[51] It is primarily in *created* freedom, not in God, that we first and constantly discover the two "poles" of self-determination and consent, and, Balthasar says, these poles are an image of the Triune God.[52]

Balthasar begins this tracing of created freedom first by following the lineaments of the "autonomous motion" of the free subject, that is, the ability each subject has to determine itself in some way. He finds this claim everywhere in the patristic tradition and notes how it allies self-determination with self-knowledge—willing with rationality—an alliance that is, as we have already seen through Siewerth, discoverable in Thomas as well.[53] When he turns to Thomas, therefore, Balthasar again highlights the unity of willing

---

50. He recalls this logic again in *TD* 5, here to try an outline a further relationship between the economic and immanent Trinity through further analogies of being, participation, and eternity. See *TD* 2, 267; *TD* 4, 244–46.

51. See, for example, *TD* 2, 261.

52. *TD* 2, 240.

53. *TD* 2, 218. On Irenaeus: "To deny that man has autonomous motion is to deny him rationality. Here we have a clear statement of the inseparability of reason and freedom, on which Thomas will place such weight."

and reasoning, which are related reciprocally.[54] Indeed, this reciprocal relationship between knowing and willing, between being and the good, is anchored in the subject by its natural desire to reach the totality of being and goodness. As we have identified above with Siewerth, no finite thing will do.[55]

Here, Balthasar relies on *Summa contra gentiles*. For Balthasar, the first key passage is book 3, q. 25, where Thomas argues that, just as "the ultimate end of each thing is God," so also "an intellectual substance tends to divine knowledge as an ultimate end." The second citation is book 3, q. 50, which describes the natural desire to know as unable to be satisfied by any finite thing. These are the same citations that Siewerth uses to establish a similar basic description of the finite subject. Balthasar is explicit in his reliance on Siewerth here, not only for the basic Thomistic logic but also for a further description of the autonomous subject: there is a (relative) "absoluteness" in finite freedom, since it "can neither get back to its own origin, insofar as finite freedom is present 'as a given,' nor (therefore) can it reach its goal by pursuing the totality of goods and values to be found in the world, be they personal or impersonal."[56] Balthasar uses Siewerth as a reader of Thomas and as a thinker in his own right, and what is helpful about Siewerth's analysis is his ability to hold in tension the dynamic integrity of willing and knowing in the finite subject *and* the infinite toward which that willing and knowing strives.

Balthasar stresses the unity of knowing and willing within finite freedom, a unity that is autonomous in a limited sense, and this unity of knowing and willing is one that Balthasar considers especially important to Thomas.[57] But Thomas also provides the other pole of freedom in Balthasar's schema, which

---

54. *TD* 2, 225: "Autonomous motion always involves positing the '*logikon*,' that is, it involves insight into being in its totality and the act of judging every existing thing and every value under the aspect of being and of the good per se; so much so that the two elements can only be grasped in a reciprocal priority."

55. *TD* 2, 225–26: "But because the '*motus*' of freedom is inseparable from the '*causa sui*,' because there is thus in the will a natural longing (*desiderium naturale*) for complete, exhaustive self-possession, which would have to coincide with the "possession" of being as such, we arrive at the Thomist paradox . . . : man strives to fulfill himself in an Absolute and yet, although he is '*causa sui*,' he is unable to achieve this by his own power or by attaining any finite thing or finite good. Precisely this, according to Thomas, constitutes man's dignity."

56. *TD* 2, 226. This argument also appears in "Truth as Freedom" in *TL* 1, 79–103 and is repeated on 235–36. See also *TD* 4: "Although we cannot deny that finite freedom has an absolute aspect, it has power over neither its own ground nor its own fulfillment. It does possess itself, yet it is not its own gift to itself: it owes itself to some other origin" (139).

57. Balthasar also draws from *De veritate* to say: "Only human reason is able to 'judge its own judgment' and thus 'be a cause of its own self not only in autonomous motion (that is, in spontaneity) but also in judging.'"

is that of consent and which conditions any claims to an absolute autonomy. Here, Balthasar moves back-and-forth between the two poles, as they are not separate moments or movements but are together constitutive of finite freedom. When he speaks of freedom as "consent," Balthasar focuses on how it is that finite freedom exists *from out of*, because of, within the boundlessness of, infinite freedom.[58] Freedom is "given" as well as enacted, and it is given by infinite freedom. This givenness is the aspect of consent. Human freedom is at once "its own" and an affirmation of the infinite freedom that makes it effective. But this givenness is inseparable from what is given—being itself. For Balthasar, this is explicitly understood in terms of Thomas. A particular passage deserves our attention here:

> Thus, insofar as self-being [*Selbst-Sein*] in principle discloses all reality, it means that everything real that is encountered in the realm of being, insofar as it participates in being, is posited as worthy of recognition (as true) and worthy of approval (as good). This posits an irreducible bipolarity in (individual) self-consciousness, indicating that this consciousness does not coincide with the totality of Being but only participates in it, that is, it is a contingent and factually existing consciousness.[59]

So every being, inasmuch as it knows itself, implicitly knows all of being, because it participates in being.[60] Remember that a finite being only "has" being in a secondary sense, and only God can be said to *have* and *be* being.[61] Inasmuch as I am, inasmuch as I am in act, I am so because I share in God's being and acting (which are one).[62] With this in mind, Balthasar desires to

---

58. So, for example, to continue the citation above: "In answering the question of how infinite freedom can indwell finite, in order to allow it to be genuine, finite freedom, we must return once more to the primal act of self-knowledge (which is a knowledge of being) and recall that, in grasping our own being, we also grasp all being whatsoever, which goes beyond all particular beings" (*TD* 2, 239).

59. *TD* 2, 239. He repeats the logic of participation later in *TD* 5, 67–68, and echoes the second volume deliberately on pp. 75–81, which he emphasizes in order to include some kind of "eternal movement" (not, he stresses, becoming) in the Trinity. This makes way for "areas of freedom" in God in *TD* 2 and "joy/surprise" in God in *TD* 4.

60. He says in *TL* 1, 229–30: "There is no aspect of worldly truth that simply rests in itself. . . . It is true, of course that in this first act the subject takes the measure of itself and of being as a whole, God can be glimpsed, in however veiled and indirect a fashion, as the necessary ground of all worldly truth."

61. Again, in *TL* 1: "There is no alien matter upon which God impresses his ideas; the only preexistent 'matter' out of which God creates the world is his free will and his eternal idea" (234). He cites *De veritate* q. 8, a. 13 ad 18.

62. In *TL* 1, this becomes the "groundlessness" of created truth, which does not emerge without God's truth, and yet, by virtue of its groundlessness, shares in an analogous way in the "groundlessness" of God's truth (231).

appropriate a metaphysical emphasis that he considers peculiar to Thomas, which "concerns the mediation of Being, which permeates and is at work in all finite being, the most unique as well as the most general."[63] Here, Balthasar references the fundamental meaning of "being" in the Thomistic sense, which I earlier established alongside Siewerth and te Velde: "being" does not refer to a being or a scale of beings but rather to the unity of essence and existence in God, which a finite being participates in according to (as Siewerth reminds us) the act by which that thing is.

But Balthasar then adds to this Thomist ground the stratum of consciousness, so that the supposedly "external" categories of metaphysics apply to the inward disposition of the conscious subject.[64] For Balthasar, participation in being leads logically to the "letting be" of other beings, which is a Heideggerian theme.[65] Just as the knowing mind participates in the fullness of being, so too must it participate in that same "letting be" that is structurally an aspect of creation itself. Balthasar writes, "the soul, precisely because it possesses itself in freedom, necessarily respects all other beings on account of their freedom (they are true and real) and *lets them be*."[66] If self-possession is, at least in part, knowledge of my own existence and goodness, and through it a knowledge of being in general, then by dint of that same principle, I must also acknowledge the being and freedom of others. The logical move is significant in the sense that it is important to Balthasar, but more so in the sense that Balthasar has to make a deliberate turn against the pressures of Heidegger and even Thomas, pressure to remain at the level of either the individual or the metaphysical. Here, he instead insists that the logic of both, to be consistent, demands acknowledgment of other human beings.[67] In other words, Balthasar could have remained within the confines of Dasein and/or Thomistic metaphysics, but he does not. This is, though not directly attributable to Siewerth, nevertheless Siewerth's position in, for example, *Metaphysik der Kindheit*.

---

63. *TD* 2, 239.

64. This is not necessarily an addition, strictly speaking, to Thomas, since Balthasar roots himself in the likes of *Summa contra gentiles* and *De veritate*, which are also preoccupied with the knowing subject. Balthasar's emphasis is decidedly on this consciousness, and in that sense, we see him taking up Heidegger's call to grasp the situation of finite being rather than a static set of relations to being. This is so all while it is impossible to understand what Balthasar means here without also understanding "being" and "participation" as Thomas does.

65. This agreement between Balthasar and Heidegger on "letting be" is explicit elsewhere. See especially *TL* 1, 63–67, 110–11.

66. *TD* 2, 240.

67. He does the same in "Positivity of the 'Other'" in *TD* 5, 81–85 and in "The Individual" in *TD* 3, 447–64.

Balthasar insists that the "origin" of finite being's self-possession, while in some way found in the finite being, is *also* found in "the very ground of Being," such that "Spiritual being is one form, a highest form, of participation in Being."[68] This reiterates the tension of the poles of finite freedom, undergirded by Thomas: the finite being has its own freedom, a freedom given by the infinite freedom it participates in. For Balthasar, these poles are not ultimately opposed to one another.[69] This claim echoes Siewerth's insistence that the "movement" of being out of its ground only to "return" to it is not an addition to being but rather is the "manifestness" of being itself. The same can be said for Balthasar, who, when he moves to consider infinite freedom, is more emphatically theocentric: "the creature, man, suspended in the medium of God's freedom, is anchored—objectively—solely in God's truthfulness and—subjectively—in his own attitude of trust."[70]

Notice how, while speaking in the context of God's freedom, Balthasar returns to the situation of finite freedom. If in Thomas a finite form resembles the good in at least two ways, through the likeness it has to God by virtue of the form that is intrinsic to it (and so it is intrinsically good) and through its participation in the good (by virtue of efficient causality), then Balthasar continues this logic by expanding the manner in which the finite form bears a likeness to its creator. This allows Balthasar to stress this likeness in a fully Trinitarian mode, and it allows Balthasar to explain how it is that finite freedom is a participation in infinite freedom without also being an erasure of its own, intrinsic freedom—again in a fully Trinitarian mode:

> If *letting-be* belongs to the nature of infinite freedom—the Father *lets* the Son be consubstantial God, and so forth—there is no danger of finite freedom, which cannot fulfill itself on its own account . . . becoming alienated from itself in the realm of the Infinite. It can only be what it is, that is, an image of infinite freedom, imbued with a freedom of its own, by getting in tune with the (trinitarian) "law" of absolute freedom (of self-surrender): and this law is not foreign to it—for after all it is the "law" of absolute Being—but most authentically its own.[71]

If human freedom is self-possessed *and* an affirmation of the infinite act that makes it effective, then Balthasar argues that this infinite act itself, the Trinity,

---

68. *TD* 2, 240.

69. *TD* 2, 242. In *TL* 1, a resonance tension appears between knowledge and its inherent fragmentary status, which presents us with a (perhaps discouraging) "infinity" of questions, and yet this infinity is "an inverse mirror image of the true, but never graspable, infinity of God" (253).

70. *TD* 2, 253.

71. *TD* 2, 259.

is—as free—self-possessed *and* affirmed: God knows himself and loves himself and is himself in the same act. And so Balthasar attempts a Trinitarian elaboration of God as pure act, where God knows himself to be and loves himself as and himself is triune. This elaboration is pressed to its maximum: the processions and relations are the divine nature knowing, loving, and being three Persons by an infinite act of "letting be" that, since personal, is described distinctly with respect to each Person (thus, neologistic phrases receive their meaning: "the Father lets the Son be," etc.).

With this essential metaphysical scaffolding in place, Balthasar is able to establish a theo-drama that is, while not solely or strictly metaphysical, nevertheless a drama that bears an intelligible relationship to metaphysics. Because Balthasar has so thoroughly amplified the Trinitarian dimension of the gift of being and the infinite freedom within the Trinitarian relations, freedom is now also amplified as a constitutive aspect of being itself. Balthasar is able to say, with all seriousness, that "every worldly dramatic production" finds its ultimate image in the eternal, Triune "coincidence of freedom and obedience or of self-being and consciously acknowledged dependence."[72] That is, every worldly drama is an image of the divine one. This is so much the case that even when finite freedom arises as "its own," and so in "opposition" to the divine freedom (because it is *not* the divine freedom) in a dramatic dialogue, we can nevertheless understand what Balthasar means by this without positing a rupture in the universe wherein the two kinds of freedom become comparable objects to one another, and so involved in a mythic struggle.[73]

The above argument has been, for all its length, compacted in its description of the undercurrents of Balthasar's claim that there are "areas of freedom" in God. So, the implications of my explorations deserve some final highlighting and repetition. In the first place, Balthasar fully appropriates the Thomistic sense of "being," with its attendant sense of "participation." Thus, the (economic) theo-drama played out on the stage of the world is not identical with the immanent Trinity, though salvation is the work of one and the same God, *and also* the creature's dramatic dialogue with God is not the elevation of human beings into some kind of identity or equality with the immanent Trinity. Second, Balthasar—like Thomas—sets out to describe God in order to

---

72. *TD* 2, 268.

73. Cf. *TD* 2, 271–72. My argument would thus challenge not only Lösel's thesis that Balthasar destroys the economy by lifting it into the immanent Trinity (see n. 9) but also would challenge elements of Ben Quash's claim that Balthasar's theo-dramatics is an "epic" drama in the Hegelian sense. See Ben Quash, *Theology and the Drama of History* (New York: Cambridge University Press, 2005), 41–42, 132–37 and "'Between the Brutally Given, and the Brutally, Banally Free': Von Balthasar's Theology of Drama in Dialogue with Hegel," *Modern Theology* 13 (1997): 293–318.

understand creation, which frames his interest in the divine "areas of freedom." This is our major analogical movement. Its foundation is the goodness that God is, which is shared with creaturely being via intrinsic form and participation, thereby funding the analogy that persists between the two orders of being. The analogy's elaboration is "letting be" in God, which accommodates or spans (in God) the two "poles" of Balthasarian freedom: autonomous motion and consent. The "location" of the letting-be is, precisely, the "areas of freedom" in the Trinity, mapped onto the divine Persons. This allows Balthasar to follow the analogical movement to its end: as these poles are in God, so by analogy we find them in the rational subject. Balthasar thus elaborates on the Thomist position by applying its logic to Trinitarian reflection, both in God and in the created images of God, human beings.

CONCLUSION

We have spent our time in an extended study of Gustav Siewerth's Heideggerian Thomism in order to understand the metaphysical aspects of Balthasar's claim that there are areas of infinite freedom in the Persons of the Trinity. Balthasar adapts Heidegger's claim that truth requires an attitude or comportment of "letting be," applying it both to the created subject and (analogously) to the Persons of the Trinity. Heidegger receives sharp critique since Dasein is so intensely individualistic, a critique that Siewerth employs at length. For Siewerth, being and community are linked to one another, and Thomas Aquinas's understanding of being is better able to account for both. Thomas uses being to primarily mean the unity of essence and existence in God, a unity that the created being participates in according to the manner of its existence. Balthasar, presuming a Thomistic account of being highly similar to that of Siewerth, situates the relation of finite freedom to infinite freedom. Within this relation, this participation, Balthasar expands on the way in which finite (rational) form bears a likeness to God. This likeness is found in the "bipolarity" of creaturely consciousness, suspended between freedom as autonomy and consent. In the Trinity, this image is found in how each Person "is" uniquely (that is, is not the others), and how at the same time each consents to the others in an act of eternal surrender. This surrender is achieved from out "areas of freedom" by which each gives over divinity entirely to the others, in modes or relations unique to each Person. The result of this complex set of appropriations and claims is a metaphysically intelligible framework for an eternal, divine drama that all earthly drama mimics, and for a metaphysically intelligible relation between the earthly and the divine dramas. This metaphysical frame is but the scaffolding upon which Balthasar builds, essential to understand and yet not identical with the whole form of the theo-drama.

BIBLIOGRAPHY

Aquinas, Thomas. *Summa Contra Gentiles*. Translated by Anton C. Pegis, James F. Anderson, Charles J. O'Neil, and Vernon J. Bourke. New York: Hanover House, 1955–57.

Cummings, Owen T. "Divine Refusal: An Aspect of the Internal Link Between God and Truth in Heidegger." *International Journal of Philosophy and Theology* 74 (2013): esp. 183–84.

Dalzell, Thomas G. "Lack of Social Drama in Balthasar's Theological Dramatics." *Theological Studies* 60 (1999): 457–75.

Hadley, Christopher. *A Symphony of Distances: Patristic, Modern, and Gendered Dimensions of Balthasar's Trinitarian Theology*. Washington, DC: The Catholic University of America Press, 2022.

Heidegger, Martin. "Letter on 'Humanism.'" In *Pathmarks*, edited by W. McNeil, translated by F. A. Capuzzi, 239–76. New York: Cambridge University Press, 1998.

———. "On the Essence of Truth." In *Pathmarks*, edited by W. McNeill, translated by J. Sallis, 136–54. New York: Cambridge University Press, 1998.

Lochbrunner, Manfred. *Hans Urs von Balthasar und seine Philosophenfreunde: Fünf Doppelporträts*. Würzburg: Echter Verlag, 2005.

Long, D. Stephen. *The Perfectly Simple Triune God: Aquinas and His Legacy*. Minneapolis, MN: Fortress Press, 2016.

Lösel, Steffen. "Murder in the Cathedral: Hans Urs von Balthasar's New Dramatization of the Doctrine of the Trinity." *Pro Ecclesia* 5 (1996): 427–39.

———. "Unapocalyptic Theology: History and Eschatology in Balthasar's Theo-Drama." *Modern Theology* 17 (2001): 202.

Orr, James. "Edith Stein's Critique of Sociality in Early Heidegger." *Neue Zeitschrift für systematische Theologie und Religionsphilosophie* 55, no. 3 (2013): 379–96.

Pöggeler, Franz. "Gustav Siewerth—Wirk und Wirken." In *Innerlichkeit und Erziehung: In memoriam Gustav Siewerth*, edited by F. Pöggeler, 4–6. Freiburg: Herder, 1964.

Quash, Ben. "'Between the Brutally Given, and the Brutally, Banally Free': Von Balthasar's Theology of Drama in Dialogue with Hegel." *Modern Theology* 13 (1997): 293–318.

———. *Theology and the Drama of History*. New York: Cambridge University Press, 2005.

Siewerth, Gustav. *Das Schicksal der Metaphysik: von Thomas zu Heidegger*. Einsiedeln: Johannes Verlag, 2003.

———. *Der Thomismus als Identitätssystem*. Frankfurt: Verlag Gerhard Schulte-Bulmke, 1961.

———. *Metaphysik der Kindheit*. Einsiedeln: Johannes Verlag, 1957.

Te Velde, Rudi. *Participation and Substantiality in Thomas Aquinas*. New York: Brill, 1995.

Tourpe, Emmanuel. *Siewerth apres Siewerth: Le lien idéal de amour dans le Thomisme spéculatif de Gustav Siewerth et la visée de réalisme transcendental.* Paris: Louvain, 1998.
von Speyr, Adrienne. *The World of Prayer.* San Francisco: Ignatius Press, 1985.

Revelation

CHAPTER 3

On the Wisdom of Faith and the Salvific Power of Christ's Prophetic Office

Thomas Aquinas on Revelation

ROGER NUTT

IN AN ESSAY ON THE TOPIC OF REVELATION, Hans Urs von Balthasar cites a comment by Thomas Aquinas in his *Catena aurea* that affirms that "One who does not nourish himself on the word of God is no longer living." Remarking on the significance of this passage, Balthasar notes, "The word of scripture is above any other word concerning God; in virtue of its Christo-logical form it is a word opening into God and leading to him."[1] Without glossing over the differences that exist between thinkers separated by seven hundred years of thought and controversy, Balthasar's statement on scripture touches many central aspects of Aquinas's doctrine of revelation.[2] While St. Thomas does not stress the transcendental of beauty that is so integral to Balthasar's entire project,[3] and while Aquinas does not concur with some of Balthasar's conclusions about the death of Christ revealing an inner-Trinitarian distance, Thomas Aquinas's doctrine of revelation systematically mediates and

---

1. "The Word, Scripture, and Tradition," in *ET* 1, 24–25.

2. Steffen Lösel argues that Balthasar's treatment of the cross's revelatory and theo-logico-aesthetical value is founded upon "his Thomistic theory of perception and its two key concepts 'form' and 'splendor.'" See Lösel's "Love Divine, All Loves Excelling: Balthasar's Negative Theology of Revelation," *The Journal of Religion* 82, no. 4 (2002): 589. For general treatments of various aspects of Aquinas's theology of revelation, see Wil-helmus G. B. M. Valkenberg, *Words of the Living God: Place and Function of Holy Scripture in the Theology of St. Thomas Aquinas* (Leuven: Peeters, 2000) and Lawrence Feingold, *Faith Comes from What Is Heard: An Introduction to Fundamental Theology* (Steubenville, OH: Emmaus Academic, 2016).

3. For a treatment of the status of beauty as a transcendental in Aquinas, see Thomas Joseph White, OP, "Beauty, Transcendence, and the Inclusive Hierarchy of Creation," *Nova et Vetera* (English edition) 16, no. 4 (2018): 1215–26.

develops the first millennium's doctrine of the interconnectedness between the nature of God (*theologia*) and the unfolding of the plan of salvation (*oikonomia*) culminating in Christ.[4] The vast majority of what each thinker contributes to our understanding of the nature of revelation can be read in a complimentary fashion.[5]

For Aquinas, the teaching of the Christian faith manifest in scripture and summarized in the creeds depends on a freely bestowed divine communication—revelation is fundamentally gratuitous. Despite his great acumen as a philosopher, Aquinas insists on the epistemological superiority of revealed truth over that of demonstrative knowledge.[6] It is revelation that contains this divinely bestowed sacred teaching.[7] Without gainsaying his firm confidence in reason to know metaphysical truths, Aquinas affirms that while faith's knowledge is not "seen" in the sense of a demonstrative proof, it is a true mode of knowing that surpasses the horizons of unaided human wisdom.[8] Revelation, therefore, as contemplated by Aquinas, makes knowing God in his fullness possible, scientifically cogent, and certain.[9]

Because of the well-ordered formality of Aquinas's theological thought, his doctrine of revelation is not enclosed within just one treatise of his corpus.[10] Aquinas discusses revelation "sometimes as an operation of salvation," René Latourelle explains:

---

4. For an exposition of Aquinas's doctrine of revelation in relation to his theology of the temporal missions of the Son and the Holy Spirit, see Matthew Levering, *Engaging the Doctrine of Revelation: The Mediation of the Gospel through Scripture and the Church* (Grand Rapids, MI: Baker Academic, 2014), 37–43. Levering also provides a helpful presentation on Balthasar's position on this point at pp. 43–49.

5. For a thoughtful summary of Balthasar's thoughts by a Thomist theologian, see Battista Mondin, *I Grandi Teologi del Secolo Ventesimo*, vol. 1, *I Teologi Cattolici* (Turin: Borla editore, 1969).

6. See Roger W. Nutt, "Are Aristotelian-Thomists Rationalists? On *Thomism*, the *Praeambula Fidei*, and Theological Faith," in *Theology Needs Philosophy: Acting against Reason Is Contrary to the Nature of God*, ed. Matthew L. Lamb (Washington, DC: The Catholic University of America Press, 2016), 116–34.

7. See Albert Paretsky, "The Influence of Thomas the Exegete on Thomas the Theologian: The Tract on Law (Ia-IIae, qq. 90–108)," *Angelicum* 71, no. 4 (1994): 549–78.

8. For a discussion of Thomas's understanding of the scientific nature of revealed teaching, see James Weisheipl, "The Meaning of *Sacra Doctrina* in *Summa Theologiae* I, q. 1," *The Thomist* 38, no. 1 (1974): 49–80.

9. See John I. Jenkins, *Knowledge and Faith in Thomas Aquinas* (Cambridge: Cambridge University Press, 1997). See also Lawrence Dewan, "Communion with the Tradition: For the Believer Who Is a Philosopher," *Science et Esprit* 40, no. 3 (1988): 315–25.

10. For a general treatment of revelation in Aquinas, see V. White, "Le concept de révélation chez S. Thomas," *L'année théologique* 11 (1950): 1–17, 109–32.

proceeding from the free love of God and furnishing man with all the lights that are indispensable or simply useful for the pursuit of his salvation; sometimes as an historical event, unrolling in time and touching men of all centuries through a complex economy of intermediaries, stages, and modalities; sometimes as a divine activity penetrating into the psychological life of the prophet and, as a consequence . . . sometimes as a sacred doctrine communicated through Christ to His apostles and handed down by them, a doctrine contained in Scripture and proposed, through the preaching of the Church . . . sometimes, finally, as a degree of knowledge which he lines up in relation to the other types of knowledge: natural knowledge, knowledge of faith, knowledge of vision.[11]

Aquinas's doctrine of revelation therefore permeates the entirety of his theological thought. Furthermore, Aquinas's doctrine of revelation, like most of his developed teaching, is treated analogically.[12] The completion of revealed knowledge is found only in the vision of heaven, while the pilgrim journey of faith also includes a mediated participation in the realities known fully only by the blessed. "Prophecy is by way of being," Aquinas teaches, "something imperfect in the genus of Divine revelation: hence it is written (1 Cor 13:8) that "prophecies shall be made void" and that "we prophesy in part," that is, imperfectly. The Divine revelation will be brought to its perfection in heaven; wherefore, the same text continues (1 Cor 13:10): "When that which is perfect is come, that which is in part shall be done away."[13]

This chapter will tie together the many aspects of Aquinas's teaching on revelation in the context of salvation in Christ, which is the telos of revelation.[14]

---

11. René Latourelle, *Theology of Revelation* (New York: Alba House, 1987), 159.

12. On Aquinas's doctrine of analogy, with explicit discussion of how analogy is developed in revelation, see Steven A. Long, *Analogia Entis: On Analogy, Metaphysics, and the Act of Faith* (Notre Dame, IN: University of Notre Dame Press, 2011), 97–106; Charles Journet, *The Wisdom of Faith: An Introduction to Theology*, trans. R. F. Smith (Westminster, MD: The Newman Press, 1952), 19–21; and Roger W. Nutt, "On Analogy, the Incarnation, and the Sacraments of the Church: Considerations from the *Tertia pars* of the *Summa theologiae*," *Nova et Vetera* (English edition) 12, no. 3 (2014): 989–1004. For Balthasar's defense of the Catholic doctrine of the analogy of being against the criticisms of the reformed theologian Karl Barth, see his *The Theology of Karl Barth* (San Francisco: Ignatius Press, 1992). For a treatment of Balthasar's attempt to reconcile Barth's rejection of the analogy of being with the classical doctrine of Aquinas, see Gregory Rocca, *Speaking the Incomprehensible God* (Washington, DC: The Catholic University of America Press, 2004), 97–103.

13. Thomas Aquinas, *Summa theologiae*, ed. John Mortensen and Enrique Alarcon, trans. Laurence Shapcote, *Opera Omnia*, vols. 13–20 (Lander, WY: The Aquinas Institute for the Study of Sacred Doctrine, 2012), 2–2.171.4 ad 2. Translations of the *Summa theologiae* will be taken from this edition, unless otherwise noted.

14. For Balthasar's articulation of the connection between Christ's death and the pattern of Christian life, see *MCW*.

REVELATION AND SOTERIOLOGY

Perhaps the most recurrent theme in Aquinas's teaching on revelation is its saving significance. A helpful place to start, therefore, is by considering Aquinas's answer to the question of whether or not divine revelation is necessary for the human race. Given the power of reason to come to know truth, why not simply allow humankind to seek its final end by means of its natural capacities? "Because man is directed to God," Aquinas answers, "as to an end that surpasses the grasp of his reason. . . . But the end must first be known by men who are to direct their thoughts and actions to the end."[15] For Aquinas, the direction of humanity to the supernatural end of God himself requires a divinely bestowed knowledge—revelation—for the sake of properly directing humanity to this end. "Hence it was necessary," Aquinas argues, "for the salvation of man that certain truths which exceed human reason should be made known to him by divine revelation. . . . Therefore, in order that the salvation of men might be brought about more fitly and more surely, it was necessary that they should be taught divine truths by divine revelation."[16] The use of the word "necessary" by Aquinas in this passage is meant to be absolute in the sense that salvation would not merely be difficult without revelation, but it would be impossible for human beings to know and love God adequately had God not manifest the truth about himself.

The inclusion of truths that can be known by reason within divine revelation, Aquinas insists, makes the full truth of the providential order, and hence salvation, accessible to all by faith. "Beneficially, therefore," Aquinas explains, "did the divine Mercy provide that it should instruct us to hold by faith even those truths that the human reason is able to investigate."[17] This divine generosity gives a participation in the knowledge of God: "In this way, all men would easily be able to have a share in the knowledge of God, and this without uncertainty and error."[18]

By noting that truths of the natural order are taken up in divine revelation Aquinas in no way intends to conflate supernatural mysteries with truths proportionate to humanity's natural capacities. The rational creature could not participate in God's Trinitarian knowledge had it not been revealed. Nevertheless, Aquinas argues that salvation is furthered by the revelation of those truths that can be known by reason without divine assistance: "Even as regards those truths about God which human reason could have discovered, it was

---

15. *ST* 1.1.1.

16. *ST* 1.1.1.

17. Thomas Aquinas, *Summa contra gentiles, Book One: God*, trans. Anton C. Pegis (Notre Dame, IN: University of Notre Dame Press, 1975), 1.4.6, 68.

18. *SCG* 1.4.6.

necessary that man should be taught by a divine revelation; because the truth about God such as reason could discover, would only be known by a few, and that after a long time, and with the admixture of many errors."[19]

Even truths of the natural law may be not known only by means of unaided human reason, or they may be known only confusedly. "Objects which are the subject-matter of different philosophical sciences," such as natural truths pertain to philosophy, Aquinas explains, "can yet be treated of by this one single sacred science under one aspect precisely so far as they can be included in revelation. So that in this way, sacred doctrine bears, as it were, the stamp of the divine science which is one and simple, yet extends to everything."[20]

Revelation as a Salvific Participation in God

Revealed knowledge, Aquinas holds, communicated through the gratuitous infusion into the soul of theological virtue of faith animated by charity, constitutes a participation in the God's own knowledge of himself and things as they relate to him. This sharing by God of his own knowledge of himself, makes the truths known by theological faith what Aquinas terms "co-natural" to the believer. Thomas views the infused gift of wisdom as an especially deep share of the divine realities with the believer: "the wisdom which is a gift of the Holy Ghost enables us to judge aright of Divine things, or of other things according to Divine rules, by reason of a certain connaturalness or union with Divine things, which is the effect of charity."[21]

The knowledge, therefore, given by God in revelation and accepted by the gift of faith constitutes for Aquinas one of three possible degrees by which humankind can come to know God:

> There is, then, in man a threefold knowledge of things divine. The first is that in which man, by the natural light of reason, ascends to a knowledge of God through creatures. *The second is that by which the divine truth—exceeding the human intellect—descends on us in the manner of revelation* . . . as something spoken in words to be believed. The third is that by which the human mind will be elevated to gaze perfectly upon the things revealed.[22]

That the rational creature is able to know God's existence through the powers of reason is a pivotal truth in Aquinas's doctrine of revelation. The capacity to

---

19. *ST* 1.1.1.

20. *ST* 1.1.3 ad 2.

21. *ST* 2–2.45.4. See Brendan Case, "Judging according to Wisdom: Sacra Doctrina in the Summa Theologiae," *New Black Friars* 98, no. 1077 (2017): 582–98.

22. *SCG* 4.1.5, 37.

know truth by the natural light of reason stands as the foundation for how truth is known in the elevated modes. If there is nothing in humanity that can know some level of truth by the power of a natural light within its nature, then having truth revealed would also be futile. "If this [natural] light," Aquinas argues,

> because it is created, is not adequate to know the truth, but needs a new illumination, the added light with equal reason will not suffice, but will require another light, and so on to infinity. . . . And so it will be impossible to know any truth. Therefore we must depend on the first light, so that the human mind can see the truth by its natural light without anything being added.[23]

Thomas's famous conviction that grace does not destroy but rather perfects and presupposes nature also plays out in his doctrine of revelation:

> The existence of God and other like truths about God, which can be known by natural reason, are not articles of faith, but are preambles to the articles; *for faith presupposes natural knowledge, even as grace presupposes nature, and perfection supposes something that can be perfected.* Nevertheless, there is nothing to prevent a man, who cannot grasp a proof, accepting, as a matter of faith, something which in itself is capable of being scientifically known and demonstrated.[24]

The natural ability to know the truth is precisely what is elevated by the revelation of truth from a higher source. Aquinas even places the knowledge possessed by the "old woman" (*vetula*) with firm faith above the knowledge of the philosophers prior to the coming of Christ.[25] "No one of the philosophers," Aquinas argues, "before the coming of Christ could, through his own powers, know God and the means necessary for salvation as well as the old woman since Christ's coming knows him through faith."[26]

The saving significance of revelation is a point that unites Aquinas and Balthasar. "God's message is theological, or better theo-pragmatic," Balthasar affirms, "It is an act of God on man; an act done for and on behalf of man— and only then to man, and in him. It is this act that we must say: it is credible

---

23. Thomas Aquinas, *Super de Trin.* 1.1 s.c., in *Faith, Reason, and Theology: Questions I–IV of his Commentary on the De Trinitate of Boethius,* trans. Armand Maurer (Toronto: Pontifical Institute of Mediaeval Studies, 1987), 15–16, hereafter cited as "Maurer."

24. *ST* 1.2.2 ad 1. Emphasis added.

25. See Bruce Marshall, "Quod scit una vetula": Aquinas on the Nature of Theology," in *The Theology of Thomas Aquinas,* ed. Rik Van Nieuwenhove and Joseph Wawrykow (Notre Dame, IN: University of Notre Dame Press, 2005), 1–35.

26. Thomas Aquinas, *In Symb. Ap.* prol., in *The Catechetical Instructions of St. Thomas Aquinas* (Manila: Sinag-Tala Publishers, Inc.), 2.

only as love—and here we mean God's own love, the manifestation of which is the manifestation of the glory of God."[27]

Revelation and Hierarchical Mediation in History

For Aquinas, the soteriological efficacy of divine revelation is ordered by the pedagogy of divine wisdom to unfold through historical mediations culminating in Christ.[28] Revelation is thus progressively communicated by the divine initiative through mediations and mediators.[29] Following the categories set forth in scripture, Aquinas associates the gift of prophecy with revelation: "prophetic knowledge is bestowed by Divine enlightenment and revelation."[30] The order through which this illumination is brought about corresponds to the hierarchies outlined in the work of the Syrian monk Dionysius, to whom Aquinas's thought is deeply indebted.[31] "Now the Divine ordering," Aquinas explains, "according to Dionysius, is such that the lowest things are directed by middle things."[32] The first mediation, therefore, in the divine pedagogy is angelic: "Now the angels hold a middle position between God and men, in that they have a greater share in the perfection of the Divine goodness than men have. Wherefore the Divine enlightenments and revelations are conveyed from God to men by the angels."[33]

Originating in God, Aquinas explains that revelation reaches lower orders through mediators of a higher order: "Now Divine revelation reaches those of lower degree through those who are over them, in a certain order; to men, for instance, through the angels, and to the lower angels through the higher, as Dionysius explains."[34] Despite being mediated through creatures, the gift of revelation remains "divine," Aquinas argues, because "The work of the instrument is ascribed to the principal agent by whose power the instrument acts. And since a minister is like an instrument, prophetic revelation, which is conveyed by the ministry of the angels, is said to be Divine."[35]

---

27. Hans Urs von Balthasar, *Love Alone: The Way of Revelation* (London: Sheed and Ward, 1968), 7–8.

28. On this point, too, Aquinas and Balthasar are in substantial agreement. See *C*, 90–105.

29. For a treatment of Thomas's doctrine of the development of revelation, see A. Hayen, "Le thomisme et l'histoire," *Revue thomiste* 62 (1962): 51–82.

30. *ST* 2–2.172.2.

31. For a presentation of the Dionysius's doctrine of revelation and its influence on Aquinas's thought, see Fran O'Rourke, *Pseudo-Dionysius and the Metaphysics of Aquinas* (Notre Dame, IN: University of Notre Dame Press, 2005), 3–61.

32. *ST* 2–2.172.2.

33. *ST* 2–2.172.2.

34. *ST* 2–2.2.6.

35. *ST*, 2–2.172.2 ad 3.

Aquinas recognizes that the same hierarchical ordering follows in the transmission of divine revelation from angels to human beings:

> the unfolding of faith must needs reach men of lower degree through those of higher degree. Consequently, just as the higher angels . . . have a fuller knowledge of Divine things than the lower angels . . . so too, men of higher degree, whose business it is to teach others, are under obligation to have fuller knowledge of matters of faith, and to believe them more explicitly.[36]

With this line of reasoning, Aquinas clearly has in mind the progression that takes place from angelic mediation through the prophetic revelations of the Old Testament to those of Christ and the Apostles in the New Testament.

The relationship between salvation history, the advancement of revelation, and hierarchical mediation is spelled out by Aquinas directly in the following passage:

> Whatever the prophets knew by revelation of the mysteries of grace, was revealed in a more excellent way to the angels. And although God revealed in general to the prophets what He was one day to do regarding the salvation of the human race, still the apostles knew some particulars of the same, which the prophets did not know. Thus we read (Eph 3:4–5): "As you reading, may understand my knowledge in the mystery of Christ, which in other generations was not known to the sons of men, as it is now revealed to His holy apostles." Among the prophets also, the later ones knew what the former did not know.[37]

When explaining authority in theological argumentation, Aquinas appeals directly to the nature of divine revelation. While sacred doctrine makes use of philosophical authorities and arguments "as extrinsic and probable arguments," it "properly uses the authority of the canonical Scriptures as an incontrovertible proof."[38] The authority of biblical revelation, Aquinas teaches, is derived from the fact that "faith rests upon the revelation made to the apostles and prophets who wrote the canonical books."[39] As he tersely says in his commentary on Peter Lombard's *Sentences*, "The believer believes a human being not insofar as he is a human being but insofar as God speaks in him."[40]

---

36. *ST* 2–2.2.6.

37. *ST* 1.57.5 ad 3.

38. *ST* 1.1.8 ad 2.

39. *ST* 1.1.8 ad 2.

40. *Super Sent.* 3.23.2.2.2 ad 3, cited in Bruno Niederbacher, "The Relation of Reason to Faith," in *The Oxford Handbook of Aquinas*, ed. Brian Davies and Eleonore Stump (New York: Oxford University Press, 2012), 346, n.13.

Revelation and the Mediation of Christ

Aquinas understands God's revelatory pedagogy in history to tend toward and culminate in the mediation of Christ: "There is one true God and one mediator between God and man, the man Jesus Christ" (1 Tim 2:5). Following this Pauline teaching, Aquinas explains that

> The office of a mediator is to join together and unite those between whom he mediates: for extremes are united in the mean. Now to unite men to God perfectively belongs to Christ. . . . And, consequently, Christ alone is the perfect Mediator of God and men, inasmuch as, by His death, He reconciled the human race to God. Hence the Apostle, after saying, "Mediator of God and man, the man Christ Jesus," added: "Who gave Himself a redemption for all."[41]

Unlike that of the interventions of angels, the priests of the Old Law, or Moses, Christ's mediation serves the unique salvific role of uniting God and humanity in himself.

A point of difference between Aquinas and Balthasar is the revelatory content of Christ's death on the cross. Balthasar maintained that Christ's cry of abandonment on the cross was a revelation of an inner-Trinitarian distance founded upon the infinite eternal freedom in the relations between the Father, Son, and Holy Spirit.[42] "Yet this "infinite distance," Balthasar argues, "which recapitulates the sinner's mode of alienation from God, will remain forever the highest revelation known to the world of the diastasis (within the eternal being of God) between the Father and the Son in the Holy Spirit."[43] While Aquinas and Balthasar agree broadly that Christ's death is the supreme revelation of God's love, they make opposite conclusions about the content of this revelation. For Aquinas, Christ's superlative exercise of the offices of priest and mediator on the cross reveals a unity in love, and not a distance. In Christ's assuming the penalty for sin and offering himself as a sacrifice for it, Aquinas sees a revelation of the eternal union between Christ and the Father. "The office proper to a priest is to be a mediator between God and the people," Aquinas explains,

---

41. *ST* 3.26.1.

42. For a fair but critical engagement with Balthasar's doctrine of revelation vis-à-vis the cross and Trinitarian theology, see Guy Mansini, "Balthasar and the Theodramatic Enrichment of the Trinity," *The Thomist* 64, no. 4 (2000): 499–519. See also Matthew Levering, *Scripture and Metaphysics: Aquinas and the Renewal of Trinitarian Theology* (Malden, MA: Blackwell Publishing, 2004), 120–43.

43. *TD* 3, 228.

to wit, inasmuch as He bestows Divine things on the people . . . and again, forasmuch as he offers up the people's prayers to God, and, in a manner, makes satisfaction to God for their sins. . . . Now this is most befitting to Christ. For through Him are gifts bestowed on men. . . . Moreover, He reconciled the human race to God, according to Colossians 1:19–20: "In Him" (i.e., Christ) "it hath well pleased (the Father) that all fullness should dwell, and through Him to reconcile all things unto Himself."[44]

In his preface to the third part of the *Summa theologiae*, which treats of Christ, Thomas explains the connection between the Incarnation of the Word and the full revelation of the truth: "Our Savior the Lord Jesus Christ, in order to *save his people from their sins* (Matt 1:21), as the angel announced, showed unto us in His own Person the way of truth."[45] For St. Thomas, the Incarnation of the Word himself establishes a special aspect of certitude for the Christian faith: "with regard to faith, which is made more certain by believing God Himself Who speaks."[46] The hierarchal mediations of salvation history culminating in Christ's priestly sacrifice on the cross reveal, Aquinas explains, a movement of the Son toward the Father in love. The notion of a revealed, inner-Trinitarian distance is foreign to the charity animating Christ's self-offering and the Father's acceptance of that offering that Aquinas sees playing out on the cross.[47]

Christ the Teacher of Revelation

As the Word of God Incarnate, St. Thomas understands Christ to be the principal teacher of revelation in the economy of salvation and the center of history.[48] Revelation for St. Thomas is not merely a body of truths but also a teaching by which those truths are made known. Each of the events of Christ's life are received by Aquinas as a further clarification of the salvific telos of the Incarnation.[49] For example, one of Thomas's reasons for the necessity of the Christ's Resurrection is: "in order to complete the work of our salvation:

---

44. *ST* 3.22.1.

45. *ST* 3 prol.

46. *ST* 3.1.2.

47. Balthasar does have a well-developed doctrine of revelation vis-à-vis the love of Christ. It is distilled concisely in the sixth chapter of *LAC*, "Love as Revelation," 68–80.

48. For an exposition of the role of Christ as teacher in Aquinas's theology, see Michael Dauphinais, "Christ the Teacher: The Pedagogy of the Incarnation" (PhD diss., University of Notre Dame, 2000).

49. For a presentation of Thomas's understanding of time and history in relation to the Incarnation, see G. M. Salvati, "Cristo e il tempo: Prospettive di teologia tomistica della storia," *Angelicum* 80, no. 3 (2003): 527–37.

because, just as for this reason did He endure evil things in dying that He might deliver us from evil, so was He glorified in rising again in order to advance us towards good things."[50] The universality of Christ's saving mission also clarifies for Thomas why he sent his Apostles to teach "all nations": "Christ was given to be the light and salvation of the Gentiles through His disciples, whom He sent to preach to them."[51]

Furthermore, one of the reasons that Aquinas appeals to for Christ's possession of the so-called "gratuitous graces" like prophesy is precisely his role as the primary teacher of the Christian faith. "The gratuitous graces," Aquinas argues, "are ordained for the manifestation of faith and spiritual doctrine. For it behooves him who teaches to have the means of making his doctrine clear. . . . Now Christ is the first and chief teacher of spiritual doctrine and faith."[52] This is also one of the reasons why Aquinas affirms Christ's beatific knowledge.[53] Christ was not taught the Christian faith from some other mediator; the Christian faith and salvation in Christ are derived from his fullness. "Men are brought to this end of beatitude," Aquinas affirms, "by the humanity of Christ. . . . And hence it was necessary that the beatific knowledge, which consists in the vision of God, should belong to Christ pre-eminently, since the cause ought always to be more efficacious than the effect."[54] For Aquinas, this truth is essentially economic: there is no middle ground between the "unseen" nature of faith, which must be mediated, and beatitude, which consists in the vision of God. Christ either possessed the truths that he taught, or he needed to be taught them by faith.

Thomas also recognizes a revelatory significance in the manner of life Christ adopted. "Christ's manner of life had to be in keeping with the end of His Incarnation," Thomas argues, "by reason of which He came into the world. Now He came into the world, first, *that He might publish the truth.*"[55] His revelatory mission explains why Christ did not live a cloistered life: "Hence it was fitting not that He should hide Himself by leading a solitary life, but that He should appear openly and preach in public. Wherefore (Lk 4:42–43) he says to those who wished to stay him: "To other cities also I must preach the kingdom of God: for therefore am I sent.""[56]

---

50. *ST* 3.53.1.

51. *ST* 3.42.1 ad 1.

52. *ST* 3.7.7.

53. For a summary of contemporary objections to Thomas's position and a response, see Benedict Ashley, "The Extent of Jesus' Human Knowledge," in *Reading John with St. Thomas,* ed. Michael Dauphinias and Matthew Levering (Washington DC: The Catholic University of America Press, 2005), 241–53.

54. *ST* 3.9.2.

55. *ST* 3.40.1.

56. *ST* 3.40.1.

For Thomas, therefore, the Incarnation is not simply an isolated divine intervention into human history but the fullest pedagogical means by which God reveals himself to humankind. In his *Commentary on John*, Aquinas draws an analogy between the way in which human beings reveal their interior thoughts by "letters or sounds" and God's mode of teaching in the Incarnation: "wanting to be known by us, [God] takes his Word, conceived from eternity, and clothes it with flesh in time."[57] The Incarnation also makes it possible for the Word of God to be heard by means of Christ's preaching and oral teaching: "in order for us to hear the divine Word directly, the Word assumed flesh, and spoke to us with a mouth of flesh."[58]

Commenting on John 18:37: "For this I was born, and for this I have come into the world, to bear witness to the truth," St. Thomas paraphrases Christ's words as follows: "that is, to myself, who am the truth, 'Even if I do bear witness to myself, my testimony is true' (8:14). And to the extent that I manifest myself, the Truth, to that extent I establish my kingdom. For this cannot be done without manifesting the truth, which can only be done fittingly by me, who am the light: 'The only Son, who is in the bosom of the Father, he has made him known' (1:18)."[59] Revelation of the truth in Christ is, therefore, coextensive with the inauguration of the kingdom of God in the plan of salvation history.

Stages of Revelation and the Unity of the Economy of Salvation

Thomas recognizes that the movement toward the consummation of God's salvific plan in Christ is realized through progressive stages of revelation.[60] The progression of divine revelation demarks the movement of history according to Aquinas: "[prophetic revelation] progressed according to three divisions of time, namely before the law, under the law, and under grace."[61] This movement in revealed knowledge over the course of salvation history is not on the part of God somehow realizing himself through history.[62] Rather,

---

57. Thomas Aquinas, *Super Ioh.* 14.2 (para. 1874), in *Commentary on the Gospel of John*, vol. 3, chaps. 13–21, trans. Fabian Larcher and James Weisheipl (Washington DC: The Catholic University of America Press, 2010), 57, hereafter cited as "Larcher."

58. Aquinas, *Super Ioh.* 8.3 (para. 1183; Larcher 3:119).

59. Aquinas, *Super Ioh.* 18.6 (para. 2359; Larcher 3:222).

60. On how God accommodates himself to the pedagogical needs of humanity, see Stephen D. Benin, *The Footprints of God: Divine Accommodation in the Jewish and Christian Thought* (Albany: State University of New York Press, 1993), 182–85.

61. *ST* 2–2.174.6.

62. For a study of the relationship between the thought Hegel and Balthasar's thought, which is not unrelated to the topic of development and progress, see Cyril

the progress in revelation happens in the knowledge of humankind, according to the wisdom of God's pedagogy. "The master," Aquinas argues, using the analogy of a human teacher,

> who has perfect knowledge of the art, does not deliver it all at once to his disciple from the very outset, for he would not be able to take it all in, but he condescends to the disciple's capacity and instructs him little by little. It is in this way that men made progress in the knowledge of faith as time went on. Hence the Apostle (Gal 3:24) compares the state of the Old Testament to childhood.[63]

Thomas maintains that progress in revelation does not constitute a mutability of revealed truth and the content of faith. Aquinas sees the Christian faith to be included implicitly in the monotheism knowable by reason and revealed in the Old Testament. "All the articles," Aquinas maintains,

> are contained implicitly in certain primary matters of faith, such as God's existence, and His providence over the salvation of man, according to Hebrews 11: "He that cometh to God, must believe that He is, and is a rewarder to them that seek Him." For the existence of God includes all that we believe to exist in God eternally, and in these our happiness consists; while belief in His providence includes all those things which God dispenses in time, for man's salvation, and which are the way to that happiness.[64]

Aquinas understands that the progress of revelation is one of growth by way of clarifications and illuminations amplifying the previous deposit.[65] The Apostles' triune knowledge of "He who is" most certainly completed the knowledge of God revealed in the Old Testament.

Thomas also distinguishes progress made in revelation from the advance in understanding of the nature of God and the Incarnation by believers.[66] For example, comparing David and Moses in relation to the revelation that each received as prophets of the Old Law, Aquinas argues that "The prophecy of David approaches near to the vision of Moses, as regards the intellectual

---

O'Regan, *Anatomy of Misremembering: Von Balthasar's Response to Philosophical Modernity*, vol. 1, *Hegel* (Chestnut Ridge, NY: Crossroad Pub. Co., 2014).

63. *ST* 2–2.1.7 ad 2.

64. *ST* 2–2.1.7.

65. For a presentation of Aquinas on doctrinal development, see Francisco Marin-Sola, *L'évolution homogène du dogme catholique* (Fribourg: Librarie de l'Oeuvre de Saint-Paul, 1925).

66. On this point, see Matthew Levering, *Paul in the Summa Theologiae* (Washington, DC: The Catholic University of America Press, 2014), 109.

vision, because both received a revelation of intelligible and supernatural truth, without any imaginary vision. Yet the vision of Moses was more excellent as regards the knowledge of the Godhead; while David more fully knew and expressed the mysteries of Christ's incarnation."[67]

The relation of the Old Law to the New Law is also articulated by Thomas in these terms:

> Now the end of every law is to make men righteous and virtuous . . . and consequently the end of the Old Law was the justification of men. The Law, however, could not accomplish this: but foreshadowed it by certain ceremonial actions, and promised it in words. And in this respect, the New Law fulfils the Old by justifying men through the power of Christ's Passion. . . . And in this respect, the New Law gives what the Old Law promised . . . in this respect, it also fulfils what the Old Law foreshadowed . . . in other words, the reality is found in Christ. Wherefore the New Law is called the law of reality; whereas the Old Law is called the law of shadow or of figure.[68]

Thus, Thomas sees the saving power of revelation, as it progresses from the Old toward fulfillment in the New, is united, in history, by Christ.

Revelation, Authority, and Faith

Christ's Incarnation also consummates the bestowal of divine revelation.[69] "The ultimate consummation of grace was effected by Christ," Aquinas teaches, "wherefore the time of His coming is called the 'time of fulness' (Gal 4:4). Hence those who were nearest to Christ, wherefore before, like John the Baptist, or after, like the apostles, had a fuller knowledge of the mysteries of faith."[70]

The ministry of the Apostles and the teaching office of the church, therefore, derive their dignity from their proximity to Christ in Aquinas's teaching.[71] It is on this account that he places John the Baptist above Moses as a mediator of revelation: "John belongs to the New Testament, whose ministers take precedence even of Moses, since they are spectators of a fuller revelation."[72]

---

67. *ST* 2–2.174.4 ad 1.

68. *ST* 1–2.107.2.

69. See Henk Schoot, *Christ the "Name" of God: Thomas Aquinas on Naming Christ* (Leuven: Peeters Press, 1993).

70. *ST* 2–2.1.7 ad 4.

71. See Serge-Thomas Bonino, "The Role of the Apostles in the Communication of Revelation according to the *Lectura super Ioannem* of St. Thomas Aquinas," in *Reading John with St. Thomas*, 318–46.

72. *ST* 2–2.174.4 ad 3.

The proximity to revealed truth is also what locates the teaching of the church within the scope of the infused virtue of faith even though faith's proper object is first truth itself, according to Aquinas. That is, even though the church and her teachings are distinguishable from God as first truth, the teaching of the church maintains a special authority in the life of faith. This is so, Aquinas maintains, precisely because magisterial teaching is related to what has been revealed. What makes a teaching heretical, for Aquinas, is its failure to be measured by church teaching, which originates with first truth and is revealed in sacred scripture:

> Now the formal object of faith is the First Truth, as manifested in Holy Writ and the teaching of the Church, which proceeds from the First Truth. Consequently *whoever does not adhere, as to an infallible and Divine rule, to the teaching of the Church, which proceeds from the First Truth manifested in Holy Writ, has not the habit of faith, but holds that which is of faith otherwise than by faith.* . . . Now it is manifest that he who adheres to the teaching of the Church, as to an infallible rule, assents to whatever the Church teaches; otherwise, if, of the things taught by the Church, he holds what he chooses to hold, and rejects what he chooses to reject, he no longer adheres to the teaching of the Church as to an infallible rule, but to his own will.[73]

The heretical rejection or abandonment of a particular church teaching, therefore, according to Thomas, is an evacuation of the of the gift of faith because the church's understanding of revelation is the proper index of faith. "Faith adheres to all the articles of faith by reason of one mean," Thomas teaches, "on account of the First Truth proposed to us in Scriptures, according to the teaching of the Church who has the right understanding of them. Hence whoever abandons this mean is altogether lacking in faith."[74]

This understanding also extends to Thomas's presentation of the authority and multiplicity of the church's creeds and doctrines. The various creeds are proposed by the church as the proper explanation of the faith that has been revealed. The multiplicity of the creeds results from the pedagogical needs of the faithful and the living nature of the church's faith:

> The same doctrine of faith is taught in all the symbols. Nevertheless, the people need more careful instruction about the truth of faith, when errors arise, lest the faith of simple-minded persons be corrupted by heretics. It was this that gave rise to the necessity of formulating several

---

73. *ST* 2–2.5.3.
74. *ST* 2–2.5.3 ad 2.

> symbols, which nowise differ from one another, save that on account of the obstinacy of heretics, one contains more explicitly what another contains implicitly.[75]

According to Aquinas, the multiplicity of the creeds is due to the sinful imperfections of human beings that taint the reception of revelation. "The truth of faith is sufficiently explicit in the teaching of Christ and the apostles," Aquinas, explains, "But since . . . some men are so evil-minded as to pervert the apostolic teaching and other doctrines and Scriptures to their own destruction, it was necessary as time went on to express the faith more explicitly against the errors which arose."[76]

Aquinas's doctrine of faith is often associated with his dictum that the object of faith is not the propositions of faith but the realities themselves to which those propositions intend. A full appreciation of Aquinas's teaching on the theological virtue of faith requires a consideration of the full passage from which this dictum is derived:

> The symbol mentions the things about which faith is, in so far as the act of the believer is terminated in them, as is evident from the manner of speaking about them. Now the act of the believer does not terminate in a proposition, but in a thing. For as in science we do not form propositions, except in order to have knowledge about things through their means, so is it in faith.[77]

The saving significance of faith, therefore, is not that it merely gives revealed truths cast in propositions for the believer to ponder. Rather, in addition to constituting an infused habit of right thinking about God, Thomas holds, the revealed truths of faith establish a participatory form of knowing the realities themselves.[78] When Aquinas explains that the "act" of the believer terminates in the realities, he indicates that faith is a divine motion by which the believer is given contact with the things that are revealed. The interior, infused reality of grace is for Thomas the essence of the New Law of the Gospel that brings the plan of salvation to fulfillment. "Now that which is preponderant in the law of the New Testament," Aquinas teaches, "and whereon all its efficacy is based, is the grace of the Holy Ghost, which is given through faith in Christ.

---

75. *ST* 2–2.1.9 ad 2.

76. *ST* 2–2.1.10 ad 1.

77. *ST* 2–2.1.2 ad 2.

78. For a presentation of Thomas's teaching on the unity of theology with significant engagement with trends in German theology from the last 40 years, see Reinhard Hütter, "Theological Faith Enlightening Sacred Theology: Renewing Theology by Recovering its Unity as Sacra Doctrina," *The Thomist* 74, no. 3 (2010): 369–405.

Consequently the New Law is chiefly the grace itself of the Holy Ghost, which is given to those who believe in Christ."[79]

For this reason, too, Thomas annexes the gifts of knowledge and understanding to the theological virtue of faith. These gifts aid the believer in being more docile to the interior movements of the Holy Spirit within the life of faith. "Man needs a supernatural light," Aquinas argues, "in order to penetrate further still so as to know what it cannot know by its natural light: and this supernatural light which is bestowed on man is called the gift of understanding."[80]

THE POLYMORPHIC NATURE OF REVELATION ACCORDING TO ST. THOMAS

Part of the wisdom of the divine pedagogy that Thomas recognizes is the manifold (or polymorphic) way in which God discloses himself.[81] The general category of "revelation" includes many diverse forms of disclosure adopted by God.

The "Many" and "Various" Modes of Divine Revelation

St. Thomas sees the manifold nature of revelation indicated by the words "in many and various ways God spoke" in the first line of the Letter to the Hebrews.[82] In his commentary on this passage, Thomas labors to underscore this point. The author of Hebrews, he argues, says "In many ways," "referring first of all to various persons, because God spoke not to one person but to many, namely, Abraham, Noah and others."[83]

Furthermore, Thomas notes, that "many" refers "to the times and always with the same certitude: 'He went out early in the morning. . . . And about the third hour. . . . And again about the sixth hour' (Mt 20:1 ff.). The 'many' also indicates the matters treated, namely, divine things: 'I am who am' (Ex 3:14)"; the diverse temporality of revelation: ". . . and future events: 'She knows signs and wonders before they be done' (Wis 8:8); and

---

79. *ST* 1–2.106.1.

80. *ST* 2–2.8.1.

81. In his *Theology of Revelation*, Latourelle uses the word "polymorphous" to explain how Thomas sees that "God did not overlook any form of communication" in making Himself known (162).

82. For a treatment of Aquinas's commentary on Hebrews, see *Aquinas on Scripture: An Introduction to His Biblical Commentaries*, ed. Daniel Keating and Thomas Weinandy (New York: T&T Clark, 2005).

83. Thomas Aquinas, *Super Heb.* 1.1 (para. 9), in *Commentary on the Letter of Saint Paul to the Hebrews*, trans. Fabian Larcher (Lander, WY: The Aquinas Institute for the Study of Sacred Doctrine, 2012), accessed at https://aquinas.cc/la/en/~Heb.

promises of future benefits, at least in figure: 'Many things are show to you above the understanding of men' (Sir 3:25)." The author's use of "many" also indicates "the variety of figures; because at one time he uses the figure of a lion, at another the figure of a stone: 'A stone was cut out of a mountain without hands' (Dan 2:34), 'That he might show you that his law is manifold' (Jb 11:6)."[84]

Along with the diverse aspects of revelation indicated by the word "many," Thomas also recognizes an importance to the second part of the passage: "various ways." "This refers," says Thomas,

> to the three kinds of vision: first, ocular vision: "In the same hour there appeared fingers, as it were the hand of a man writing over against the candlestick upon the surface of the wall" (Dan 5:5); secondly, imaginary vision: "I saw the Lord sitting upon a throne high and elevated" (Is 6:1); thirdly, intellectual vision, as to David: "I have had understanding above the ancients" (Ps 119:100).[85]

In addition to the various forms of vision employed by God to reveal himself, "It refers also to the various ways He spoke," Thomas continues, "because sometimes He spoke plainly and sometimes obscurely. In fact, there is not manner of speaking that has not been employed in the writings of the Old Testament, . . . Thirdly, because He spoke by rebuking the wicked, by enticing the just, and by instructing the ignorant: 'All scripture, inspired of God, is profitable to teach, to reprove, to correct, to instruct in justice' (2 Tim 3:16)."[86]

The Hidden and Figurative Aspects of Revelation

Thomas also understands God's use of figures in scripture to be an important part of the way in which God teaches humankind. "The things of God are not to be revealed to man," Thomas argues, "except in proportion to his capacity: else he would be in danger of downfall, were he to despise what he cannot grasp. Hence it was more beneficial that the Divine mysteries should be revealed to uncultured people under a veil of figures, that thus they might know them at least implicitly by using those figures to the honor of God."[87]

---

84. Aquinas, *Super Heb.* 1.1 (para. 9), in *Commentary on the Letter of Saint Paul to the Hebrews.*

85. Aquinas, *Super Heb.* 1.1 (para. 9), in *Commentary on the Letter of Saint Paul to the Hebrews.*

86. Aquinas, *Super Heb.* 1.1 (para. 9), in *Commentary on the Letter of Saint Paul to the Hebrews.*

87. *ST* 1–2.101.2 ad 1.

A similar line of argument is used by Thomas to defend the use of metaphor, analogy, and images in sacred scripture.[88] "It is befitting Holy Writ to put forward divine and spiritual truths," Thomas insists

> by means of comparisons with material things. For God provides for everything according to the capacity of its nature. Now it is natural to man to attain to intellectual truths through sensible objects, because all our knowledge originates from sense. Hence in Holy Writ, spiritual truths are fittingly taught under the likeness of material things. This is what Dionysius says: "We cannot be enlightened by the divine rays except they be hidden within the covering of many sacred veils." It is also befitting Holy Writ, which is proposed to all without distinction of persons . . . that spiritual truths be expounded by means of figures taken from corporeal things, in order that thereby even the simple who are unable by themselves to grasp intellectual things may be able to understand it.[89]

Finally, one of the modes of revelation that Thomas recognizes is the frequency in which the exact meaning of the words and events communicated in scripture are hidden. This feature of revelation, in Aquinas's estimation, is employed by the divine pedagogy to invite the rational creature to prayerful contemplation and the pursuit of wisdom by carefully reflecting on the teaching of revelation.[90] Since written documents can be read by anyone who obtains them, the meaning of sacred scripture is not always evident on the surface: "Because a written book can fall into the hands of anybody," Aquinas argues, "these matters should be concealed with obscure language, so that they will benefit the wise who understand them and be hidden from the uneducated who are unable to grasp them."[91]

REVELATION AND PROPHETIC ILLUMINATION

It is important to note that while Aquinas's understanding of the gift of prophecy is intimately related to his teaching on revelation, he never conflates

---

88. See Scott W. Hahn and John A. Kincaid, "The Multiple Literal Sense in Thomas Aquinas's Commentary on Romans and Modern Pauline Hermeneutics," in *Reading Romans with St. Thomas Aquinas,* ed. Matthew Levering and Michael Dauphinais (Washington, DC: The Catholic University of America Press, 2012), 163–82.

89. *ST* 1.1.9.

90. On the contemplative aim of theological speculation with several comparisons between Aquinas and Balthasar, see Levering, *Scripture and Metaphysics,* 12–46. See also Gilles Emery, "Trinitarian Theology as Spiritual Exercise in Augustine and Aquinas," in *Aquinas the Augustinian,* ed. Michael Dauphinais, Barry David, and Matthew Levering (Washington DC: The Catholic University of America Press, 2007), 1–40.

91. Aquinas, *Super de Trin.* 2.4 (Maurer, 54).

the more common gift and revelation vis-à-vis the deposit of faith.[92] "At all times," Aquinas affirms, "there have not been lacking persons having the spirit of prophecy, not indeed for the declaration of any new doctrine of faith, but for the direction of human acts."[93] The distinction between the prophetic or spiritual inspiration given to faithful, especially the saints and doctors of the church, and the hierarchy of authorities that can be appealed to in theological argumentation, is important for Aquinas to clarify: "For our faith rests upon the revelation made to the apostles and prophets who wrote the canonical books, and not on the revelations (if any such there are) made to other doctors."[94]

Scholastic theology was frequently criticized by various twentieth-century Catholic theologians for treating revelation in an ahistorical and propositional fashion. However true this criticism may have been of certain neo-scholastics writing in the manual genre, it is certainly not reflective of Aquinas's doctrine of revelation. "Since everything which is revealed is revealed under some light," Aquinas teaches, "those things which are made known to man above ordinary knowledge must be made known by some higher light. This is called the prophetic light and by receiving it one is established as a prophet."[95]

Because prophetic knowledge pertains to matters that go beyond humanity's natural powers, it relies especially on the agency of God's illuminative action in the soul.[96] Prophecy is thus not akin to a habit abiding in the soul in Aquinas's teaching. Rather, prophecy is a "light [that] stays in the mind of the prophet only when it is actually being divinely inspired."[97]

The fact that St. Thomas consistently maintains that prophesy is not a habit accentuates his conviction that revelation is historically mediated to humankind through particular individuals by the economic work of the Holy Spirit:

---

92. For an introduction to Aquinas's thinking on "biblical inspiration and prophetic mission," see Matthew L. Lamb, Introduction, Thomas Aquinas, *Commentary on Saint Paul's Epistle to the Ephesians*, trans. Matthew L. Lamb (Albany, NY: Magi Books, 1966), 6–11.

93. *ST* 2–2.174.6 ad 3.

94. *ST* 1.1.8 ad 2.

95. Thomas Aquinas, *De ver.* 12.1 co., in *Quaestiones disputatae*, vol. 1, *De veritate*, ed. R. Spiazzi; Rome: Marietti, 1949), 235. The translation is my own: "Cum autem omne quod manifestatur, sub lumine quodam manifestetur, ut etiam haberi potest ab apostolo, Ephes. V, 13, oportet ut ea quae manifestantur homini supra cognitionem communem, quodam altiori lumine manifestentur, quod lumen propheticum dicitur, ex cuius receptione aliquis propheta constituitur."

96. For a development of the prophetic and sanctifying aspects of Aquinas's teaching on revelation, see Charles Journet, *What Is Dogma?* trans. Mark Pontifex (San Francisco: Ignatius Press, 2011), 23–32.

97. *De ver.* 12.1 co.

> It is requisite to prophecy that the intention of the mind be raised to the perception of Divine things. . . . This raising of the intention is brought about by the motion of the Holy Ghost. . . . After the mind's intention has been raised to heavenly things, it perceives the things of God. . . . Accordingly inspiration is requisite for prophecy, as regards the raising of the mind. . . . while revelation is necessary, as regards the very perception of Divine things, whereby prophecy is completed; by its means the veil of darkness and ignorance is removed.[98]

In this passage, Thomas traces a movement of divine agency within the soul that ends with a greater intimacy between the soul and God by the elimination of the darkness that kept the truth about God hidden.

The knowledge that results from the infusion of the prophetic light is not just more reliable than a knowledge without this light. Rather, for Aquinas, prophetic knowledge is a specific participation in the divine light that issues from the act of revelation. "Prophecy is a kind of knowledge," Thomas teaches, "impressed under the form of teaching on the prophet's intellect, by Divine revelation."[99]

The participation in the divine knowledge that results from the revelation and infusion of prophetic knowledge creates, according to Thomas, a likeness within the creature to God.[100] "The truth of knowledge is the same in disciple and teacher," Aquinas argues, "since the knowledge of the disciple is a likeness of the knowledge of the teacher, even as in natural things the form of the thing generated is a likeness of the form of the generator."[101] This is especially true of the Apostles, and among them St. John, to whom the Lord granted an especial knowledge of his teachings. "John is described as to privilege," Aquinas explains,

> since, among the other disciples of the Lord, John was more loved by Christ. Without mentioning his own name John refers to himself . . . as "the disciple whom Jesus loved." And because secrets are revealed to friends, "I have called you friends because everything I have heard from my father I have made known to you (below 15:15), Jesus confided his secrets in a special way to that disciple who was specially loved.[102]

Even though many things are included in divine revelation, what unites all of the diverse material elements of revelation in Aquinas's teaching is the divine

---

98. *ST* 2–2.171.1 ad 4.

99. *ST* 2–2.171.6.

100. Balthasar, in fact, adopts and summarizes Aquinas's teaching on this matter: revelation "is a certain participation in God's self-contemplation and in the vision of God which the blessed have." See *C*, 49.

101. *ST* 2–2.171.6.

102. Aquinas, *Super Ioh.* prol. (para. 11; Larcher 3:6).

luminosity by which they are made known. "The formal element in prophetic knowledge," Aquinas argues, "is the Divine light, which being one, gives unity of species to prophecy, although the things prophetically manifested by the Divine light are diverse."[103]

Revelation, therefore, exceeds any kind of immanent inspiration, such as that enjoyed by poets. Rather, "the gift of prophecy," Thomas teaches, "confers on the human mind something which surpasses the natural faculty."[104] From this perspective, "human teaching may be likened to prophetic revelation" in regards to the use of species that represent this to the mind, but not with respect to the interior illumination that God bestows with revelation: "For a man represents certain things to his disciple by signs of speech, but he cannot enlighten him inwardly as God does."[105] Even though revelation constitutes a scientific body of knowledge for Aquinas, its principal aspect is the illuminative action of God upon the soul. The truths revealed can be taught by God in lower (images and representations) and higher (intellectual vision) manners, but each mode of revelation is accompanied by the corresponding interior movement of the divine light.

Thomas takes certain perplexing cases of salvation history, such as Abraham's willingness to sacrifice his son Isaac, as a clear indication that the inner movement of the divine light also accompanies revelation, and that both the truth revealed and the inner prompting confirm the recipient in certitude. The interior prompting of the divine light, Thomas reasons, "may be gathered from the fact that Abraham being admonished in a prophetic vision, prepared to sacrifice his only-begotten son, which he nowise would have done had he not been most certain of the Divine revelation."[106] This is also why those who receive inspired revelations can proclaim with confident certitude things which extend beyond their own natural ability to grasp.

REVELATION AS SPEECH AND WORD ACCORDING TO ST. THOMAS

Aquinas stands firmly within the tradition in his use of the analogy of speech and the spoken word to clarify the nature of divine revelation. Aquinas identified several modes of word and speech by which God discloses himself. In Jesus' words in John 5:37, "the Father who sent me has himself given testimony on my behalf, but you have neither heard his voice, nor seen his image," Aquinas sees, "three ways in which God reveals things. This is done either by a sensible

---

103. *ST* 2–2.171.3 ad 3.
104. *ST* 2–2.173.2.
105. *ST* 2–2.173.2.
106. *ST* 2–2.171.5.

voice, as he bore witness to Christ in the Jordan and on the mountain. . . . Or, God reveals things through a vision of his essence, which he reveals to the blessed. . . . Thirdly, it is accomplished by an interior word through an inspiration."[107] The analogy of speech stands for Aquinas as the basic point of reference for understanding revelation: "for to speak to another only means to make known the mental concept to another."[108] The speaking that takes place in divine revelation, therefore, is the making known, on the part of God, of his eternal Word, accommodated to the human capacity for learning.[109]

CONCLUSION

Crafting a meaningful conclusion to a chapter that has traced Aquinas's teaching on revelation through so many nuances is a difficult task. Indeed, Balthasar, too, found it challenging to offer a concluding word on the topic of revelation. "Where revelation is concerned," Balthasar observes, "it is best to avoid speaking of a "'conclusion.'" The word "conclusion," Balthasar explains, "is inappropriate since the completion of fullness is not so much an end as a beginning. It is the beginning of the infinite pouring out of Christ's fullness into that of the church, of the church's growth into the fullness of Christ and of God."[110] Here again, Aquinas and Balthasar are in agreement. This chapter has demonstrated that Aquinas views revelation as a luminous grace, received in faith, fully manifested and historically mediated in the life and teaching of Christ, and bestowed for the sake of human salvation, which is begun in this life and brought to perfection in the next.[111] It is the fullness of Christ's mediation in history, toward which the history of salvation is ordered, and from which the church derives both her teaching and ministerial authority, around which each aspect of Thomas's teaching on revelation revolves.

BIBLIOGRAPHY

Ashley, Benedict. "The Extent of Jesus's Human Knowledge." In *Reading John with St. Thomas*, edited by M. Dauphinias and M. Levering, 241–53. Washington, DC: The Catholic University of America Press, 2005.

---

107. Aquinas, *Super Ioh.* 5.6 (para. 321; Larcher 1:302).

108. *ST* 1.107.1.

109. See also Beryl Smalley, *The Gospels in the Schools c. 1100–c.1280* (London: The Hambledon Press, 1985), 257–71.

110. Balthasar, "The Word, Scripture, and Tradition," 26.

111. For a summary of how Aquinas's position developed in relation to his commentary on the *De Trinitate* of Boethius, see Lawrence J. Donohoo, "The Nature and Grace of Sacra Doctrina in St. Thomas's *Super Boetium de Trinitate*," *The Thomist* 63 (1999): 343–401.

Benin, Stephen D. *The Footprints of God: Divine Accommodation in the Jewish and Christian Thought.* Albany: State University of New York Press, 1993.

Bonino, Serge-Thomas. "The Role of the Apostles in the Communication of Revelation according to the *Lectura super Ioannem* of St. Thomas Aquinas." In *Reading John with St. Thomas,* edited by M. Dauphinias and M. Levering, 318–46. Washington, DC: The Catholic University of America Press, 2005.

Case, Brendan. "Judging according to Wisdom: Sacra Doctrina in the Summa Theologiae." *New Black Friars* 98, no. 1077 (2017): 582–98.

Dauphinais, Michael. "Christ the Teacher: The Pedagogy of the Incarnation." PhD diss., University of Notre Dame, 2000.

Dewan, Lawrence. "Communion with the Tradition: For the Believer Who Is a Philosopher." *Science et Esprit* 40, no. 3 (1988): 315–25.

Donohoo, Lawrence J. "The Nature and Grace of Sacra Doctrina in St. Thomas's *Super Boetium de Trinitate.*" *The Thomist* 63 (1999): 343–401.

Emery, Gilles. "Trinitarian Theology as Spiritual Exercise in Augustine and Aquinas." In *Aquinas the Augustinian,* edited by M. Dauphinais, B. David, and M. Levering, 1–40. Washington, DC: The Catholic University of America Press, 2007.

Feingold, Lawrence. *Faith Comes from What Is Heard: An Introduction to Fundamental Theology.* Steubenville, OH: Emmaus Academic, 2016.

Hahn, Scott W., and John A. Kincaid. "The Multiple Literal Sense in Thomas Aquinas's Commentary on Romans and Modern Pauline Hermeneutics." In *Reading Romans with St. Thomas Aquinas,* edited by M. Levering and M. Dauphinais, 163–82. Washington, DC: The Catholic University of America Press, 2012.

Hayen, A. "Le thomisme et l'histoire." *Revue thomiste* 62 (1962): 51–82.

Hütter, Reinhard. "Theological Faith Enlightening Sacred Theology: Renewing Theology by Recovering Its Unity as Sacra Doctrina." *The Thomist* 74, no. 3 (2010): 369–405.

Jenkins, John I. *Knowledge and Faith in Thomas Aquinas.* Cambridge: Cambridge University Press, 1997.

Journet, Charles. *What Is Dogma?* Translated by M. Pontifex. San Francisco: Ignatius Press, 2011.

———. *The Wisdom of Faith: An Introduction to Theology.* Translated by R. F. Smith. Westminster, MD: The Newman Press, 1952.

Lamb, Matthew L. "Introduction to St. Thomas Aquinas." In *Commentary on Saint Paul's Epistle to the Ephesians,* translated by M. L. Lamb. Albany: Magi Books, 1966.

Latourelle, René. *Theology of revelation, including a commentary on the constitution "Dei verbum" of Vatican II.* New York: Alba House, 1966.

Levering, Matthew. *Engaging the Doctrine of Revelation: The Mediation of the Gospel through Scripture and the Church.* Grand Rapids, MI: Baker Academic, 2014.

————. *Paul in the Summa Theologiae.* Washington, DC: The Catholic University of America Press, 2014.

Levering, Matthew. *Scripture and Metaphysics: Aquinas and the Renewal of Trinitarian Theology.* Malden, MA: Blackwell Publishing, 2004.

Long, Steven A. *Analogia Entis: On Analogy, Metaphysics, and the Act of Faith.* Notre Dame, IN: University of Notre Dame Press, 2011.

Lösel, Steffen. "Love Divine, All Loves Excelling: Balthasar's Negative Theology of Revelation." *The Journal of Religion* 82, no. 4 (2002): 589.

Mansini, Guy. "Balthasar and the Theodramatic Enrichment of the Trinity." *The Thomist* 64, no. 4 (2000): 499–519.

Marin-Sola, Francisco. *L'évolution homogène du dogme catholique.* Fribourg: Librarie de l'Oeuvre de Saint-Paul, 1925.

Marshall, Bruce. "Quod scit una vetula": Aquinas on the Nature of Theology." In *The Theology of Thomas Aquinas,* edited by R. Van Nieuwenhove and J. Wawrykow, 1–35. Notre Dame, IN: University of Notre Dame Press, 2005.

Mondin, Battista. *I Grandi Teologi del Secolo Ventesimo,* vol. 1, *I Teologi Cattolici.* Turin: Borla editore, 1969.

Nutt, Roger W. "On Analogy, the Incarnation, and the Sacraments of the Church: Considerations from the *Tertia pars* of the *Summa theologiae.*" *Nova et Vetera* (English edition) 12, no. 3 (2014): 989–1004.

O'Regan, Cyril. *Anatomy of Misremembering: Von Balthasar's Response to Philosophical Modernity,* vol. 1, *Hegel.* Chestnut Ridge, NY: Crossroad Pub. Co., 2014.

O'Rourke, Fran. *Pseudo-Dionysius and the Metaphysics of Aquinas.* Notre Dame, IN: University of Notre Dame Press, 2005.

Paretsky, Albert. "The Influence of Thomas the Exegete on Thomas the Theologian: The Tract on Law (Ia-IIae, qq. 90–108)." *Angelicum* 71, no. 4 (1994): 549–78.

Rocca, Gregory. *Speaking the Incomprehensible God.* Washington, DC: The Catholic University of America Press, 2004.

Salvati, G. M. "Cristo e il tempo: Prospettive di teologia tomistica della storia." *Angelicum* 80, no. 3 (2003): 527–37.

Schoot, Henk. *Christ the "Name" of God: Thomas Aquinas on Naming Christ.* Leuven: Peeters Press, 1993.

Smalley, Beryl. *The Gospels in the Schools c. 1100–c.1280.* London: The Hambledon Press, 1985.

Valkenberg, Wilhelmus, G. B. M. *Words of the Living God: Place and Function of Holy Scripture in the Theology of St. Thomas Aquinas.* Leuven: Peeters, 2000.

Weisheipl, James. "The Meaning of *Sacra Doctrina* in *Summa Theologiae* I, q. 1." *The Thomist* 38, no. 1 (1974): 49–80.

White, V. "Le concept de révélation chez S. Thomas." *L'année théologique* 11 (1950): 1–17, 109–32.

CHAPTER 4

The Double Unveiling

Balthasar's Monastic Theology of Revelation

JONATHAN CIRAULO

IN ORDER TO SPEAK OF A REVELATION, of an unveiling (*revelatio*, ἀποκάλυψις), one must presuppose that something must have been previously out of sight, too distant to behold, or perhaps hidden from view (*objectum fidei est res divina non visa*).[1] If hidden, then the object of revelation is by definition not the immediate property of the public at large (the realm of *ratio*). If there is to be any meaningful distinction between faith and reason, theology and philosophy, this at least should be read as a truism. Revelation is, in this quite traditional and schematic reading, essentially *esoteric*, something that exceeds the basic equipment of humanity. Nominating revelation as a form of esotericism may be scorned as a needless provocation, especially as esotericism is a category that emerged in France only in the nineteenth century, with its romantic sympathy for secret societies.[2] It must be noted, however, that "revelation" likewise did not become a separate theological category until roughly the same time, specifically as a response to Enlightenment Deism, and before the sixteenth century, theological usage of the term "revelation" often meant "an extraordinary psychic occurrence in which hidden things are suddenly made known," something that sounds very much like the esoteric, indeed.[3]

---

1. *ST* III, q. 7, a. 3, co.

2. See Jean Borella, *Christ the Original Mystery: Esotericism and the Mystical Way*, trans. G. John Champoux (Brooklyn, NY: Angelico Press, 2018), 14ff. for a brief history of the term "esoteric," from its early usage as a distinction between the popular and the technical writings of Aristotle to its later form as a noun, beginning around 1828.

3. Avery Dulles, *Models of Revelation* (New York: Orbis, 1992), viii, 19. And even for Aquinas, "revelation" is a topic usually covered under the topic of prophetic knowledge and thus cannot be reduced to a simple distinction between objects discovered by reason versus those discovered by supernatural faith, but rather includes an interesting psychological investigation of the illumination of the prophet. See also Jean-Yves Lacoste, "Revelation," in *Encyclopedia of Christian Theology*, vol. III, ed. Jean-Yves Lacoste (New York: Routledge, 2005), 1383–391, particularly his analysis of the role of nominalism in the shift toward a view of revelation as information.

Hans Urs von Balthasar believes that if we are to rightly understand revelation in modernity, which means understanding it with the same basic contours that Thomas Aquinas earlier formulated (albeit with important modifications), then we must consider revelation to be something like the esoteric. Thus, for Balthasar, revelation, both in its content (*fides quae creditur*) and its reception (*fides qua creditur*), is comprehensible only for those who are initiated, those who refuse a purely rationalistic *logos* to dictate the terms of experience and knowledge, and thus those who also hold to Christianity's particular *mythos*. Yet, as we will see at the end of this chapter, esotericism for Balthasar is always directed toward the exoteric, and the former in fact is the hermeneutical key for the latter. We will proceed by first examining Balthasar's interpretation of the historical interaction between philosophy, myth, and theology, a history in which Aquinas functions paradigmatically. Then, following this genealogical account, we will evaluate Balthasar's linking of revelation to the esoteric and the mythic, specifically as this relates to his use of Origen of Alexandria. Thus, of particular concern is his particularly monastic conception of revelation. All the while, we will attend to a host of issues that surround the question of revelation, such as the respective roles of the intellect and will, the analogical relationship between the gift of revelation and its finite reception, and the legitimate place of theological pluralism, particularly the tension between monastic and scholastic theological tendencies. Finally, we will see that for Balthasar, revelation is a double unveiling: not only of God to the creature, but of the creature to God.[4]

Aquinas's Synthesis: Distinguishing in Order to Unite

Understanding Balthasar's analysis of Aquinas on the subject of revelation is not straightforward due to the fact that Balthasar rarely has only one Aquinas in mind. Balthasar is highly interested in the thirteenth-century Dominican and turns to his thought as authoritative with great frequency, but Balthasar sees in the angelic doctor far more than a "historical Thomas." Balthasar's Aquinas is one that provided something like a perfect synthesis of philosophy and theology in his own time, but one who also sowed the seeds for later corruption and aberration. Though Balthasar usually distances Aquinas from his later corruptions, Balthasar does not entirely exonerate him, either. Though something of a *ressourcement* theologian, Balthasar is certainly of the opinion that although contemporary theology has everything to gain

---

4. For a much fuller account of Balthasar's theology of revelation, see Larry Chapp, *The God Who Speaks: Hans Urs von Balthasar's Theology of Revelation* (Bethesda, MD: International Scholars, 1997).

by drinking deeply from the wells of the patristic and scholastic past, it has everything to lose if it in any way attempts to reproduce the forms of thought of a previous age, including that of the angelic doctor. Thus, Balthasar's reading of Aquinas is quite frequently of the archeological sort, but it is also always aware of the ways that Aquinas is later developed, maligned, and corrupted, as well as sensitive to how his thought sounds to ears that have already heard Kant, Hegel, Schelling, Husserl, and Heidegger.

Balthasar provides an account of the history of metaphysics in *The Glory of the Lord* IV and V, with special concern for the aesthetic. As one would expect, this is largely a survey of the development of philosophy and theology, but it is quite an unconventional survey in that there is a third category that looms as large as the others: that of the realm of the mythic (roughly, all that is autochthonous and categorical, that which is so locally true that it stubbornly resists the universal and transcendental). From pre- to post-Christian thought, Balthasar evaluates various levels of success and failure in which philosophy, theology, and myth are integrated into a coherent whole. Not that Balthasar thinks that this is a self-evidently easy task, for we have some good reason to think that reason and revelation may very much be at odds with one another. Though he only follows Barth so far, he at least grants that revelation will very often appear to reason as a condemning judge, and because reason necessarily strives for the infinite, it quite often remains hostile to any encroachment from above. Myth, as well, even in antiquity, is not readily synthesized with either philosophy or classical religion, and it is only the greatest luminaries (here Balthasar highlights Virgil and especially Plotinus) who achieve any convincing level of integration.[5]

It is only after the Incarnation, according to Balthasar, that we can speak of the faith-reason or philosophy-theology pair. The mythic no longer functions as a third category after Christ, for it is now entirely an element of (ideally) both philosophy and theology. The mythic cannot be destroyed without simultaneously destroying human nature and the orthodox Christology that supports it. For Balthasar, much of the drama of thought *post Christum* is not only the perennial balance of faith and reason but also innumerable attempts to properly integrate or actively dispel the realm of *mythos*. Christianity for Balthasar must remain as mythic as it is philosophical, at least if it is to remain human:

Indeed Christians may well delude themselves if they imagine that in the present age they have put myth completely behind them, ancient religion

---

5. "Myth rested on tradition which had to be received in faith and in the same act of faith justified prayer as cult and rite: it was not its nature to stray into the realm of knowledge. There is no 'fundamental theology' of myth." See *GL* 4, 155. See also *GL* 4, 280–313, esp. 291, for Balthasar's take on Plotinus.

half and philosophy almost completely behind them, so as to lay out its unique fare on this tabula rasa. . . . We may indeed do so announcing with Karl Barth in tones of loud conviction that Christianity is not a religion, or, with Kierkegaard, that it is not a philosophy, or, with Bultmann, that it is not a mythology. But God would not have become human if he had not come into positive inner contact with these three forms of thought and experience.[6]

Thus, to simply stipulate the matter at this stage, whatever "revelation" is for Balthasar, it is decidedly not in fundamental opposition to anything that constitutes human nature, including the propensities for speculative thought, imagistic representation, and religious cult.

Even if the antique world, in Balthasar's estimation, was by and large ontologically monistic, it never achieved a union of religiosity and philosophical speculation. Insofar as piety and popular religion remained philosophically underdetermined, philosophy and theology were indistinguishable. Heidegger will make the same claim, of course, noting how Aristotle's analysis of being qua being also necessarily resorts to the *primum movens*. But whereas Heidegger views Christianity as simply a later iteration of the original ontotheological catastrophe, Balthasar recoils from this procrustean presentation. For Balthasar, Aquinas, in particular, achieves a distinction between philosophy and theology that was unmatched at his time, a distinction that has never been adequately reformulated since. With Aquinas, and in consonance with his patristic predecessors, there occurs a clear conceptual distinction between philosophy and theology but, simultaneously, also their harmoniously interrelation. These are both distinguished and held together only by his commitment to the *desiderium naturale*, which Balthasar takes to be so assuredly the only proper way of reading Aquinas that he dispenses himself from citing Maurice Blondel or Henri de Lubac.[7] We will return to the natural desire later, but here it is essential to note that no sooner did Aquinas achieve his synthesis that it was thereafter lost. What he distinguished would later be ripped apart. Considering Aquinas as a *kairos* in his ability to hold philosophy and theology as separate yet complementary is not a Balthasarian invention, but it has been stated before and after Balthasar, often with greater historical notation.[8]

---

6. *GL* 4, 242–43. See also Erich Przywara, "Image, Likeness, Symbol, Mythos, Mysterium, Logos," in *Analogia Entis: Metaphysics: Original Structure and Universal Rhythm*, trans. John R. Betz and David Bentley Hart (Grand Rapids, MI: Eerdmans, 2014), 430–62, esp. 445, regarding the same point about Christianity's inherent ties to *mythos* and *myterium*, which the Enlightenment rejects as antithetical to "pure Logos."

7. *GL* 4, 14.

8. Étienne Gilson makes the case in numerous places, perhaps most succinctly in *Reason and Revelation in the Middle Ages* (New York: Charles Scribner's Sons, 1938).

Aquinas is kairotic for Balthasar principally because of his ability to hold together various tensions without allowing the poles to collapse into a monistic identity or separate into a hard, dualistic contradiction. These tensions include the faith/reason pair, the antinomy of a natural desire for God that in no way places a burden upon God to give such a gift, and the methodological division that we today label the distinction between monastic and scholastic theology, or the relative prioritizing of either *voluntas* or *intellectus*. Aquinas thinks of these tensions analogically, and as Balthasar will interpret him, notes that man's dignity is his "state of suspension" between opposing pairs. All of Balthasar's greatest teachers taught him that only by holding these pairs in their inherent tension can a clearing be opened for truly fertile thought about God: this is as true for Erich Przywara with his *analogia entis* and the *Spannungs-Einheit* between essence and existence as it is for Romano Guardini with his understanding of truth as an oppositional polarity (*Gegensatz*) rather than as contradictory (*Widerspruch*),[9] as well as the whole of Henri de Lubac's thought as operating within a "suspended middle."[10] One could also add Martin Buber's dialogical *Ich-du* as another instance of this type of tensile thinking.[11]

The key for our question about revelation is that Balthasar interprets Aquinas as already avoiding the hardened options that emerge into the light only at the end of the nineteenth century, namely, what Blondel labeled in

---

Gilson demonstrates the difficulty of Aquinas's achievement, especially in light of the context of Averroism, and its ephemerality, with subsequent deformations of scholastic thought and the eventual repudiation of speculative theology by the *devotio moderna*. In addition to *GL* 4 and 5, Balthasar's best small accounts of the historical tension between philosophy and theology, with Aquinas's special status always noted, are "Theology and Sanctity," in *ET* 1, 181–209, and "Philosophy, Christianity, Monasticism," in *ET* 2, 333–72. Jean-Yves Lacoste's *From Theology to Theological Thinking*, trans. W. Chris Hackett (Charlottesville: University of Virginia Press, 2014) repeats much of the same timeline but stresses to an even greater extent the briefness of his synthesis and the impossibility of its permanence. See esp. 44–45 and 52: Aquinas is a "brilliant exception." Lacoste is explicitly indebted to Balthasar on numerous points in this book.

9. Romano Guardini, *Der Gegensatz: Versuche zu einer Philosophie des Lebendig-Konkreten* (Mainz: Matthias Grünewald, 1925). See Balthasar's brief commentary of this text in *RG*, 22–24.

10. See Balthasar's *THL*. This is a phrase that John Milbank adopts for his book on de Lubac, though Milbank attempts to use this phrase against Balthasar: *The Suspended Middle: Henri de Lubac and the Debate Concerning the Supernatural* (Grand Rapids, MI: Eerdmans, 2005), 11–14 and 62–78. It is interesting to note that Milbank repeatedly refers to Balthasar as "mythological," a phrase we can sanction, though not with Milbank's polemical intention, given that Balthasar does indeed want to restore genuine human *mythos*. Note *GL* 4, 396, where Balthasar speaks of Aquinas's attention to this "state of suspension."

11. See Hans Urs von Balthasar, *Martin Buber and Christianity: A Dialogue between Israel and the Church* (New York: Macmillan, 1961), esp. 89–110.

his 1904 *Histoire et Dogme* the "historicism" of modernism and the "extrinsicism" of the then-regnant scholasticism.[12] While the modernism of figures such as Alfred Loisy and George Tyrrell tended to view the content of revelation as simply the inevitable fruit of the longing of the human heart, the "veterist" model was content to see that revelation made no infringements whatsoever on human nature, that without the offer of grace, one would have no more inclination toward revelation than one would toward speaking Esperanto. It is obvious here how much the conjugation of faith and reason is bound up with a decision regarding the *desiderium naturale*. In Balthasar's reading, Aquinas's solution to the problem of revelation's relative function regarding the confirmation, elevation, and condemnation of the human spirit (and thus faith's relation to reason) is the "bold paradox" of holding that the "nobility of human nature" consists in the fact that "we can attain perfection in our *desiderium naturale* for the very Highest only through a free self-disclosure of God."[13] The anthropological picture is something of a tragic one, especially in Blondel's rendition of the issue,[14] not one in which the human is happily open to supernatural fulfillment but rather one in which humanity strives in vain for a finality that it inevitably betrays by falling into myriad forms of superstition. The same applies, *mutatis mutandis*, to how reason blindly feels its way for something like supernatural revelation but must patiently wait in darkness for the light to appear. Thus, the good intuition of the "extrinsicist," or what Avery Dulles calls the "propositionalist," model of revelation is affirmed: revelation must be a gift given from outside the self.[15] Yet, Balthasar (and he brings Aquinas, Blondel, and de Lubac along with him) then takes another step to affirm the valid intuition of modernism: revelation

---

12. English translation by Alexander Dru and Illtyd Trethowan in Maurice Blondel, *The Letter on Apologetics & History and Dogma* (Grand Rapids, MI: Eerdmans, 1994), 211–87.

13. *GL* 4, 14–15. Balthasar here cites *ST* I-II, q. 5, a. 5, ad 2, where Aquinas confirms that humans need assistance in order to attain to "the perfect good of happiness."

14. De Lubac notes that Blondel's perspective is "quite different" from Aquinas's, stemming from different difficulties that they were trying to solve. See *The Mystery of the Supernatural* (New York: Crossroad, 1988), 187. Blondel's famous formulation, his "doubly imperious conclusion," is the following: "it is impossible not to recognize the insufficiency of the whole natural order and not to feel an ulterior need; it is impossible to find within oneself something to satisfy this religious need. *It is necessary,* and *it is impracticable.*" See *L'Action (1893): Essay on a Critique of Life and a Science of Practice*, trans. Oliva Blanchette (Notre Dame, IN: University of Notre Dame Press, 2003), 297. Balthasar states it similarly: "Man of his own self has no 'claim' he can make on God, not even though in the last resort he is unable to fulfill himself without God's free revealing of himself." See *EG*, 67.

15. Dulles, *Models of Revelation*, 36–52.

must fulfill the interior dynamism of the human spirit. Thus, revelation is essentially esoteric, unable to be known by the uninitiated but, once it is seen, lights up the dark paths that one had been walking all along.

Concomitant to remaining in between the modernist and propositionalist dialectic is that Balthasar sees Aquinas, perhaps contrary to popular opinion, as a representative of "monastic" theology as much as the more obviously "scholastic" type. That is to say, Aquinas avoids the potential errors of a purely affective monastic theology (which Balthasar clearly reads as a harbinger of later modernism) and the coming reign of scholasticism's tendencies toward arid rationalism. Aquinas's monastic/scholastic synthesis means that he refuses what was a temptation in figures such as Diadochus and William of St. Thierry ("the element of experience threatened to swallow up the whole of objective dogmatics"[16]) while also giving experience a privileged role in the theological task. Balthasar's 1954 commentary on *ST* II-II, qq. 171–82 (on the gratuitous graces, such as prophecy) clearly shaped his later work in *Herrlichkeit*, in which he sees in Aquinas's writing on the gifts of the Holy Spirit the establishment of "an autonomous and even Christian psychology."[17] That is to say, for Aquinas, and for any genuine theology of experience, revelation is the ultimate end of both the intellective as well as volitional dynamism of human nature, but it is an end that can be reached only when the person has gained a *compassio sive connaturalitas* with things divine. In other words, to see revelation aright, according to Aquinas, one must be initiated into divine wisdom, or to use the Areopagite's phrase, one must suffer divine things: *patiens divina*.[18] Balthasar's Aquinas is highly Dionysian[19] precisely in the unity between subjective holiness and the objectivity of revelation, such that the latter represents the full flowering and consummation of the former: "Christian experience confirms the

---

16. *GL* 1, 285. It should be added, however, that Balthasar's worry about the tendencies of monastic theology is only when "the criterion of subjective evidence" is taken out of the monastic and contemplative milieu from which it originated (283).

17. *GL* 1, 285. See *Besondere Gnadengaben und die Zwei Wege Menschlichen Lebens* (Gemeinschaftsverlag, 1954).

18. See *ST* II-II, q. 45, a. 2, co. The phrase from Denys comes from *The Divine Names* II, but it also echoes a saying from Aristotle. For a nice history of the term, see Vivian Boland, OP, "Non Solum Discens Sed Et Patiens Divina: The Wanderings of an Aristotelian Fragment," in *Roma, Magistra Mundi, Itineraria Culturae Medievalis: Mélanges offerts au Père L. E. Boyle à l'occasion de son 75e anniversaire*, ed. Jacqueline Hamesse, 55–69 (Louvain-la-Neuve, 1998).

19. And recent studies have argued in this direction with much greater force. See, particularly, Fran O'Rourke, *Pseudo-Dionysius & the Metaphysics of Aquinas* (Leiden: Brill, 1992) and Bernhard Blankenhorn, *The Mystery of Union with God: Dionysian Mysticism in Albert the Great and Thomas Aquinas* (Washington, DC: The Catholic University of America Press, 2015).

axiom *gratia supponit et elevat naturam*, even while preserving the radical newness of divine revelation."[20] To repeat, revelation is necessary but impossible. If somehow made possible, those who receive it would, as a matter of course, be confirmed in their creaturely finitude while also coming to participate in the life of God. Theology would then be, for Aquinas as much as for Balthasar, intimately bound to holiness, scholasticism to monasticism, *theoria* to *praktike*. The two are distinguished, to be sure, as holiness is not de facto theology, nor is *theoria* equivalent to *praktike*. But Aquinas's genius, and what for Balthasar makes him *the* authority on this particular issue, is that he is able to distinguish between faith and reason only in order to unite them more closely together.[21]

Revelation as Esoteric

Having briefly noted some of the more salient ways that Balthasar largely exonerates Aquinas from any blame regarding later rationalistic decadence, and points to him as the last (and in some sense the first) to successfully balance faith and reason, we can turn to Balthasar's account of the hardening opposition between philosophy and theology and his own proposal for conceptualizing revelation as esoteric. While the "metaphysics of Aquinas is thus the philosophical reflection of the free glory of the living God of the Bible and in this way the interior completion of ancient (and thus human philosophy)," metaphysics after Aquinas entirely loses the sense of "that all-embracing mystery of being which surpasses the powers of human thought, a mystery pregnant with the very mystery of God."[22] The thread uniting creaturely being and the Infinite God is severed, and thought either drifts toward the jealous exclusivity of finitude, in which the mythic and the revelatory are forbidden entrance, or toward a hypertrophic speculative idealism that subsumes the particularity of the finite into a theo-cosmic evolution. If Aquinas is to be blamed for any of this, it is simply due to his successful application of reason to the givens of revelation: a method that, when it lacks Aquinas's ecclesial sense of theological proportion, will lead to an unscrupulous and titanic reduction of things divine to the all-discerning eye of reason.

To turn now more directly to Balthasar's own understanding of revelation, we can begin by examining his use of the category of the esoteric.

---

20. *GL* 1, 288. After the next sentence, Balthasar cites Blondel and says that in *L'Action*, "the theological *a priori* and the *vérité expérimentale* of the rightness of faith are finally discovered" (288, n. 111).

21. The phrase "distinguish in order to unite" is Jacques Maritain's preferred designation of Aquinas's thought. See *Distinguish to Unite, Or, The Degrees of Knowledge* (Notre Dame, IN: University of Notre Dame Press, 1995).

22. *GL* 4, 407.

Though Balthasar did, in fact, have an interest and sympathy for the esoteric or the hermetic *sensu stricto*, this has been analyzed elsewhere and concerns our topic only accidentally.[23] Instead, we will examine how and why Balthasar chose to validate the categories of the esoteric, the hermetic, and the mythic, with major qualifications, as appropriate to Christian revelation and what fruits and clarifications are gained thereby. In *Glory of the Lord* 1, after discussing the difficulty that the world has in understanding the saints, the holy fools, and thus the *maior dissimilitudo* between the rapturous effect of natural beauty and Christ's glory, he writes the following:

> For at this point one must have seen the same thing as [the saints] if one is to understand them, and *this, therefore, is where the esoteric begins and where the proofs for its truth bear the character of a ritual initiation*, as the *Symposium* showed long ago. Even so truly a "church of the people" as the Catholic Church does not abolish genuine esotericism. The secret path of the saints is never denied to one who is really willing to follow it. But who in the crowd troubles himself over such a path?[24]

This appeal to the esoteric comes indeed from the same Balthasar who wrote *Razing the Bastions,* which called for the deconstruction of the walls separating "the sacred interior" of the church and the "profane exterior," which would seem to suggest that everything about the church is now exoterically available.[25] Balthasar affirms both these facts based on his understanding of revelation. Scripture and the writings of the church fathers and other ecclesial luminaries are indeed publicly available texts, and the liturgy no longer excludes the uninitiated. The *disciplina arcani* has been revoked, and Balthasar has no desire to see it reinstituted. The church is exposed almost mercilessly before the prodding eyes of the world. Yet there also remains "the secret path of the saints," which does not provide new, hermetic teachings unavailable to outsiders but rather provides the lens by which any of the exoteric teachings could be understood

---

23. See Kevin Mongrain's highly illuminative "Rule-Governed Christian Gnosis: Hans Urs von Balthasar on Valentin Tomberg's *Meditations on the Tarot,*" *Modern Theology* 25, no. 2 (April 2009): 285–314. The principal text for Mongrain's discussion is Balthasar's foreword to the aforementioned text, the English translation of which is *Meditations on the Tarot: A Journey into Christian Hermeticism* (New York: Tarcher, 2002): 659–65.

24. *GL* 1; 33; *Herrlichkeit*, 31. Italics added for emphasis. The English translation has been greatly altered, especially where it strangely attempts to qualify Balthasar's language. What I translated quite literally as "where the esoteric begins" is simply *beginnt das Esoterische*, whereas the English translation is "is the point where a certain esotericism is unavoidable."

25. *RB*, 101. It is important to note that even in this controversial book, Balthasar says that even if the separating walls need to be brought down, a distinction must remain between world and church, nature, and grace.

at all.[26] As is one of the main themes of Balthasar's *Herrlichkeit*, the only way to see what the saint sees is through *initiation* (baptismal, to be sure, with equal emphasis on the *opus operantis* as the *operatum*), which includes but is far more than notional acknowledgement of doctrinal pronouncements.

The real locus of Balthasar's reflection on genuine Christian esotericism stems from his writing on Origen of Alexandria. His work on Origen in the 1930s, both his anthology of Origen's writings, *Geist und Feuer* [1938], and his articles that were later compiled as *Parole et mystère chez Origène* [1957], provides Balthasar with a theological "style" that stays with him and guides his evaluation of the history of philosophy and theology.[27] That style is a particularly "monastic" one.[28] More than just from Origen, but equally from Plato and Plotinus, as well as Augustine and Denys, Balthasar learned that truth concerns far more than an *adaequatio mentis ad rem*, if *mens* or *intellectus* is interpreted as detached mental computation, or if the entire phrase is tritely encapsulated by the catchphrase: "getting at the facts."[29] Truth is not "just the facts," and this applies equally to truths of revelation as to truths of creation. For all these thinkers, Aquinas included, the idea of *adaequatio* implies not only that the object is brought into the purview of the intellect but also that the mind is made adequate, made worthy, for its object. Plato's *Letter VII* expresses this with words that one could be forgiven for confusing with Cardinal Newman: "neither quickness of learning nor a good memory can make a man see when his nature is not akin to the object, for this knowledge never takes root in an alien nature."[30] It is Origen above all who demonstrates how this basic epistemological law remains in force even when, or rather especially when, we are dealing with supernatural mysteries.

Truth then takes on an ineluctably moral element, which leads to Balthasar elevating rather than diminishing the esoteric element in Origen's thought. In *Parole et Mystère*, this takes the form of insisting on the "centre du véritable ésotérisme d'Origène," and in his introduction to *Geist und*

---

26. Aquinas himself explores this topic nicely in *In Boet. De Trin*, I, q. 2, a. 4. See Balthasar's interpretation of the *disciplina arcani* in Denys's thought in *GL* 2, 152–54.

27. *Origenes: Geist und Feuer: Ein Aufbau aus seinen Schriften*, translated into English by Robert J. Daly as *OSF*. The two essays, entitled "Le Mystère d'Origène," were published in consecutive issues of *Recherches de science religieuse*: 26 (1936): 514–62, and 27 (1937): 38–64. They were later included in the book *PM*.

28. As Jean Leclercq notes, "in every period or place where there was a monastic renewal, there was a revival of Origen." See *The Love of Learning and the Desire for God: A Study of Monastic Culture* (New York: Fordham University Press, 1961), 94.

29. And in this regard, Alasdair MacIntyre puts it best: "But facts, like telescopes and wigs for gentlemen, were a seventeenth-century invention." See *Whose Justice? Which Rationality?* (Notre Dame, IN: University of Notre Dame Press, 1988), 357.

30. Plato, *Letter VII*, 344a.

Feuer, a positive defense of Origen's esotericism.[31] In the latter text, Balthasar refuses to avoid some of the more difficult positions held by Origen, or at least held as theological possibilities, and is content with noting the variously heterodox positions not adopted or explicitly rejected by later church teaching. Thus, Balthasar allows that admiration for Origen can also reject some of his more extravagant positions. Nevertheless, Balthasar does not allow this strategy to apply to the question of esotericism, one of those elements in Origen that Balthasar acknowledges as likely to be excused or excised by his admirers. We can quote and gloss some of Balthasar's key statements on this subject: "A second error in criticism would seem to be the fundamental rejection of Origen's esotericism. This esotericism is grounded in his doctrine of being itself and is thus not to be disposed of by an external comparison with pagan mystery cults." Being itself has the quality of a progressive self-disclosure and an esoteric core, and if Aquinas's *non tollit* means anything, it must mean that revelation likewise shares this characteristic of all beings. "The esotericism of Origen is rather only the consequence he has fearlessly drawn from the Christian idea that true knowledge is only attained by action, and that consequently the anticipation of a higher knowledge by someone still unpurified and unprepared can be harmful and even existentially false for such a person." *Theoria* not only flows into *praktike*, but as Origen knew as well as Pascal, action is often the precondition for knowledge (*fac et videbis*): "Later theology gave up this esotericism. It could do this only at the price of a progressive separation between school theology and mystical (or existential experience-) theology, both of which form a strict unity in Origen."[32] For Balthasar, renouncing Christianity's esoteric core is tantamount to endorsing a firm rupture between spirituality and dogmatic theology, and thus the way to heal their rupture is to once again, in the footsteps of Origen, highlight the price of admission for gaining access to revelation.[33]

---

31. *PM*, 33.

32. *OSF*, 17. Though written in 1938, this interpretation of the separation of mysticism and theological speculation is continued and greatly specified thirty years later in *GL* 4 and 5. With regard to Balthasar's genealogy, not only is Aquinas blameless in this regard, but it is above all Nicholas of Cusa who brings a renewal of "the esoteric character of all theology." See GL 5, 223.

33. At the end of *PM*, he admits that while Origen was "already very close to this solution," it is "only Gregory of Nyssa" who best articulates a solution to the tension between desire and knowledge (114–15). Naturally, this is given greater expression in *Presence and Thought*, where Balthasar again concludes with the unity of action and thought: "[Life] then becomes the realization of thought through action, which is the proof of conceptual truth. . . . Far from being opposed to one another, dogmatic theology and mystical theology are inseparable. Indeed, if theology is conceived of as a dynamic realization, they are identical" (171–72).

To gain some measure of precision, we can move from speaking about revelation in the abstract to speaking briefly about the main witness to revelation, namely, scripture. Scripture quite clearly evinces the exoteric/esoteric tension that we have been addressing, and this tension is in some sense the guiding principle for all theologically responsible biblical hermeneutics. To state the matter so plainly as to verge on the banal: scripture admits of better and worse interpretations, not only regarding historical accuracy and philological finesse but especially regarding the theandric origins of the text. To claim that there is a revelatory, truly theological meaning beyond the mere *littera* is to suggest that scripture hides as much as it reveals, that its exoteric shell is as likely to blind as it is to illuminate. There is thus good theological reasoning for directing financial resources to efforts other than placing bibles in hotel dressers. Such an approach is the evangelical, *sola scriptura* equivalent to the scholastic theory of revelation as *locutio Dei ad homines*, as if revelation were purely its textual manifestation in scripture and/or the documents of tradition.[34] Instead, Balthasar thinks that a solely exoteric understanding of revelation is as philosophically dubious as it is an easy retreat from the very difficult question about the uncontrollable site of revelation. It is clear why Balthasar was so enlivened in his protest against an overweening historical-critical approach to scriptural interpretation. The problem is that it has often operated with an *a priori* exclusion of any canonical unity or revelatory coherence. For Balthasar, however, the aggregate of all the various parts that make up scripture and tradition do not in themselves equal the total form of revelation. The words that constitute the gospels, even those of the original Greek, do not provide in themselves the form of Christ, the *Gestalt Christi*, which is instead accessed only via initiation. Even scripture then, for Balthasar, is properly understood as an esoteric text, a text with layers of signification and meaning hidden from the uninitiated, who only see words on a page and not the living Person to whom they refer.

Here again, we return to the crux mentioned above: if revelation is not to be equated with scripture, then we again seem to run the risk of either positing revelation as the official dogmatic decisions regarding scripture's content (Blondel's "extrincisism") or again as coterminous with the believing spirit (modernism), which alone has access to the privileged core. Instead, Balthasar's answer is the following: revelation is not grasped or judged ultimately by the intellect but by love, a love that accepts the form of the beloved in the mode

---

34. And though these scholastics, such as Christian Pesch and Hermann Dieckmann, do note the necessity of a supernatural instinct, "Revelation" strictly speaking is not that instinct but is "contained in the verbal testimonies of Scripture and tradition" (Dulles, *Models of Revelation*, 43).

in which the beloved is given.[35] This implies that the "content" of revelation is not firstly a matter of fodder for the intellectual appetite. As *Dei Verbum* made clear, and Aquinas would no doubt agree, Christ himself is the "mediator and the sum total of revelation."[36] Whatever the role of the text of scripture and the clarifications and specifications of later tradition, and for Balthasar these are essential, they are necessarily subservient to Christ, who is excessive of even the most accurate propositions and descriptions. But secondly, this also means that knowing Christ (or any person, we might add) operates in a quite different register from knowing facts. Knowledge of revelation, then, requires charity. As he concludes his study of Origen, he notes that "Origen knows that the true knowledge [*savoir*] is love: 'friendship with Christ in the Holy Spirit, such is, indeed, the knowledge [*connaissance*] of God.'"[37] Or if one is averse to Origen, and as a way to return to the theme of scripture, it is clear that Augustine himself taught much the same. For Augustine, love (for God and neighbor) is the one irreplaceable hermeneutical principle that must guide all scriptural interpretation. For even if one errs in interpretation, the charitable reading demonstrates that the reader has already arrived at the goal to which scripture was directing.[38] While the data of revelation are indeed publicly available, namely scripture and the teaching of the church, the only means of seeing them for what they are is to move into the esoteric heart, which is through charity. Balthasar interprets Origen to mean that just as God is the transcendent ground of creaturely flux, and so is not then reducible to it, so also the spiritual meaning of scripture is to its material expression: "For just as there the (God-) Spirit lies unmoved behind the change of material things, so here does the esoteric spiritual meaning lie ready, clear and motionless so to speak behind the image of the letter."[39] For Balthasar, as well as for Origen and Augustine, a subjective disposition of loving adherence to Christ is an infinitely more precious thing (and more theologically reliable) than a capacious intellectual grasp of all of scripture and tradition.

Balthasar's proximity to modernism at this point is palpable, as is Aquinas's, it should be added.[40] Yet for Balthasar and Aquinas, unlike Loisy

---

35. Blankenhorn also notes the following of Aquinas: "Hence loving God is greater than knowing him. . . . Faith's cognition serves charity as an essential guide, but charity's perfection goes beyond such cognition, for its only 'measure' is God" (*The Mystery of Union with God*, 288).

36. *Dei Verbum*, 2. See René Latourelle's commentary on *Dei Verbum* in *Theology of Revelation* (Alba House, 1967), 453–88. Note also *ST* III, prologue: *viam veritatis nobis in seipso demonstravit.*

37. *PM*, 116.

38. *De Doctrina Christiana*, I.39–41.

39. *OSF*, 19.

40. See *ST* I, q. 1, a. 9, co. and ad 2.

or Tyrrell, the truths of revelation are not simply means, and potentially hazardous ones, for arriving at an amorphous, nonthematic religious sentiment that would "make consciousness and revelation synonymous."[41] The priority of love that Balthasar accords to the reception of revelation does not imply that revelation is strapped to the procrustean bed of human longings and thus confined to merely validating creaturely *eros*. Again, he requires both parts of Blondel's paradox: revelation is necessary for the fulfillment of the creature but likewise remains impossibly beyond its reach. Human *eros* for the divine is not negated (*non tollit*) but rather perfected into a form of supernatural rapture. As human *eros* strives after the infinite, it finds that it has been met by a descending *eros*, and thus for Balthasar we need to posit a "*doppelte beidseitige Ekstase—Gottes zum Menschen und des Menschen zu Gott*: a double and reciprocal ekstasis—of God to men and of men to God."[42] Following Denys, Balthasar says that it was first God who is "drawn out of himself by *eros* into creation, revelation, and Incarnation," and thus the creature's erotic return to God is a secondary movement of response. The subjective impulse is then met, and completed by, the objective deeds of the Incarnate God, which give *eros* an object that exceeds its natural capacities. The descending *eros* therefore *enthuses* human love with a divine capacity (call it the *lumen fidei*, Rousselot's *les yeux de la foi*, or even an authentically Christian *gnosis*): "All divine revelation is impregnated with an element of 'enthusiasm' (in the theological sense)."[43] To then summarize how Balthasar attempts to hold together this tension of subjective dynamism with its objective referent, we could say the following: for Balthasar, while the inexhaustible Person of Christ is himself the unsurpassable form of revelation, he also holds that scripture, tradition, and the magisterium are indeed indispensable witnesses to, and instantiations of, that revelation. Further, a true lover, one who is truly enthused for things divine, desires the beloved not solely as a *mysterium tremendum et fascinans* but in the concrete, particular modes of divine self-expression. However, on their own, without the enthusiasm that gives one a vision of the whole, these can be nothing but *littera*, hieroglyphs without a Rosetta stone.

While it was Aquinas's particular charism to firmly establish the provinces of faith and reason and thus to coordinate their mutually beneficial interaction, Balthasar writes at a time when faith and reason had been torn asunder, when philosophy (predominantly) claims that only the exoteric, the publicly available, can demand serious consideration. As is the case with all divorces, it is the children that suffer: in this case, the element of *mythos*. Whether or not the third leg of the stool, *mythos*, is relegated to the hinterland of faith or is

---

41. Pius X, *Pascendi Dominici Gregis*, 8.
42. *Herrlichkeit*, 118; *GL* 1, 122.
43. *GL* 1, 120.

allowed to remain with reason (even if just on the weekends) is one way of reading the contemporary division between philosophical temperaments, the analytic and the continental. The task for theology today, according to Balthasar, is to insist that revelation lays claims on reason and on our penchant for the mythic, and that, in fact, the realm of the esoteric, where perhaps only few enter, is the secret heart of public *ratio* and the innate strivings of the will. That is to say, revelation not only gives extra knowledge than what we can garner with our own intellectual powers but also opens up the depths of being itself, exposes what lays hidden before our eyes, and provides a clue into the subtlety and unexpected depths of being.[44] The esotericism of revelation, as Balthasar understands this, is not another form of extrincisism, as if this "secret knowledge" given from above has only an internal coherence and self-referential frame of reference. It is rather an open secret, a secret openly proclaimed but seldom heard. Thus, the *connaturalitas* required to receive the self-disclosure of God is not only *fides*, not only an intellectual enlightening, but ultimately *caritas* (as purified *amor*). Revelation is then esoteric only because real love is rare, while the embryonic stages and simulacra of love are ubiquitous. The genuine, striving forms of love are everywhere present, and when present, are mirrors of the infinite. But for Balthasar, the esoteric heart of revelation is reserved for true lovers.

Finally, it must be noted that the "double ekstasis" of the Dionysian tradition (of which both Aquinas and Balthasar are heirs) means that revelation is also double: the self-disclosure of the hidden depths of God, which elicits an unveiling, an apocalypse, of the finite spirit to God. Heidegger's rendering of truth as *aletheia* is partially validated, but for Balthasar, this unconcealment does not ultimately occur within an entirely immanent clearing (*Lichtung*) but to God in a spirit of adoration and confession: "The ontological unveiling of the creature before God guarantees that the truth of this world is in fact true. Truth is the unconcealment of being, while the full notion of this unconcealment requires someone to whom it is unconcealed."[45] Revelation, then, is that circular movement in which the Triune life is laid bare before a creature in all humility, and the creature in turn offers everything, its *ratio*, its *voluntas*, its capacity for the poetic word, back to God in confession and adoration. In

---

44. Just as Aquinas knew and Vatican I affirmed, the fields of revelation and reason overlap. See *SCG* I.4 and *Dei Filius* 2. Balthasar takes this much further, following an insight he found in Romano Guardini, by noting the contours of being that *could* have been discovered by reason but, as a simple matter of historical chronology, have only been discovered in cultures infused with Christian faith. See *TL* 1, 13; *TL* 2; and *RG*, 21. For a complementary notion of theology as the *entelechy* of philosophy, which likewise refers to Vatican I, see Przywara, *Analogia Entis*, 172–74.

45. *TL* 1, 269.

this creaturely unconcealment, the depths of "nature" are seen as if for the first time. In this exchange, the beloved not only learns about the Divine Lover through its act of love but also discovers itself precisely *as* a beloved, as something that had been brought into existence by another.

CONCLUSION: THE KISS

Although we have highlighted their relative proximity to one another on the issue of revelation, it is not the case that there are not fundamental and perhaps irresolvable differences between Aquinas and Balthasar, not only on this issue but on numerable others.[46] While there is considerable agreement between Aquinas and Balthasar regarding the fact that revelation is neither reducible to nor infinitely removed from its manifestation in scripture and tradition (we should say, rather, that there is an analogical relationship between the esoteric and exoteric), each takes this division to mean something slightly different for the theological task. We have already seen how Balthasar nominates Aquinas as a synthesis of scholastic and monastic theology, but it should be clarified that Aquinas *is* indeed a scholastic theologian first and foremost, but in such a manner that complements rather than contradicts (again, Guardini's *Gegensatz* rather than *Widerspruch*) monastic theology. His understanding of theology is one that looks primarily for intellectual elaboration of the givens of revelation, to show the coherence and fecundity of Christian faith. Balthasar, on the other hand, if one must choose, is more monastic than scholastic. Thomas Merton recognized as much, writing the following in a letter in 1964: "Dom Leclercq mentioned lately that he thought Von Balthasar was the one who came closest to a monastic theology in our day. I very much agree."[47] Merton also knew that this monastic theological style had something to do with Balthasar's reading of Origen. Hence, he wrote earlier, to Balthasar himself: "But you are an Origenist: how can you fail to be alert to the seriousness of the poetic word, which has its own special place

---

46. Other differences that should at least be flagged regarding revelation include Thomas' insistence, following Hebrews 11:1, on the incompatibility of faith and sight (e.g., *ST* II-II, q. 1, a. 4) and Balthasar's use of sight as the primary metaphor for the act of faith. This also means that Aquinas thinks that knowing and believing are mutually exclusive while Balthasar, much like Newman, thinks that knowledge and faith are always bound up with one another at the most basic epistemological level. For a nice summary of this second point, see "Kenotic Faith: Hans Urs von Balthasar," in Francesca Murphy, Balázs M. Mezei, and Kenneth Oakes, *Illuminating Faith: An Invitation to Theology* (New York: T&T Clark, 2015): 109–13.

47. Letter to Father Columba Halsey on October 29, 1964 (*The School of Charity*, 248). The "Dom Leclercq" is, of course, Jean Leclercq, OSB, author of *The Love of Learning and the Desire for God*.

in the world of the sons of God since Adam was appointed to name the animals. . . . Theoria demands not just gazing but response and statement. Don't you agree?"[48] Though there are indeed important biographical reasons for Balthasar's affinity to monastic thought,[49] for our purposes here, the essential point is that Balthasar's conception of theology is one that robustly takes into account "the poetic word" and spiritual experience as much as dogmatic definitions and scriptural affirmations. It is a theology that attempts to consider the totality of witnesses to the center of revelation, which includes the official sources as well as the experience of saints, mystics, and novelists, and is meant to foster not only an intellectual apprehension of the faith, but a loving adherence and admittance to its esoteric core. Yet, this is not a flight into the irrational, for Balthasar also aimed for a harmony with the insights gained from the rigorous application of *ratio* that is so characteristic of scholasticism. Only the obdurate insist that Aquinas and Balthasar are mutually exclusive theological styles, no matter how one evaluates their specific theological decisions. Revelation is indeed given so that one may *know* the truth. Here, Aquinas is dominant and Balthasar recessive. But *knowing* involves loving, involves the entire person, including the will and even the body. Here, Aquinas is recessive, and Balthasar dominant.

Aquinas is not a rationalist, and Balthasar is not a modernist or a voluntarist, and any argument for either claim would be comically polemical. They do, however, tend toward the logical and the sapiential, respectively, but these two emphases are nothing more than the two lips of which Saint Bernard wrote: "He who understands truth without loving it, or loves without understanding, possesses neither one nor the other. Thus this kiss leaves no room for error or for lukewarm feelings. To receive the holy kiss of this two-fold grace, the spouse must prepare two lips: reason for intelligence, will for wisdom."[50] For Balthasar, revelation is the unveiling of the Triune life of God to the world, which occurs paradigmatically in the nuptial union between Christ and the church. The response of the bride to the bridegroom must likewise be a revelation, a laying bear of creation itself. It is thus an offering of reason and will, the philosophical genius and the religious and affective

---

48. Letter to Balthasar on July 3, 1964 (*The School of Charity*, 219). Also note the following in another letter to Balthasar two years later (after Merton had given up reading *Herrlichkeit* in the original German and resigned himself to the French translation) on September 12, 1966: "Yes, I feel it is very important for us other monks to show gratitude towards a theologian such as you, who are, after all, more contemplative and more 'monastic'" (*The School of Charity*, 312).

49. Like Aquinas, Balthasar studied with the Benedictines as a youth (at Engelberg), and later, after leaving the Jesuits, Balthasar renewed his priestly vows at Maria Laach, to name just two significant points.

50. *Sup. Cant.* 8.5–6, cited in Leclercq, *The Love of Learning*, 228.

dynamism of the spirit, as well as a eucharistic exchange of flesh. The kiss, if it is to be ecclesial, must be monastic and scholastic, Balthasarian and Thomist. The one without the other, at least considering the two as forms or styles of the theological task, would be a kiss offered begrudgingly, with pursed lips. The viability of either contemporary Thomist or so-called Balthasarian positions will depend on whether either (and ideally both) can be expansive enough to affirm and integrate the myriad ways in which the Divine Self-Gift can be and has been received: *Wer mehr Wahrheit sieht, hat mehr recht.*[51]

BIBLIOGRAPHY

Balázs, Francesca, M. Mezei, and Kenneth Oakes, eds. *Illuminating Faith: An Invitation to Theology.* New York: T&T Clark, 2015.

Balthasar, Hans Urs von. *Besondere Gnadengaben und die Zwei Wege Menschlichen Lebens.* Freiburg: Gemeinschaftsverlag, 1954.

————. *Martin Buber and Christianity: A Dialogue between Israel and the Church.* New York: Macmillan, 1961.

————. *Meditations on the Tarot: A Journey into Christian Hermeticism.* New York: Tarcher, 2002.

Blankenhorn, Bernhard. *The Mystery of Union with God: Dionysian Mysticism in Albert the Great and Thomas Aquinas.* Washington, DC: The Catholic University of America Press, 2015.

Blondel, Maurice. *L'Action (1893): Essay on a Critique of Life and a Science of Practice,* trans. Oliva Blanchette (Notre Dame, IN: University of Notre Dame Press, 2003).

————. *The Letter on Apologetics & History and Dogma.* Translated by A. Dru and I. Trethowan. Grand Rapids, MI: Eerdmans, 1994.

Boland, Vivian. "Non Solum Discens Sed Et Patiens Divina: The Wanderings of an Aristotelian Fragment." In *Roma, Magistra Mundi, Itineraria Culturae Medievalis: Mélanges offerts au Père L. E. Boyle à l'occasion de son 75e anniversaire,* edited by J. Hamesse, 55–69. Louvain-la-Neuve, 1998.

Borella, Jean. *Christ the Original Mystery: Esotericism and the Mystical Way.* Translated by G. J. Champoux. Brooklyn, NY: Angelico Press, 2018.

Chapp, Larry. *The God who Speaks: Hans Urs von Balthasar's Theology of Revelation.* Bethesda, MD: International Scholars, 1997.

De Lubac, Henri. *The Mystery of the Supernatural.* New York: Crossroad, 1988.

Dulles, Avery. *Models of Revelation.* New York: Orbis, 1992.

Gilson, Étienne. *Reason and Revelation in the Middle Ages.* New York: Charles Scribner's Sons, 1938.

---

51. "Whoever sees more truth is more correct," an axiom of Balthasar (see *EP*, 15, 43), though not of Balthasarian origin (he calls it a "well-known proverb"). This idea is explored in greater depth in *TS*.

Guardini, Romano. *Der Gegensatz: Versuche zu einer Philosophie des Lebendig-Konkreten.* Mainz: Matthias Grünewald, 1925.

———. *Reform from the Source.* San Francisco: Ignatius, 2010.

Lacoste, Jean-Yves. *From Theology to Theological Thinking.* Translated by W. C. Hackett. Charlottesville: University of Virginia Press, 2014.

———. "Revelation." In *Encyclopedia of Christian Theology,* vol. III, edited by J.-Y. Lacoste, 1383–391. New York: Routledge, 2005.

Latourelle, René. *Theology of Revelation.* New York: Alba House, 1987.

Leclercq, Jean. *The Love of Learning and the Desire for God : A Study of Monastic Culture.* New York: Fordham University Press, 1982.

MacIntyre, Alasdair. *Whose Justice? Which Rationality?* Notre Dame, IN: University of Notre Dame Press, 1988.

Maritain, Jacques. *Distinguish to Unite, Or, The Degrees of Knowledge.* Notre Dame, IN: University of Notre Dame Press, 1995.

Milbank, John. *The Suspended Middle: Henri de Lubac and the Debate Concerning the Supernatural.* Grand Rapids, MI: Eerdmans, 2005.

Mongrain, Kevin. "Rule-Governed Christian Gnosis: Hans Urs von Balthasar on Valentin Tomberg's *Meditations on the Tarot.*" *Modern Theology* 25, no. 2 (April 2009): 285–314.

O'Rourke, Fran. *Pseudo-Dionysius & the Metaphysics of Aquinas.* Leiden: Brill, 1992.

Przywara, Erich. "Image, Likeness, Symbol, Mythos, Mysterium, Logos." In *Analogia Entis: Metaphysics: Original Structure and Universal Rhythm,* translated by J. R. Betz and D. Bentley Hart, 430–62. Grand Rapids, MI: Eerdmans, 2014.

Christology

CHAPTER 5

The Father's Perfect Image Became Our Perfect Mediator

The Christology of Thomas Aquinas

REV. ANDREW LIAUGMINAS

"PROPERLY SPEAKING, the office of a mediator is to join together those between whom he mediates: for extremes are united in the mean. Now to unite men to God perfectively belongs to Christ, through whom men are reconciled to God." It is with these words that Thomas Aquinas begins his response in the *Summa theologiae* to the question of whether it belongs to Christ to be the Mediator of God and men (*ST* 3.26.1). Thomas shows the importance of the question by locating it "in the mean" of his Christological treatise in the *Tertia Pars*: namely, at the conclusion of his consideration of "the mystery of the Incarnation itself, whereby God was made man for our salvation" in *ST* 3.1–26 and immediately prior to his discussion of "such things as were done and suffered by our Savior, that is, God Incarnate" in 3.27–59 (*ST* 3 *pr.*).

Since the doctrine of Christ's mediatorship sits at the intersection of Thomas's consideration of the ontology of the Word Incarnate and his saving work in the *Summa theologiae*, the understanding of Christ as Mediator of God and man provides a helpful focal point in considering Thomas's mature Christology. While several other works of Thomas could also serve as a foundation to discuss his Christology, the relatively late place which the *Summa* occupies in Thomas's *corpus* reflects the Angelic Doctor's most-developed positions on the principal questions of Christology and thus affords the reader a natural point of departure for considering the place that Christ occupies overall in his thought. It is from this position that we can incorporate the contributions that Thomas's other works offer in the realm of Christology.

A NOTE ON THE PLACE OF CHRIST IN THE SUMMA

When considering the Christology of Thomas Aquinas in the contemporary context, one of the first points to emerge is the question of why Thomas placed his Christological treatise seemingly at the end of the *Summa* rather than in the

95

middle. Critics have argued that his decision to place his treatise on Christ in the final part of the *Summa*'s three principal parts turns Christology into a footnote on the discussion of God and man.[1] Since "the final goal of human life, the grace offered to fallen humankind, and our moral life, all receive their concrete shape and form through Christ," as Roch Kereszty argues, the treatise on Christ should have *preceded* the treatise on man and not followed after it.[2] Given this, how should one understand Thomas's decision to treat human action and divine grace *before* considering the person and mission of Christ?

In response, defenders of Thomas's synthesis have pointed out that his decision to locate the treatise on the Incarnate Word in the *Tertia Pars* does not mean that Christ appears only at the end of his synthesis. From the Son's personal role in the Trinity in the *Prima Pars* to the central place Christ has in the discussions of virtue, the New Law, and grace in the *Secunda Pars*, it is evident that the Second Person of the Trinity appears throughout the *Summa*.[3]

Moreover, a study of the global organization of Thomas's synthesis in the *Summa* reveals that the work moves from considering God as he is in himself (*theologia*) to considering God as "the beginning of things and their last end" (*economia*), and then—within the last element—moving "from God the creator to God who returns in Christ to take man with Him into glory," in the words of Jean-Pierre Torrell.[4] Seen in this way, it emerges with clarity how the mature Christology of the *Tertia Pars* serves as the "consummation" of Thomas's theological project in the *Summa*, which is exactly what he states in the prologue (*ST, pr.*).[5]

When Thomas arrives at his study of the Incarnate Word in the *Tertia Pars*, his treatise on Christ stands out among medieval *summae* for its eminently biblical foundation and salvation-historical setting—a true "innovation" in its time, as Joseph Wawrykow notes.[6] Considering the broader archi-

---

1. See, for example, *KB*, 263–65.

2. Roch A. Kereszty, *Jesus Christ: Fundamentals of Christology*, 3rd ed. (Staten Island, NY: St. Paul's—Communio Book, 2002), 278.

3. See the argument of Jean-Marc Laporte in "Christ in Aquinas's *Summa Theologiae*: Peripheral or Pervasive?" *The Thomist* 67, no. 2 (2003): 221–48.

4. Jean-Pierre Torrell, *Saint Thomas Aquinas*, vol. 1, *The Person and His Work*, trans. R. Royal (Washington, DC: The Catholic University of America Press, 2005), 153. Notably, Thomas is building on a neo-Platonic *exitus-reditus* schema; on this, see M.-D. Chenu, "Le plan de la Somme théologique de saint Thomas," *Revue Thomiste* 45 (1939): 93–107.

5. On this, see John F. Boyle, "Is the Tertia Pars of the Summa Theologiae Misplaced?" in *Proceedings of the PMR Conference*, vol. 18 (Villanova, PA: Augustinian Historical Institute, 1996), 103–9.

6. Joseph Wawrykow, "The Christology of Thomas Aquinas in its Scholastic Context," in *The Oxford Handbook of Christology*, ed. Francesca A. Murphy (Oxford: Oxford University Press, 2016), 239.

tecture of the *Summa* and Thomas's profound incorporation of scripture, Edward T. Oakes observes that "Thomas's treatment of Christ, even in [the *Summa Theologiae*], is strikingly *biblical* and therefore *narrative* in its approach . . . more so perhaps than is often recognized. . . . And because . . . the Bible never narrates its events except in the highly pitched tones of a cosmic *drama*, Thomas's Christology, too, is often cast in dramatic terms."[7] The "drama" of the Incarnation and redemption, following the principal lines of Thomas's presentation in the *Summa theologiae*, begins his discussion of the Person of Son in the *Prima Pars*. His consideration of the ontological constitution of Christ, found at the beginning of the *Tertia Pars*, follows next. Finally, Thomas concludes his Christological treatise in the *Tertia Pars* with the mysteries of the life of Christ. For Thomas, the Incarnate Word, *as God*, is one of the Holy Trinity—the Divine Son who is the "perfect Image of the Father" (*ST* 1.35.2 ad 3; cf. 3.59.1)—and, *as man*, is the "perfect Mediator," "through whom men are reconciled to God" (3.26.1).

THE PERSON AND MISSION OF THE SON

To situate the Christology of the *Summa* in its proper context, one must begin with Thomas's treatment of the person and mission of the Second Person in the *Prima Pars*. While we recognize the sonship of the Second Person in the order of knowing by virtue of the fact that he proceeds eternally as the Only-Begotten of the Father, what constitutes the hypostasis of the Second Person in eternity, according to Thomas, is his subsisting *relation of filiation*.[8]

The Son's unique and eternal relation allows us to employ certain appellations for the Second Person as "personal names" (*nomina propria*), if and only insofar as those names reflect his relationship of origin within the Trinity. Names such as "Son" (1.27.2, 1.33.3), "Word" (1.34), "Splendor" (1.34.2 ad 3), "Image" (1.35), and "Wisdom Begotten" (1.39.7 ad 2; cf. 1.37.1) are personal names of the Second Person for this reason.[9] While all these names express the filiation of the Second Person, they do so in distinct ways, with each name expressing an aspect of the unique relationship that constitutes him in eternity.[10]

---

7. Edward T. Oakes, *Infinity Dwindled to Infancy: A Catholic and Evangelical Christology* (Grand Rapids, MI: William B. Eerdmans, 2011), 198–99. Emphasis in original.

8. *ST* 1.30.2, 1.40.4. See also *ST* 1.28, 1.40.1 ad 1. For a comprehensive study of Thomas's Trinitarian thought, see Gilles Emery, *The Trinitarian Theology of St Thomas Aquinas*, trans. Francesca A. Murphy (Oxford: Oxford University Press, 2007).

9. For a study of various linguistic and theological issues surrounding the naming of Christ, see Henk J. M. Schoot, *Christ the "Name" of God: Thomas Aquinas on Naming Christ* (Leuven: Peeters Publishers, 1993).

10. *ST* 1.32.3, 1.34.2 ad 3. See also *Super Ioh.* 1.1, paras. 41–42.

While Thomas limits the personal names of the Second Person to those that speak exclusively of his personal property of filiation, he also acknowledges that we can fittingly make use of certain essential attributes of God to help manifest the Son to our reason by way of *appropriation* (1.39.7). While the essential attributes of God do not belong to any one divine Person but are shared in common, insofar as certain attributes are particularly congruent with the Person of the Son, they can be fittingly appropriated to him. For example, Thomas posits that "beauty" bears a fitting likeness to the personal property of the Son insofar as beauty's constitutive elements—*integritas, consonantia*, and *claritas*—harmonize with the Second Person's consubstantiality with the Father (as Son), his perfect expression of the Father (as Image), and the manner in which he is "the light and splendor of the intellect" (as Word).[11]

Since the Second Person proceeds within the Trinity by way of intellect (1.27.2), it is fitting that his economic mission—even in its preincarnate, "invisible" stage—would gravitate around the enlightenment of human intellects (1.43.2; also 1.43.7 ad 4), and would specifically involve that illumination "which breaks forth into the affection of love" (1.43.5 ad 2).[12] Moreover, given that the Son's characteristic work *ad extra* involves enlightening-created intellects, it is fitting that his invisible mission would become manifest (i.e., as his "visible mission") by means of a nature that is essentially *rational*.[13] Indeed, it was right that the "Author of Sanctification"—another, often-overlooked name that Thomas associates with the Son—should be sent visibly "according to a rational nature to which *it belongs to act*, and which is *capable of being sanctified*."[14] These lines from the *Prima Pars* not only foreshadow but also lay the foundation for Thomas's treatise on the Incarnate Word later in the *Summa*.

---

11. *ST* 1.39.8. See also *ST* 1.34.2 ad 3; *Super Sent.* 1.31.2.1 co. Two notable contributions in the study of Thomas on beauty include Umberto Eco, *The Aesthetics of Thomas Aquinas*, trans. H. Bredin (Cambridge, MA: Harvard University Press, 1988) and Brendan T. Sammon, *The God Who Is Beauty: Beauty as a Divine Name in Thomas Aquinas and Dionysius the Areopagite*, Princeton Theological Monograph Series 206 (Eugene, OR: Pickwick, 2013).

12. As "Love" is the personal name of the Holy Spirit (*ST* 1.37.1), this affirmation reflects Aquinas's attention to the deep interrelationship between the missions of the Son and the Spirit in the divine economy. On this, see *ST* 1.43.5 ad 3, 1.93.7, and Dominic Legge, *The Trinitarian Christology of St. Thomas Aquinas* (Oxford: Oxford University Press, 2017), 131–231.

13. For a study of the argument from fittingness (*convenientia*) in Thomas's thought in dialogue with the place of beauty in Balthasar's thought, see Gilbert Narcisse, *Le Christ en sa beauté*, vol. 1, *Christologie: Hans Urs von Balthasar, Saint Thomas d'Aquin* (Magny-les-Hameaux: Soceval, 2005).

14. *ST* 1.43.7 ad 4, emphasis added. See also *SCG* 4.55; *ST* 1–2.114.6, 3.4.1.

As Thomas approaches the mystery of the Incarnation in the *Tertia Pars*, he reaffirms the fittingness of the Incarnation, considering God's self-communicating Goodness and man's rational nature (3.1.1). Yet now, his reflections on the fittingness of the Incarnation take, as their starting point, the actual state of postlapsarian man. Indeed, says Thomas, God *could have* accomplished man's salvation in a different manner than by sending his Son (e.g., 3.3.3–8),[15] but—because of our actual *need* for liberation from the "tyrant," forgiveness of our sins, and restoration of our relationship with God (3.1.2–3)—"there was no more fitting way of healing our misery" than the way God *did* choose: namely, to send his Son to take on our flesh so that he might reveal the Father,[16] atone for our sins, and bring us the gift of adopted sonship in God.[17]

---

15. This question (i.e., *ST* 3.3) has become one of the most debated facets of Thomas's Christology because, in the course of this question, Thomas grants the theoretical possibility of various counterfactuals for the Incarnation (3.3.2–7), including the thesis that the Father or the Spirit could have become incarnate instead of the Son (3.3.5). Responding to this affirmation, Karl Rahner famously remarked that if any member of the Trinity could have become incarnate, "then the fact of the incarnation of the Logos 'reveals' properly nothing about the Logos *himself*, that is, about his own relative specific features within the divinity," and "sonship in grace would in fact have absolutely nothing to do with the Son's sonship, since it might equally well be brought about without any modification by another incarnate person" (Rahner, *The Trinity*, trans. J. Doncel [London: Burns and Oates, 1970], 28–29). In response, Thomists have observed that Thomas' reasoning in *ST* 3.3 is a meditation on "the actual Christian dispensation," a fact that becomes evident in 3.3.8 (Joseph Wawrykow, "Wisdom in the Christology of Thomas Aquinas," in *Christ Among the Medieval Dominicans*, ed. K. Emery, Jr. and Joseph Wawrykow [Notre Dame, IN: University of Notre Dame Press, 1999], 182). Overall, it is evident that Thomas's reflections in *ST* 3.3 (as well as those in 3.1.3) have prompted important debates about the revelatory dimension of the work of the Trinity in the economy, the centrality of the Second Person in God's plan of creation and redemption, and the specifically filial identity of the One who was sent for our salvation.

16. According to Thomas, the Son's singular and complete knowledge of the Father makes him the most apt teacher of the things of God (e.g., *Super Ioh.* 1.11, para. 217–19; 8.1, para. 1118–124). See also Pawel Klimczak, *Christus Magister: Le Christ Maître dans les commentaires évangéliques de saint Thomas d'Aquin*, Studia Friburgensia 117 (Fribourg: Academic Press Fribourg, 2014).

17. *ST* 3.1.2, 3.3.8. See also 1.33.3. Regarding the gift of adopted filiation, Thomas states that it belongs to "the very end of the Incarnation of Christ . . . that men might be reborn as sons of God" (*ST* 3.28.1; see also *Super Ioh.*, 1.6, paras. 148–64). For a study of this theme, see Luc-Thomas Somme, *Fils adoptifs de Dieu par Jésus Christ: la filiation divine par adoption dans la théologie de saint Thomas d'Aquin*, Bibliothèque Thomiste 49 (Paris: J. Vrin, 1997).

Christ, the True and Perfect Mediator

Having affirmed the fittingness of the Incarnation of the Son to serve the work of salvation given the actual state of man, in the third part of the *Summa*, Thomas undertakes a careful consideration of the Incarnation and the ontology of the Incarnate Word, the mysteries of the life of Christ, and how Christ's actions and sufferings brought about our salvation. At the nexus of his study of the Incarnation in 3.1–25 and his consideration of the life of Christ in 3.27–59 lies the question of Christ's mediatorship (3.26).

What does it mean to say that Christ is the *mediator* of God and men?[18] First, the Christian Faith affirms that "Christ alone is the perfect Mediator of God and men" because it is *in* Christ that God reconciles the world to himself (2 Cor 5:19). Thomas argues that Christ *is* the mediator of God and man not only because of the mediatory actions he performs in the flesh but also because—by virtue of the Incarnation and precisely *in his humanity*—the "one mediator of God and man, Christ Jesus" (1 Tim 2:5) joined together in himself "those between whom he is a mediator: for extremes are united in the mean [*in medio*]" (*ST* 3.26.1 co.).[19]

Before considering how in Thomas's thought Christ as man is the "true and perfect Mediator" (3.26.1 ad 1) and how he reconciled us with God, it is necessary to consider first how he is constituted such that the One who made "peace by the blood of his cross" (Col 1:20) is also the One in whom "all the fullness of God was pleased to dwell" (Col 1:19).

The Assumption of Human Nature

Aquinas firmly builds his discussion of the ontology of the Word Incarnate upon the foundation established by the fathers of the church and its

---

18. While the formulation "mediator *between* God and men" might sound more natural to the English speaker, Thomas typically uses the Latin genitive case when speaking about Christ's unique mediatory role: *mediator Dei et hominum*, "mediator *of* God and *of* men" (*ST* 3.26). Notably, he distinguishes this from the mediatory role the priests of old fulfilled as *mediatores inter Deum et homines* (3.26.1; cf. *Super Heb.* 7.1, para. 329). Among other reasons, Thomas might be using the double genitive (*Dei et hominum*) instead of "*inter* + accusative" (*inter Deum et homines*) to avoid an Arian misreading of Christ's mediatorship.

19. According to Thomas, it is in Christ's *humanity*, and not his divinity, that he is the "*mediator*" (*ST* 3.26.2; see also *ST* 3.22.2). See also *Super Heb.* 7.4, paras. 366–68. For a close study of Christ's mediatory role, see Gilles Emery, "Le Christ médiateur: l'unicité et l'universalité de la médiation salvifique du Christ Jésus suivant Thomas d'Aquin," in *Christus—Gottes schöpferisches Wort: Festschrift C. Schönborn*, ed. G. Augustin, M. Brun et al. (Freiburg i.B.: Herder, 2010), 337–55.

early Ecumenical Councils.[20] Following the church's conciliar tradition, Thomas draws a fundamental distinction between the ontological categories of person and nature. In the Incarnation, the Second Person of the Trinity unites an individuated human nature to himself so that, while continuing to subsist in his divine nature, he now begins to subsist also in his assumed human nature.[21] This "union according to the hypostasis"—to use Cyril's signature phrase, affirmed by the Council of Ephesus and confirmed in the Second Council of Constantinople—maintains the ontological distinction between the two natures in the Incarnation while affirming that the sole subsisting subject of the Incarnation is the Person of the Word.[22] Thomas understands the resulting constitution of the Word after the Incarnation in a thoroughly Chalcedonian manner: acknowledging "one and the same Christ, Son, Lord, Only-Begotten in two natures," while affirming that the union of the two natures in the one person did not abolish the distinction between the natures but preserved intact the properties of each nature in the one Person of the Word.[23]

As Thomas incorporates the teachings of the Fourth Ecumenical Council, he also engages the developments of the Fifth Ecumenical Council, which he translates into the philosophical language of his time.[24] Just as the assumed human nature does not have its own hypostasis but was hypostasized in the hypostasis of the Son, so, too—Thomas argues—the assumed human nature does not have a separate act of being (*esse personale*) but receives its personal

---

20. Jean-Pierre Torrell observes that Thomas is "the first Latin theologian to quote literally the acts of the first five ecumenical councils" (*Saint Thomas Aquinas*, 1:139). For Thomas's use of patristic sources, see Leo J. Elders, "Thomas Aquinas and the Fathers of the Church," in *Reception of the Church Fathers in the West: From the Carolingians to the Maurists*, ed. Irena Backus, vol. 1 (Leiden: E. J. Brill, 1997), 337–66.

21. *ST* 3.2.4 co. See also *ST* 3.2.6, 3.17.1–2; *De un. Verb.*, aa. 3–4. For a study of Thomas's theology of the Incarnation in the *Commentary on the Sentences* and the *Summa Contra Gentiles*, see Francis Ruello, *La Christologie de Thomas d'Aquin*, Théologie Historique 76 (Paris: Beauchesne, 1987), 21–274.

22. For a recent study of Thomas' understanding of the Hypostatic Union, see Michael Gorman, *Aquinas on the Metaphysics of the Hypostatic Union* (Cambridge: Cambridge University Press, 2017).

23. Council of Chalcedon, *Definition*, in *Compendium of Creeds, Definitions, and Declarations on Matters of Faith and Morals*, 43rd ed., ed. H. Denzinger and P. Hünermann (San Francisco, Ignatius Press, 2012), 302. See also *ST* 3.2.4. For a study of Thomas's use of Chalcedon, see C. G. Geenen, "En marge du concile de Chalcédoine. Les textes du Quatrième Concile dans les œuvres de saint Thomas," *Angelicum* 29, no. 1 (1952): 43–59.

24. See Martin Morard, "Une source de saint Thomas d'Aquin: Le deuxième concile de Constantinople (553)," *Revue des sciences philosophiques et théologiques* 81, no. 1 (January 1997): 21–56.

act of being in the uncreated *esse personale* of the Son.[25] By virtue of this, the distinctly *filial* identity that characterizes the Son in the Trinity also came to characterize his existence in the flesh from the moment in which the human nature was "elevated to God."[26] Thomas identifies this gratuitous exercise of God's will as a grace (i.e., *gratia unionis*) from the perspective of the assumed nature (*ST* 3.2.10, 3.6.6).

When seen from the perspective of the divine Person, the Incarnation means that the Son—while continuing to subsist truly and fully as God—now comes to subsist truly and fully *as man*. As a result, the singular divine subject is both "perfect in divinity and perfect in humanity," and operates by virtue of the proper principles of *each nature* to win our salvation. Here, Thomas follows closely the logic of Leo's *Tome*. In the Incarnate Word, both natures "do what is proper to each in union with the other": in his divinity, he carries out what is proper to divinity; in his humanity, he carries out what is proper to humanity.[27] In both natures, he wills and works our salvation, and in either nature, the One who acts and wills is the singular Person of the Word.

"Full of Grace and Truth" (Jn 1:14)

As Thomas considers additional implications of the Incarnation, he continues to operate by the Chalcedonian principle that the two natures of the Incarnation, while united inseparably in the Person of the Word, always retain their respective properties—or, as John Damascene succinctly states, "the created remains created, and the uncreated, uncreated."[28] Applying this principle to the question of the *grace* of Christ's soul, Thomas argues that Christ's soul—precisely insofar as it is a *human* soul—requires the divine assistance that all men need to perfect the powers of the soul, as they are moved by the Holy Spirit to allow man to will and to act in accord with God. That assistance takes the form of the infused gift of "habitual grace" (*gratia habitualis*).[29] As

---

25. *ST* 3.6.6, 3.17.2. See also *ST* 3.2.10, 3.4.1 ad 2, and 3.8.5 ad 3. Thomas holds what appears to be a notably different position in the disputed question *De un. Verb.*, a. 4. For further discussion on this point, see Roger Nutt, "Christ's Esse and Filiation: Interpreting St. Thomas on the Metaphysical Status of Christ's Human Nature," in *Redeeming Philosophy: From Metaphysics to Aesthetics*, ed. J. J. Conley (Washington, DC: The Catholic University of America Press, 2014), 115–29.

26. *ST* 3.2.10; see also *ST* 3.7.11. Yet, cf. *ST* 3.33.3 ad 3.

27. Pope Leo I, *ep.* 28.4 (DH 294). See also *ST* 3.19.1.

28. John Damascene, *De Fide Orthodoxa* (Cerbani versio), c. 47, ed. Eligius Buytaert (St. Bonaventure, NY: The Franciscan Institute, 1955), 395. Thomas quotes this in *ST* 3.10.1.

29. *ST* 3.7.1. See also *ST* 1–2.109.2–6, 1–2.110.2, 1–2.111.2, 3.2.10, 3.6.6, and 3.7.11.

Thomas associates the gift of grace with the person and mission of the Holy Spirit (see *ST* 1.38.2, 1.43.3), his articulation of the distinct place that habitual grace occupies in the Son's mission highlights the inextricable interrelationship of the missions of the Son and the Spirit in the economy.[30] With the plenitude of grace in his soul, Christ also had the fullness of the virtues, "which perfect the several powers of the soul [as they are moved by reason] for all the soul's acts" (3.7.2). Thus, Christ is the perfect exemplar of the moral life that Thomas outlined in *Secunda Pars*.[31]

Echoing the Evangelist's affirmation that the Incarnate Word was not only "full of grace and truth" (Jn 1:14) but also came so that "of his fullness we might all receive grace upon grace" (v. 16), Thomas holds that the fullness of Christ's grace pertains not only to himself but also to us, for "the soul of Christ so received grace that, in a manner, it is poured out from it upon others; and hence, it behooved him to have the greatest grace" (*ST* 3.7.9). When the superabundance of Christ's grace is considered from the point of view of the members of his Mystical Body, to whom the grace of the Head (3.8.1–6)[32]—the "font of all grace" (3.22.1 ad 3)—flows forth, it is called the "capital grace" of Christ (*gratia capitis*).

Thomas's consideration of the fullness of grace in Christ's soul serves an important role in his understanding of Christ's mediatory priesthood, for it is essential to the office of the priest to communicate "divine things" to the people—the greatest of which is participation in the divine life, made possible purely by God's grace (*ST* 3.22.1; cf. 1–2.109.5). Thus, as Christ is the "high priest of the good things that have come" (Heb 9:11), "it was right for him to have grace that would overflow upon others" (*ST* 3.7.1). In these ways, Thomas's discussion of the workings of the Incarnation and the fullness of grace in Christ's human soul not only speaks to the constitution of the nature that was assumed by the Word but also prepares the stage for his discussion of the role Christ's particular humanity plays in mediating *our participation* in grace.

---

30. See *ST* 1.43.6 ad 3, 1.43.7 ad 6, and 3.7.13. See also *ST* 3.32.1–3. On the Trinitarian foundations of Thomas's discussion of Christ's habitual grace, see Legge, *The Trinitarian Christology of St Thomas Aquinas*, 131–71; cf. our observations in Andrew Liaugminas, "The Trinitarian Christology of St Thomas Aquinas (Review)," *Gregorianum* 99, no. 3 (2018): 668–69.

31. For a study of this topic, see Joseph Wawrykow, "Jesus in the Moral Theology of Thomas Aquinas," *Journal of Medieval and Early Modern Studies* 42, no. 1 (Winter 2012): 13–33.

32. See also *ST* 3.8.3; *Super Rom.* 12.2.

The Knowledge of Christ

Just as in his discussion of Christ's grace, when Thomas approaches the question of Christ's *knowledge*, he recognizes what can be said distinctly of each of the two natures in the Incarnate Word. Starting with his divine nature, Thomas affirms that the Word *inquantum Deum* never ceases to know as God (*ST* 3.9.1 ad 1), for "to be [divinely] intelligent belongs to the Son in the same way as it belongs to him to be God" (1.34.2 ad 4). Since Christ knows all things in his divine nature, it might seem that "any other knowledge would have been superfluous in him" (3.9.1, obj. 1). Yet, Thomas remains attentive to the fact that the Word united to himself a *complete* human nature that "was not destroyed by being divinized, but remained in its own state and kind," as the Sixth Ecumenical Council confesses.[33] This not only proscribes any denial of the full integrity of his human intellect (as in Apollinarianism)[34] but also, as Thomas affirms, precludes any functional bracketing of it (3.9.1 ad 1). Taking seriously the human mind of Christ thus requires us to render a full account of what Christ knew *as a man*.

In this regard, Thomas affirms that Christ, in his human soul, by virtue of "a light participated from the Divine Nature," beheld the Beatific Vision in an immediate vision from the moment of his conception (*ST* 3.10, 3.9.2, 3.34.4). For Thomas, this affirmation does not represent an addition to the theology of the Incarnation but follows as its necessary corollary, for "every created intellect knows in the Word . . . so many more things the more perfectly it sees the Word," and no created intellect has a greater vision of the Word than the human soul of the Word himself (3.10.2). For Thomas, this does *not* mean that Christ's human mind "comprehended" the Divine Essence (3.10.1), for such a task would be impossible for any finite human intellect to do. However, it does mean that Christ possessed *beatific knowledge* by which he "knows in the Word all things existing in whatever time, and [knows] the thoughts of men, of which he is the Judge" (3.10.2).

Aquinas's understanding of Christ's beatific knowledge has been the subject of significant critique in the contemporary context. Karl Rahner commented that statements such as these "sound almost mythological today" and "seem to be contrary to the real humanity and historical nature of Our Lord."[35] However, Thomas's Christological epistemology revolves around a

---

33. Constantinople III (681), *Definition of Faith* (DH 556).

34. See Cyril of Alexandria, *ep.* 4 (DH 250); Chalcedon, *Definition* (DH 302).

35. Karl Rahner, "Dogmatic Reflections on the Knowledge and Self-Consciousness of Christ," in *Theological Investigations*, vol. 5, *Later Writings*, trans. K.-H. Kruger (London: Darton, Longman & Todd; Baltimore: Helicon, 1966), 194–95. See also *TD* 3, 191–202.

profound appreciation for the full integrity of the assumed nature, as he affirms from the start of his treatment of this question in the *Summa* (3.10.1). In fact, Thomas takes great care to explain that Christ's "beatific knowledge" is always the knowledge *of a man*: after all, it is a type of knowledge that *all* blessed humans, together with the angels, will possess in beholding the Beatific Vision. Unlike contemporary writers, however, Thomas does not see any difficulties in affirming that a man living in human history and sharing in everyday human experience can behold this Vision while still on earth; quite the opposite, Thomas believes that such affirmations—radical as they may be—are the necessary results of taking seriously the fact that a full and intact human nature is enhypostasized in the hypostasis of the Word.

Far from being ahistorical, this understanding of Christ's beatific knowledge radically reaffirms the relationship between human history and the Beatific Vision. Thus, it seems that the real difference between Thomas and his contemporary critics on this point lies not in varying convictions about the need to take seriously the real humanity of the Word—in fact, here they appear to agree—but in differing understandings of the *implications* of that conviction. Moreover, as Nicholas Healy demonstrates, a closer investigation of the question reveals that Thomas's understanding of Christ's beatific knowledge reflects a profound appreciation for the "missional" quality of the Son's filial knowledge of the Father and the soteriological importance of his humanity for our access to that vision.[36]

It might seem that Christ's divine knowledge (in his divinity) and beatific knowledge (in his humanity) would encompass everything there would be to say about the knowledge of the Incarnate Word. However, still attentive to the full integrity of Christ's human intellect, Thomas posits two other forms of human knowledge in the Word, relative to the passive and active intellects of man, as discussed in the *Prima Pars* (see 1.79). He reasons that, by the operation of grace upon his passive intellect, Christ had the gift of *infused knowledge*, by which the soul of Christ "knows things in their proper nature by intelligible species proportioned to the human mind" (3.9.3; see also 3.11).[37] Moreover, Thomas argues that Christ had *acquired knowledge* arising from the natural engagement of his active (or "agent") intellect in the act of

---

36. Nicholas J. Healy, Jr., "Simul viator et comprehensor: The Filial Mode of Christ's Knowledge," *Nova et Vetera* (English edition) 11, no. 2 (2013): 341–55. For a full study of this question, see Simon Gaine in *Did the Saviour See the Father? Christ, Salvation, and the Vision of God* (London: T&T Clark, 2015). See also Oakes's *excursus* on this topic in *Infinity Dwindled to Infancy*, 210–21.

37. For an engagement of this topic in dialogue with contemporary theology, see Simon Gaine, "Is There Still a Place for Christ's Infused Knowledge in Catholic Theology and Exegesis?" *Nova et Vetera* (English edition) 16, no. 2 (Spring 2018): 601–15.

knowing and which speaks to his experiential knowledge (3.9.4, 3.12). While one can distinguish between Christ's beatific, infused, and acquired knowledge, all three are properly knowledge *of a man*—again affirming the integrity of Christ's human nature in all its aspects.

Thomas's portrait of Christ as man further comes to life in his affirmation that Christ experienced genuine wonder (3.15.8). Indeed, we see this in the Gospels when Christ marveled at the faith of the centurion (Mt 8:10; Lk 7:9) and at the people's unbelief (Mk 6:6). While the affirmation of Christ's wonder may carry little controversy in the present day, Thomas was one of the first medieval masters to propose that Christ could experience genuine wonder. Moreover, he was among the first to argue that Christ had acquired knowledge on the basis of his earthly experiences.[38] The fact that Wisdom Begotten *could* progress in knowledge while on earth and *could* experience of genuine wonder during his earthly sojourn are often-overlooked epistemological corollaries of Thomas's Christology that affirm the enduring significance of human history in the life of the Eternal Word.

"A Man of Suffering and Acquainted with Infirmity" (Is 53:3)

While Thomas dedicates most of his attention in this section of the *Summa* to the perfections of the nature assumed by the Word, he also considers how the Word subjected himself to certain "defects" (*defecta*) or weaknesses of the human body, such as hunger, thirst, bodily pain, and ultimately, death (3.14).[39] In addition to assuming these corporeal deficiencies, Christ also assumed various passions of the soul, including pain, fear, sorrow, and even anger (3.15).[40] The bodily weaknesses and passions of the soul that he assumed willingly (3.14.3) also played a central role in his mediatory priest-

---

38. Thomas notably changed his opinion on this question from the start of his career (see *Super Sent.* 3.14.3.5), at which point he had agreed with the prevalent position of his contemporaries. Yet in the *Summa theologiae*, Thomas informs the reader that his thinking has developed and that he now holds that Christ *did* have acquired knowledge based on his experience (*ST* 3.9.4, 3.12.2). For a critical appraisal of this "revolutionary" point in Aquinas's Christology, see Simon Gaine, "Christ's Acquired Knowledge According to Thomas Aquinas: How Aquinas's Philosophy Helped and Hindered his Account," *New Blackfriars* 96, no. 1063 (May 2015): 255–68.

39. While we might see hunger and thirst as part of the ordinary functioning of a human body, and death as an inescapable part of the human lifecycle, when seen in the light of scripture, they are understood as consequences of the Fall (see Gen 3:16–19). Thus, Thomas understands them as "defects" that "flow from the common sin of the whole nature" (*ST* 3.14.4; see also 3.1.4 ad 2).

40. For a full study of this topic, see Paul Gondreau, *The Passions of Christ's Soul in the Theology of St. Thomas Aquinas* (Scranton, PA: University of Scranton Press, 2009).

hood, for it was by enduring his sufferings voluntarily that he merited our salvation (3.48.1, 3.49.5). Moreover, the fact that Christ bore these "defects" gives him profound solidarity with those for whom he is interceding: "because he himself has suffered and been tempted, he is able to help those who are tempted" (Heb 2:18; cit. at 3.14.1). Finally, Christ's sufferings also had a moral-exemplary value for us (3.15.1), for he gave us "an example of patience by valiantly bearing up against human passibility and defects" (3.14.1; Heb 12:3; 1 Pt 2:21).

Understanding the ways in which the Savior was "full of grace and truth" (Jn 1:14) but also how he shared in our weaknesses (Heb 2: 4:15–5:10) prepares us to understand the One whom we encounter in the Gospel, the pivotal events of whose life Thomas considers in the next part of his study of Christ.

THE LIFE OF CHRIST, THE SUPREME MEDIATOR

The Christology of the *Tertia Pars* reaches its midpoint with the question of Christ the Mediator (*ST* 3.26). As seen, this question stands structurally *in medio* between Thomas's consideration of the unique ontological constitution of the Incarnate Word, who is both God and man, and his consideration of the mysteries of the life of Christ, through whom God reconciled mankind to himself. His questions on Christ's life are far from an appendix to his systematic Christology, for it is in the context of the mysteries of Christ's life that Thomas "fleshes out" the doctrine of the Incarnation that he expounds in the first half of the *Tertia Pars*.[41]

Christ's Entry into and Progression through the World

Thomas moves from his consideration of the mystery of the Incarnation itself to the mysteries of the life of Christ by means of several questions on the Blessed Virgin Mary (3.27–30), through whom the Word entered the world.[42]

---

41. Eleonore Stump's claim that Thomas's explanation of the Incarnation "is not successful in giving a complete analysis of the doctrine" (*Aquinas* [London: Routledge, 2005], 425) does not seem to account for the fact that Thomas's treatment in the *Summa theologiae* of Christ's ontological constitution in the Incarnation (3.1–26) is but a prelude to his treatise on the mysteries of Christ's life, death, and Resurrection (3.27–59). It is in the latter context—as well as his many scripture commentaries and sermons—that Thomas explores the lived reality of the Mystery of the Incarnation. See also Jean-Pierre Torrell, *Le Christ en ses mystères: La vie et l'oeuvre de Jésus selon Saint Thomas d'Aquin*, 2 vols., Jésus et Jésus-Christ 78 (Paris: Desclée, 1999); Étienne Vetö, *Du Christ à la Trinité: Penser les mystères du Christ après Thomas d'Aquin et Balthasar* (Paris: Cerf, 2012).

42. While Thomas argues against the Doctrine of the Immaculate Conception of the Virgin Mary—at least partially as a result of his understanding of the universality of

Christ—who is *caput Ecclesiae*—was born of a virgin mother according to the flesh, "so as to signify that his members would be born of a virgin Church according to the Spirit."[43] The parallel Thomas draws in these articles between Mary and the church suggests a profound insight into Mary's spiritual maternity vis-à-vis her Son's Mystical Body.[44] Thomas's theological reflections on the conception of Christ, his nativity, and the life of the infant Christ child (3.31–36) build firmly upon his previously established theses. For example, Thomas draws upon principles he outlined in his discussion of the divine missions in the *Prima Pars* (i.e., 1.43) to explain the work of the Trinity in the conception of Christ (3.32), and he draws upon the principles he established in his discussion of the perfections of Christ (3.7–13) to discuss the perfection of the child conceived in Mary's womb (3.34).

Showing how Christ is the perfect fulfillment of the Law of old, Thomas treats two questions regarding how the precepts of the Jewish Law were observed in Christ's infancy (3.37–38, 3.40.4).[45] However, as Thomas's focus at this point is on "those things that pertain to [Christ's] coming into the world" (3.27 *pr.*), he passes over other events of the hidden years of Christ's life—such as his childhood in Nazareth[46] (Lk 2:39–40, 2:51–52), the finding in the Temple (Lk 2:41–50), and the sojourn in Egypt (Mt 2:13–15)—proceeding directly to Christ's baptism, when his public ministry began (3.39).[47]

---

mankind's need for redemption in Christ (*ST* 3.27.2)—he does affirm that Mary was sanctified while still in her mother's womb (a. 1), that she never committed a sin, and that she received the fullness of grace (aa. 4–5). Given Thomas's unequivocal deference to the Magisterium and the fact that he prefaces his first response to the first question on Mary (i.e., 3.27.1 s.c.) with a recourse to the authority of the church's liturgy, there is little doubt that he would have accepted the Immaculate Conception had he lived after its formal definition in 1854.

43. *ST* 3.28.1, citing Augustine, *uirg.* 6.

44. For a point of dialogue with the theology of Hans Urs Balthasar, see *OP*, 195–242.

45. For a full study of this question, see Matthew Levering, *Christ's Fulfilment of Torah and Temple: Salvation According to Thomas Aquinas* (Notre Dame, IN: University of Notre Dame Press, 2002).

46. However, Thomas did deliver a notable academic sermon on Luke 2:52. See "Sermon 08: *Puer Jesus*," in *The Academic Sermons*, trans. M.-R. Hoogland, The Fathers of the Church, 11 (Washington, DC: The Catholic University of America Press, 2010), 87–107.

47. Thomas views Christ's baptism more in terms of what the event reveals *to us* than what it did for Christ, "since he was filled with the grace of the Holy Spirit from the beginning of his conception" (*ST* 3.39.2; see also 1.43.6 ad 3, 1.43.7 ad 6). This contrasts with the growing trend in contemporary Christology to see the baptism of Christ as a significant moment of Messianic anointing (e.g., Luis F. Ladaria, *La Trinità, mistero di comunione*, trans. M. Zappella [Milan: Paoline, 2004], 232–72).

Here, Thomas draws a connection between the Father's voice at Christ's baptism and the Father's voice at his Transfiguration, affirming that "both in his Baptism and in his Transfiguration, the natural sonship of Christ was fittingly made known by the testimony of the Father" (3.45.4 co.) to manifest "the diverse modes in which men can be partakers of the likeness of the eternal Sonship" (3.45.4 ad 1; see also 3.39.8 ad 3).

Between these two epiphanic events, Thomas depicts the earthly ministry of Christ as a life lived "fitting with the ends of the Incarnation, according to which he came into the world": namely, to manifest the truth, to liberate us from sin, and to grant us access to God through himself (3.40.1). Even the weaknesses we observe in Christ's body and soul (3.14–15) serve the salutary purpose of strengthening us against temptations, providing us with an example of how to overcome them, and filling us with "with confidence in his mercy," for—as Thomas reminds us—"we have not a High Priest who is unable to have compassion on our infirmities, but One who is tempted in all things like as we are, without sin" (3.41.1; cit. Heb 4:15). Against this background, Thomas sees Christ's miracles as confirmations of the divine origin of his teaching and manifestations of God's presence in him by the grace of union (3.43.1; Jn 2:11).

Christ's Departure from the World

While Christ's words and actions left us an example and pattern to follow in our own lives, Thomas is clear that the Incarnation was ultimately "ordained by God as a remedy for sin" (*ST* 3.1.3), and thus it was finally the events of his Paschal Mystery that opened the way to our participation in the life of God (cf. 1 Pet 2:21–25). At the outset of Thomas's study of the Passion, it is helpful to recall the quote from Pope Leo the Great that he cites at the beginning of the *Tertia Pars*: the Incarnate Word was so constituted that "one and the same Mediator of God and men might die in one [nature] and rise in the other, for this was our fitting remedy" for sin (*ST* 3.1.2). At the same time, Thomas contextualizes this Christological dyophysitism within a wider Trinitarian perspective in which the saving action originates in the Trinity, extends from God to mankind, and returns to the Triune God. Importantly for Thomas, God carries out this saving action *through* the complete humanity of Jesus Christ, that is, utilizing all the actions and passions of his soul and body. In this sense, Thomas understands Christ's humanity to play a causally *instrumental* role in man's salvation (3.48.6, 3.19.1).[48] Behind this

---

48. This is the background for Thomas's affirmation that the humanity of Christ is the "instrument of the divinity" (e.g., *ST* 1–2.112.1 ad 1–2, 3.7.1 ad 3, 3.8.1 ad 1, and 3.19.1; *SCG* 4.41.12–13; *De un. Verb.* 5 ad 1). Thomas employs this concept more to

affirmation lies profound respect for the integrity of Christ's human willing and acting that follows closely the dyothelitism of Maximus the Confessor and the Third Council of Constantinople.[49]

In Thomas's reading, the primary "action" of the Passion occurs among the members of the Trinity as "the Father handed over Christ, and Christ handed over himself out of love" (*ST* 3.47.3 ad 3).[50] The "logic" that orders Christ's handing over of himself, for Thomas, is governed by *love* and *obedience*, "for he fulfilled the precepts of love out of obedience, and he was obedient to the Father's command out of love" (3.47.2 ad 3). As Thomas's study of the Passion unfolds, love increasingly comes to the foreground, for—as Thomas argues—"Christ's Passion was the offering of a sacrifice, insofar as he endured death of his own free-will, out of love" (3.47.4 ad 2; cf. 3.22.4 ad 2). Christ suffers out of love for the Father (3.47.2 co.), "and this voluntary enduring of the Passion was most acceptable to God, as coming from love" (3.48.3 co.).

By enduring those sufferings "out of love and obedience," Christ offered a recompense to God greater than man's offense, and thereby satisfied the debt of the penalty (*poena*) that mankind had incurred in justice before God (*ST* 3.48.2, 3.49.3). Moreover, his Passion was the price that redeemed mankind from the servitude due to the guilt (*culpa*) associated with man's willful enslavement to sin (3.48.4–5, 3.49.2).[51] Christ's Passion not only freed man *from* the penalty and guilt associated with sin but also freed him *for* union

---

affirm the place of Christ's humanity in God's work than to marginalize it. In this sense, it could be read along the lines of Paul's statement that "God was *in Christ* reconciling the world to himself" (2 Cor 5:19). For a study of this topic, see Paul G. Crowley, "*Instrumentum Divinitatis* in Thomas Aquinas: Recovering the Divinity of Christ," *Theological Studies* 52, no. 3 (1991): 451–75. For Balthasar's appreciative appraisal, see *A Theology of History* (San Francisco: Ignatius—Communio, 1994), 17–18, 73–74.

49. See *ST* 3.19. For a study of Thomas's use of the Sixth Ecumenical Council, see Aaron Riches, "Theandric Humanism: Constantinople III in the Thought of St. Thomas Aquinas," *Pro Ecclesia* 23, no. 2 (May 2014): 195–218. For wider studies of this question, see Corey Barnes, *Christ's Two Wills in Scholastic Thought: The Christology of Aquinas and Its Historical Contexts* (Toronto: Pontifical Institute of Medieval Studies, 2012).

50. Original: "*Pater enim tradidit Christum, et ipse seipsum, ex caritate....*" Thomas's language around Christ's self-surrender and the Father's handing over of Christ suggests a point of dialogue with the Passiology of Hans Urs Balthasar. However, it should be noted that Thomas fundamentally views the "handing over" of the Son as an action *of the entire Trinity*. On this, see *ST* 3.47.3 ad 2.

51. Thomas's articulation of the latter point creatively restructures the patristic concept of redemption so that the price of redemption is not paid to the devil but *to God* (*ST* 3.48.4 ad 3). Indeed, Thomas affirms that the devil held man unjustly, and thus, with regard to the devil, Christ redeemed man as a victor and not as a debtor (3.48.4 ad 2; see also 3.46.3 ad 3, 3.49.2, and 3.57.6).

with God in the reconciliation that came through his sacrifice (3.48.3, 3.49.4). This liberating and finally reconciling action, in turn, opens man to receive the communication of grace—the fruits of salvation—and prepares him ultimately to receive the gift of participation in his glory that Christ extends to those configured to him (3.46.3, 3.49.5).[52] For the free decision of that innocent man to suffer "for the sake of justice" gained for him merit that "overflows" from him and flows out to the members of his Body, the church (3.48.1; see also 3.19.3–4).

In this saving action, Christ exercises the fullness of both aspects of the priesthood that Thomas outlines in *ST* 3.22.1. By offering himself as victim on the cross, Christ perfectly carries out the *ascending* dimension of priesthood, offering a satisfaction to God for man's sins, with the goal of reconciling man with God. Thomas ultimately locates this ascending dimension within the wider *descending* dimension of Christ's priesthood: conveying sacred gifts to his people, with the goal of their ultimate divinization.[53] At the center, we find the Son at work in every dimension of his incarnate ontology: *as God*, sharing with the Father and Spirit in the efficient agency of the saving action (3.48.6); as man, in his *soul*, meriting man's salvation by willingly suffering for the sake of justice (a. 1); and in his *body*, accomplishing the saving action that freed man from the penalty due to his sin (by satisfaction; a. 2). He freed man from his tragic self-conscription into sin's servitude (by redemption; aa. 4–5) and freed him for eternal communion with God (a. 3) by the reconciling sacrifice he freely offered out of "love for his Father" and "love for his neighbor" (3.47.2 ad 1).[54]

Extending the Benefits of Christ's Redemption to All

If the logic of the Passion is based on the free self-offering that Christ makes to God, on our behalf and out of love and obedience to the Father, then—for Thomas—the consummation of that sacrifice on the cross (Jn 19:30) brings to fulfillment our reconciliation with God (*ST* 3.49; Eph 2:16). Still, while Christ's Passion is "a kind of universal cause of the forgiveness of sins, it needs to be applied to each individual for the cleansing of personal sins" (3.49.1 ad 4). Notably, Thomas holds that this activity of applying the power of the Passion to individuals—a work that continues to

52. For a closer consideration of Thomas's study of the Passion, see Aidan Nichols, "St Thomas Aquinas on the Passion of Christ: A Reading of Summa Theologiae IIIa, Q. 46," *Scottish Journal of Theology* 43, no. 4 (1990): 447–59.

53. See also *ST* 2–2.86.2 and 3.82.3.

54. For a full study of Christ's priesthood in the *Summa*, see Jean-Pierre Torrell, "Le sacerdoce du Christ dans la Somme de théologie," *Revue Thomiste* 99 (1999): 75–100.

animate the church to this day—began on Holy Saturday when Christ, as a "dead man" (3.50.4), descended into Hell, "by visiting it and enlightening it" (3.52.1).[55] While the effects of Christ's presence in Hell extended to every part therein, only those "united to his Passion through faith quickened by love" (3.52.6) were disposed to receive the power of the Passion when Christ came to extend it to them. Those ready to receive him were liberated from the devil's captivity and became joyful participants in Christ's glory (3.52.4–5).

Thomas draws together all the strands of the priestly and mediatory work of the Incarnate Word in his reflections on the *pro nobis* meaning of Christ's Resurrection and Ascension. The Resurrection, in Thomas's soteriological vision, compliments and completes the saving work initiated in the Passion (*ST* 3.53.1 ad 3). The unity of the two can be seen in the fact that the body that rose in glory and then ascended to the Father still bore the scars of his Passion, which, Thomas notes, "will always remain on his body" (3.54.4 ad 3). Finally, Christ ascends into heaven because "just as the High Priest (*pontifex*) in the Old Testament entered the sanctuary to stand before God on behalf of the people, so also Christ entered into heaven 'to make intercession for us' [see Heb 7:25, 9:24]," and thus "being established in his heavenly seat as God and Lord, he might send forth gifts upon men" (3.57.6; see also 3.49.5; Eph 4:4–13). Yet, unlike the priests of old who passed along divine things to those standing *outside* the sanctuary, Christ the High Priest communicates divine gifts by drawing people *into* the sanctuary: by incorporating them into his Body, wherein they can receive the "gifts" of grace that effect an ever-greater configuration to the Head (3.49.3 ad 3; cf. Eph 1:17–23, Heb 10:5–14).[56] Christ continues to extend the power of his Passion to the living "through spiritual contact: that is, through faith and the Sacraments of the Faith" (3.48.1 ad 2; see also 3.62.5). Herein lies the mission of the church: to call the whole world into participation in his Body through the Sacrament of Baptism, to draw mankind into ever-greater union with God in the Eucharistic Sacrifice, which "contains Christ himself, the author of our sanctification" (1–2.101.4 ad 2), and to work for the reconciliation of man with God by offering the

---

55. While Thomas affirms that Christ's death and burial could not win any further merit for us—since merit can only be earned by a living man (*ST* 1–2.114, 3.34.3) and Christ was dead during this time (3.50.4)—Thomas also verifies that Christ's death and burial *did* play an efficacious role in how God brought about our salvation in Christ (3.50.6; see also 3.51.1 ad 2).

56. Bernhard Blankenhorn, *The Mystery of Union with God: Dionysian Mysticism in Albert the Great and Thomas Aquinas*, Thomistic Ressourcement Series 4 (Washington, DC: The Catholic University of America Press, 2015), 268–69. On the church as the "mystical body of Christ," see *ST* 3.8.1 and 3.49.1.

Sacrament of Penance.[57] From this late point in the *Summa*, the reader can understand the full meaning of what Thomas stated at the very beginning of his work: that Christ, as man, is "the way leading us back to God" (1.2, *pr.*).[58]

CHRISTOLOGY: THE "CONSUMMATION" OF THOMAS'S THEOLOGY

It was while working on the questions of the *Summa* that treat Christ's Passion that Thomas—during an early morning period of private prayer—is said to have received this locution from the cross: "Thomas, you have written well of me; what reward would you receive from me for your labor?" To that, Thomas gave his famous reply: "Nothing but you, Lord."[59] These words—*non nisi te, Domine*—reveal the interiority of the theologian who identified Christology as "the consummation of the entire theological endeavor" (*ST* 3 *pr.*). This is the same preacher who proclaimed that "whoever wishes to live perfectly should do nothing but disdain what Christ disdained on the Cross, and desire what he desired, for the Cross exemplifies every virtue."[60] This is the same professor who taught that Christ bore his cross like "a teacher [bearing] his candelabrum, in which rested the light of his teaching, because the message of the Cross is the power of God for believers" (*Super Ioh.* 19.3, para. 2414). This is the same priest whose Eucharistic hymns and liturgical texts have an enduring place in the church's commemoration of the Body and Blood of Christ. And this is the same theologian who saw the Word's Incarnation as integrally oriented to the work of redemption, and his work of redemption as an essential part of Christ's priestly mediation, which aims to reconcile man with God and to communicate to mankind the gift of eternal life.

BIBLIOGRAPHY

Barnes, Corey Ladd. *Christ's Two Wills in Scholastic Thought: The Christology of Aquinas and Its Historical Contexts.* Studies and Texts 178. Toronto: Pontifical Institute of Medieval Studies, 2012.

---

57. Hence, in the Sacraments, we experience both aspects of Christ's priesthood: we enter into his sacrifice on the cross, by which he reconciled us with the Father, and we receive through him heavenly gifts, the greatest of which is the gift of divine life and filiation.

58. *ST* 1.2 *pr.* See also Jean-Pierre Torrell, "Christ in the 'Spirituality' of St. Thomas," in *Christ and Spirituality in St. Thomas Aquinas,* trans. Bernhard Blankenhorn, Thomistic Ressourcement Series 2 (Washington, DC: The Catholic University of America Press, 2011), 74–109.

59. Torrell, *Saint Thomas Aquinas,* 1:285.

60. Aquinas, *In Symb. Ap.* 6.4.

Blankenhorn, Bernhard. *The Mystery of Union with God: Dionysian Mysticism in Albert the Great and Thomas Aquinas.* Thomistic Ressourcement Series 4. Washington, DC: The Catholic University of America Press, 2015.

Boyle, John F. "Is the Tertia Pars of the Summa Theologiae Misplaced?" In *Proceedings of the PMR Conference*, vol. 18, 103–09. Villanova, PA: Augustinian Historical Institute, 1996.

Chenu, Marie-Dominique. "Le plan de la Somme théologique de saint Thomas." *Revue Thomiste* 47 (1939): 93–107.

Crowley, Paul G. "Instrumentum Divinitatis in Thomas Aquinas: Recovering the Divinity of Christ." *Theological Studies* 52, no. 3 (1991): 451–75.

Eco, Umberto. *The Aesthetics of Thomas Aquinas.* Translated by H. Bredin. Cambridge, MA: Harvard University Press, 1988.

Elders, Leo J. "Thomas Aquinas and the Fathers of the Church." In *Reception of the Church Fathers in the West: From the Carolingians to the Maurists*, ed. Irena Backus, vol. 1, 337–66. Leiden: E. J. Brill, 1997.

Emery, Gilles. "Le Christ médiateur: l'unicité et l'universalité de la médiation salvifique du Christ Jésus suivant Thomas d'Aquin." In *Christus—Gottes schöpferisches Wort*, Festschrift C. Schönborn, edited by G. Augustin, M. Brun et al., 337–55. Freiburg i.B.: Herder, 2010.

———. *The Trinitarian Theology of St Thomas Aquinas.* Translated by Francesca A. Murphy. Oxford: Oxford University Press, 2007.

Gaine, Simon F. "Christ's Acquired Knowledge According to Thomas Aquinas: How Aquinas's Philosophy Helped and Hindered his Account." *New Blackfriars* 96, no. 1063 (May 2015): 255–68.

———. *Did the Saviour See the Father? Christ, Salvation, and the Vision of God.* London: T&T Clark, 2015.

———. "Is There Still a Place for Christ's Infused Knowledge in Catholic Theology and Exegesis?" *Nova et vetera* (English edition) 16, no. 2 (Spring 2018): 601–15.

Geenen, Godefroid. "En marge du concile de Chalcédoine. Les textes du Quatrième Concile dans les œuvres de saint Thomas." *Angelicum* 29, no. 1 (1952): 43–59.

Gondreau, Paul. *The Passions of Christ's Soul in the Theology of St. Thomas Aquinas.* Scranton, PA: University of Scranton Press, 2009.

Gorman, Michael. *Aquinas on the Metaphysics of the Hypostatic Union.* Cambridge: Cambridge University Press, 2017.

Healy, Jr., Nicholas J. "Simul viator et comprehensor: The Filial Mode of Christ's Knowledge." *Nova et Vetera* (English edition) 11, no. 2 (2013): 341–55.

Kereszty, Roch A. *Jesus Christ: Fundamentals of Christology.* 3rd ed. Staten Island, NY: St. Paul's—Communio Book, 2002.

Klimczak, Pawel. *Christus Magister: Le Christ Maître dans les commentaires évangéliques de saint Thomas d'Aquin.* Studia Friburgensia 117. Fribourg: Academic Press Fribourg, 2014.

Ladaria, Luis F. *La Trinità, mistero di comunione*. Translated by M. Zappella. Milan: Paoline, 2004.

Laporte, Jean-Marc. "Christ in Aquinas's *Summa Theologiae*: Peripheral or Pervasive?" *The Thomist* 67, no. 2 (2003): 221–48.

Legge, Dominic. *The Trinitarian Christology of St Thomas Aquinas*. Oxford: Oxford University Press, 2017.

Levering, Matthew. *Christ's Fulfilment of Torah and Temple: Salvation According to Thomas Aquinas*. Notre Dame, IN: University of Notre Dame Press, 2002.

Liaugminas, Andrew. "The Trinitarian Christology of St Thomas Aquinas (Review)." *Gregorianum* 99, no. 3 (2018): 668–69.

Morard, Martin. "Une source de saint Thomas d'Aquin: Le deuxième concile de Constantinople (553)." *Revue Des Sciences Philosophiques et Théologiques* 81, no. 1 (1997): 21–56.

Narcisse, Gilbert. *Le Christ en sa beauté*. Vol. 1, *Christologie: Hans Urs von Balthasar, Saint Thomas d'Aquin*. Collection méditer. Magny-les-Hameaux: Soceval, 2005.

Nichols, Aidan. "St Thomas Aquinas on the Passion of Christ: A Reading of Summa Theologiae IIIa, Q 46." *Scottish Journal of Theology* 43, no. 4 (1990): 447–59.

Nutt, Roger W. "Christ's *Esse* and Filiation: Interpreting St. Thomas on the Metaphysical Status of Christ's Human Nature." In *Redeeming Philosophy: From Metaphysics to Aesthetics*, edited by John J. Conley, 115–29. Washington, DC: The Catholic University of America Press, 2014.

Oakes, Edward T. *Infinity Dwindled to Infancy: A Catholic and Evangelical Christology*. Grand Rapids, MI: William B. Eerdmans, 2011.

Rahner, Karl. "Dogmatic Reflections on the Knowledge and Self-Consciousness of Christ." In *Theological Investigations*, vol. 5, *Later Writings*, translated by K.-H. Kruger, 193–215. London: Darton, Longman & Todd; Baltimore: Helicon, 1966.

———. *The Trinity*. Translated by J. Doncel. London: Burns and Oates, 1970.

Riches, Aaron. "Theandric Humanism: Constantinople III in the Thought of St. Thomas Aquinas." *Pro Ecclesia* 23, no. 2 (May 2014): 195–218.

Ruello, Francis. *La Christologie de Thomas d'Aquin*. Théologie Historique 76. Paris: Beauchesne, 1987.

Ryan, Thomas. "Jesus—'Our Wisest and Dearest Friend': Aquinas and Moral Transformation." *New Blackfriars* 97, no. 1071 (September 2016): 57—90.

Sammon, Brendan Thomas. *The God Who Is Beauty: Beauty as a Divine Name in Thomas Aquinas and Dionysius the Areopagite*. Princeton Theological Monograph Series 206. Eugene, OR: Pickwick, 2013.

Schoot, Henk J. M. *Christ the "Name" of God: Thomas Aquinas on Naming Christ*. Leuven: Peeters, 1993.

Somme, Luc-Thomas. *Fils adoptifs de Dieu par Jésus Christ: la filiation divine par adoption dans la théologie de saint Thomas d'Aquin*. Bibliothèque Thomiste 49. Paris: Vrin, 1997.

Stump, Eleonore. *Aquinas.* London; New York: Routledge, 2005.

Torrell, Jean-Pierre. *Le Christ en ses mystères: La vie et l'œuvre de Jésus selon Saint Thomas d'Aquin.* 2 vols. Jésus et Jésus-Christ, 78. Paris: Desclée, 1999.

———. "Christ in the 'Spirituality' of St. Thomas." In *Christ and Spirituality in St. Thomas Aquinas,* translated by Bernhard Blankenhorn, 74–109. Thomistic Ressourcement Series 2. Washington, DC: The Catholic University of America Press, 2011.

———. "Le sacerdoce du Christ dans la Somme de théologie." *Revue Thomiste* 99 (1999): 75–100.

———. *Saint Thomas Aquinas.* Vol. 1, *The Person and His Work,* 3rd ed. Translated by Matthew K. Minerd and Robert Royal. Washington, DC: The Catholic University of America Press, 2023.

Vetö, Étienne. *Du Christ à la Trinité: Penser les mystères du Christ après Thomas d'Aquin et Balthasar.* Paris: Cerf, 2012.

Wawrykow, Joseph. "The Christology of Thomas Aquinas in its Scholastic Context." In *The Oxford Handbook of Christology,* edited by Francesca A. Murphy, 233–49. Oxford: Oxford University Press, 2015.

———. "Jesus in the Moral Theology of Thomas Aquinas." *Journal of Medieval and Early Modern Studies* 42, no. 1 (Winter 2012): 13–33.

———. "Wisdom in the Christology of Thomas Aquinas." In *Christ Among the Medieval Dominicans: Representations of Christ in the Texts and Images of the Order of Preachers,* edited by K. Emery, Jr. and Joseph Wawrykow, 175–96. Notre Dame, IN: University of Notre Dame Press, 1998.

CHAPTER 6

The Dramatic Christology of Hans Urs von Balthasar

FRANCESCA ARAN MURPHY

INTRODUCTION: GAUDIUM ET SPES 22

BALTHASAR'S PRESENTATION OF JESUS CHRIST is dramatic. Within his trilogy, the first section deals with Christ as revealed beauty, the object of contemplative faith. The Theological Aesthetics section is methodological, seven volumes about doing theology on one's knees that embed Christology within the objective faith of the church. The final section, the *Theo-Logic*, offers Balthasar's most lucid exposition of Trinitarian theology. Doing theology on one's knees leads to adoring the truth of the Trinity, and to the theological virtue of love. Truth comes after virtue. Truth can become the object of knowledge after our practical appetites have been trained in goodness and we have become contestants for the Olympian prizes in virtuous deeds (2 Tim 4:7). The middle section is the hinge of the trilogy. The *Theo-Drama* is about the hopeful, desirous pursuit of the good. The centerpiece of the trilogy presents Balthasar's most capacious discussion of Christology, in the context of divine and human drama, the goodness that the Trinity shares in eternity and communicates in the economy.

A drama is a single action[1]; the Greek word *dromenon*, for drama, means something done. The *Theo-Drama* tells us what Christ does. The pursuit of the good is dramatic, entailing twists, about turns, reversals, abrupt transitions, and gasps of surprise and recognition. A dramatic protagonist has a pressing need to achieve some goal, to find something out or complete some deed. For the spectator, the drama consists in learning what happens to the actor as he or she follows the course dictated by this inner drive, finding out whether they can be true to their determination no matter where it leads, and discovering whether they can face up to their chosen destiny.

Moral action is free action because it is responsible action, action for which we claim ownership. So free action is self-owning action, action in

---

1. Aristotle, *Poetics* XXIII.

117

which we possess ourselves, own what we do, and belong to ourselves. Drama is about becoming oneself, attaining authentic self-possession or freedom, wherever the quest takes us.

Dramatic personae face off: but against what? The fundamental feature of drama is not precisely conflict, or face-to-face confrontation, but rather the working out of a tension. Like everything the Greeks liked and were best at, drama is a contest, an *agon*. The dramatic element in human life is a contest over which interior impulses and gravitations will win out in each person's pursuit of the good. Drama is propelled by dialogues, not monologues. These indicate forces outside of the lead character, for instance, Dionysius's hypnotizing effect on Pentheus in *The Bacchae*, or simply fate, in *Oedipus Rex*. The protagonist is caught on a hook that drags him.

In *L'Action*, Maurice Blondel described the human being as possessed by such a tension, a finite actor propelled by a surplus energy whose source is invisible to him. The drama of Blondel's Everyman is his search for the source of his own boundless energy. Everyman is oriented and driven beyond his finitude, but he knows not why. Blondel's philosophical anthropology is dramatic, but as a philosophy, it is modest about naming its source: the actor knows only, by a process of elimination, that every finite source of inspiration is insufficient to account for his surplus, infinite drive. The Blondelian actor is a dramatic character in that he needs to find out who he is and where his infinite drive is coming from. As a theological acolyte of the philosopher, Henri de Lubac alludes to a calling, or vocation: our propulsion toward infinitude is spurred by the gravitational pull of a call.[2]

In classical Catholic thinking, the good is the object of desire. Balthasar's *Theo-Drama* is pervaded with cryptic allusions to the boundlessness of human desire, like perfume in Shalimar. The human being is described as a finite actor caught in the lure of infinite freedom, or pulled to and fro between autonomy and authentic self-possession. One can spend years diligently reading these volumes trying to spell out what they tell us about the natural desire for the supernatural. There is no immanent quest for the good here, no transcendental argument from the infinite human quest to "The Infinite," or God. Rather, this is a theological anthropology in which Christ is the one who has best exercised the interplay of finite and infinite freedom, achieving his good by carrying out his call or mission to be who God calls him to be. In this theological anthropology, the weight falls not on the human quest to find itself but on the divine gift of a name and role, and the consequent performance of this role. Christ is the lead actor who enables other human beings to play their

---

2. Henri de Lubac, *Surnaturel: études historiques* (Paris: Desclée de Brouwer, 1991 [Original French, 1946]), 486–87.

parts, to reconcile their finite freedom with the lure of infinite freedom by recognizing self-donation as authentic self-possession.

The Thomisms of the late nineteenth and early twentieth century were drawn by the interior dynamic of leaning on the "How do we know?" question into various transcendental Thomisms in which God becomes the object of the infinite desire to know. Maurice Blondel was no Thomist, but, as an in-depth reader of German idealism, he developed his own philosophy of the transcendental question: how does the finite source of human energy and volition produce a boundless desire that is satisfied by no finite object? The method for Balthasar's trilogy prohibits him from founding his Christology in a transcendental anthropology, even a dramatic one. The theological is about the beauty of Christ, presented to human vision in an act of faith that is illuminated and given form by Christ himself. The *Theo-Drama* sets out one, the human quest for a role or "name," only to show that it humanly fails: the first volume concludes by contending that the sole way to legitimate the uniqueness of the person is theologically, by taking it that God gives each person an individual name that fits. Here Balthasar turns to Martin Buber and, especially, Franz Rosenzweig's proposal that it is only in dialogue with the divine Thou that the human "I" is drawn out of itself and authentically named. The *Theo-Drama* oscillates between the Buber-Rosenzweig contention that our unique naming comes only from God, from the drama of Christ's achievement of his own name, as the Son, and the Blondelian picture of Everyman as in dramatic pursuit of itself. Hence, the centrality of anthropology in Balthasar's Christology: the *Theo-Drama* enables humanity to be fully itself. This gives us a soteriology that turns on Galatians 4:16 and Romans 8:15. Because *Abba*-Father names Christ as Son, we are liberated into adopted "sonship."

Following what he calls Buber and Rosenzweig's rediscovery of biblical revelation,[3] Balthasar argues that we do not *achieve* a unique person[a] but rather we are given it as a "name" and calling from God.[4] Every human being knows implicitly that they owe their self-hood to having been called out and named by another human person (usually by our mother), who in turn owes their existence to another: freedom or self-possession is passed on to me by others because, like the good, it tends to communicate itself. That infinite freedom, which God is, is communicative. Authentic freedom is a transcendental property of being: to experience it is to experience the self-possession of numberless other finite persons. We experience authentic freedom in company. The communicative property of self-possession is an image of the Trin-

---

3. See Francesca Aran Murphy, "Whence Comes this Love as Strong as Death: The Presence of Franz Rosenzweig's 'Philosophy as Narrative' in Von Balthasar's Theo-Drama," *Literature and Theology* (September 1993): 227–47.

4. *TD* 1, 626–28, 636–38.

ity; to know myself as self-possessed in response to the commanding call of another is to recognize the "Eternal Thou" [Buber] within the finite Thou. This experience of freedom as an analogical, transcendental property is an experience of the I-Thou dialogical structure of the Trinity. To know myself as free when I obey the call of infinite freedom is to know myself as sent, as given a role by God. The exemplary dramatic actor in whom this self-knowledge is perfected is Jesus Christ.[5]

"Drama" is the most significant artistic genre here because human beings sense in the predicament of the actor upon the stage the best approximation to what their lives are like and what they aspire to be. We are actors and mimics from the time we begin to speak. No human activity is unscripted; every human activity requires that we assume roles. We feel as if the actor's performance upon a stage is a projection of our ordinary lives. The actor is making a performance and judged by whether he makes a good or a bad fist of it. He is constantly evaluated, up there on stage. His free decisions are embodied in his historical life. He knows that his performance, his quest for freedom, with its prevarications, right and wrong turns, and short-lived conversions will be judged. He longs for a rating on his performance, despite knowing he falls short. He knows that what he makes of his life is a performance and knows that it must be judged.

God judges each performance and its success in finding and embodying the good. Christ's role as exemplary actor in the theo-drama is to achieve divine justification, and by so doing to make it possible for all others to perform their humanity in like manner. Balthasar's Christ makes it possible to "play the part of man": this is the central fact of his Christology. Christ enables us to uncover the mystery of ourselves, that is, to find the source of our freedom and thus our humanity, by being fully human and fully divine, the perfect union of finite and infinite freedom.

This gives us a "Gaudium et Spes 22" Christology:

> Only in the mystery of the incarnate Word does the mystery of man take on light. For Adam, the first man, was a figure of Him Who was to come, namely Christ the Lord. Christ, the final Adam, by the revelation of the mystery of the Father and His love, fully reveals man to man himself and makes his supreme calling clear. He Who is "the image of the invisible God" (Col 1:15) is Himself the perfect man. . . . by His Incarnation the Son of God has united Himself with every man. He worked with human hands, He thought with a human mind, acted by human choice and loved with a human heart.[6]

---

5. *TD* 3, 457–58.

6. Vatican II, *Gaudium et Spes*, December 7, 1965, 22.

Dramatic Christology

To be human is to struggle to find one's self by relating one's finite freedom, the basic expression of self-hood, to its infinite source. This infinite source is like a point of light shining within every human who walks toward the light, falls off course, and, upon acknowledging its mistake, is led back on track. Every Adam and Eve spends a lifetime repeating the three basic human gestures of converting back to the light, being forgiven, and being offered hope in return.[7] For Balthasar, penance has a sacramental centrality as the sacrament in which we personally confess our guilt and are given forgiveness.[8] No human being, however much of a saint, succeeds in fully connecting with the light source, the infinite freedom at the root of their personal being. To be human is to face this lifelong contest to connect interior freedom with illuminating, infinite freedom. The world, the flesh and the devil tempt it with multiple distractions, and the real human "agony," the mortal combat in which fallen Everyman fights, is to reconnect its own will with the infinite will that gives it authentic personal freedom to be itself.

The individual human being does not struggle alone: infinite freedom seeks to gift it with a dynamic name that imparts each individual's personal task in life, his "mission." To connect one's finite freedom, expressing one's personal make-up, with God's infinite vitality is to be given a role in life that uniquely fits and exhibits one's personality. No matter how well or ill we match up to our vocation, it remains a gift, not a given. We must do what is not of our own making to achieve self-possession in God. The unique calling fits us perfectly without being ontologically our own. The wind of the infinite, divine will at our back graciously perfects our course.

Jesus Christ shares fully in the universal human "agony," and uniquely among all human beings, he bonds his finite freedom and autonomy with infinite freedom. The Holy Spirit, who calls human creatures and gives them charismatic gifts, *is* Jesus' own Spirit. What comes to others as an interior gift from outside comes to Jesus as an interior gift from within his identity. The gift of the Spirit to Jesus, his own Spirit, makes him infinitely free,[9] making his finite freedom overflow entirely into transcendent, infinite freedom, opening him from tip to toe for his calling or mission. In Jesus as in no other, finite human freedom or volition is wholly in congruity with the infinite, divine will. The character's search for its author who is sending him on his journey is achieved in the complete matching of Jesus' human finite and infinite divine

---

7. *TD* 4, 111–15.

8. Here Balthasar follows Adrienne von Speyr, *Confession*, translated by Douglas W. Stott (San Francisco: Ignatius Press, 1985).

9. *TD* 4, 198–99.

will. Jesus alone completes the Herculean labor and finds himself in God. This volitional return of the creature to its Creator-source in Jesus Christ is the perfect exhibition of the *analogia entis,* the analogy of personal creature to personal Creator. He is the analogizing of being in the "unconfused, undivided" two natures united in his person.[10] This interplay of finite and infinite being is the theo-drama.

Jesus alone is his own identity, his own mission or calling. The extent to which a human being carries out his moral calling is the extent to which he becomes himself, the self which God wills. The creaturely human identity is found in its moral calling, which is a gift of God. Jesus' mission and identity is his own, not a gift but part and parcel of his divine being: in Jesus Christ, Balthasar says,

> the "I" and the role become uniquely and ineffably one in the reality of his mission, far beyond anything attainable by earthly means. . . . Thomas Aquinas described this identity by saying that in Christ the procession within the godhead which constitutes the Son as the Father's dialogue partner, is identical, in God's going-out-from-himself toward the world, with the *missio,* the sending of the Son to mankind. (This *missio* is completed by the sending of the Spirit into the world, proceeding from both Father and Son.). . . . the Spirit is two things: he is most interior to the "I," making the person a son, and causing him to cry "Abba, Father"; and he is the socializing "between," rooting human fellowship in a (trinitarian) personal depth that cannot be realized by purely earthly means.[11]

The world is a drama from the moment of creation. God gifts Adam (humanity) with a freedom that is genuinely Adam's *own,* that is, a genuine autonomy. He gives Adam and humanity its own "space" in which to be free. God relinquishes his omnipotence in gifting Adam with "divine freedom: this is a first kenosis. He will let Adam be himself, and Adam replies by attempting to achieve self-possession, or to own for himself the divine freedom that God has leased to him. God "covenants" with Adam, further restricting by this promise to be with Adam the divine exercise of power and control. The "first act" of the drama between God and the world leaves it there.[12]

In the second act, the play becomes fully "theo-dramatic." The achievement of the "analogy" of divine and human wills in Jesus Christ, the perfect fruition of human nature that he effects, turns the bumbling, postlapsarian relations between God and humanity into a theo-drama. We might imagine that the resolution of the human mystery in Jesus Christ dead-ends the story and

---

10. *TD* 4, 198–99, 380.

11. *TD* 1, 645–47.

12. *TD* 4, 67.

forecloses any further drama, but that is because we unconsciously impose an immanent frame on the notion of drama (or have a closed, undramatic notion of drama). The bumbling efforts toward drama in the "first act" become wholly theo-dramatic in the second act, especially when God acts on the cross.

Human history after Christ is a battle of the Logos, as depicted in the book of Revelation. Full humanity has been achieved, and this confronts each human being with an existential decision unknown to pre-Christian humanity. The drama is now heightened to the point of choosing eternal life or eternal death: will we follow Christ's exhibition of the possibility of how to be fully human, or will we try to be gods on our own volition? Will we try to possess our divine freedom for ourselves and use it at our own volition, or will we find ourselves by tracing our freedom back to its source and handing it over to its author for naming? Once Christ has shown that finite human and personal identity is achieved by self-surrender to the call of the infinite from within one's humanity, once Christ has been and achieved such an identity, each human being must accept or reject such a task. This is the authentic drama of humanity after the cross.

In Act I of the drama, God creates human creatures, calling each of them through the mystery of their humanity. If the "primal kenosis" is the Father's eternal begetting of the Son, the Creator's giving freedom (a divine property) to the creature is a second kenosis:

> In creation, God fashions a genuine creaturely freedom and sets it over against his own, thus in some sense binding himself. It is possible to call this creation, together with the Covenant associated with it—in Noah, and . . . in Abraham and Moses—a new "kenosis" on God's part, since he is thereby restricted, implicitly, by creaturely freedom and explicitly by the covenant and its stated terms. He is "bound" in two ways. First, he has endowed man with a freedom that, in responding to the divine freedom, depends on nothing but itself. Like the ultimate ground that cannot have some further rationale beyond itself and is hence groundless—that is, the Father's self-surrender to the Son and their relationship in the Spirit—human freedom participates in divine autonomy, both when it says Yes and when it says No. This is analogous to the way in which the Son receives the autonomy of the divine nature in the mode of receptivity (not, like the creature, in being created): the Father "has granted the Son also to have life in himself" (Jn 5:26).[13]

Humanity has been given real freedom, and makes a poor fist of it, seeking to use its quasideity on its own terms (like the tenants in Mark 12 who refuse to pay the landlord and kill his delegates who are sent to collect the rent) rather

---

13. *TD* 4, 328.

than to exercise it responsively. There is an old joke to the effect that God created humanity and then lost control of events: this is funny to the degree that it resonates with vague recollections of the Old Testament stories, like the wandering in the desert after the Exodus. God gives orders and commands, and most human beings busy themselves finding ways to disobey. The biblical God exercises his omnipotence through a creative powerlessness or kenosis, punishing aberrant human beings but declining to exercise his omnipotence by compelling human beings to obey the commands and to do the right thing.[14] A less omnipotent God, a tyrant who exercised compulsion upon his creatures and made them to be good automatically and robotically, would be less open to the satirical humor of sceptics than the God of the Old Testament, but more open to the Nietzschean objection that a living God deprives human beings of the freedom that belongs to them. Act I furnishes multiple examples of humanity fruitlessly seeking escape from the God who has been all too generous with giving human beings freedom:

> Whenever the self tries to prescind from its rootedness in God and establish its own autonomy, it is attempting to consolidate its freedom; it is attempting to seize power. And so long as God appears primarily in the form of power—omnipotence—the self can use this as an excuse . . . to set itself up, likewise, as a "power" over against God. . . . it is not the "image" of God? What is needed . . . is the second level of reflection. . . . This facilitates the insight that God may disclose and give himself, thus transcending the notion that freedom means power; true freedom is thus seen in self-giving.[15]

Why create a dramatic Christology? Why would it matter that the perfect accord of the human and divine wills of the person Christ exhibits the core of the analogy between creature and Creator? Balthasar creates a dramatic Christology to show that Christ can be followed, because he achieves what every human being is constantly trying to do, in his sallies toward and away from the beckoning "Light." Christ achieves what every human being wants most, self-possession, by giving himself away to the Father. What drives human beings toward, and away from, the good, is what drives Jesus Christ, and he embodies and fulfils the natural human desire for God. Balthasar writes:

> Man's own experience teaches him that, if he is to know God inwardly, it can only come about through God's self-disclosure. At this . . . point we have the final paradox of the human being; Thomas Aquinas perceived and formulated it with utmost clarity and Henri de Lubac (*Surnaturel*,

---

14. *TD* 4, 331.
15. *TD* 4, 147.

1946) has brought it to the center of attention once more. Put simply: man is dependent on the free self-disclosure of his fellow human beings if he is to be himself—and he cannot force this self-disclosure . . . since man is created to be receptive to absolute truth and goodness, he is dependent on God's self-disclosure: it is not something he can postulate.[16]

If finite freedom, then, is to grasp

> itself *as freedom*, it cannot see itself as purely autonomous but must also realize that it is a gift, owing its existence to some other source. This highest act of freedom in no ways means that freedom should be defined as . . . "freedom to choose" (*liberum arbirtrium*) "between good and evil." But as Henri de Lubac has shown in his *Surnaturel*, it does mean that God cannot create a freedom that is so confirmed in the good that it does not need to choose; such a freedom . . . would have been robbed of its supreme *dignity*. That is why . . . we spoke of a necessary "latency," according to which God initially keeps his free, inner self hidden: thus he gives the creature the opportunity to lay hold of its own freedom, a freedom that both is its own *and* comes from an external source. "It is not simply a case of doing all the good one wants to do, and of deciding to do it in an act of free good will. The important and hard thing is to do it in the right manner, in a spirit of humility and calm, sensing the presence of another will by which one has to take one's bearings" (Blondel, *L'Action*, 1893, 396). Here, for Blondel, lies the choice between losing and gaining one's freedom; here, too, therefore, is the original locus of perversity, or moral evil in the world.[17]

God veils himself, makes himself somewhat latent, so that human beings can make an authentically free choice for the light, a choice that, if they make it aright, will enable each of them to be what the French call "un homme libre," a free man whose choices are not dictated by others, right down to the decision for self-sacrifice.

Drama in the form of sacrifice has become necessary because sin has perverted freedom "for God" into freedom for oneself. Human nature becomes "agonal," riven against itself as a result of sin. This is the story of the first act, and the tension cannot be resolved from within the terms as played in the Old Testament: God cannot continue to receive sacrifice from behind the veil of the Temple when what is now needed is a deeper entry into sacrifice itself, an entry by God into the "agonal" state of the human being, into its "greatness and misery" (Pascal). Act I has created a drama in which human beings cannot respond to the call of God. They cannot adequately take up the roles given

---

16. *TD* 4, 142.
17. *TD* 4, 150–51.

to them by God and thus can neither be good and justified in his sight, a basic human need, nor be liberated into personhood. From Genesis 3, history has been a play in which God judges humans who fail to respond to their call. The only way forward is the dramatic route: the one who *is* his role will enter the state, making of the play of world history an actual *Theo-Drama*. Christ is both imitable and unique:

> We are only acquainted with a single case where role and person coincide absolutely: that of the God-man. The point of identity is his mission from God (*missio*), which is identical with the Person *in* God and *as* God (*procession*). . . . The Son of God, in order to carry out his mission, does not look at himself . . . but at the Father's will, which is set before him anew at every moment by the Holy Spirit, or—using the stage metaphor—at the Holy Spirit's prompting.[18]

Jesus Christ embraces his identity as Son by embracing the Father's will.[19] Human beings having lost their gifted "sonship," forfeited their quasidivine liberty. The Son of God becomes human in order to make human creatures divine once more, restoring the freedom that made them akin to God.

In the third act, human beings have been enabled by Incarnation and cross to imitate Christ's proper wielding of his freedom. They are enabled to be good but are also capable of much deeper perversion than the cartoon villains who provoke God's wrath in the Old Testament. They must now decide for or against Christ and his exemplary demonstration of how to achieve deification, through sacrifice and self-abandonment to God. Once "'a God'" [has] step[ped] onto the stage . . . as 'a person,'" "theo-drama is possible"[20]: now, what modern philosophers like Blondel describe in universal, abstract terms as the human quest for identity becomes the deciding thread of history: "The closer a man comes to his identity, the more perfectly does he play his part . . . the saints are the authentic interpreters of theo-drama."[21]

Jesus Christ Makes Tragedy and Comedy Possible

The notion of a primal kenosis within God, followed by a second kenosis or self-limitation on God's part in permitting created freedom to be free, is not part of the classical, Aristotelian and Thomistic notion of God. Nor in that tradition does the work of Christ engage him in abandonment by God the Father. In classical Thomistic Christology, the begetting of Christ by the

---

18. *TD* 3, 458; *TD* 4, 532–33.
19. *TD* 3, 199–200.
20. *TD* 2, 189.
21. *TD* 2, 14.

Father is not an aboriginal, eternal sundering from the Father, which is the condition for his economic self-surrender on the cross, in which Christ suffers separation from the Father to redeem and justify sinful humanity.

One very striking line of criticism of Balthasar's notion of Christ's abandonment and surrender on the cross was made by the Rahner scholar Karen Kilby. Kilby invented a memorable parable: if a woman burns her house down with her children inside but goes and sits in the house and burns to death alongside them, what good does it do the children to know that their mother shares their pain by burning to death alongside them, when their death was caused by her arson? Against the all-too-common refrain that "only the suffering God can help," Kilby's parable protests that a cosuffering God offers no help by cosuffering. It leaves the sufferer no better off to be suffered alongside by God.[22] If Balthasar's insistence on taking Cyril at his word when he states that "One of the Trinity suffered" is supposed to be a theo-dicial litigation, a defense of God against the problem of evil, Kilby's response is that the evil is not diminished by God's suffering it as well, nor is the theo-dicial problem. The Thomist theologian Thomas Joseph White expands on Kilby's complaint in Thomistic style when he avers that introducing worldly evil or suffering into God makes the theo-dicial problem even worse and, in fact, insoluble, because human union with a suffering God will no longer elevate out of the realm of suffering, evil and death, if these are also present in God.[23]

Balthasar seems to think that where postlapsarian history was always a play, it is elevated to a theo-drama—a God-Drama—at the Incarnation and the Crucifixion of the God-man. The drama Jesus Christ thus recreates in and for human nature becomes the standard and regulatory point of analogy and mediation between humanity and God. He expresses this idea by calling Jesus Christ "the acting area," that is, the platform or stage upon which all human calling and role-play takes place, and by describing Jesus as the condition for the possibility of all drama.[24] One Balthasarian response to Kilby's objection is to say that by in some sense sharing in our most ultimate terrors and joys, by constructing the stage on which these dramas will be performed, Jesus Christ makes tragedy and comedy possible for us. At a simple level, he makes it possible for us to articulate the realization of our nightmares as *tragedy*, and not simply as disaster. He does not simply cosuffer but reframes and thus rearticulates the experience of unendurable horror. He likewise makes it possible for us to name our great, undeserved good fortunes as comedy. The

---

22. Karen Kilby, "Evil and the Limits of Theology," *New Blackfriars* 84, no. 983 (2003):13–29.

23. Thomas Joseph White, OP, *The Incarnate Lord: A Thomistic Study in Christology* (Washington, DC: The Catholic University of America, 2017), 351.

24. *TD* 3, 41, 51.

fallen human condition seems to call out for a description of the misery and the greatness of our experience as tragedy and as comedy. These are generic names for what appears as literature in Homer, in the Athenian dramatists, and in Shakespeare. But the two literary genres resonate with us because they are true to our human experience at its two furthest extremes. Tragedy and comedy seem to be there, under the muddle of fallen human experience: Jesus Christ, in his death-in-abandonment and in his equally helpless Resurrection validates these experiences by recreating them in relation to the supernatural God. He makes tragedy and comedy into more than just worldly experiences, within a closed immanent frame, and turns them into active analogates or pointers to a connection between ourselves and God. When we cosuffer with Christ, or become helpless with laughter in Christ's own acting area, we are participating in super-tragedy and super-comedy, analogates which his death and Resurrection have generated.

Here we need to consider a page-long reflection in the second volume of the *Theo-Drama* on the change Christ makes to tragedy and comedy. I will slip in a few illuminating lines from authors who have influenced Balthasar's view of tragedy, but Balthasar's words here form a single, continuous citation. He writes: "Thus Jesus Christ, the Beloved before all worlds . . . who became obedient to the Father for us unto death on the Cross and so was exalted above everything in heaven, on earth and under the earth (Phil 2:9 f.)—this Jesus Christ, in his dramatic role, which encompasses all dimensions of the world and of history, becomes the norm of every real and possible drama in the personal and public domains."[25] This means that, without Christ, drama has no normative, canonical form.
Balthasar continues:

> Insofar as every individual drama must first be lifted up to him, the Head, in order to discover its meaning, the conflicts that exist within the world are, at best, *provisionally* soluble. Thus, comedy has a happy ending because the tensions which create it are not pressed too far, and tragedy can give the relatively satisfying appearance of a certain immanent justice, even when the hero is doomed: it summons us to face up to the abiding tragic dimension of all existence. In comedy, the "gracious" good fortune prevails which, in tragedy, could equally well be denied and, one day, *will* be denied—in death, "the last enemy." To that extent, tragedy is the deeper truth of existence that underlies every comedy.[26]

Here Balthasar is saying that inner worldly tragedy and especially comedy do not really work. Within an immanent frame, justice tends only to be a

---

25. *TD* 2, 83.
26. *TD* 2, 83.

karmic, objective ordering—"the relatively satisfying appearance of a certain justice"—and comedy is escapist entertainment, a dessert course that evades the deeper truth of human life, which is death.

In the immanent frame, then, neither tragedy nor comedy is ultimately satisfying: comedy because its good fortune can last only so long, and tragedy because it consists in bowing to necessity. This reflection may remind readers of de Lubac's *Drama of Atheist Humanism*. He writes that with the coming of the Christian idea that every human being is made to the image of God, "man was freed, in his own eyes, from the ontological slavery with which Fate burdened him . . . mankind . . . took cognizance of its royal liberty. No more circle! No more blind destiny! No more *Moira*! . . . Transcendent God . . . revealed in Jesus, opened for all a way that nothing would ever bar again."[27] Tragedy for the great Athenians, and for all postlapsarian human experience, is being trapped between the Scylla of necessity (the commands and will of the gods) and the Charybdis of one's own freedom. This is the experience of fallen human beings, unable to achieve authentic human freedom. Balthasar describes Sophocles's Oedipus as a type of fallen Adam.[28]

Balthasar continues by describing the recreation and renewal of tragedy and comedy through the normative "super-drama" of cross and Resurrection. He seems to say that because Jesus Christ enters into the "super-tragedy" of divine abandonment and is then graciously Resurrected from the dead by his Father, *comedy*, or "super-comedy," becomes the normative form of drama. As in all comedies, "grace and reconciliation carry the day," but they do so now by defeating "the last enemy":

> If the once-for-all drama of Christ is to be exalted as the norm of the entire dramatic dimension of human life, two things must happen simultaneously: the abyss of all tragedy must be plumbed to the very bottom (which no human tragedy can do); and, in it and transcending it, we must discern the element of gracious destiny that genuinely touches human existence (and not merely *seems* to touch it). Thus the dramatic aspect of existence yields postulates addressed to Christology, although they can only be meaningful if they have already encountered the revelation concerning Christ. First, there is the postulate that Christ's being is of such a kind that he is able to descend into the abyss of all that is tragic—far beyond the ability of any tragic hero (who only bears his *own* destiny)—and hence that the tragic overstretching of his person must be absolute, that is, divine. (For "demi-gods" are self-contradictory.) The

---

27. Henri de Lubac, *The Drama of Atheist Humanism*, translated by Edith M. Riley, Ann Englund Nash, and Mark Sebanc (San Francisco: Ignatius Press, 1995 [Original French, 1944]), 22–23.

28. *GL* 4, 129.

other postulate is that, precisely in this abyss of unsurpassable tragedy, the element of grace asserts itself, that grace which encompasses existence and can persist and penetrate into the conciliatory aspect of tragedy. Both together lead to the absolute Christological paradox: in the horror of dissolution—under the weight of the world's guilt and of forsakenness by God—we are delivered from the meaninglessness of the world's suffering, and grace and reconciliation carry the day. John brings both aspects together in his concept of "exaltation" (exaltation on the Cross and exaltation to God's presence) and "glory." "Glory" is the manifestation of the Father's love for the world in the Son's bearing of the world's sin: by an inner necessity, this pure obedience to the Father calls for the Father to glorify the Son and announces it in advance.[29]

There is an element of innerworldly "karmic" justice in our sufferings: the weight of sin creates an immanent, cosmic justification for suffering. By taking the burden of sin upon himself, Christ renders it karmically weightless, displacing our "inner worldly tragedy" into the super-tragedy of his death-in-abandonment. Balthasar's reflection concludes:

> In Christ, therefore, penetrating the whole doomed predicament of human existence and being obedient to the Father's direction are simply one and the same. The movement of Incarnation, according to the Father's purpose, does not come to an end until all man's remoteness from God, all his guilt and pain, have been endured and undergone in performance of this obedience. This obedience is freely given, but the monstrous content laid upon Christ.... is positively explosive. While the world's tragedy "oppresses" the Suffering Servant under its weight, the prophecy of Isaiah 53 is fulfilled: he has "humbled himself"; "he makes himself an offering for sin"; "he shall see the fruit of the travail of his soul and be satisfied; . . . my servant (shall) make many to be accounted righteous." All norms, ultimately, come down to the Son's (unlimited) capacity for obedience: the Father asks him to give tangible proof of the divine love for the world and loads upon him the totality of men's free turning away from God.[30]

So far as this is intended as theodicy, it removes the element of justice in inner-worldly tragedy, justice as karmically merited punishment for sin, and replaces it with the divine justice, where Christ justifies us, by enduring our tragedy, the death that sin has merited, and transforming it into resurrection, new life.

It seems that Kilby's hapless cosuffering Deity only entered into immanent tragedy, participating in human suffering without assuming it into the

---

29. *TD* 2, 83–84.
30. *TD* 2, 84–85.

life of God. This is no way to help anyone. Kilby's hypothetical Deity does not help because it does not recast immanent tragedy as an analogue to the divine life, as "super-tragedy." As Balthasar conceives the Christic experience of abandonment, it is not a matter of God entering into human worldly suffering or tragedy because God is not involved in worldly suffering.[31]

On the one hand, then, the first "kenosis" of the begetting of the Son, in which he figuratively "goes out" from the Father and figuratively "returns," giving thanks for his begetting, is the exemplary "permission" or opening for all the suffering and tragedy of the created world. Just as his simultaneous Eucharistic thanksgiving, the "return" is the Trinitarian ground for the comedy of the created human condition. The primal Trinitarian kenosis does not import evil into God, making it inescapable for us from the get-go; rather, the kenosis creates the space in which tragedy and comedy can occur in created human life. God is not the protagonist of a tragic role within creation. Instead, creation's tragedies reflect Trinitarian kenosis and are thus not untouched by or external to God.[32] There is no history in God, whether good or evil, but human history is embraced by God, taking its course within the grounds created by the Trinitarian processions.

CHRIST CAN BE FOLLOWED BY DISCIPLES

The way in which Jesus Christ unites divine and human nature in one person and this persona's path through the economy enables him to be imitated. The point of constructing a "dramatic" Christology is to show how human beings can follow in Christ's footsteps, how believers can make "the body of Christ" live within history. A dramatic Christ is an imitable Christ, not simply as a moral leader but as the exemplary body within which repeat performances are presented. The metaphor of drama for Christology is in large part intended to show that Christ offers an imitable analogue for believers rather than someone, like an Olympic athlete, whose imitation is beyond their sights or capabilities. If Christ's deified humanity is to be, as Aquinas has it, the final cause of the deified humanity of believers, if he is to sanctify us and make us like him, then he must beat out the path for us by the mode and method of his Incarnation.

The analogy between believing follower and Christ is the role or persona. Jesus Christ *is* his role; he *is* the Son of God, homoousios with the Father. By being taken into the body of Christ in baptism, each believer is graced with a unique role or persona. To be the God-man is to perfectly perform the role of Sonship within the economy. To follow him is to be gifted and tasked with

---

31. *TD* 4, 324.
32. *TD* 4, 324, 331.

achieving that unique self-hood that fulfills our search for identity and that is the ideal persona God wants us to become. We have the freedom to act our roles well or badly, just as Christ, in the lowly "status examinatus," was open to temptation and had the freedom to will to play his filial role.

The unity of the two natures in the one person of the God-man is the highest point of analogy between God and humanity because the point of analogy in Christ is personal and therefore free. The two natures acting in unison in one person effects an analogy of divine and human freedoms. The God-man presents an example for imitation in a way that engages human freedom. Giving a believer a character role to adopt and become is positioning each person in a way that they can exercise their finite freedom. The name or character is our destiny, written on the "white stone" in the book of Revelation, but we are not automatically "destined" to become it without the exercise of our freedom. The Christ into whose death baptized believers die and are reborn is character forming: his work is being a character, the Son, and imparting character is what he does. Using the dramatic metaphor for Christology makes us understand the central importance of the two wills in Christ, and it gives us a way of conceiving adoption into God, deification, by analogy to the unity of the two wills in him. Our finite freedom is not commandeered or press-ganged by assumption into the body of the God-man, when the God-man is thus conceived. Grace is an "offer" and an "accompaniment," when we conceive of Christ as playing the role of Christ in response to the cues of the Holy Spirit.[33]

As the norm of divine-human unity, Christ the Son becomes the "acting area" within which all vocations are given and shaped. Each unique human vocation interlocks with every other, analogizing with the most diverse callings, working together to form the history of the one church, because all are given in the common mediating ground of Christ's body. Each person is "sent," in emulation of Christ's mission. The dramatic metaphor for Christology enables us to think of deification as person-forming, speaking to the human need to find a source for one's own personal uniqueness and an arena in which that uniqueness can complimented by company.

BECAUSE IT IS DRAMATIC, FREEDOM IS CONSTITUTIVE OF CHRISTOLOGY

Friedrich Schleiermacher raised a question worth considering when he protested against the Chalcedonian Christology belief that two natures, one finite and one infinite, cannot exist alongside one another. Human and divine

---

33. *TD* 3, 19–21.

natures are not static entities or limited quantities that can be stacked one top of one another.[34] The Blondelian answer, that human nature is blindly groping toward the horizon of divinity, is helpful in that it indicates that human nature is internally related to God. But we have to go further, in a personalist direction. Not even a single nature operates automatically within a person: all personal natures operate volitionally, freely choosing to be themselves, or denying themselves. If we ask with Schleiermacher how two natures, divine and human, can be seated alongside each other, the theo-dramatic answer is personally, that is, by the continuous choice of a free personality. The two natures are "activated" as themselves by the free volition of the divine person in whom they act.

For Balthasar, the most important agency of the divine or human person is the exercise of freedom. Many features of his Christology arise from the significance of freedom in his conception of personality. Its freedom is what makes a character dramatic, in that a free personality always exists in a tension toward an Other in which it can resist or acquiesce. For example, the finite creature has to remain itself, at a distance from Creator, but it has to simultaneously remain in creaturely relation to the Creator.

Free personalities are unpredictable and take risks. There was a risk involved in God's creation of the angels and of human beings, which we know since some of the former and all of the later originally resisted their tension to their Creator to the breaking point. Freedom involves risking the choice to snap or break the tension that constitutes the personality. The misuse of freedom damages the personality.

The business of human social life involves playing roles in which, with partial pretense and partial authenticity, we play act our functional relationships. All human life is conducted off-off Broadway. We project this social necessity of "acting" onto the theatrical stage and enjoy watching actors act because the acting itself resonates with our everyday lives.

For all the Greek etymology, acting is not hypocrisy and deceit: we can be our authentic selves only by playing roles. There is no authentic self without a role through which to mediate it. There is a mixture of authenticity and masking in the performance of any human social role, and no one can put the whole of himself or herself into a socially generated role. That leaves us without a means of fully becoming ourselves. Our social roles are generated to set up finite tensions between finite personae, enabling us to know how to act with our equals, inferiors, and superiors: plumbers and their desperate clients, professors and their students, salespeople and buyers. No social role entirely fits its bearer because each human person needs not a finite, immanent tension

---

34. Friedrich Schleiermacher, *The Christian Faith*, translated by H. R Macintosh (Edinburgh: T&T Clark, 1928), pt. II, sects. 95–96.

to be herself but a finite-infinite tension. The off-off Broadway of immanently framed social drama is too small a stage. We are not quite comfortable in the skin of our social roles, since they do not permit the whole of the dramatic tension that our finite freedom requires to operate.

Stage drama mimics a man or a woman's becoming their personae. The perfect unity of the dramatic character with his or her part, the perfectly played theatrical role, is a signpost that we can be liberated by *some* kind of role. Theatrical drama is an ideal model of emancipatory acting because it is what we wish that off-stage real life could be.

Thus, Balthasar speaks of Jesus Christ as the "truth" of dramatic character, the undisguised achievement in the flesh of what stage character shows by the use of disguise. The Swiss theologian claims that

> in the identity of Jesus' person and mission, we have the realization . . . of what is meant by a dramatic "character": namely a figure who, by carrying out his role, either attains his true face or . . . unveils his hidden face. In the case of Jesus Christ we have, . . . in real life, the truth of what is found on the stage, that is, the utter and total identification of the character as a result of his utter and total performance of his mission . . . in theo-drama, he is . . . the model for all other actors.[35]

We know that this "truth" to the role is an economic replay of the eternal, Trinitarian drama: "this identity is only possible if the Person has been given a mission, not accidentally, but as a modality of his eternal personal being; if, as Aquinas says, the Son's *mission* is the economic form of his eternal *procession* from the Father."[36] For this to happen, the finite free will of Jesus' human nature must choose to enact this drama and to perfectly perform his filial role. His finite freedom, his human willing and desire must give itself entirely to this role just as his "infinite freedom," the divine will, does. The divine person of Jesus Christ synthesizes his finite and infinite will, and both finite and infinite will freely choose the necessity of playing the Son. Though "the synthesis" of the two wills "is a free act of the divine Person";[37] each will is itself, finite and creaturely on the one hand, and infinite on the other.

The person of the Incarnate Son is a dramatic interplay of finite and infinite freedoms, and it contains real, dramatic tension. The Incarnation of the Son is not a theatrical stage performance of the perfectly achieved tension between finite and infinite freedom, which means the finite freedom of Jesus Christ has to learn out how to put his role into practice in each of the concrete

---

35. *TD* 3, 201.
36. *TD* 3, citing Thomas Aquinas, *ST* 1.43.1.
37. *TD* 3, 223.

situation of his life, just as every individual human freedom in search of the good has to work out in the concrete how to do the right thing in each particular time and place. Unless he has to struggle to figure out how best to perform his role, to "do the good thing here and now," Jesus Christ does not really exercise human free will, and he is not a model that other human beings can follow. If our human free will is to be implanted in the humanity of Jesus Christ, his must be a humanity that genuinely exercises human freedom and experiences faith and hope as we will do. He must give us the capacity to experience the best use of our freedom, in charity, and with faith and hope. This explains in part why Balthasar claims that the Savior does not see the Father in the beatific vision: Jesus Christ must, in his human freedom, choose to live by faith in the Father and will to act in faith in the Father just as his human followers will do. The Christ who the believer seeks to emulate is a Person in possession of a finite free will who puts his freedom at the disposal of the Father, just as he asks his disciples to do:

> since Jesus does not see the Father in a *visio beatifica* but is presented with the Father's commission by the Holy Spirit, that is his awareness of his mission is only indirect, it is possible for him to be tempted. Though he is exposed in this way. . . . "being able to sin" is not part of his freedom. . . . fully resolved as he is to carry out his mission, he is exposed to temptation as we are. This is only possible if, with his entire task in his mind's eye, he has to use his own freedom to search for ways of implementing it in detail; for only then can there be any attraction in the suggestion that he avoid the hard path, the path of humiliation and earthly failure, by taking the short-cut put forward by human calculation. As man, he must continually measure the partial visions that present themselves against the totality of the mission, of his Father's will; when he does this, the direction he is to take—the hardest course— becomes luminous. He sees the totality of the Father's will, and hence of his mission shining forth from this partial value. . . . and such luminous radiance is only possible within his total, free availability. It is then that, although he cannot sin, his obedience is meritorious. His merit is that he himself anticipates nothing . . . Jesus is the perfect example . . . of faith and hope.[38]

The perfect tension between finite and infinite freedom in the person of Jesus is hard won and an act of merit.

Freedom is constitutive of Balthasar's Christology because he wants to show that Christ fully enters into Adam's humanity. Jesus Christ is Alpha and Omega, the Creator norm of sonship aimed at in the first Adam and the cre-

---

38. *TD* 3, 200.

ative norm of human sonship as the second Adam. Adamic humanity fully becomes itself and achieves its desires in the second Adam. As the second Adam, Christ liberates Adamic humanity to be itself. As Balthasar puts it,

> The man who is reborn in Christ is given a share in the analogy of Christ's freedom: freed for a responsibility before God and the world, that is genuinely within his grasp, he possesses the Holy Spirit, who enables him to be a docile follower of absolute, divine freedom. In the exercise of this analogy, we see the perfecting of something that was present in germ in creaturely freedom: for, if Adam was created really free, he was not fettered in that way . . . characteristic of man's fallen state . . . he was not imprisoned with a freedom that can only circle round and round within the confines of the world, relating only itself, its advantage and its achievements. His gift of freedom came from the creative Logos and thus imparted a real possibility of transcending the internal world and heading for God. Now . . . since the Logos . . . took on fallen Adam's "likeness of sinful flesh" (Rom 8:3) . . . the Christian is liberated to enjoy a freedom that . . . outstrips Adam's. He is freed from the chains of a freedom that circles around itself and endowed by the Son of God with the freedom of the sons of God (Jn 8:36; Gal 5:1).[39]

There is a real tension in the dramatic interplay of finite and infinite freedom that *is* the person of the Incarnate Son.

From a worldly perspective, or metaphysically speaking, within the closed immanent frame, power is the opposite of helplessness or vulnerability. To say that God is free means in part that even in the Incarnation he does not get onto the grounds of the "immanent frame": he always acts, even in the Incarnation, in sovereign transcendence of how things work for finite entities. Thus, God can be intimate with human beings, and Christ can offer human persons intimacy with the divine, without overpowering their human freedom. This is because the divine omnipotence is free of the inner-worldly necessity of being a greater power than all others. God leaves human

> freedom . . . intact, even when perverted into sin. God does not overwhelm man; he leads him to his goals. . . . This indicates no inability on God's part. . . . It arises from the power-lessness that . . . is identical with his omnipotence: he is above the necessity to dominate, let alone use violence. This identity of powerlessness and omnipotence sheds . . . light on . . . John's use of the term "glorification," where the powerlessness of the Cross and the omnipotence of the Resurrection are seen together.[40]

---

39. *TD* 4, 476–77.
40. *TD* 4, 331–32.

DRAMATIC SOTERIOLOGY

Many disputed questions are best answered with a "no, but," or with a distinction. The answer to the question "does the crucified Christ become sin for our sake and to be punished as such by the Father?" is not perhaps best answered by setting it aside as Lutheran heresy. The "no, but," often favored by Thomas Aquinas in the *Summa* is the best way forward here. His notion of the work of Christ is a great achievement of accumulating *all* of the insights of scripture and tradition. Rather than largely focusing on deification and the defeat of the devil and death, with the Fathers and much Eastern tradition, or putting all of the weight on satisfaction, as Anselm had done, Aquinas gives due attention to most of the biblical metaphors for Christ's work of reparation. Perhaps even Luther's slightly dotty theory, which seems in places to identify Christ with sin and the devil in a God-almighty struggle with the Father, ought to be answered with a distinction and not flat rejection.

Gustav Aulen described the "devilward" conception of atonement as the "dramatic" theory of atonement,[41] and he was not wrong to think of it as more dynamic than substitution theories. Balthasar argues that in order to be dramatic as the scripture metaphors themselves are, a theory of Christ's work must include five elements: the Christ; the Son must hand himself over for the world's salvation; he must exchange his own sinless person for the sinful collective persona of humanity; human beings must be liberated and adopted into the Triune communion; and, fifth, this process must be an expression of God's love.[42] The work of Christ is dramatic in two ways.

In the first, multiple tensions are involved: three opposed parties are at play, each with their own appropriate gravitational pull. The dramatic characters are the triangle of Holy God, sinful humanity, and the demonic forces in which humanity is entangled. Standing crucified between all three, representing God to humanity in his divine nature and human nature to God, is Christ, who is anointed for this act of mediation. If we take out any one element, the drama loses its tension. Why would we remove the punitive element, the idea that Christ is punished on our behalf for the sins against which God's anger is sparked? First, to avoid saying that humanity moves God to act, and second, to protect Christ's sinlessness, since God's punitive anger is aroused against sin. According to Balthasar, both Anselm and Aquinas ameliorate and diminish the idea that God the Father punishes Christ on our behalf so as to avoid tarnishing the sinless One with our sin.[43] If he were punished for our sakes, the justice of that would be

---

41. Gustav Aulen, *Christus Victor: An Historical Study of the Three Main Types of Atonement Theory*, translated by A. G. Herbert (London: SPCK, 1970), 4.

42. *TD* 4, 317.

43. *TD* 4, 260–63.

that he became sinful for our sakes. Balthasar wants to say that the work is neither the offering of the sinless instead of sinners (Anselm), which restores the balance of cosmic justice, nor Christ's being made to sin for us (Luther).[44]

Balthasar's conception of "super-tragedy," as discussed earlier, is intended to create a "no, but" for Luther's attempt to redramatize the banalization of evil seen in an accountant's notion of atonement-and-reconciliation as a sinless substitution, absent the demonic forces, which is channeled into works of human reparation. In the system Luther challenges, Christ emerges triumphant from the grave without having gotten his hands dirty while he sinlessly pays the price of divine justice. Luther calls on the old "defeat of the devil" metaphor as an alternative, but here, the "third angle" of the triangle, the demonic forces, and the "second angle," humanity itself, both collapse into God. The atonement therefore becomes a struggle, a "tragic" battle between good and evil within God himself, between Son and Father. That gives us not only a weird gnostic mythology but a hyperdrama that takes place above and beyond the heads of creatures, whether fallen angels or human beings, who are, after all, responsible for evil.

Both Luther's heaping of sin interiorly into Christ and the conception of Christ's work as a rectification of divine justice in which the sinless Christ is offered as a ransom-equivalent for sinful humanity removes the God-creature drama. In Balthasar's conception, Christ really enters into the tragedy, subjectively accepting as punishment what objectively—in terms of objective divine justice—cannot actually be punishment. He enters into the tragedy of the creature's separation from God and really experiences it for what it is. He suffers real forsakenness, the forsakenness of those who chose exile from God. He selflessly enters into the interior of the human tragedy and experiences God-forsakenness from within, without deserving it, and thereby reorients the tragedy into something that meaningfully belongs within God, the "super-tragedy" within the Trinitarian relations. Balthasar states that

> the Crucified does not bear the burden as something external: he in no way distances himself from those who by rights should have to bear it. . . . Subjectively . . . he can experience it as "punishment," though objectively speaking, in his case, it cannot be such. The sufferings of Christ on man's behalf are far above all possible sufferings entailed by sin. . . . If we realize the ground-lessness of man's free No in the face of the purely gracious . . . Yes of God's love, it is clear that the expiation of this ground-less sin must involve a transfiguration through suffering that is surpassingly "ground-less" . . . in a way we cannot image.[45]

---

44. *TD* 4, 336.
45. *TD* 4, 337–38.

Christ transfigures the tragedy of human sin from within: this is Balthasar's "no but" for Martin Luther.

The second way in which the atonement is dramatic is that the two great freedoms, divine and human, are both equally active. The atonement is a work of God and of humanity, in Christ's human nature. Both creature and Creator really are players in the work of atonement: each has its own sovereign part. If we fully respect human freedom, the freedom of the whole human person, and fully acknowledge that nothing happens outside God's work, we cannot let fleshly humanity endure the suffering while God pulls the strings from beyond the play, nor, in a mirror image of that, let the performance happen weightlessly and mythologically within God. Balthasar asks:

> Are the systems hitherto attempted sufficiently dramatic? Or have they always failed to include . . . one element . . . that is essential to the complete dramatic plot. For no element may be excluded here: God's entire world drama is concentrated on and hinges on this scene. This is the theo-drama onto which the world *and* God have their ultimate input: here absolute freedom enters into created freedom, interacts with created freedom, and acts *as* created freedom. God cannot function here as a mere Spectator, allegedly immutable and not susceptible to influence; he is not an eternal, Platonic "sun of goodness," looking down on a world that is seen as a "vast perpetual scene of slaughter." Nor . . . can man, guilty as he is in God's sight, lie passive and anaesthetized on the operating table while the cancer of his sin is cut out.[46]

CONCLUSION: NOT ENOUGH DRAMA?

An interesting criticism of Balthasar's kenotic Christology is that it builds too much on two or three verses in Paul's letter to the Philippians. Gilbert Narcisse asks whether Balthasar is wise to build his Christological edifice on kenoticism when the biblical foundation for it is so sparse.[47] This is a good question, since it is easy to forget that *ekenōsen* occurs but once in the Christian scripture (Phil 2:7).

Another biblical image other than *ekénōsen* is that of the covenant: this recurs in scripture from the Noachic covenant, to the covenants with Abraham and Moses, down to the last supper discourses in the Synoptics. For God to "covenant" with his people is to bind himself, freely to avow to restrict his actions, to be governed by his own promises to his people. The idea of Israel

---

46. *TD* 4, 318.

47. Gilbert Narcisse, "Christology and Revelation," in *The Oxford Handbook of Divine Revelation*, ed. Francesca Murphy and Balazs Mezei, 154–69 (Oxford: Oxford University Press, 2021).

and then the church as the "bride" of the Lord flows from the image of a free avowal of loyalty between God and his people. Balthasar's kenotic Trinity is the God of the covenant.

Balthasar's notion of Christ's work revolves around a nexus of dynamic Pauline images, including especially his idea of Christ as the "new man" or the new Adam. Balthasar's use of Philippians 2:7 is interwoven with the Adam-Christ typology in Romans 5:12–21. The central idea of his dramatic Christology is that Christ is the mysterious, surprising, and yet awaited fulfillment of human nature. Perhaps the two most important Pauline words in the Balthasarian script are "*en Christo.*" Everything that happens to Adam and Eve happens "in Christ."

It is perturbing, then, to learn from Thomas Joseph White that Balthasar's conception of Christ's descent into hell to retrieve lost souls destroys the "drama" of the embodied human being having a finite stretch of time in which to choose for or against God. He thinks that interpreting Christ's descent into hell as an event outside of chronological time, in which Christ can meet and rescue the damned sinner at any moment of his choosing, opens the way to replacing the given "finitudes" of hell with neo-Gnostic purgatorial cycles. He claims that by detemporalizing the embodied mortal soul's decisions for or against Christ, we replace a dramatic, horizontal conception of divine judgement with an undramatic, cyclical conception, where judgement is endlessly deferred until all prisoners finally achieve release.[48]

Balthasar praises Homer for giving his heroes a finite life-span, thereby heightening their tragedy and grandeur, and for not giving any leeway to reincarnation of souls.[49] It is in Homer's tragic conception of life, he thinks, that we see a real analogy to the biblical view and not in the all too soul-ful reincarnation theories of Plato and Pythagoras. He seems to appreciate White's perspective.

But perhaps White is privileging chronological time over Christic time. The "stage" or "acting area" on which each human being must strut, and be judged, is the "body of Christ." The moral standard to which each son and daughter of Adam is held is Christ himself, their model. What makes the decision dramatic is not the brevity of the temporal span in which they must perform but the comparison to the model. We are not to envisage each fallen soul being given aeons of years to decide for or against Christ: in every case, Balthasar says, Christ makes the judgement. The light falls from Christ onto the sinner, judging him and seeing him for what he is.[50] It is not the chronological time in which we have to play our role that makes it dramatic, forcing

---

48. White, *The Incarnate Lord*, 423–26.

49. *GL* 4, 47.

50. *GL* 7, 117–21.

us to make our choice before the final act, but rather the encounter between the Savior and his fallen image.

Balthasar does not intend to import a primal tragedy into the Trinity, or even a primal comedy (in the Holy Spirit's eternal bridging of the Father and Son). He wants to say that the created world exists *within* this Trinitarian Mercy Seat (*Gnadenstuhl*) and human-created tragedy is not outside of God, randomly permitted by God but interior to God. The Trinity is not the source of tragedy but instead the great backdrop to human tragedy (and comedy). It is, as it were, its inscape.

BIBLIOGRAPHY

Aristotle, *Poetics*. Edited by R. McKeon. *The Basic Works of Aristotle*. New York: Random House, 1941.

Aulen, Gustav. *Christus Victor: An Historical Study of the Three Main Types of Atonement Theory*. Translated by A. G. Herbert. London: SPCK, 1970.

De Lubac, Henri. *The Drama of Atheist Humanism*. Translated by Edith M. Riley, Ann Englund Nash, and Mark Sebanc. San Francisco: Ignatius Press, 1995.

———. *Surnaturel: études historiques*. Paris: Desclée de Brouwer, 1991.

Kilby, Karen. "Evil and the Limits of Theology." *New Blackfriars* 84, no. 983 (2003): 13–29.

Murphy, Francesca Aran. "Whence Comes this Love as Strong as Death: The Presence of Franz Rosenzweig's 'Philosophy as Narrative' in Von Balthasar's Theo-Drama." *Literature and Theology* 7, no. 3 (September 1993): 227–47.

Narcisse, Gilbert. "Christology and Revelation." In *The Oxford Handbook of Divine Revelation*, edited by F. Murphy and B. Mezei, 154–69. Oxford: Oxford University Press, 2021.

Schleiermacher, Friedrich. *The Christian Faith*. Translated by H. R Macintosh. Edinburgh, T&T Clark: 1928.

von Speyr, Adrienne. *Confession*. Translated by Douglas W. Stott. San Francisco: Ignatius Press, 1985.

White, Thomas Joseph. *The Incarnate Lord: A Thomistic Study in Christology*. Washington, DC: The Catholic University of America, 2017.

Trinity

CHAPTER 7

Should the Cross Be the Sole Revelation of the Trinity?

REV. EMMANUEL DURAND, OP
TRANSLATED BY REV. JOHN BAPTIST KU, OP

THE QUESTION FORMULATED in the title of this chapter justifies major reworkings of Trinitarian theology from the contemporary period. More precisely, such a question could spark a debate, from a distance, between Hans Urs von Balthasar and Thomas Aquinas. Over and above the centuries, it would be possible to bring them face to face concerning their different ways of conceiving, for example, person and mission, the fruitfulness of the Father, the role of the Spirit, etc.

I prefer, however, to note a more radical divergence on the epistemological plane, with respect to the foundation of a Trinitarian analogy, and then to illuminate the Trinitarian function of the mysteries of Jesus, which preoccupied each theologian in his own time. Thomas Aquinas and Hans Urs von Balthasar are indeed two great theologians who undertook an integral theological rereading of the life of Jesus. I do not propose to undertake a textual exegesis of Aquinas as a response critical of "troubling" or "doubtful" innovations from Balthasar. In concert with St. Augustine, I will begin by sketching out the issue at hand. Next, I will charitably read and interpret the thought of Balthasar concerning this matter, yielding some benefits and raising a fundamental problem. Finally, I will close by drawing an insight from Thomas Aquinas in order to make a forward-looking proposal.

THE MOMENTS OF TRINITARIAN WITNESS, ACCORDING TO AUGUSTINE OF HIPPO

To clarify the unity and aim of my overall proposal, centered on the mode of Trinitarian revelation and manifestation, let us begin by gathering the logic of the rule of Trinitarian faith handed on by Augustine and briefly recall several points. At the beginning of his treatise *De Trinitate*, Augustine declares his intention to defend the substantial or essential unity of the Father, the Son, and the Spirit. In the first books, he tries to respond to the Arian objections in opposition to the unity and equality of the three Persons.

To begin, he recalls and reformulates the rule of Trinitarian faith such as he has received it through the fathers and his other predecessors.[1] It possesses an elaborate and instructive theological structure that I render as follows:

- The unicity of God: one single substance, indivisible, whence one single God.
- The distinction of the three Persons through the incommunicable properties of each: the Father alone begets; the Son alone is begotten; the Spirit alone belongs to both the Father and the Son.
- The differentiated action or manifestation proper to each in the New Testament: the birth of the Son, his crucifixion, burial, Resurrection, and Ascension; the manifestation of The Spirit at the baptism and at Pentecost; the manifestation of the Father at the baptism, the transfiguration, and the announcement of glory.
- The inseparability of the three Persons in their differentiated but conjoined action-manifestation.

According to the structure of the rule of faith handed on by Augustine, the distinction of the three Persons does not depend on their differentiated manifestation but, rather, on the eternal acts and properties enunciated above. Nevertheless, their eternal distinction is attested by certain events in the history of salvation. Augustine assembles the following events under this or that facet: birth, baptism, transfiguration, announcement of glory, Crucifixion, burial, Resurrection, Ascension, and Pentecost.

In virtue of the inseparability of the three Persons, each of these scenes could no doubt be studied as an integral Trinitarian unveiling,[2] but Augustine suggests here that what is proper to each is attested in a determinate, concrete way in this or that event. This or that revelatory facet of the mysteries of Christ, in reality, pertains to the singular mode of presence or action of one of the three. There is no moment *par excellence* for the Trinitarian manifestation, even less an exclusive moment. None of the events mentioned appear to loom brightly over the others. For Augustine, the sequence of public Trinitarian attestation extends from Christ's birth to Pentecost. It thus practically embraces the whole trajectory of Christ Jesus such as it is recounted in the four Gospels and then in the Acts of the Apostles.

Through the remainder of the first four books in *De Trinitate*, Augustine shows that the theophanies of the Old Testament do not afford sure access to the distinction of the three Persons. It is only through the Incarnation and Pentecost that the Son and the Spirit are identifiable as sent by the Father.

---

1. See Augustine, *De trin.* I.7.
2. See Augustine, *De trin.* IV.30.

The economy of Trinitarian revelation thus stretches between the two beacons of the Incarnation of the Son and the Pentecost of the Spirit.

Augustine's rule of faith is a common foundation that makes it possible to frame our background question: how is God the Trinity engaged in the mysteries of Jesus? The mysteries here are understood in the broad sense of salvific events related to the incarnation, life, and Passover of Christ Jesus.

Such an inquiry makes it possible to situate and honor the contribution of several contemporary Trinitarian theologies. In my opinion, there has not been a radical reshaping of triadology since Basil of Caesarea or Augustine of Hippo. If we step across a few centuries for a moment to consider contemporary Trinitarian theologies, leapfrogging over Bonaventure and Thomas Aquinas, and then Luther and Calvin, one of the main concerns of recent theologians has been to take a fresh look at a strong link between the eternal Trinity and the economy of salvation. Let us now question the theologian Hans Urs Balthasar about the deployment of the relationship between the Trinity and the cross.

THE CROSS, THE PROPER PLACE OF TRINITARIAN REVELATION IN BALTHASAR

In *Theo-Drama IV: The Action*, Balthasar states that the doctrine of the Trinity can be developed only by beginning with the cross. The cross will then be understood to include the Resurrection, though it will designate, above all, the abandonment lived in fidelity to Calvary.[3] In *Mysterium Paschale*, Balthasar stated more clearly that the revelation of the Spirit ultimately shines forth in the Resurrection. This led him to conclude that, while being prepared by the opposition of wills during the agony and the abandonment by the Father on the cross, the revelation of the Trinity is properly accomplished by the Resurrection.[4] Comparatively, in the *Theo-Drama*, the Trinitarian exposition seems almost exclusively centered around the moment of Calvary. Indeed, Balthasar judges that there, "for the first time," the "distance" between the Father and the Son is made manifest in the dereliction of Jesus. The terms chosen are decisive: the theologian seeks the "first" explicit Trinitarian epiphany, and he traces it to when Father and Son are presented under the mode of distance. Two questions arise: Why such a focus on the cross? Why such an attraction to "distance"?

---

3. See *TD* 4, 317–32.

4. See "Mysterium Paschale," in *Mysterium Salutis III*, 269–81.

From the Impasse of the Image to the Law of Gift

Balthasar is disappointed by the scholastic and modern avatars of the Augustinian analogy (mind, knowledge, love; memory, intellect, will, etc.). This image has led to the formalism of a Trinity conceived according to the cleavage of the human mind: the begetting of the Son by way of intellectual operation, and the procession of the Spirit by way of a voluntary impulse. Thomas Aquinas and his epigones were thus caught in the snare of the *mens* (mind). The moderns have only accentuated the projection of solipsism onto God. They have rethought the Trinity by the yardstick of the absolute subject who takes possession of himself according to a simple divine self-mediation. They have plunged deeper into the same rut that ensnared scholastic thinkers.

At the beginning of his article entitled "Der Heilige Geist als Liebe" ("The Holy Spirit as Love"), Balthasar emphasizes the thinness (or weakness) of the scriptural foundations of the Augustinian analogy, according to which the Son is begotten by way of knowledge, while the Spirit proceeds by way of love.[5] In Johannine literature, love is the love of the Father for the world and for the Son, manifested to the world by the sending and the offering of the Son, while the Spirit has rather a function of teaching and discernment. In Pauline literature, the appropriation of love to the Spirit is not applied in a clear and unequivocal way. The Spirit is often associated with the power (*dunamis*) of God. He also makes it possible to confess and recognize the Lord.

The Augustinian analogy thus seems to be a gratuitous theological fabrication. There is nothing normative about it, but it is substituted for New Testament revelation by governing the Western representation of the Trinity. For Balthasar, the Trinitarian unfolding is explained entirely by the ecstatic and fecund love of the Father, which seems more in conformity with the New Testament, where love runs through the whole Trinitarian economy but without being appropriated to the Spirit.

To reconnect with the New Testament economy of Trinitarian revelation is to recognize that the Father's love is at the beginning of all Trinitarian fructification. Love is the heart of the Trinity, and, like absolute love, it is the eternal gift of self. The Father is identical to this gift. He does not lose himself, nor does he reserve himself. He is gift as dispossession of self to extreme abandonment. In a word, paternal love is eternally primordial kenosis (*Urkenosis*).

The only support mentioned by Balthasar for treating the Father's "self-exteriorization" as kenosis is the idiosyncratic thought of Sergei Bulgakov. Surprisingly, Balthasar does not seek to base such an intuition on the New

---

5. See Hans Urs von Balthasar, "Der Heilige Geist als Liebe," in *Skizzen zur Theologie III: Spiritus Creator* (Einsiedeln: Johannes Verlag, 1967), 106–22. My attention was drawn to this text by Vincent Holzer, *Hans Urs von Balthasar* (Paris: Cerf, 2012), 136–39.

Testament. It must be recognized that the assertion of a primordial kenosis of the Father ultimately comes from the way in which the theologian conceives the intrinsic logic of extreme love in the act of giving: excess or plenitude, abandonment or kenosis, and envelopment.[6] It belongs in some way to the internal law of love given to pass through self-abandonment. Applicable to us, it would also be applicable in the highest degree to the Trinity, starting with the Father.

The Salvific Function of an Infinite Distance Eternally Overcome

Thus, the begetting of the Son by the Father implies a paternal abandonment. For Balthasar, it is the establishment of an "infinite distance" in the sense that the Son is "infinitely other" than the Father. Why speak here of otherness in terms of distance? This is fully illuminated by the salvific function attributed to the eternal distance between the Father and the Son. If the distance between the Son and the Father is the greatest of all, it eternally includes every possible separation of God from free creatures. The infinite distance between the Father and the Son is eternally maintained in openness and communion through the Spirit. It is, so to speak, eternally overcome in God himself. This is precisely what is made manifest on Calvary: the Son, abandoned by the Father on account of being identified with sin as separation from God, is nevertheless maintained in fidelity and communion with the Father through the Spirit. The event of the cross is thus the temporal epiphany of the eternal Trinitarian event. In *The Glory of the Lord: The New Covenant*, with respect to the Paschal glorification of the obedient Christ, Balthasar already referred to the Spirit as "the agent of the reciprocal immanence of the love between Christ and the Father," or even as "the personal identity of the personal difference in the divinity."[7]

The cross reveals, therefore, that the Trinity envelops the world. The whole drama of created freedoms in conflict with God is eternally included and embraced in the internal drama of the Trinitarian life, where the infinite distance is always already overcome in love. In other words, the reconciliation of all possible separations from God, sinners though they be, is already

---

6. On the law of gift or extreme love, see Pascal Ide, *Une Théologie de l'Amour. L'amour, centre de la* Trilogie *de Hans Urs von Balthasar* (Brussels: Lessius, 2012); Ide, *Une Théo-logique du Don. Le don dans la "Trilogie" de Hans Urs von Balthasar* (Leuven: Peeters, 2013); and Michele M. Schumacher, *A Trinitarian Anthropology: Adrienne von Speyr and Hans Urs von Balthasar in Dialogue with Thomas Aquinas* (Washington, DC: The Catholic University of America Press, 2014).

7. See Hans Urs von Balthasar, *Herrlichkeit*, III.2. *Neuer Bund* (Einsiedeln: Johannes Verlag, 1969), 243: "als dem Wirker des gegenseitigen In-eins der Liebe zwischen Christus und dem Vater," "als der personalen Identität der personalen Differenz in der Gottheit."

acquired in its eternal foundation. Such a Trinitarian conception of reconciliation is the main justification for the daring language of absolute and infinite distance between the Father and the Son.[8] It is at the cross that such a distance is found to be revealed on the world stage.

Undoubtedly, Balthasar takes some methodological precautions. He does not mean to confuse God with mutable, intramundane events, nor to project an eternal suffering onto God. On several occasions, he asserts that it is necessary first to exclude all suffering from God and then lay the foundation in him, the condition of possibility, for the drama of the world. A moment of negative theology must thus precede the affirmation of an eternal foundation. The whole history of freedom and covenant is made possible by the primordial otherness-distance of the Father and the Son, the foundation of the otherness-distance of creatures, consumed on the cross. To the question, "Why is the cross the proper place of the trinitarian unveiling in Hans Urs von Balthasar?" I ultimately answer: so that every separation from God through created freedom might be reconcilable in God the Trinity, where infinite distance is eternally reconciled.[9]

Competing Analogies and Scriptural Foundations

Balthasar's option for the cross as the quintessential place for Trinitarian epiphany can be questioned (rather than challenged) on several points: the relationship between concepts and metaphors; the supposition of an archetypal eternal drama of the cross; the theological status of an immanent law of love; and the scriptural foundation of an eternal kenosis proper to each divine Person. Such points of discussion have in common that they ultimately involve theologico-epistemological presuppositions. In other words, they come under the subject of knowing how this or that theology can account for its way of progressing in knowledge and making intellectual decisions. I will treat the last two points together.

Balthasar has distanced himself from the Augustinian analogy, and that is legitimate and well-founded. He is right to underscore the difficulty of rigorously anchoring such an analogy in the New Testament. Given the almost autonomous development of the Augustinian *analogon* in medieval scholasticism, there was cause for concern. To safeguard the right function of the triads

---

8. This is confirmed by Hans Urs von Balthasar in *TD* 5, 95.

9. As a counterpoint, Martin Bieler has brought to my awareness the dependence of Balthasar on Ferdinand Ulrich regarding another logic: "separation" (*Trennung*) as a condition for a relation of the recipient of a gift to the giver. See Ferdinand Ulrich, *Leben in der Einheit von Leben und Tod*, in *Schriften*, vol. II, ed. Martin Bieler and Stefan Oster (Freiburg i.B.: Johannes Verlag, 1999), 71–72.

mind-knowledge-love or memory-intellect-will in the Western tradition, it is, however, useful to issue two reminders, which do not erase the real problem:

- In Augustine, triads are first and foremost mere likenesses illustrating how three figures can at the same time be consubstantial and relative, distinct and inseparable. The use of these illustrations is not primarily oriented toward the identification of each term with one of the three Persons.[10]
- In Thomas Aquinas, the reprise of the Augustinian likeness has a precise and limited function: beginning with the natural sequence between knowledge and love, to conceive a real order and a relation of origin between the Spirit and the Son, so as to envision theologically their real distinction.[11]

In other words, neither in Augustine nor in Thomas is the Augustinian analogy supposed to acquire a descriptive function of the immanent life of the Trinity. This, however, leaves the whole objection concerning the lack of a scriptural foundation for the analogy.

It is true that to envision the whole Trinitarian unfolding, both economic and immanent, in terms of love seems more in conformity with the New Testament (at the very least with the Johannine literature). Balthasar is probably right to want to reimagine the Trinity as love. One must be aware, however, that he creates a Balthasarian *analogon*, competing with the Augustinian *analogon* and exposed to the same risk.

We could call it the law of extreme love that gives itself: plenitude or excess, abandonment or kenosis, and envelopment. It is thus that Balthasar gives an account of the Father's love before showing that the Son and the Spirit live in turn, in an original way, their own abandonment or kenosis. In this way, the Trinitarian person is fundamentally conceived as a being in kenotic relation. Yes, it is quite possible that extreme human love almost always involves this kind of relation. However, is it a fitting analogy for approaching the love inside the life of the Trinity?

Thus, we see here the question of scriptural foundation. The Johannine literature clearly expresses that the love of the Father is manifested by the Son and that it is extended in the fraternal life of the disciples, inhabited by the Spirit of truth (see 1 Jn 4). The conceptual transition from such an economy of manifested love to an understanding of the immanent life of the Trinity in terms of love (and what is more, as kenotic love) is not immediately obvious. That amounts to a free creation comparable to that of the Augustinian *analogon*.

---

10. See Augustine, *De trin.* 4.30, 9.4–8.

11. See Aquinas, *ST* 1.27,3, ad 3.

The main criterion for receiving or not receiving a kenotic theology of the immanent Trinity should be, in my view, the quality of its scriptural foundation. In this regard, it is instructive to reread the section entitled "Kenosis" in *The Glory of the Lord: The New Covenant*. The problem raised is as follows. The identification of Christ with the condition of sin supposes a prior divine decision that pertains to the preexistent Son. To show that an "abandonment of the *forma Dei*" is possible, Balthasar rules out a first explanation based on the power that the divine nature would have to render itself powerless because he favors another explanatory path, directly based on the interpersonal relations in God the Trinity.[12] Immediately, Balthasar refers to Bulgakov's intuition that the foundation of everything is "the selflessness [*Selbstlosigkeit*] of the divine persons, as of pure relations in the love within the Godhead." This is translated as creative kenosis, at the risk of created freedom, carried to its climax by the kenosis of the cross. And so returns the Trinitarian epiphany already exposited: "the Spirit . . . uniting them now only in the expressive form of the separation [*Trennung*]."[13]

The cross is thus silhouetted in the creative kenosis itself. However, Balthasar immediately challenges the idea that the kenosis of God would merely be the amplification of some intramundane law. It is indeed necessary to safeguard the nonnecessity of the kenosis of God in the economy of salvation. It is only because God has actually lowered himself that we can recognize that such an economy in fact corresponds to his own essence, that is, to the immanent life of the Trinity where the Persons are in a kenotic relationship.

God can seek out and save the created freedom that wrecks itself into nothingness because he is already, in the person of the Son, "the emptiness of love's absolute obedience for the unconditional command."[14] The humanity of Jesus, however, is not from its origin identified with the suffering of the cross. It is led there through a true human life of full availability, although its entire existence be determined by the kenosis of God, attested in Philippians 2:7 and Romans 8:3 (by allusion).

Thus, the sole scriptural foundation for the "kenosis of God" is found at the outcome of theological reasoning, once the being-in-relation of the divine Persons has been qualified as kenotic by recourse to other references. This poses two serious questions: Is the Balthasarian *analogon* of extreme love as a kenotic relationship theologically valuable by itself, in an autonomous fashion? And does the kenosis of Philippians 2:7 found not only a kenosis of the Son in view of the cross but also a kenosis of the Father, the Son, and the

---

12. See *GL 7*, 211–28; Sergei Bulgakov, *The Lamb of God*, trans. Boris Jakim (Grand Rapids, MI: Eerdmans, 2008).

13. *GL 7*, 214.

14. *GL 7*, 214, 216.

Spirit in the immanent life of the Trinity? I will leave the first question to qualified interpreters of Hans Urs Balthasar. I will try to shed light only on the second question, which to my eyes seems even more decisive.

THE BACKGROUND DECISION BETWEEN TWO TYPES OF CHRISTOLOGIES

There are two basic options in Christology. I call them the Chalcedonian paradigm and the ascending path.[15] The Chalcedonian paradigm holds the unity of the subject Christ and the duality of natures in the form of a paradox. The human nature and the divine nature of Christ are not in a direct relationship of transparency or correspondence. They are incommensurable and are united by the one subject of subsistence and operation who is the Son of God in history. The divine nature is the proper nature of the Son, while the human nature is really appropriated to him as being assumed. In such a perspective, the conditions and properties of Christ in his humanity maintain a paradoxical relationship to the properties of his divinity: impassible, he is nevertheless passible; eternal, he is nevertheless mortal; omnipotent, he is nevertheless reduced to impotence, etc. Impassibility is not revealed in passibility. There are two distinct sources of knowledge that are combined by way of paradox in Christology: on one hand, a biblico-metaphysical doctrine of the names and attributes of God,[16] and on the other hand, the teaching of the whole economy of the Son in the flesh.

Such a paradigm was overthrown by Martin Luther, based on his reflection on the Eucharist. The divinity of the Son is not recognized or predefined from any other source than his flesh. Only the abased humanity of the Son gives access to the proper content of his divinity. This is not in conformity with a divine essence knowable in advance. Through the economy of the Son in the flesh, what is proper to his divinity is unveiled or reflected in transparency. The divinity of the Son is abasement, obedience, consent, etc. In this way, the humanity and divinity of Christ no longer maintain an indirect and paradoxical relationship. They are in a relation of correspondence and fittingness. Initiated by Luther,[17] such a Christology of corre-

---

15. For a development of the genesis and the consequences of these two options, see Emmanuel Durand, *L'Offre universelle du salut en Christ* (Paris: Les éditions du Cerf, 2012), 213–39.

16. See Janet M. Soskice, "Athens and Jerusalem, Alexandria and Edessa. Is there a Metaphysics of Scripture?" *International Journal of Systematic Theology* 8 (2006): 149–62; see also Matthew Levering, *Scripture and Metaphysics: Aquinas and the Renewal of Trinitarian Theology* (Oxford: Blackwell, 2004), 23–74, 110–43.

17. See Martin Luther, *Disputatio Heidelbergae habita*, props. 19–22, in *Weimarer Ausgabe* I (Weimar: Böhlau, 1883), 354.

spondence was brilliantly implemented by Karl Barth in paragraph 59 of his *Church Dogmatics* IV/1, dealing with the kenotic obedience of the Son of God.

As we have seen, Balthasar does not really seek to found his conception of the kenotic being of each of the three divine Persons, beginning with the Father, on the kenosis of the Son of God, attested by Philippians 2:7. To rise from the kenotic state of Christ in the flesh to the kenotic being of God is then an implementation of the ascending path such as I have qualified it. The kenotic obedience of Christ is the direct revelation of his kenotic being as Son in the bosom of the immanent Trinity. Such an assertion is possible, but going any further is not justified. Even in the logic of the ascending path, the kenosis of Philippians 2:7 does not allow us to affirm that the Father himself is the abandonment of self in his singular manner of being a person. It is divinity such as it is possessed and exercised by the Son that is revealed in the abased humanity of Jesus and not the divinity or the being-a-person of just any of the three divine Persons. In my view, the *Urkenosis* of the Father remains completely unfounded on the scriptural level.

Having confronted the Augustinian *analogon* and the Balthasarian *analogon*, some conclusions can be formulated:

- On a scriptural level, the Balthasarian *analogon* is no better founded than the Augustinian *analogon*.
- These are, in reality, two competing speculative developments. Their validity is rather to be sought in their reception and their fruitfulness.
- The fruitfulness of the Augustinian *analogon* is widely demonstrated, notably by its capacity to found a real participation of human beings in the Trinitarian life.
- The reception of the Balthasarian *analogon* is still in progress, as the debate attests.

Up to this point, I have argued especially with Hans Urs von Balthasar. Can we, drawing support from Thomas Aquinas, provide a different treatment of the initial question concerning proper places of Trinitarian attestation, also posing to ourselves the question of the nature of such an attestation: Is it a manifestation or an inference? If it is a manifestation, is it for both the senses and the mind? Under what objective and subjective conditions?

The Trinitarian Function of the Mysteries of Jesus: Revelation or Manifestation?

Let us then return to our initial question. We were asking what the proper places are of Trinitarian attestation in the mysteries of Jesus. The vocabulary of the attestation here remains relatively indeterminate, while suggesting a preliminary knowledge of the Trinity. Augustine includes in the economy of Trinitarian revelation all the manifestations proper to one of the three, situated between birth and Pentecost. For his part, Balthasar places the emphasis on the cross, then Resurrection as the Trinitarian revelation of the distance between the Father and the Son carried in the Spirit of communion.

Additional light can be drawn from the treatise on the life of Jesus by Thomas Aquinas (*ST* III, qq. 27–59). When he treats this or that mystery, Aquinas willingly points out the personal implication of the Spirit, the Son, or the Father. In the mysteries of the childhood, the Spirit is often invoked as an actor. It is with respect to the birth and the baptism that Aquinas tackles in the most direct way an economy of manifestation. It is striking that he then speaks of manifestation (*manifestare, manifestatio*) and not of revelation (*revelare, revelatio*).[18]

Concerning the manifestation of Christ by his birth, Aquinas distinguishes three kinds of manifestations, when he considers the role of the angels and the star.[19] As a general rule, the manifestation occurs through the mediations closest to the addressees. For the righteous, the truth is taught from within through the inspiration of the Spirit of prophecy, without manifestation by sensible sign, as was the case with Anna and Simeon. For the pagans, sensible signs are, by contrast, required and adapted to their own conditions, like the star intended for Magi, who Aquinas thinks were astronomers. For the Jews, finally, the angels are regular messengers to whom they were accustomed, including for the eminent gift of the Law.

In the strict sense, revelation refers to the interior teaching of salvific truth to be believed, brought about by the inspiration of the Holy Spirit. Manifestation requires observers to rise from signs to the truth, while revelation offers the divine truth to the adherence of living faith through the interior action of the Spirit. In the natural order, a sign can maintain proportion to the truth it manifests. In the supernatural order, such a proportion could not exist.[20] The signs become effective only when they encounter in the witnesses an interior perception in faith of the truth manifested by the

---

18. See Etienne Vetö, *Du Christ à la Trinité. Penser les Mystères du Christ après Thomas d'Aquin et Balthasar* (Paris: Cerf, 2012), 98–104. Vetö considers Aquinas's opting for mere manifestation as a limitation of his system. A close study of Aquinas's works would nevertheless show that revelation and manifestation are not sharply divided and, indeed, sometimes overlap.

19. See Aquinas, *ST* 3.36.5 co., with Jean-Pierre Torrell, *Encyclopédie Jésus le Christ chez saint Thomas d'Aquin* (Paris: Cerf: 2008), 609n69.

20. See Aquinas, *ST* 3.39.8, ad 2, concerning the difference in nature between the voice and the Father, the humanity and the Son, and the dove and the Spirit, although these are manifestations proper to each of the three.

signs. In this way, the economy of manifestation by signs is relative to an economy of interior revelation by the Spirit.

In the Trinitarian economy, this translates as follows. The mysteries of Jesus are privileged places for a Trinitarian manifestation in the proper sense, especially in the time of his childhood and baptism, but such a manifestation presupposes an adherence in faith to God the Trinity, made possible through an interior inspiration by the Holy Spirit. Now, such an interior event of inspiration and recognition is precisely what we call a Trinitarian revelation in the proper sense. In this respect, our own epistemic conditions in general differ from those of Jesus' own contemporaries, for they had to be driven from his manifold manifestation—mainly, the words and deeds he performed in his humanity—to the internal revelation of his identity, whereas we are usually led from that interior revelation—mediated by being initiated into the rule of faith—to the contemplation of the Lord's manifestations.

From this perspective, it is not appropriate to rummage through the mysteries of Jesus to look for the perfect moment where the Trinity would reveal itself for the first time in a clear and unmistakable way. Rather, we must recognize that all the mysteries of Jesus are marked by a Trinitarian manifestation for the one who benefits from Trinitarian revelation. Through Christian initiation and the tradition of the rule of faith, revelation is, from our perspective, prior to the economy of manifestation. It is because believers receive the interior inspiration of the Spirit (the *lumen fidei*, and possibly the *lumen propheticum*) and the tradition of Trinitarian faith that the successive events of the life of Jesus become for them a Trinitarian manifestation adjusted to revelation. In my view, the Trinitarian rule of faith handed on by Augustine illustrates such a link between Trinitarian revelation and Trinitarian manifestation.

An Inversion of the Relationship between Light and Form or Figure

Compared to the theology of faith and prophecy established by Thomas Aquinas, Hans Urs von Balthasar has consciously inverted the relationship between *lumen* and *species*, light and form. This is very clear and recurrent in *The Glory of the Lord: Seeing the Form*. In Aquinas, the *lumen* (of faith or prophecy) is the power of supernatural illumination without which no form or figure can become revelation. The proper angle of revelation always comes from a new *lumen* bestowed by the Holy Spirit in the intimacy of the human intellect thus elevated. In Balthasar, the *lumen* is deliberately rendered relative to the objective evidence of the figure (the *Gestalt* taking over from the *species*). In favor of his theological aesthetics, the Swiss theologian knows perfectly well that he is inverting the order of priority formerly established by Thomas Aquinas between *lumen* and *species*.[21] There is an epistemological coherence proper to Balthasar's theological project, and it underlies the project's progressive focusing of Trinitarian revelation on objective evidence of the Trinitarian drama of the cross.

According to the theology of faith and prophecy of Thomas Aquinas, it would be futile to seek to identify the first moment of Trinitarian revelation. There is always an anteriority of Trinitarian faith, a response to the interior revelation by the Spirit, to the Trinitarian epiphany really attested in the life and Passover of Jesus. For us wayfaring pilgrims, it is not yet a question of seeing God the Trinity but of believing in him and, consequently, of contemplating him in rich signs in the life and Passover of Jesus. From his birth to Pentecost, we recognize that Jesus is the center of a Trinitarian epiphany precisely because his very identity is relational. He unceasingly presented himself to human beings as the one sent by the Father and as the herald of the Spirit, whom he finally poured out.

BIBLIOGRAPHY

Balthasar, Hans Urs von. "Kommentar." In *Besondere Gnadengabe und die zwei meschlichen Lebens,* 250–472. Berlin: De Gruyter, 1954.

Bulgakov, Sergei. *The Lamb of God.* Translated by Boris Jakim. Grand Rapids, MI: Eerdmans, 2008.

Durand, Emmanuel. *L'offre universelle du salut en Christ.* Paris: Les éditions du Cerf, 2012.

Holzer, Vincent. *Hans Urs Von Balthasar 1905–1988.* Paris: Cerf, 2012.

Ide, Pascal. *Une Théologie de l'Amour. L'amour, centre de la* Trilogie *de Hans Urs von Balthasar.* Brussels: Lessius, 2012.

———. *Une Théo-logique du Don. Le don dans la "Trilogie" de Hans Urs von Balthasar.* Leuven: Peeters, 2013.

Levering, Matthew. *Scripture and Metaphysics: Aquinas and the Renewal of Trinitarian Theology.* Oxford: Blackwell, 2004.

Luther, Martin. *Disputatio Heidelbergae habita.* In *Weimarer Ausgabe* I. Weimar: Böhlau, 1883.

Schumacher, Michele M. *A Trinitarian Anthropology: Adrienne von Speyr and Hans Urs von Balthasar in Dialogue with Thomas Aquinas.* Washington, DC: The Catholic University of America Press, 2014.

---

21. See *GL* 1, 118–19, 151, and 177–78. Balthasar knows all the more what he is doing, given that he commented in detail on Thomas Aquinas's treatise on prophecy: see Hans Urs von Balthasar, "Kommentar," in Thomas von Aquin, *Besondere Gnadengabe und die zwei meschlichen Lebens* (Heidelberg: Die deutsche Thomas-Ausgabe, 1954), 250–472.

Soskice, Janet M. "Athens and Jerusalem, Alexandria and Edessa. Is there a Metaphysics of Scripture?" *International Journal of Systematic Theology* 8 (2006): 149–62.

Torrell, Jean-Pierre. *Encyclopédie: Jésus le Christ chez saint Thomas d'Aquin.* Paris: Cerf: 2008.

Ulrich, Ferdinand. *Leben in der Einheit von Leben und Tod.* In *Schriften*, vol. II, edited by Martin Bieler and Stefan Oster. Freiburg im Breisgau: Johannes Verlag, 1999.

Vetö, Etienne. *Du Christ à la Trinité. Penser les Mystères du Christ après Thomas d'Aquin et Balthasar.* Paris: Cerf, 2012.

CHAPTER 8

Balthasar and St. Thomas on the Trinity

MICHELE M. SCHUMACHER

FOR THOSE OF US WHO STUDIED THEOLOGY during the long pontificate of St. John Paul II (1978–2005)—at least for those of us who read him regularly—one passage of the Second Vatican Council remains almost engrained in our minds, acting as a common point of reference not only for Christian anthropology and ethics but also for theology, properly speaking. That passage—"of course"—is *Gaudium et Spes*, no. 24[1]:

> Indeed, the Lord Jesus, when he prayed to the Father, "that all may be one. . . . as we are one" (Jn 17:21–22) opened up vistas closed to human reason, for he implied a certain likeness between the union of the divine Persons, and the unity of God's sons in truth and charity. This likeness reveals that man, who is the only creature on earth which God willed for itself, cannot fully find himself except through a sincere gift of himself (cf. Lk 17:33).

Because the "model for this interpretation of the person"—as "achieved *'through a sincere gift of self'*"—is, as Pope John Paul II commented upon this passage, "God himself as Trinity, as a communion of Persons,"[2] it was simply taken for granted for many of us that the God who reveals himself as "love" (cf. 1 Jn 4:8, 16) is "a mystery of personal loving communion,"[3] which is to say that "the Three Persons love each other in the intimate mystery of the one divine life." We unquestionably took John Paul at his word when he wrote: "Only in this way [in the presentation of the three divine persons as 'lov[ing] each other in the intimate mystery of the one divine life'] can we

---

1. See Pascale Ide, "Une théologie du don. Les occurrences de *Gaudium et spes*, nr. 24, § 3 chez Jean-Paul II," *Anthropotes* 17, no. 1(2001): 149–78; 17, no. 2 (2001): 313–44.

2. John Paul II, *Mulieris Dignitatem*, Apostolic Letter on the Dignity and Vocation of Women (August 15, 1988), no. 7.

3. John Paul II, *Familiaris Consorti*, Apostolic Exhortation on the Role of the Family in the Modern World (November 22, 1981), no. 11.

159

understand the truth that God in himself is love."[4] We were, moreover, exonerated when the Catechism, too, presented "God's very being" as "love": "By sending his only Son and the Spirit of Love in the fullness of time, God has revealed his innermost secret: God himself is an eternal exchange of love, Father, Son, and Holy Spirit, and he has destined us to share in the exchange" (no. 221; cf. nos. 2331, 2205).

From this particular image of the Trinity and our destined participation therein, it is a short step to the affirmation of Hans Urs von Balthasar, borrowed from Gregory the Great, that love "can only be *agape, caritas,* if it reaches out toward the other. . . . Where God is defined as love, he must be in essence perfect self-giving, which can only elicit from the Beloved, in return, an equally perfect movement of thanksgiving, service and self-giving."[5] More foreign to us—ironically enough, given the importance that it assumed throughout most of the western Christian tradition—was the Augustinian analogy of the Trinity drawn from human psychology (*mens, notitia, amor*) and inspiring the analogy of Aquinas: "the intelligible word . . . proceeds from the speaker, yet remains in him" (*ST* I, 27, a. 1), and love proceeds from the will, without its object ever wandering from the lover's heart (*ST* I, a. 3; q. 37, a. 1).

Having been captivated by John Paul II's phenomenological realism, which pointed a way beyond the "gnosiological attitude"[6] that had reigned for centuries in philosophy and more recently in theology, we were unlikely to subscribe to an analogy that seemed to draw upon a self-referential view of knowledge and will. Despite all due regard for the "greater dissimilitude" (DS 806) than similitude implied in any analogical discourse about God, it was, to be more specific, the necessarily immanent character of the Augustinian-Thomistic analogy that failed to address a generation vaccinated against enlightenment epistemologies. Still captivated by the lingering influence of nominalism, however, and (all too easily) misunderstanding John Paul II's personalism, we were struck by the disparity between Aquinas's analogy of God—*in the* admittedly *limited manner in which it was understood*—and the call launched by the Council and so persistently by John Paul II to pattern our relationships and the mode of our self-fulfillment after the self-giving love

---

4. John Paul II, *Mulieris Dignitatem,* no. 7.

5. *TD* 5, 82 (*Theodramatik* IV. *Das Endspiel* [Einsiedeln: Johannes Verlag, 1983], 71, 72: "Und dies erhellt gemäß der Offenbarung daraus daß Gott die Liebe ist, die nach dem Satz Gregors des Grossen *agape, caritas* nur sein kann, wenn sie auf den andern hinstrebt. . . . Wohingegen Gott als Liebe definiert wird, muß er in sich vollkommene Hingabe seiner selbst sein, was von seiten des Geliebten nur mit ebenso vollkommener Rückwendung in Dank, Verfügbarkeit, Hingabe beantwortet werden kann.").

6. Karol Wojtyła, *Person and Community, Selected Essays,* trans. Theresa Sandok (New York: Peter Lang, 1993), 226.

of the divine persons. It was, at any rate, obvious to us that the "plentitude" of divine being "requires," as Balthasar reasoned, "the reciprocal ecstasy of the [divine] 'Persons' in order to unfold itself as absolute love and, in doing so, as absolute truth."[7] "Love," we heartedly agreed, "supposes the one, the other and their unity."[8]

St. Thomas's Analogy of the Trinity: Personalist and Essentialist

Of course, when St. Thomas presents the procession of the Word from the Father in his own version of the Augustinian analogy, he has in mind—to complete the analogy as it bears upon the procession of the Holy Spirit—that this is "not any sort of word, but one Who breathes forth Love" (*ST* I, q. 43, a. 5, ad 2). To see it otherwise would be to call into question the value of the analogy itself, for the processions are distinguished by their order: the Son proceeds from the Father, while the Spirit proceeds from the Father and the Son. Hence, although St. Thomas admits that "will and intellect are not diverse in God," he nonetheless insists upon the analogy whereby "nothing can be loved by the will unless it is conceived in the intellect" as pointing to this Trinitarian order (*ST* I, q. 27, a. 3, ad 3).[9] "From the very fact of saying that the Holy Spirit proceeds by way of will and the Son by way of intellect it follows that the Holy Spirit is from the Son. For love proceeds from a word: we are able to love nothing but that which a word of the heart conceives" (*SCG* IV, chap. 24, no. 3617).

Not only does this analogy of "a Word breathing love" illuminate the mystery of the divine processions, it also serves to describe the "intellectual illumination [of the believer, caused by the revealed Word of God], which breaks forth into the affection of love, as is said (Jn 6:45): *Everyone that hath heard from the Father and hath learned cometh to Me.*" Hence, to perceive the Word of God, as such—to recognize its divine origin—"implies a certain experimental knowledge," which is "properly called wisdom" (*ST* I, q. 43, a. 5, ad 2). The Word-made-flesh thus initiates the faithful into two sorts of knowledge, as St. Thomas explains in his commentary of John 17:26:

---

7. *TL* 5, 180 (*Theologik* II. *Wahrheit Gottes* [Einsiedeln: Johannesverlag, 1985], 165: "der gegenseitigen Ekstasis der 'Personen' bedarf, um als absolute Liebe und darin als schlechthinnige Wahrheit sich auszufalten").

8. *MW*, 118 (*Mein Werk—Durchblicke* [Einsiedeln: Johannes Verlag, 1990], 96: "die Liebe den Einen, den Andern und ihre Einheit voraussetzt").

9. St. Thomas continues: "the procession of love [in God] occurs in due order as regards the procession of the Word" (*ST* I, q. 27, a. 3, ad 3; see also q. 27, a. 4, ad 1). On the distinction of the divine persons according to origin or, rather, relations of origin, see also q. 40, a. 2.

> First, is that of doctrine, and he refers to this by saying, *I have made known to them your name,* teaching them by my external words: *no man has ever seen God: the only begotten Son, who is in the bosom of the Father, has made him known* (John 1:18). . . . The other knowledge is from within, through the Holy Spirit. . . . The fruit of this knowledge is *that the love wherewith you loved me; may be in them, and I in them.* (*In Ioan.* c. 17, lect. 6, no. 2269, 2270)

In short, as Dominic Legge explains, "sanctifying knowledge of the truth accounts for the indwelling of the Son and, consequently, for the gift and indwelling of the Holy Spirit."[10] For where there is the Word of God, there is also necessarily the Spirit of God, whose name is "Love" (*ST* I, q. 37) or "Gift" (q. 38).

St. Thomas thus recognizes that his psychological analogy of the Trinity is best understood by one who has been initiated into the holy mystery: by one in whom God is present "as the object known is in the knower, and the beloved in the lover" (*ST* I, q. 43, a. 3; cf. q. 37, a. 1). It is, in other words, by participating in the processions themselves—by knowing as God knows, namely, by the impression of his Word within the intellect, and by loving as God loves, in virtue of the indwelling of the Holy Spirit—that one can finally be said to know the love of God (cf. *ST* I, q. 93, a. 6). "I, your Word, will be in them; and by the fact that I am in them," St. Thomas comments, *"the love wherewith you love me may be in them,* that is, will be given to them, and you will love them as you have loved me" (*In Ioan.,* c. 17, lect. 6, no. 2270). Or, as Gilles Emery explains, "the Love through which both Father and Son are together one is also the Love through which they net us into their communion."[11]

The genius of St. Thomas is such that he thus employs the same analogy (the correlation of knowledge and will) to illustrate the mystery of the Holy Trinity and the Christian's initiation therein: his or her graced participation in the Trinitarian processions, which presupposes man's spiritual nature. For "as the uncreated Trinity is distinguished by the procession of the Word from the Speaker, and of Love from both of these," so also, St. Thomas explains, does there exist "an image of the uncreated Trinity" in the rational creature "wherein we find a procession of the word in the intellect, and a procession of the love in the will" (*ST* I, q. 93, a. 6). Because, moreover, "the Word of God is born of God according to the knowledge of Himself; and Love proceeds from God according as he loves himself . . . the image of God is found in the soul according as the soul turns to God, or possesses a nature that

---

10. Dominic Legge, *The Trinitarian Christology of St. Thomas Aquinas* (Oxford: Oxford University Press, 2017), 230.

11. Gilles Emery, *The Trinitarian Theology of St. Thomas Aquinas,* trans. Francesca Murphy (Oxford: Oxford University Press, 2007), 340. Cf. *ST* I, q. 37, a. 2 c; ad 3.

enables it to be drawn to God" (a. 8). It follows that, "human intellect and will are shown" by St. Thomas, as Anna Williams perceives, "to have been fashioned on the basis of deifying intentions."[12] Hence, as Jean-Pierre Torrell puts it so well, creation "is not external to, but at the heart of the Trinitarian communion," that is to say, "of the *circulatio* that passes from the Father through the Son and returns toward him, through and in the Spirit, in drawing the universe into his love [cf. *ST* I, q. 38, a. 2]."[13]

The Regretful Overshadowing of Trinitarian "Personalism" by Essentialism

Clearly, such a personal, even mystical, vision of the Trinity appears far from the cold and calculated idea of God—more philosophical than theological, Balthasar explains[14]—as a perfectly self-contained monism who understands and loves himself and all else on account of his own goodness. Such, as André Malet described the common impression of St. Thomas's teaching in 1954, is a sort of "*Urgottheit* [original divinity]" from which "gushes forth the triune God."[15] Indeed, for the reader who picks up the *Summa* for the first time—assuming that this is his first introduction—God is encountered as One (!), whose love is evident in this: he has will. For "in whomsoever there is will," Thomas reasons, "there must also be love" (*ST* I, q. 20, a. 1), and "there must be will in God, since there is intellect in Him." After all, "will follows upon intellect" (*ST* I, q. 19, a. 1). As for the "seductive power"[16] of the Augustinian presentation of love as a binding force, it is taken by St. Thomas to mean—at least in the first instance[17]—that the good that God "wills for Himself, is no other than Himself, Who is good by His essence" (*ST* I, q. 20, a. 1, ad 3). Indeed, divine beatitude consists in God's perfect knowledge of himself (cf. *ST* I, q. 26).

Such an apparently solipsistic vision of God is not necessarily dispelled, moreover, when one enters more properly into Thomas's treatise on the Trinity, for the immanent processions are brilliantly crafted in view of maintaining

---

12. Anna N. Williams, "Deification in the *Summa theologiae*: A Structural Interpretation of the *Prima Pars*," *The Thomist* 61 (1997): 219–55, at 254.

13. Jean-Pierre Torrell, *Saint Thomas Aquinas*, II: *Spiritual Master*, trans. Robert Royal (Washington, DC: The Catholic University of America Press, 2003), 90; see also Emery, *The Trinitarian Theology of St. Thomas Aquinas*, 358.

14. See *KB*, 262–65 (*Karl Barth: Darstellung und Deutung seiner Theologie* [Einsiedeln: Johannes Verlag, 1976], 275–77).

15. André Malet, "La synthèse de la personne et de la nature dans la théologie trinitaire de saint Thomas," *Revue thomiste* 54, no. 3 (1954): 483–522, at 484.

16. Torrell, *St. Thomas, Spiritual Master*, 184.

17. For a more properly Trinitarian instance of the image, see *ST* I, q. 37, a. 1, ad 3.

the divine unity (cf. *ST* I, q. 27, a. 3); whence our return to the idea of a God who loves himself: "when anyone understands and loves himself he is in himself, not only by real identity but also as the object understood is in the one who understands, and the thing loved is in the lover" (*ST* I, q. 37, a. 1). To be sure, the mutual love between the Father and Son in the Holy Spirit is not entirely lacking (cf. *ST* I, q. 37, a. 1, ad 3; q. 36, a. 4, ad 1), nor is the rich mystical and biblical doctrine of the circumincession (cf. *ST* I, q. 42, a. 5), which is arguably at the heart of his Trinitarian theology.[18] Apparently—if not intentionally[19]—absent in his Trinitarian theology is nonetheless the ecstatic character of love that is developed in his treatise on the virtues, for example (cf. *ST* I-II, q. 28, aa. 3, 4), for it is "not admissible to say that God is placed outside of Himself" (*ST* I, q. 20, a. 2, obj. 1).[20] To be sure, St. Thomas does invoke the force of love "to move and impel the will of the lover towards the object loved" in his account of the name chosen for the Holy Spirit. Because *spirit* designates "impulse and motion" (*ST* I, q. 36, a. 1) in corporeal things, it is fitting that the One who proceeds from love should be so named, he reasons. We could hardly be further from Balthasar's own argument that "if God is defined as love, he must be so not only in an 'intransitive' sense but [he] must [also] love the [divine] Other 'transitively.'"[21]

Similarly, given the immanent structure of the Word within St. Thomas's Trinitarian theology, "Word" is not to be understood dialogically: that is to say, as analogical to the manner whereby the human spirit "goes beyond subjectivity and reaches out to other persons" in view of "communion and mutual intercourse," as Balthasar proposes in his own analogy, as influenced by Adrienne von Speyr.[22] Instead, by "word" is meant in St. Thomas's analogy of the

---

18. See chapter 12 of Gilles Emery's *The Trinitarian Theology of St. Thomas Aquinas*, 298–311; Emmanuel Durand, *La périchorèse des personnes divines: Immanence mutuelle. Réciprocité et communion, préface par Vincent Holzer* (coll. *Cogitatio Fidei*, 243) (Paris, Cerf, 2005).

19. St. Thomas's presentation of the Spirit's procession by love is recognized by Gilles Emery as drawing upon the idea of love's gravitational pull, whereby the beloved is "present in a dynamic mode." For "love carries the will outside of itself toward the beloved good." The Swiss Dominican nonetheless admits that "St. Thomas himself did not always put it forward as clearly as this (Emery, *The Trinitarian Theology of St. Thomas Aquinas*, 66, 67).

20. For a thorough explanation of St. Thomas's preference for the psychological model of the Trinity over the interpersonal model of mutual love, see Emery, *The Trinitarian Theology of St. Thomas Aquinas*, 233–45.

21. *TD* 5, 82 (*Theodramatik* IV. *Das Endspiel*, 71–72: "Aber wenn Gott Liebe sein soll, kann er es nicht nur intransitive sein, sondern er muß auch transitive den Je-Andern lieben.").

22. *ET* 1, 81 (*Verbum Caro, Skizzen zur Theologie* I [Einsiedeln: Johannes Verlag, 1960], 86: "er ja schon die Subjektivität überstiegen hat zum Du (grundsätzlich jedem Du) und als Intersubjektivität existiert. Er ist Kommunion und Austausch"). See also

Trinity that which is uttered internally by the spirit and signified by the vocal word: an interior word, or "a conception of the object understood." From Balthasar's perspective, however, any such "word of the heart" (*ST* I, q. 27, a. 1) must assume a transitive mode if it is to be an authentic word *of love*: "The *verbum mentis* that has its source in inmost being, and the love that causes and accompanies it, do not turn the person in on himself (as a superficial interpretation of Augustine's *imago trinitatis* might lead one to think), but rather reveal the mystery of being through the mutuality of knowledge in love."[23] In short, if we are to take seriously the scriptural affirmation that "God is love" (1 Jn 4:8, 16), this love "must presuppose," Balthasar argues, "not numerical, but transcendental plurality": that is to say, "if it is to go beyond mere self-love (*dilectio*) and become *caritas*—the highest of the perfections created by God and which is found supereminently in him."[24]

This is not to suggest that Balthasar would have us simply substitute the interpersonal model of the Trinity, as proposed by Richard of St. Victor, for example, since he recognizes that it "cannot attain the substantial unity of God."[25] On the other hand, he does call into question St. Thomas's decision to order the processions according to the principle that something cannot be loved unless it is known (cf. *ST* I, q. 27, a. 3, ad 3). This, Balthasar argues— ironically enough, given the quantity of similar criticisms launched at his own theology on precisely this point[26]—is simply "an importation from the created order into the divine world."[27]

Michele M. Schumacher, *A Trinitarian Anthropology: Adrienne von Speyr & Hans Urs von Balthasar in Dialogue with Thomas Aquinas* (Washington, DC: The Catholic University of America Press, 2014), 41–63, 366–71.

23. *ET* 1, 81 (*Verbum Caro*, 86–87: "das Verbum Mentis, das im innersten Sein entspringt, und die Liebe, die es entspringen lässt und begleitet, nicht etwas ist, was die Person solipsistisch auf sich zurückbiegt (wie eine oberflächliche Deutung der Imago Trinitatis bei Augustin glauben machen könnte), sondern das Seinsgeheimnis selbst in der Gegenseitigkeit der Bewusstheit in der Liebe eröffnet.").

24. *TL* 3, 217–18 (*Theologik* III, *Der Geist der Wahrheit* [Einsiedeln: Johannes Verlag, 1987], 199: "wenn keine zahlenhafte, so doch transzendentale Vielheit voraussetzt, wenn sie bloße Selbstliebe (*dilectio*) in *caritas*—die höchste der von Gott geschaffenen Vollkommenheiten, die ihm eminent zukommen muss—übersteigen soll."). See also *TL* 2, 39–42; 82. Cf. Augustine, *De Trinitate* VIII, chap. 8, 12; Aquinas, *De Pot* 9,9.

25. *TL* 2, 38 (*Theologik* II, 35: "kann die substantielle Einheit Gottes nicht erreichen.").

26. See Schumacher, *A Trinitianarian Anthropology*, 310–56, 376–83; "Criticisms of Balthasar's Theology," in *The Oxford Handbook of Hans Urs von Balthasar*, ed. Mark J. McInroy, Anthony Sciglitano, and Cyril O'Reagan (Oxford: Oxford University Press, 2023), forthcoming.

27. *TL* 2, 162 (*Theologik* II, 149: "etwas aus der geschöpflichen in die göttliche Welt hinein Getragenes."); see also 164.

There is an order here: love presupposes knowledge, while knowledge presupposes being. But the love that stands at the end of the sequence as the goal of its unfolding stands, in another perspective, at its beginning as the basic impulse underlying it [*ST* I, q. 5, a. 2, ad 1]. Eternity is a circulation in which beginning and end join in unity. By the same token, everything that has a ground, every truth claim that needs grounding, occurs within this order, but the order itself is sustained by the ultimate ground, which is love. To be sure, God is eternal truth and by this truth all other things are true and meaningful. But the very existence of truth, of eternal truth, is grounded in love.[28]

THE CHRISTOLOGICAL REVELATION OF THE GOD OF LOVE

Herein might be discerned Balthasar's primary concern: defending the specifically Christian revelation that "God is love" (1 Jn 4:8, 16), as revealed in the "indissoluble unity of the figure of Jesus."[29] "Eternal Love is not only present in this man but also, in him, manifests and interprets its very nature and renders it visible," "not" as a simple "*metaphor* of Eternal Love, but eternal Love itself."[30] By this statement, Balthasar points to the figure of Christ as one in whom "the 'super-essential' [*hyperousion*] mystery of triune love becomes evident, both on the basis of this figure's constitution"—he is always the loving Son of the loving Father, who reveals "the mutual, exclusive knowledge" between them—"as well as because of the radiating grace that it in turn radiates outward."[31] "By no means" does the Incarnate Son reveal "the Father (economically) only *per modum intellectus*," for "what the Son reveals is,"

---

28. *TL* 1, 272 (*Theologik* I: *Wahrheit der Welt* [Einsiedeln: Johannes Verlag, 1985], 312: "Es gibt jene Fundierungsordnung, daß die Liebe Erkenntnis voraussetzt, die Erkenntnis das Sein. Aber was am Ende der Reihe als Ziel der Entfaltung steht, das hat doch, in einer anderen Perspektive, am Anfang als Anstoß gestanden. Im Kreislauf der Ewigkeit schießen sich Anfang und Ende zusammen, und während alles Begründete, als Wahrheit zu Begründende innerhalb der Fundierungsreihe steht, wird die ganze Reihe von dem letzten Grund getragen, welcher die Liebe ist. Es gibt dies ewige Wahrheit Gottes, durch die alles wahr ist und sinnvoll erklärt werden kann. Aber *daß* es überhaupt Wahrheit und ewige Wahrheit gibt, das hat seinen Grund in der Liebe.").

29. *EP*, 96 (*Epilog* [Einsiedeln: Johannes Verlag, 1987], 75: "die unauflösbare Einheit der Gestalt."). See also Pascal Ide, *Une théologie de l'Amour. L'amour, centre de la* Trilogie *de Hans Urs von Balthasar* (Bruxelles: Editions Lessius, 2012).

30. *PR*, 184 (*Das betrachtende Gebet* [Einsiedeln: Johannes Verlag, 1955], 163: "nicht nur ein erhabenes *Gleichnis* der ewigen Liebe sichtbar, sondern die ewige Liebe selbst, deren Gegenwart in diesem Menschen auch ihr Wesen Kundtut, es auslegt und anschaulich macht.").

31. *EP*, 97 (*Epilog*, 76: "das Überwesentliche" (hyperousion) Mysterium der dreieinigen Liebe . . . sowohl aufgrund ihrer Beschaffenheit wie aufgrund des auf sie fallenden und von ihr ausstrahlenden Gnadenlichts.").

Balthasar argues, "primarily the Father's love,"[32] not excepting the Spirit's mission of "bringing to light and searching (1 Cor 2:10) the ever-deeper abysses of the renunciatory love of Father and Son."[33] This does *not* mean, Balthasar admits, that "the absolutely incomprehensible reality that 'God is love' has become graspable in the form of Christ, for it is without analogy."[34] Nonetheless, for Balthasar, the Incarnate Word "always remains the starting point and the abiding substratum of the upward movement toward the 'Word [who is] with God,'"[35] and his actions "only make sense if they are seen and expounded as expressing the nature of divine love."[36]

It is thus "on the basis of Jesus' trinitarian relationship with God" that, Balthasar suggests, we "should construct a picture of the divine 'essence' and 'being.'" The Incarnate Son "does not speak about God in general," he explains, "but shows us the Father and gives us the Holy Spirit."[37] Similarly, on the basis of Christ's own words about his relationship with the Father, it is "clear" to Balthasar "that they interpenetrate in their reciprocal loving self-surrender."[38] In the Gospel of St. John, for example, the same concept of receptivity is used to describe both the Son's terrestrial mission and obedience (cf. Jn 10:18; 14:31, etc.) and the mutual indwelling of the divine persons (cf. Jn 14:10, 17:21, etc.).[39] The Swiss theologian thus invites us to recognize the Incarnate Word as one who affirms that the very form of his existence "is the uninterrupted reception of everything that he is, of his very self, from the Father." It is his "essence as Son to receive life ([Jn] 5:26), insight (3:11), spirit (3:34–35), word (3:34; 14:24), will (5:30), deed (6:9),

---

32. *TL* 3, 162 (*Theologik* III, 149: "Keineswegs offenbart der Sohn ökonomisch den Vater nur "*per modum intellectus,*" sondern er offenbart . . . primär die Liebe des Vaters.").

33. *TL* 3, 227 (*Theologik* III, 209: "die immer tiefere Ab-gründigkeit der verzichtenden Liebe von Vater und Sohn auflichtet.").

34. *EP,* 96 (*Epilog,* 75: "Man kann nicht sagen, daß in der Analogielosigkeit der Gestalt Christi das absolut Unfaßliche, daß "Gott Liebe ist," faßlich geworden sei.").

35. *TL* 3, 195 (*Theologik* III, 179: "das fleischgewordene Wort immer der Ausgangspunkt und das bleibende Substrat der Emporbewegung zum 'Wort bei Gott' bleibt.").

36. *PR,* 184 (*Das betrachtende Gebet,* 163: "erhalten sie doch ihren Sinn nur, wenn sie als Ausdruck des Wesens göttlicher Liebe gelesen und gedeutet warden.").

37. *TD* 5, 67 (*Theodramatik* IV, 58: "wir uns vom trinitarischen Gottesverhältnis Jesu au sein Bild über das "Sein" und "Wesen" Gottes machen sollen "; "Jesus spricht nicht über Gott im allgemeinen, sondern zeigt uns den Vater und schenkt uns den Heiligen Geist.").

38. *TL* 3, 226 (*Theologik* III, 208: "deutlich"; "Ineinanderschlagen ihrer gegenseitigen Liebeshingabe").

39. *LAC,* 87 (*Glaubhaft ist nur Liebe* [Einsiedeln: Johannes Verlag, 1963, 20198], 57); *TL* 2, 137; *GL* 1, 467–80, esp. 479 (*Herrlichkeit: Eine theologische Ästhetik* I: *Schau der Gestalt* [Einsiedeln: Johannes Verlag, 1961], 449–62, esp. 461); and *CS,* 79 (*Christlicher Stand* [Einsiedeln: Johannes Verlag, 1977], 61–62).

doctrine (7:16), work (14:10), and glorification (8:54; 17:22, 24) from another." Of course, all of this is received "in such a way that he has it all in himself (5:26)" and disposes of it "as of his own (10:18, 28)."[40] Nevertheless, the Incarnate Son never fails to refer everything that he has and *is* back to the Father (cf. Jn 17:10). Hence, there can be "no question," as far as Balthasar is concerned, "of Jesus as man obeying himself as God; nor does he obey the Trinity: as Son, in the Holy Spirit, he obeys the Father."[41] Similarly, Balthasar observes that, "Although he is God, he does not exposit himself in his humanity. Rather, he exposits the Father in the Holy Spirit, with whom he is identical as divine nature, but not as hypostasis."[42] It is thus possible, Balthasar reasons, to recognize the Father's love in the form of the Incarnate Son's obedience.[43]

Because, Balthasar reasons more specifically, the Son's redemptive mission "is rooted in his coming forth from the Father,"[44] he is "the ecstasy of the divine eros flowing out of itself in which God hands himself over and entrusts himself to the world."[45] Similarly, he is the "divine 'effulgence'" expressing "the entire life of the Trinity." For "in receiving himself from the Father," the Son "also receives the (natural) will to breathe forth the Spirit" and thus "to attune himself to that self-surrender which characterizes generation by the Father."[46] To be sure, the Incarnate Word "never speaks of his self-surrender in tones of ecstatic

---

40. *TH*, 30 (*Theologie der Geschichte, Kerygma und Gegenwart* [Einsiedeln: Johannes Verlag, 1959, 20046], 24: "dieser ununterbrochene Empfang von allem, was er ist, seiner selbst somit, vom Vater"; "Sein Wesen als Sohn des Vaters ist es, Leben (5,26), Einsicht (3,11), Geist (3,35), Wort (3,34; 14,24), Wille (5,30), Tat (5,19), Lehre (7,16), Werk (14,10), und Verherrlichung (8,54; 17,22.23) von einem andern, vom Vater zu empfangen.").

41. *TD* 3, 227 (*Theodramatik* II. *Die Personen des Spiels.* Teil 2: *Die Personen in Christus* [Einsiedeln: Johannes Verlag, 1978], 208: "Keinesfalls gehorcht Jesus als Mensch sich selber als Gott, er gehorcht auch nicht der Trinität, sondern als Sohn im Heiligen Geist dem Vater.").

42. *TL* 2, 312 (*Theologik* II, 285: "Und doch legt er, der Gott ist, in seiner Menschheit night sich selber aus, sondern den Vater im Heiligen Geist, mit denen er als göttliche Natur, aber nicht als Hypostase identisch ist.").

43. See *CS*, 79.

44. *TD* 4, 334 (*Theodramatik* III. *Die Handlung* [Einsiedeln: Johannes Verlag, 1980], 311: "in seinem Hervorgang aus dem Vater"); see also 326.

45. *ET* 2, 78 (*Sponsa Verbi: Skizzen zur Theologie* II [Einsiedeln: Johannes Verlag, 1961], 78: "Die Ekstase des göttlichen Eros aus sich heraus, worin Gott sich der Welt überliefert und anvertraut.").

46. *TD* 5, 75 (*Theodramatik* IV. *Das Endspiel* [Einsiedeln: Johannes Verlag, 1983], 65: "Der Logos nicht anders als mit Vater und Geist zusammen existiert und als göttlicher 'Ausdruck' das ganze trinitarische Leben ausdrückt"; "der Sohn den (Natur-) Willen zum Hauchen des Geistes in seinem Selbstempfang vom Vater her mitbekommt: nämlich in den im Zeugen des Vaters liegenden Hingabewillen miteinzuschwingen.").

eros, but rather uses almost deadpan words that point to his obedience: without ever denying his own responsibility, he refers all the initiative and the ultimate responsibility (and therefore the glory of this consummate plan) back to the Father."[47] In accord with his own teaching, he is to be understood as "essentially 'handed over' (*traditus*),"[48] that is to say, "given up by the Father": an affirmation that Balthasar invites us to consider not so much as a "substantial *noun* (substantive)" as instead a "transitive verb."[49]

> The Christ form is no statically placed memorial but is entirely to be understood as something that points beyond itself. The Cross says: "This is how much God has loved the world" (see Jn 3:16). And which God is that? God the Father, whose Word to the world is Jesus' own word in whose love the Father's love is to be "interpreted" (see Jn 1:18). And it is God the Spirit, the Spirit of love, who is continually explaining this Word of immeasurable love for us and in us. The word in Scripture: "No one has ever seen God" and the second half of that verse: "The only begotten God who dwells in the bosom of the Father has made him known" do not contradict each other: the second does not supersede or abolish the first but confirms it by interpreting it.[50]

In short, it is on the basis of the uninterrupted filiation of the Son on earth as in heaven that we have access to the mystery of God's love not only *for us* but also and still more fundamentally, Balthasar argues, *in himself* (cf. 1 Jn 4:8, 16).[51]

Presupposed to the incarnation of the Word and his salvific mission is thus, Balthasar suggests, "a Trinitarian substructure" in virtue of which "*the Son's self-surrender*" might be viewed as "the 'economic' representation of *the Father's Trinitarian, loving self-surrender.*"[52] Hence, for example, "the

---

47. *LAC*, 86 (*Glaubhaft ist nur Liebe*, 57: "Er spricht von seiner Selbsthingabe nie im Ton des ekstatischen Eros, sondern in fast klanglosen Worten, die auf Gehorsam hinweisen: ohne sich je der Verantwortung zu entziehen, führt er die ganze Initiative und letzte Verantwortung (und damit Verherrlichung durch den überschwänglichen Plan) auf den Vater zurück.").

48. *LAC*, 85 (*Glaubhaft ist nur Liebe*, 56: "wesenhaft 'geliefert' (tradiert)").

49. *TD* 5, 74 (*Theodramatik* IV, 64: "Hingegenwerden durch den Vater"; "nicht das substantielle Substantive, sondern das transitive Verb.").

50. *EP*, 96 (*Epilog*, 75: "Christi Gestalt ist kein statisch hingestelltes Denkmal, sondern versteht sich ganz als Verweis. Das Kreuz sagt: '*So sehr hat Gott die Welt geliebt*' (Joh 3,16). Gott der Vater, dessen Wort an die Welt aber Jesu eigenes Wort ist, in dessen Liebe die väterliche Liebe 'ausgelegt' wird (Joh 1,18), widersprechen einander nicht: das zweite hebt das erste nicht auf, sondern bestätigt es—auslegend.").

51. See Schumacher, *A Trinitarian Anthropology*, 320–36.

52. *TD* 4, 332. Emphasis provided by the translator (*Theodramatik* III, 309: "der Preisgabe des Sohnes » « die ökonomische Darstellung der trinitarischen liebenden

love that is, in the Son, a mission received 'by way of generation,'" is "the expression of a love that is, in the Father, a mission to generate."[53] In this way, the Son's generation from the Father is conceived by the Swiss theologian as a primordial act of love to which the Son responds "not 'passively,' as the Beloved, but (since he receives the Father's substance, as his love) actively, as a Lover, returning love, as one who responds to the totality of the Father's love and is ready to do everything in love."[54] It is the "interpenetration of love" that "elicits the identity of love, equally powerfully in all three Persons, which is both the fruit as well as the 'conclusive' manifestation of the absoluteness of divine love (once more with all this taking place within the divine identity)."[55]

AN ANALOGY OF PERSONAL SURRENDER

To be sure, Balthasar acknowledges that Augustine abandoned his own analogy of the Trinity as love (*De Trinitate* VIII, 10: "*amans et quod amatur et amor*") for the sake of preserving divine unity,[56] a concern that is perhaps not always adequately addressed in Balthasar's own theology, as numerous critics have pointed out.[57] As for Aquinas, he basically holds three things. First, the Father begets the Son (and spirates) the Holy Spirit by nature (the divine nature is the principle of generation as well as of spiration). Second, the Father begets the Son by mode of intellect, and with the Son, he spirates the Holy Spirit by mode of will or love. Thirdly, there is no more intellect in the generation of the Son than in the spiration of the Spirit, nor more love in the spiration of the Spirit than in the generation of the Son, for intellect and will here qualify the modes that allow the order between generation and spira-

---

Selbstpreisgabe des Vaters"). The original German does not speak directly of a "Trinitarian substructure" but indirectly bemoans doctrines of redemption that allow for "a so-to-speak trinitarian subversion" ("une sozusagen trinitarische Unterwanderung").

53. *CS*, 79 (*Christlicher Stand*, 61: "Liebe im Modus der gezeugten Sendung ist Ausdruck der Liebe im Modus der aktiv zeugenden Sendung.").

54. *TL* 3, 158; translation modified. Cf. *Theologik* III: *Der Geist der Wahrheit* (Einsiedeln: Johannes Verlag, 1987, 2015), 145: "nicht 'passive' als Geliebter, sondern, da er die *substantia* des Vaters als dessen Liebe empfängt, zugleich als Mitliebender, Rückliebender, dem All der väterlichen Liebe Antwortender, zu allem in Liebe Bereiter."

55. *EP* 93 (*Epilog*, 73: "Daraus folgt, daß das Ineinander der Liebe gleich (göttlich) mächtig jene Liebesidentität hervorbringt, die, nochmals innerhalb der Identität, sowohl die Frucht wie das 'abschlißende,' An-den-Tag-Treten der Absolutheit der Liebe selbst ist.").

56. See *TL* 2, 179 (*Theologik* III, 164); cf. Augustine, *De Trinitate* XV, 6, 10.

57. For more precision, see Schumacher, *A Trinitarian Anthropology*, 310–12, 333–36.

tion—and thus the real distinction of the Son and the Holy Spirit—to be manifested. It is this real order that the whole theological elaboration of St. Thomas seeks to manifest.[58]

Balthasar, on the other hand, ironically refuses for this same reason—avoiding heresy—to attribute the procession of the Son to knowledge. Barred at the outset is the idea that the Father engenders the Son so as to know himself as God and likewise the idea that he engenders the Son, because he already knows himself perfectly. "The first position would be Hegelianism," Balthasar explains; "the second, thought through consistently, would be Arianism." Instead, Balthasar suggests that "the immemorial priority of the self-surrender or self-expropriation thanks to which the Father *is* Father cannot be ascribed to knowledge but only to groundless love, which proves the identity of love as the 'transcendental par excellence.'"[59]

Of course, two different questions about the divine processions are being posed by these authors: the "how" of Aquinas and the "why" of Balthasar. The latter nonetheless recognizes that the two questions are not unrelated, given the identity of will and nature in God. Indeed, his own Trinitarian theology seeks to reunite the two in the aftermath of nominalism's destructive influence upon Western thought. God's freedom "coincides with the act-quality of his nature," Balthasar insists.[60] Following the lead of Adrienne von Speyr, he thus proposes a "'recapitulation' of the nature-based processions in a divine freedom that goes to their very origin." Such, he explains, "ultimately excludes every ontic priority of mere necessity over divine freedom, but . . .

---

58. Thanks to Gilles Emery for this precision. Or, as he puts it in his authoritative book on the subject, "The begetting of the Son is also, and eminently, an act of love; and the procession of the Holy Spirit is not without wisdom" (*The Trinitarian Theology of Saint Thomas Aquinas*, 69–72). The most important place of reference, in St. Thomas, is probably *De potentia*, q. 10, a. 2, where it is evident that all the divine attributes contribute to the generation of the Son (and to the spiration of the Spirit). For further detail, see Emmanuel Perrier, *La fécondité en Dieu. La puissance notionnelle dans la Trinité selon saint Thomas d'Aquin* (Paris: Parole et Silence, 2009).

59. *TL* 2, 177 (*Theologik* II, 163: "das erste wäre hegelianisch, das zweite, ernsthaft durchgedacht, arianisch. Deshalb kann die Unvordenklichkeit der Selbsthingabe oder Selbstentäußerung, die en Vater allererst zum Vater macht, nicht der Erkenntnis, sondern nur der grundlosen Leibe zugeschrieben werden, was diese als das 'Transzen dentale schlechthin' ausweist."). On precisely this point, he refers to the authority of St. Thomas: "For that the Son [and not only the Spirit] is given is from the Father's love, according to the words, *God so loved the world, as to give His only begotten Son* (Jo. iii, 16)" (*ST* I, q. 38, a. 2, ad 1).

60. *TD* 2, 256 (*Theodramatik* II: *Die Personen des Spiels*. Teil I: *Der Mensch in Gott* [Einsiedeln: Johannes Verlag, 1976], 232: "fällt mit der Akthaftigkeit seines Wesens zusammen.").

also . . . every arbitrary exercise of will,"; for "God is beyond the terms 'necessity' and 'freedom.'"[61]

On the basis of this insight, Balthasar seeks to defend the proposition that God's "absolute freedom of self-possession" is, "according to its absolute nature, . . . limitless self-giving." The Swiss theologian reasons, for example, that the Father, far from losing himself in the Son's generation, "*is always himself by giving himself.*" So, too, the Son "is always himself by allowing himself to be generated."[62] As for the Spirit, he is "both the highest divine, sovereign freedom *and* perfect selflessness," one who exists "only . . . for Father and Son."[63] From this perspective, "*Ekstasis* and *enstasis* are one, simply two sides of the same thing,"[64] and divine persons "are themselves only insofar as they go out to the Others."[65]

This idea of "going out to the Others" is, in turn, illustrated—again in terms borrowed from Adrienne von Speyr—as "realms of freedom within the Godhead," which "come about both through the self-giving of the hypostases and by each hypostasis in turn 'letting' the other two 'be.'" Of course, Balthasar explains, "*we can speak these only in metaphors.*"[66] After all, "the processions in God are not free in any arbitrary sense." Nor can God be thought of as "subject to external necessity." Instead, the processions should be understood as arising "from a natural or necessary will in God, which, proceeding from Father to Son and from Father and Son to the Spirit, grounds an irreversible order."[67] These so-called "areas" of infinite freedom should not there-

---

61. *TL* 3, 163 (*Theologik* III, 149–50: "einer 'Rekapitulation' der 'naturhaften' Hervorgänge in einer bis auf den Grund gehenden göttlichen Freiheit, was letztlich jede ontische Priorität bloßer Notwendigkeit vor der Freiheit in Gott ausschließt, aber ebenso jede Beliebigkeit oder Willkür; Gott ist jenseits von notwendig und frei."). Similarly, "freedom and necessity coincide" (*TD* 5, 83 [*Theodramatik* IV, 72: "grundlose Liebe, in der Freiheit und Notwendigkeit zusammenfallen"]). See also Schumacher, *A Trinitarian Anthropology*, 41–63.

62. *TD* 2, 256 (*Theodramatik* II, 232: "die absolute Freiheit des Selbstbesitzes sich ihrem absoluten Wesen gemäß als sein grenzenloses Schenken versteht"; "er ist als der sich Schenkende *immer schon* er selbst"; "der Sohn ist immer schon er selbst, indem er sich zeugen und den Vater über sich verfügen läßt.").

63. *TL* 3, 218 (*Theologik* III, 200: "sowohl höchste göttliche, souveräne Freiheit wie vollkommene nur für Vater und Sohn daseiende Selbstlosigkeit sein kann").

64. *TD* 5, 74 (*Theodramatik* IV, 64: "so sind Ekstasis und Enstasis eins, nur zwei Seiten desselben.").

65. *TD* 5, 76 (*Theodramatik* IV, 66: "nur im Überstieg zu den Je-Andern sie selbst sind").

66. *TD* 2, 262, emphasis mine (*Theodramatik* II, 238: "sowohl durch das Sichverschenken der Hypostasen wie durch das Sein-lassen je andern sein"; "nur in Bildern reden können").

67. *TD* 5, 88 (*Theodramatik* IV, 77: "Die Hervorgänge in Gott sind ohne Zweifel nicht frei im Sinn einer Beliebigkeit, auch wenn Gott keiner ihm fremden Notwendigkeit

fore obscure the fact that "each hypostasis in God possesses the same freedom and omnipotence" and each is "codetermined by the *ordo processionis* and the Trinitarian unity."[68] With similar caution, Balthasar admits that there is only "one freedom of the divine Essence";[69] after all, "a 'personal will' destroys the very notion of the divine nature."[70] Nonetheless, this one freedom is "possessed by each Hypostasis in its own specific way,"[71] as is inferred by their *circumincessio*, which, in turn, implies their "total 'being for one another.'"[72] In short, "the hypostases determine in their circumincessio what God is and wills and does."[73]

To further illustrate the dynamic unity of the divine persons, Balthasar employs the German word *Hingabe*, as borrowed from Adrienne von Speyr.[74] Although it is generally translated into English as "surrender," this word simultaneously evokes the idea of giftedness or generosity (*Gabe* = gift)[75] and that of orientation or tendency (as conveyed by the prefix *hin-*), which is not far, as Balthasar observes,[76] from what St. Thomas presents as the 'sense' (*ratio*) of the divine relations, that is to say, their "toward" (cf. *ST* I, q. 28, a. 3). Hence, the same word can be used to express the Father's begetting of the Son and the Son's reception of the entire divine essence, including the one divine will,[77] from the Father. What is expressed in each case is thus different, so as also to be complementary in what might be considered a dynamic perspective of unity: a unity that is neither static, nor actualized—there is, after all, no potency in Balthasar's conception of God, as is sometimes claimed[78]—but a unity *in act*. Borrowing from Adrienne von Speyr, Balthasar

---

unterliegt; sie entsprechen einem Natur- oder Nezessitätswillen in Gott, der vom Vater zum Sohn und von Vater und Sohn zum Geist eine unumkehrbare Ordnung grundlegt.").

68. *TD* 2, 257, 258 (*Theodramatik* II/1, 233–34: "jede Hypostase in Gott gleiche Freiheit und Allmacht besitzt"; "durch den *ordo processionis* und die trinitarische Einheit mitbestimmt ist.").

69. *TD* 5, 485 (*Theodramatik* IV, 445: "die eine Freiheit des göttlichen Wesens").

70. *CL*, 214 (*Kosmische Liturgie. Maximus der Bekenner* [Einsiedeln: Johannes Verlag, 19883], 211: "ein 'personaler Wille' zerstört den Begriff der göttlichen Nature selbst.").

71. *TD* 5, 485 (*Theodramatik* IV, 445: "von den Hypostasen je ihrer Eigenart entsprechend besessen wird").

72. *TD* 5, 483 (*Theodramatik* IV, 443: "ihr restloses Füreinandersein").

73. *TL* 2, 148 (*Theologik* II, 137: "die Hypostasen bestimmen in ihrer 'circuminsessio,' was Gott ist und will und tut.").

74. See Schumacher, *A Trinitarian Anthropology*, 9, 59 (n. 218), 121, 221, 308–9, 313, and 335 (n. 168).

75. On the centrality of *gift* in Balthasar's work, see Pascal Ide, *Une Théo-logique du don. Le don dans la* Trilogie *de Hans Urs von Balthasar* (Leuven: Peeters, 2013).

76. See *TL* 2, 133 (*Theologik* II, 124).

77. See, for example, *TD* 5, 88 (*Theodramatik* IV, 77).

78. For more precision, see Schumacher, *A Trinitarian Anthropology*, 310–20.

explains that the "passive *actio*" of the Son with respect to the Father and of the Spirit with respect to the Father and Son "is a condition of the 'active *actio*' and imparts to the latter a certain quality of 'letting go.'"[79] Indeed, even the Father's "active *actio*" is "qualified by the 'passive *actio*' of Son and Spirit,"[80] which in no way denies but rather accents the fact that "the power of self-surrender"[81] characterizing the Son's generation by the Father is itself received by the Son from the Father and by the Spirit from the Father and Son.[82] Or, to express this mystery in the still more metaphorical language proper to von Speyr, "every Hypostasis, in its own 'decline,' causes the Other to 'arise,'"[83] in what might be considered an "eternal kenosis of the Divine Persons to one another."[84]

As this citation serves to illustrate, even the *kenosis* of Philippians 2:7 is recognized by Balthasar as a form in time, and thus a revelation, of the Son's eternal responsive surrender to the Father's own "primary kenosis":[85] the metaphorical expression of his generating of the Son, by lovingly handing over the entire divine substance, "yet without losing his Godhead in this act of self-surrender (DS 805)."[86] The Father "must not be thought to exist

---

79. *TD* 5, 86 (*Theodramatik* IV, 75: "passive *actio*"; "aktiven *actio*"; "teilt der letzern ihrerseits ein gewisses Geschehenlassen mit").

80. *TD* 5, 87 (*Theodramatik* IV, 76: "der 'aktiven *actio*' des Vater] . . . durch die 'passive *actio*' von Sohn und Geist bedingt ist"). Cf. *ST* I, q. 41, a. 6, ad 1.

81. *TD* 5, 75 (*Theodramatik* IV, 64: "Macht der Selbsthingabe").

82. The perspective of St. Thomas is somewhat different, for St. Thomas views "giving" and "receiving" in the Trinitarian God in terms of personal relations. This is why he emphasizes that there is no "passivity" in God. Passivity is not attributable to the Trinity as such (as a reality) but only to our understanding and our speaking of the Trinity (the "mode of signifying"). Indeed, for Thomas Aquinas, "It is by the same operation that the Father begets and that the Son is born from all eternity, but this operation is found in the Father and in the Son under *distinct relations*: paternity and filiation." See Gilles Emery, "La 'kenosis' chez saint Thomas d'Aquin," *Nova et Vetera* (French edition) 93, no. 4 (2018), 357–86, 376: "C'est par la même opération que le Père engendre et que le Fils naît de toute éternité, mais cette opération se trouve dans le Père et dans le Fils sous des *relations distinctes*: la paternité et la filiation.". Thomas's explanation is centered on his doctrine of the divine relation. Thanks to Gilles Emery for bringing this to my attention.

83. Emery, "La 'kenosis' chez saint Thomas d'Aquin," 478 (Emery, "La 'kenosis' chez saint Thomas d'Aquin," 439: "jede Hypostase im eigenen 'Untergehen' (als restlose Hingabe) die andere 'aufgehen' läßt.").

84. Emery, "La 'kenosis' chez saint Thomas d'Aquin," 123 (Emery, "La 'kenosis' chez saint Thomas d'Aquin," 107: "ewige Kenose der göttlichen Personen aufeinanderhin").

85. Emery, "La 'kenosis' chez saint Thomas d'Aquin," 84 (Emery, "La 'kenosis' chez saint Thomas d'Aquin," 74: "eine erste radikale "Kenose""); *TD* 4, 331 (*Theodramatik* III, 308).

86. *TL* 3, 225 (*Theologik* III, 205: "In dieser Selbsthingabe sin Gottsein nicht verliert (DS 805)").

'prior' to this self-surrender (in an Arian sense): he is," Balthasar explains, "this movement of self-giving that holds nothing back."[87] This in turn means that the Son receives from the Father "not merely 'something' (for example, the divine essence), but the self-giving Father himself, he receives the 'giving' in the 'gift.' In receiving, therefore, the Son is not only thanksgiving (*eucharistia*); he is also gift in return, offering himself for all that the Father's self-giving may require; his willingness is absolute."[88]

This, then, is the manner in which we are to understand Balthasar's bold claim that "precisely in—and *only* in—the kenosis of Christ, the *inner* mystery of God's love comes to light, the mystery of the God who 'is love' (1 Jn 4:8) in himself and therefore is 'triune.'"[89] For "if the self-giving of the Father to the Son and of both to the Spirit reflects neither an arbitrary choice nor a necessary constraint but God's inmost being, this most intimate nature—however the processions may be distinguished from one another—can in the end only be love."[90]

> The sign of the God who empties himself into humanity, death, and abandonment by God, shows us why God came forth from himself, indeed descended below himself, as creator of the world: it corresponds to his absolute being and essence to reveal himself in his unfathomable and absolutely uncompelled freedom as inexhaustible love. This love is not the absolute Good beyond being, but is the depth and height, the length and breadth of being itself.[91]

---

87. *TD* 4, 323 (*Theodramatik* III, 301: "Der Vater, der ja nicht (arianisch) als 'vor' dieser Selbsthingabe existierend gedacht werden darf, ist diese Hingabebewegung, ohne etwas berechnend zurückzuhalten.").

88. *TL* 3, 226 (*Theologik* III, 207–8: "weil der Sohn vom Vater nicht nur etwas (etwa das Gottwesen) empfängt, sondern den sich geben Vater selbst, empfängt er in der Gabe das Geben, ist er somit im Empfang ebenso umfassend nicht nur Verdankung (*eucharistia*), sondern Rückgabe, Selbstangebot zu allem, was der Vater schenkend verfügt, absolute Bereitschaft.").

89. *LAC*, 87 (*Glaubhaft ist nur Liebe*, 57: "genau in der Kenose Christi (und nur darin) erscheint das *innere* Liebes Geheimnis des Gottes, der in sich selbst 'Liebe ist' (1 Jo 4,8) und deshalb 'dreieinig.'").

90. *TL* 2, 136 (*Theologik* II, 126–27: "Und wenn das Sich-Schenken des Vaters an den Sohn und beider an den Geist weder einer freien Willkür noch einer Nötigung, sondern dem innersten Wesen Gottes entspricht, so kann dieses innersten Wesen—wie immer die Hervorgänge voneinander unterschieden werden mögen—doch schließlich nur die Liebe sein.").

91. *LAC*, 145 (*Glaubhaft ist nur Liebe*, 96: "Vom Zeichen des sich in Menschsein und Tod und Gottleere vernichtigenden Gottes aus wird deutbar, warum Gott als Weltschöpfer schon aus sich und unter sich ging: so entsprach es seinem absoluten Sein und Wesen, sich in seiner abgründigen, durch nichts genötigten Freiheit als die unauslotbare Liebe zu offenbaren, die nicht jenseits des Seins das absolute Gute ist, sondern die Tiefe und Höhe, die Länge und Breite des Seins selbst.").

Evaluation

Of course, such a presentation of the kenotic love at the heart of the immanent Trinity cannot simply be taken for granted. Notwithstanding the positive value of Balthasar's attempt "to enter more directly into the mystery of the personal Trinitarian relations qua personal,"[92] Gilbert Narcisse challenges the idea of an inner-Trinitarian kenosis as "more suggestive than demonstrative, even sometimes more doubtful than true."[93] Similarly, although Emmanuel Durand acknowledges that Balthasar's presentation of the Trinitarian processions in terms of love is "more consistent" with scripture than is the Augustinian analogy adopted by St. Thomas,[94] he nonetheless questions the biblical foundation of Balthasar's depiction of "an eternal kenosis proper to each person" and of "an eternal drama" that is an "archetype of the Cross." Balthasar is thus accused— and rightly so—of creating "a balthasarian *analogon*"—which Durand identifies as "the law of extreme love that gives itself"—"in competition with the Augustinian *analogon* and exposed to the same risks."[95]

To be sure, the Swiss theologian does acknowledge that the concept of *kenosis* "has an entirely anthropomorphic side,"[96] whence his attempt to preserve the divine immutability *precisely* by "plac[ing] God's self-surrender (which expresses his very essence) in God himself."[97] Disputable nonetheless

---

92. Gilbert Narcisse, "Participer à la vie trinitaire," *Revue thomiste* 96, no. 1 (1996): 107–28, at 128.

93. Gilbert Narcisse, "The Supernatural in Contemporary Theology," in *Surnaturel: A Controversy at the Heart of Twentieth Century Thomistic Thought*, ed. Serge-Thomas Bonino, trans. Robert Williams and Matthew Levering, 295–309, at 303 (Naples, FL: Sapientia Press, 2009).

94. Or, as Balthasar sees it: "We can certainly concede with Thomas that knowledge and love are not really distinct in God but that something can be loved only when it is known and that, in consequence, it is necessary to maintain an order of the processions (*ST* I, 27, 3 ad 3). Yet the question remains whether this kind of ordering is not in the end merely read off of the created *imago* and thence elevated to a metaphysical principle." See *TL* 2, 164 (Theologik II, 150–51: "Gewiss kann man mit Thomas zugeben, dass Erkenntnis und Wille sich in Gott nicht real unterscheiden, dass aber etwas erst geliebt werden kann, wenn es erkannt wird, und deshalb eine Ordnung der Hervorgänge eingehalten werden muss (*ST* I, 27, 3 ad 3). Aber die Frage bleibt, ob diese Art der Ordnung nicht letztlich doch nur an der geschaffenen Imago abgelesen und von dorther zu einem metaphysischen Prinzip erhoben wird.").

95. Emmanuel Durand, *Dieu Trinité. Communion et transformation* (Paris: Cerf, 2016), 202, 203, and 205.

96. *TD* 5, 513 (*Theodramatik* IV, 469: "hat eine ganz anthropomorphe Seite").

97. *ET* 4, 35 (*Skizzen zur Theologie* IV: *Pneuma und Institution* [Einsiedeln: Johannes Verlag, 1974], 32: "das Wesen Gottes enthüllende Selbsthingabe in Gott selbst hinein zu verlegen").

is Balthasar's presentation of the economic kenosis as "the revelation, in terms of the world, of the *kenosis* (or selflessness) of the love of Father and Son at the heart of the Trinity,"[98] especially when this entails a so-called "Trinitarian inversion,"[99] reversing throughout the earthly mission of Christ the order of the processions (between Son and Spirit). Such a reversal is no minor detail, of course, since it is precisely the order of the hypostases that distinguishes them. Balthasar is thus accused of introducing a rupture between the economic and immanent Trinity, thereby calling into question the revelation of the latter by means of the former.[100]

From this perspective, the decision to root analogical discourse and reasoning (from created image to divine archetype) in what he calls *katalogy* (from archetype to image)[101] is unlikely to speak in his favor, especially when the divine archetype is the subject of the most contentious of Balthasar's metaphorical depictions. He speaks, for example, of "distance," "separation," "risk," "suffering," "surprise," and even "alienation" as pointing to the distinction of the hypostases for the purpose—ironically enough—of serving the revelation of their unity and reciprocal love.[102] Such depictions give the impression that his so-called katalogical reasoning is far more earthbound than he claims, since he thereby introduces into the Godhead concepts that can only bespeak created being: concepts pointing to imperfections, unfulfillment, and potency, and thus compromising the divine nature.

As a case in point, Rowan Williams points to the "specificity of the Cross and the dereliction of the Crucified" as "anchoring" everything in Balthasar's theology.[103] I, meanwhile, have argued that his purpose is the very contrary: to found the economic kenosis—and thus the divine missions—within the eternal processions. These, in turn, precisely in their circumincession, are por-

---

98. *TL* 3, 300 (*Theologik* III, 276: "die weltliche Offenbarung der innertrinitarischen Kenose oder Selbstlosigkeit der Liebe von Vater und Sohn.").

99. See *TD* 3, 183–202 (*Theodramatik* II: *Die Personen des Spiels,* Teil 2: *Die Personen in Christus* [Einsiedeln: Johannes Verlag, 1978], 167–75).

100. See Jean-Noël Dol, "L'inversion trinitaire chez Hans Urs von Balthasar," *Revue thomiste* 100, no. 2 (2000): 201–38; Legge, *The Trinitarian Christology of St. Thomas Aquinas,* 153, no. 77.

101. See *TL* 1, 15 (*Theologik* I, xv); *TL* 2, 312–13 (*Theologik* II, 287); and Schumacher, *A Trinitarian Anthropology,* 30–31, 55, 357–66.

102. See Schumacher, *A Trinitarian Anthropology,* 200–214; 240–45; 310–36, 351–56, 364–66, 376–83, 93–97; Schumacher, "The Concept of Representation in the Theology of Hans Urs von Balthasar," *Theological Studies* 60 (1999): 53–71.

103. Rowan Williams, "Balthasar and the Trinity," in *The Cambridge Companion to Hans Urs von Balthasar,* ed. Edward T. Oakes and David Moss, 37–50, at 49 (Cambridge: Cambridge University Press, 2004).

trayed as *prototypical of all that we know as love*, for it is love that Balthasar recognizes as the greatest of God's attributes.[104]

From the perspective of these obvious limitations, it is evident that Balthasarians have need of the metaphysical precisions and dogmatic clarity that the church's common doctor has to offer: precisions that Balthasar himself willingly called upon, especially in his most recent volumes.[105] The question remains whether Thomists might likewise have something to gain from Balthasar. I would suggest that Balthasar's exaggerated personalism might help to balance the overstated essentialism that characterizes much of scholasticism in nominalism's wake, including certain strains of Thomism. Meant as an antidote, of course, this essentialist exaggeration has nonetheless led to a widespread misunderstanding of St. Thomas's teaching, whence the tendency to separate what Aquinas had strictly joined: his treatise on "*De Deo uno*" and that of "*De Deo trino*," with priority being awarded, as Gilles Emery insists, "neither to the [divine] essence nor to the mutual relationship, but instead to the [divine] *person* that unites these two dimensions."[106]

Similarly, it is likely in reaction to the long reign and enduring influence of nominalism that Catholic theology has focalized so largely upon the analogy of being (in the description of the Creator-creature relation) that it has often failed to acknowledge—as Balthasar points out—that the "creature's metaphysical and theological locus is the diastasis of the divine 'Persons' in the unity of the divine nature."[107] His point, as I previously explained, is that

> our description of God and of the creature's relation to him "should be located beyond the opposition between physic-ontic and purely personal concepts."[108] His is a "freedom that so pervades his whole Being that there cannot be a remainder of Being outside this freedom,

---

104. See Schumacher, *A Trinitarian Anthropology*, 344–50.

105. See, for example, *TL* 2 and *TL* 3.

106. Gilles Emery, *Trinity in Aquinas*, trans. Matthew Levering (Naples, FL: Sapientia Press, 2003, 2006), 28, 165–208; Malet, "La synthèse de la personne et de la nature dans la théologie trinitaire de saint Thomas."

107. *TD* 2, 288 (*Theodramatik* II/1, 262: "Der metaphysisch-theologische Ort der Kreatur ist die Diastase der göttlichen 'Personen' in der Einheit der Gottnatur."). Similarly, "The infinite distance between the world and God is grounded in the other, prototypical distance between God and God." See *TD* 2, 266 (*Theodramatik* II/1, 242: "Die unendliche Distanz zwischen Welt und Gott gründet in der anderen, urbildlichen Distanz zwischen Gott und Gott."). We are not far from the teaching of St. Thomas. See, once again, Emery, *Trinity in Aquinas*, 28.

108. *TL* 3, 235 (*Theologik* III, 217: "sollte das Verhältnis des seinem Geschöpf einwohnenden Gottes auch jenseits des Gegensatzes von physisch-ontischen und rein personalen Begriffen angesiedelt werden").

nor could some corner of his Being manage to withdraw from this freedom."[109]

[…]

If, then . . . we wish to have an adequate analogy of the one God in three persons, we must have access to both essentialist and personalist concepts, and this [in turn]. . . . implies that we must have access not only to the notion of likeness, but also to [that of] difference. . . . The divine mystery should be analogically addressed [therefore] not only in terms of the creature's unity of being (*ens*), in virtue of which it might be likened unto him who identifies with Being (*Esse est*)—terms focusing upon the divine simplicity—but also in terms of creaturely differences: terms emphasizing the plurality of the divine persons. Uniting the two— essence (unity) and persons (plurality)—in a fruitful tension is [Balthasar suggest] the key notion of surrender [*Hingabe*].[110]

Indeed, quite like St. Thomas, the Swiss theologian insists that the divine essence is "no fourth element, something common to the three Persons." It is, rather, "their eternal life itself in its processions."[111] To think otherwise is, to repeat Balthasar's insistent claim, to challenge the arguably most important Christian doctrine: *Deus Caritas Est*. Of course, this claim—in the precise manner in which Balthasar understood it—also merits patient consideration and respectful response from Thomists, especially in light of personalism's pervasive influence in popular religious belief and recent magisterial teaching. Fidelity to the master's example of constant dialogue with contemporary culture, in an honest pursuit of truth, requires as much.

BIBLIOGRAPHY

Dol, Jean-Noël. "L'inversion trinitaire chez Hans Urs von Balthasar." Revue thomiste 100, no. 2 (2000): 201–38.

Durand, Emmanuel. *Dieu Trinité. Communion et transformation*. Paris: Cerf, 2016.

———-. *La périchorèse des personnes divines. Immanence mutuelle. Réciprocité et communion*. Preface by Vincent Holzer. Collection *Cogitatio Fidei* 243. Paris, Cerf, 2005.

---

109. *EP*, 85 (*Epilog*, 66: "Eine Freiheit, die sein ganzes Sein so durchwaltet, daß kein Rest von Sein dieser Freiheit vorausläge oder sich ihr entzöge.").

110. Schumacher, *A Trinitarian Anthropology*, 54. See also my expositing (in the same work) of the various analogies, borrowed from Adrienne von Speyr, to explain the unity-in-difference of the divine persons: human freedom and divine freedom, body and spirit, individual and community, man and woman.

111. *EP*, 92–93 (*Epilog*, 72: "kein Viertes, den Personen Gemeinsames, sondern ihr in seinen Prozessionen ewiges Leben selbst").

Emery, Gilles. *The Trinitarian Theology of St. Thomas Aquinas.* Translated by Francesca Aran Murphy. Oxford: Oxford University Press, 2007, 2010.[2]

——-. *Trinity in Aquinas.* Translated by Matthew Levering. Naples, FL: Sapientia Press, 2006.

Ide, Pascale. *Une théologie de l'Amour. L'amour, centre de la* Trilogie *de Hans Urs von Balthasar.* Bruxelles: Editions Lessius, 2012.

——-. "Une théologie du don. Les occurrences de *Gaudium et spes,* nr. 24, § 3 chez Jean-Paul II." *Anthropotes* 17, no. 1(2001): 149–78; 17, no. 2 (2001): 313–44.

——-. *Une Théo-logique du don. Le don dans la* Trilogie *de Hans Urs von Balthasar.* Leuven: Peeters, 2013.

Legge, Dominic. *The Trinitarian Christology of St. Thomas Aquinas.* Oxford: Oxford University Press, 2017.

Malet, André. "La synthèse de la personne et de la nature dans la théologie trinitaire de saint Thomas." *Revue thomiste* 54, no. 3 (1954): 483–522.

Narcisse, Gilbert. "Participer à la vie trinitaire." *Review thomiste* 96, no. 1 (1996): 107–28.

——-. "The Supernatural in Contemporary Theology." In *Surnaturel: A Controversy at the Heart of Twentieth Century Thomistic Thought,* edited by Serge Thomas Bonino, translated Robert Williams and Matthew Levering, 295–309. Naples, FL: Sapientia Press, 2009.

Schumacher, Michele M. "The Concept of Representation in the Theology of Hans Urs von Balthasar." *Theological Studies* 60 (1999): 69–70.

——-. *A Trinitarian Anthropology: Adrienne von Speyr & Hans Urs von Balhtasar in Dialogue with Thomas Aquinas.* Washington DC: The Catholic University of America Press, 2014.

Torrell, Jean-Pierre. *Saint Thomas Aquinas,* II: *Spiritual Master.* Translated by Robert Royal. Washington DC: The Catholic University of America Press, 2003.

Williams, Anna N. "Deification in the *Summa theologiae*: A Structural Interpretation of the *Prima Pars.*" *The Thomist* 61 (1997): 219–55.

Williams, Rowan. "Balthasar and the Trinity." In *The Cambridge Companion to Hans Urs von Balthasar,* edited by Edward T. Oakes and David Moss, 37–50. Cambridge: Cambridge University Press, 2004.

Wojtyła, Karol. *Person and Community, Selected Essays.* Translated by Theresa Sandok. New York: Peter Lang, 1993.

Theodicy

CHAPTER 9

The Problem of Evil and the Nature of God

Divine Mercy and Sorrow in Thomas Aquinas

BRIAN T. CARL

THE QUESTION OF WHETHER AND HOW one might reconcile the existence of evil and suffering with the goodness of the divine, long considered the most formidable objection against the existence of God, was familiar to St. Thomas Aquinas.[1] The version of the problem to which St. Thomas responds, in the article containing his famous five ways, asserts succinctly an absolute opposition between the infinite goodness of God and the existence of any evil, such that if there were a God, then no evil would be found in the world.[2] To this objection, St. Thomas replies that "it pertains to the infinite goodness of God to permit evils and to draw good things out of them."[3]

As with other perennial philosophical problems, there can be as much disagreement about how to articulate the problem of evil as there is about

---

1. Cf. John F. Wippel, "Metaphysical Themes in *De malo*, I," in *Aquinas's Disputed Questions on Evil: A Critical Guide*, ed. M. V. Dougherty (Cambridge: Cambridge University Press, 2016), 12.

2. *ST* 1.2.3 obj. 1.

3. *ST* 1.2.3 ad 1. There might be a great difference between saying (a) that it pertains to God's infinite goodness to permit evils *and* to draw forth goods from them, or (b) that it pertains to God's infinite goodness to permit evils *so that he might* draw forth goods from them. Along these lines, there is a point of dispute among Thomists (both historically and recently) concerning the divine permission of sin and its relation to the good of the Incarnation. For some criticism of the idea that the sin of our first parents was permitted for the sake of the good of the Incarnation, see Jean-Hervé Nicolas, "La permission du péché," *Revue Thomiste* 60 (1960): 538–44; for a contrary view, in accordance with the more general thesis that every evil is permitted by God for the sake of a greater good, see Charles Journet, *The Meaning of Evil*, trans. Michael Barry (New York: P. J. Kennedy, 1963), 256–59; for discussion, see Gilles Emery, "The Question of Evil and the Mystery of God in Charles Journet," in *Trinity, Church, and the Human Person* (Ave Maria, FL: Sapientia Press, 2007), 249–51.

183

whether and how the problem might be resolved. St. Thomas's brief formulation of the problem, which centers on the alleged inconsistency of the existence of evils with the infinite divine goodness, leaves much room for interpretation and constructive elaboration. Furthermore, the problem of evil and the question of theodicy are closely tied to a wide range of philosophical and theological issues treated by St. Thomas and disputed among his interpreters, including divine attributes such as impassibility, eternity, foreknowledge, and providence; predestination, grace, human freedom, and the permission of sin; atonement and the redemptive character of Christ's suffering.[4] A full consideration from a Thomistic perspective of the problem of evil might seem to require engagement with all of these issues. It is no surprise that recent treatments of the problem of evil by Thomists have more often taken the form of monographs rather than articles—and in them we find widely divergent views about both the articulation of the problem of evil and what shape a Thomistic response to the problem takes.[5]

As the problem of evil concerns the apparent opposition between certain divine attributes (such as goodness and omnipotence) and the existence of evils in the world, both the articulation of the problem and any attempted resolution will depend upon how one understands these divine attributes. Brian Davies, for example, regards typical presentations of the problem of evil among contemporary philosophers of religion as having gone badly awry, insofar as they understand the goodness of God in terms of the moral goodness of human beings. Davies holds that Thomas's attribution of goodness and justice to God should not be understood in a way that would permit us to try to probe whether God has morally sufficient reasons for permitting his

---

4. In engaging with the thought of Balthasar, Thomists must also consider the relationship between the inner life of the Trinity and the Incarnation. See Dominic Legge, OP, *The Trinitarian Christology of St. Thomas Aquinas* (New York: Oxford, 2017).

5. To take just a few prominent examples from Thomistic philosophers over the last decade: Brian Davies, *Thomas Aquinas on God and Evil* (Oxford: Oxford University Press, 2011); Brian Davies, *The Reality of God and the Problem of Evil* (New York: Continuum, 2006); Eleonore Stump, *Wandering in Darkness* (Oxford: Oxford University Press, 2010); see also Eleonore Stump, *Atonement* (Oxford: Oxford University Press, 2018); John F. X. Knasas, *Aquinas and the Cry of Rachel* (Washington, DC: The Catholic University of America Press, 2013). Davies criticizes the manner in which philosophers of religion like Richard Swinburne and Stump articulate the problem of evil, insofar as Davies sees unacceptable anthropomorphism in the attribution of moral goodness to God and the investigation of whether God has "morally sufficient reasons" for permitting suffering. Knasas is critical in a different way of typical articulations of the problem of evil, finding that it is fundamentally motivated by "an inappropriate aggrandizement of persons and other things" (16). Stump's *Wandering in Darkness* is the most systematic attempt yet made to present a defense against the problem of evil in Thomistic terms in conversation with contemporary philosophy of religion.

creatures to suffer and to sin, as if the goodness of God is to be evaluated by us in terms of what we take to be God's moral obligations. Davies concludes that God should not be characterized, properly speaking, as morally good.

Davies's questioning of whether we should say that God is morally good is not the only way in which the question of theodicy leads to questions concerning the divine nature. Since the horrors of the twentieth century, many theologians outside of the Thomistic tradition have called into question whether any contemporary attempt at theodicy can fail to find a place for genuine sympathy, woundedness, and sorrow within the divine: many ask how God can be perfect love if we do not find in him any heartbreak over the horrific sins freely committed by created persons whom he wills to save.[6] Among Thomists, Jacques Maritain has attempted to find an attenuated way to attribute a sort of noble sorrow and suffering to the impassible God whose creatures freely resist him. Maritain takes as the point of departure for his reflections an element of St. Thomas's account of the divine nature that he deems less than satisfactory: St. Thomas's characterization of mercy as a divine name said only metaphorically of God, insofar as we can attribute to God the production of an effect like that produced through mercy but not the passionate sorrow of human *misericordia*.[7] Charles Journet was deeply influenced by Maritain's reflections on this point, as was Hans Urs von Balthasar.[8]

Whether in a philosophical or theological mode, the problem of evil necessarily leads us to questions concerning the divine nature. Whereas Davies removes the notion of moral goodness from what we affirm of God out of a concern for the divine transcendence, Maritain judges that we must assert that there is in God, even if in an unnamable way, something of the sorrow or suffering of a lover whose desire for his beloved is unfulfilled. Davies and

---

6. For a survey and analysis from a Thomistic perspective of several theologians who attribute sorrow or suffering to the divine, including Balthasar, see Gilles Emery, "The Immutability of the God of Love and the Problem of Language Concerning the 'Suffering of God,'" in *Divine Impassibility and the Mystery of Human Suffering*, ed. James F. Keating and Thomas Joseph White (Grand Rapids, MI: William B. Eerdmans, 2009), 27–77. See also Thomas Joseph White, "Von Balthasar and Journet on the Universal Possibility of Salvation and the Twofold Will of God," *Nova et Vetera* 4 (2006): 633–66.

7. Jacques Maritain, "Quelques réflexions sur le savoir théologique," *Revue Thomiste* 69 (1969): 5–27, esp. 14–26.

8. For discussion of Maritain's influence on Journet on this point, see Gilles Emery, "The Question of Evil and the Mystery of God in Charles Journet," in *Trinity, Church, and the Human Person* (Naples, FL: Sapientia Press, 2007), 237–62. For discussion of Maritain's influence on Balthasar, see Joshua Brotherton, "God's Relation to Evil: Maritain and Balthasar on Divine Impassibility," *Irish Theological Quarterly* 80, no. 3 (2015): 191–211. See also chap. 4 of Brotherton, *One of the Trinity has Suffered: Balthasar's Theology of Divine Suffering in Dialogue* (Steubenville, OH: Emmaus Academic 2019).

Maritain, in their views on divine moral goodness and divine mercy, represent opposite approaches to resolving the tension between the goodness of God and the existence of evil through a more nuanced understanding of the divine nature. Emphasizing the apophatic element in St. Thomas's philosophical theology, Davies denies that moral agency and moral goodness have a place among the names said properly of God, holding that we should no more call God morally good than we should call him feline.[9] Maritain, by contrast, wishes to emphasize the exemplarity of God's nature even for perfections attributed only metaphorically, reminding us that all created perfections find a supreme exemplar in the infinite divine perfection. He thus concludes that the perfection of noble suffering must find in God an unnamable exemplar, even if suffering or sorrow cannot be properly attributed to God.

I have elsewhere offered some criticism of Davies's view, particularly as an interpretation of St. Thomas.[10] In this chapter, I will explore and respond to Maritain's reflections on divine mercy and the unnamable exemplar of sorrow. The first section of the chapter will orient the later discussion by providing an overview of some of St. Thomas's philosophical and theological views relevant for consideration of the problem of evil. After introducing Maritain's position on divine suffering, I will then discuss some key elements of St. Thomas's understanding of proper, analogical divine naming and metaphorical divine naming; in light of these remarks, I will criticize Maritain's suggestion that we must posit an unnamable exemplar of human suffering within God. I will also attempt to show, however, that there are adequate resources in St. Thomas's discussions of divine mercy and sorrow, understood in light of his account of divine naming, to address the concerns that motivate Maritain's account.

THOMISTIC FUNDAMENTALS FOR THE PROBLEM OF EVIL

The foundation for everything that St. Thomas says about evil and its place within divine providence is his Augustinian metaphysical understanding of evil as a privation. Given his commitment to the transcendental character of the good—that the good is really identical and convertible with being, that to be (*esse*) is good—it cannot be that evil, as the opposite of good, can itself be a being.[11] Here some precision is necessary, however, given that we char-

---

9. Davies, *The Reality of God and the Problem of Evil*, 99. Davies offers this remark in response to criticisms by Brian Shanley, *The Thomist Tradition* (London: Kluwer Academic Publishers, 2002), 116.

10. See Brian T. Carl, "The Transcendentals and the Divine Names in Thomas Aquinas," *American Catholic Philosophical Quarterly* 92, no. 2 (2018): 236–42, esp. nn. 51–55.

11. *ST* 1.48.1.

acterize many things—suffering, illness, vicious habits and actions—as evil or bad. Addressing the question directly of whether evil is itself something (*aliquid*), St. Thomas begins by noting that just as we can distinguish between things that are white (like snow or a cloud) and what it is to be white (which we might signify abstractly as "whiteness"), so, too, we must distinguish between things that are evil and what evil is such. Since to be (*esse*) is good, it must be that evil as such is a sort of nonbeing, the privation or absence of something good. But it cannot be that simply not to be or not to exist is evil, for then the very nonexistence of anything—indeed, the nonexistence of the virtually infinite number of beings that could be created by God—would be an evil.[12] St. Thomas therefore concludes that evil as such must be "the privation of some particular good, inhering in some particular good," that is, in some being.[13] Evil, a lack of some perfection, befalls some particular being, which is always good insofar as it exists: Just as blindness, the privation of sight, befalls a living animal.[14]

God, as subsistent existence itself, is the cause of all created being and goodness, and everything besides God continuously depends upon him for existence. God loves his own goodness and wills to create for the sake of his own goodness, bringing creatures into existence and ordering them to himself, as the efficient, exemplar, and final cause of all created goodness. Divine love is not caused by created goodness: rather, it causes creatures to exist. The infinite goodness of God cannot be perfectly imitated by any one creature— not even by the highest or best of creatures—and so given God's free decision to create, by his wisdom he wills to create a universe with a variety of creatures exhibiting various modes or degrees of perfection. Indeed, although God is entirely free to create or not to create, St. Thomas holds that there are numerous general features of the universe that are conditionally necessary, insofar as something would be lacking in the completeness of the universe if it lacked, for example, immaterial, intelligent substances or material, corruptible substances. However, even though there are certain general features necessary in any universe God might create, it must also be recognized that any created

---

12. *ST* 1.48.3. In discussion below of how mercy is attributed to God, we will see that for St. Thomas, there is something of the character of mercy involved in the very act of creation. See *ST* 1.21.4 ad 3.

13. *De malo* 1.1: "Unde relinquitur quod malum, secundum quod est malum, non est aliquid in rebus, sed est alicuius particularis boni privatio, alicui particulari bono inhaerens."

14. *De malo* 1.1: "Unde dico, quod id quod est malum, non est aliquid; sed id cui accidit esse malum, est aliquid, in quantum malum privat nonnisi aliquod particulare bonum; sicut et hoc ipsum quod est caecum esse, non est aliquid; sed id cui accidit caecum esse, est aliquid." Cf. *ST* 1.48.3.

good, including the good of the entire universe, falls infinitely short of the divine goodness. For this reason, St. Thomas denies that there can be any such thing as a best possible universe: no matter how much good God creates or how good a universe he makes, he could always have willed to create more good or a universe better in some respect. Furthermore, St. Thomas consistently identifies the order of the entire universe as the highest of created goods, a claim that takes on a particular importance in his discussion of God's incidentally willing certain evils for the sake of the good of this order.

In order to sketch something of the place of evil within the good order of the created universe, we must first see how St. Thomas distinguishes different kinds of evil. We can begin with his distinction between what is evil absolutely speaking (*simpliciter*) and what is evil in a qualified way (*secundum quid*). What is evil absolutely (or evil in itself) is so because it involves the privation of something necessary for the perfection of a thing; as, for example, a sickness is an evil for an animal. But often it is the case that although something is good in itself, it nevertheless is an evil (or involves or causes evil) for another thing. For example, St. Thomas says that because fire lacks the form of water, fire—which when it acts tends to make other things to possess the form of fire like itself—is evil for water, even though fire is not evil in itself. Fire is evil, then, in this qualified way. Offering a more complex example, St. Thomas says that the order of justice requires that a sinner be deprived of some good that he desires, such that this deprivation, as a punishment, is good absolutely but an evil for the individual sinner.[15]

The example of fire being evil for water is a case of natural or physical evil, whereas Thomas's latter example involves both the moral evil of fault (*culpa*), an evil absolutely speaking, and the evil of punishment (*poena*), which is evil in a qualified way. Thomas draws the threefold distinction between the evil of natural defect, the evil of fault, and the evil of punishment when he discusses the question of whether God wills evil. Thomas approaches this question by first asserting that no appetite, whether natural or voluntary, ever wills evil as such (or *per se*), because the object of appetite is the good, whose very notion (*ratio*) is "the desirable." The only sense in which anything with appetite ever desires evil is incidentally (*per accidens*), insofar as that evil is somehow conjoined to some good that is desired.[16] For example, in a case of natural evil, a lion desires the death of a deer (an evil for the deer) not for its own sake as an evil (or *per se*), but only insofar as this death is conjoined to the good of its own nutrition; in a case of moral evil, a sinner desires the pleas-

---

15. *De malo* 1.1 ad 1.

16. There is more to be said about human appetite insofar as we are capable of misperceiving what is good—we can desire an apparent good that is not a genuine good—but we can set this aside here.

ure of fornication *per se* and the moral fault of the act only *per accidens.* St. Thomas observes that when one desires an evil *per accidens,* one prefers the good to which the evil is conjoined rather than the good of which that evil is the privation. If a man prefers the good state of his soul and union with God to the pleasure of fornication, therefore, then he will not sin.

Having analogically attributed voluntary appetite to God, Thomas extends these assertions about the relation of appetite to its object to the divine will.[17] God wills his own goodness above all things, wills created goods for the sake of his goodness, and wills some goods more than others. In every case, St. Thomas insists that God does not will evils as such or *per se,* but he does will some evils *per accidens,* insofar as they are conjoined to some good that he wills: he wills evils of natural defect, insofar as he wills the good order of nature, and he wills evils of punishment (which are, again, only evil in a qualified sense, as evils for the one punished), insofar as he wills the good of justice, which is part of the order of the universe.[18] St. Thomas is willing to assert, concerning both natural evils and evils of punishment (which are, again, evils only in a qualified sense), that God is the cause and author of such evils.[19] But with regard to sinful evils of fault, God in no way wills these evils; he only wills to permit them.[20] The claim that God is the cause of certain evils (insofar as he intends certain absolute goods to which these qualified evils are conjoined) must also be understood in light of the thesis that evil in itself is a privation rather than a being or form: to call God a *per accidens* cause of certain evils should not be taken to imply that evil is something created.

---

17. For some insightful commentary on this passage, see John F. X. Knasas, *Aquinas and the Cry of Rachel* (Washington, DC: The Catholic University of America Press, 2013), 93. Although I am not fully convinced by Knasas's interpretation of *ST* 1.48.2 and his way of distinguishing on the basis of this text what he calls "*quandoque* evils" (see chap. 3 of *Aquinas and the Cry of Rachel*), I agree with Knasas's conclusions: (1) that for St. Thomas, God wills punishments and natural evils such as corruptions, albeit *per accidens,* rather than merely permitting them, and (2) that there is in St. Thomas a distinction between natural evils like corruptions, which are a normal part of the order of nature, and natural evils like monstrous births, which involve deficiency in natural agents and are entirely outside the intention of the order of nature. For the latter distinction, see, for example, *SCG* 3.6; *De malo* 1.1 ad 8; *De malo* 3.1.

18. *ST* 1.19.9; for the characterization of the order of justice as part of the order of the universe, see *ST* 1.49.2.

19. *ST* 1.49.2; *De malo* 3.1 ad 3, ad 10.

20. *ST* 1.19.9. Charles Journet interprets "willing *per accidens*" in the case of natural evils and evils of punishment as a sort of permission, so that in general all evils are permitted only by God. For criticisms of this as a reading of St. Thomas's texts, see Knasas, 95–104. Similarly, Davies asserts that evil is for Aquinas "in no way . . . caused by God," but I do not think this can be squared with the texts cited in the previous note. See Davies, *Thomas Aquinas on God and Evil,* 69.

Although many of the evils suffered by human beings might seem to be simply instances of natural evil comparable to a deer's losing its life to a lion—so that one might try to account for much human suffering as incidental to the good of the order of nature—St. Thomas asserts as a point of Catholic faith that every evil afflicting a rational creature "is contained under either fault or punishment," indicating that there are no mere natural evils for human beings after the fall.[21] As a philosophical matter, St. Thomas advances arguments for God's special providence concerning rational creatures, who are governed by God "for their own sake," while other things are governed for the sake of rational creatures.[22] Along somewhat more detailed theological lines in his Commentary on Romans 8:28, St. Thomas claims first that, in general, any evil that occurs "turns out for the good of the universe," even if it does not always turn out for the good of the individual being that suffers the evil. He adds that evils afflicting lower parts of the universe are ordered toward "the good of the noblest parts." Going beyond the identification of the "noblest parts" of the universe with rational creatures in general, however, St. Thomas explains that among the parts of the universe, God's saints are the most excellent, so that "whatever occurs, whether to them or to other things, turns out for their good," including their own evils of punishment and fault, and "even the evils of sinners turn out for the good of the just."[23] Regarding their own punishments, St. Thomas seems to regard it as obvious that the saints profit by these, and as regards their own faults, he explains how God's permission of sin can conduce to one's ultimate perseverance.[24]

St. Thomas's views concerning the divine permission of sin and the providential willing of natural evils and evils of punishment are in many respects matters for controversy, both among Thomas's sympathetic interpreters and in conversation with other philosophical and theological approaches. What I have offered in this section amounts only to a cursory statement of certain Thomistic philosophical and theological essentials for consideration of the problem of evil. In what follows, I am going to concern myself more with the articulation of the problem of evil than its resolution, insofar as the way philosophers and the-

---

21. *De malo* 1.4. For commentary, see Wippel, 32–33, including n. 63.

22. *SCG* 3.112.

23. *Super Rom.* 8.6. In an earlier treatment of the problem of evil in St. Thomas, Stump cites this passage but seems to identify the *sancti Dei* with all created persons. See Eleonore Stump, "Aquinas on the Sufferings of Job," in *The Evidential Argument from Evil*, ed. Daniel Howard-Snyder (Bloomington: Indiana University Press, 1996), 51–52. Cf. *Wandering in Darkness*, 609, n. 16, in which Stump cites the Commentary on Romans and translates a key portion as follows: "God takes care of [human beings] in such a way that he doesn't allow any evil for them that he doesn't turn into their good."

24. *Super Rom.* 8.6.

ologians articulate the problem of evil touches on questions concerning the divine nature. Even though there is broad agreement among Thomas's interpreters concerning most of what I have stated so far, there is nevertheless tremendous disagreement among them about how to articulate the problem of evil, in light of disagreements about the nature of the God.

Jacques Maritain and the Unnamable Suffering of God

In one of his earlier works devoted to the problem of evil, Maritain highlighted what he regarded as one of "the most original of [St. Thomas's] philosophical discoveries," which concern how the human will is the originating cause of the evil of sin.[25] That original discovery on St. Thomas's part is that the defectibility of the created will is grounded in its capacity to move itself to choice in the absence of consideration by the intellect of the rule that ought to govern choice. As it is the will that would move the intellect to consider the rule, the defect that is nonconsideration is due to the will. This volitional defect is not in itself a sin, however, as it is not possible for the intellect to consider the rule (or any particular object of thought) at all times. Sin occurs when the will moves itself to a choice contrary to the rule, in a moment of nonconsideration of the rule. But what is the source of this self-movement by the will, if not God as the first mover of all things? Motivated by a concern for maintaining the absolute innocence of God with respect to sin, Maritain criticized the classical Thomistic position associated with Bañez, according to which a physical premotion to act and an antecedent permissive decree infallibly predetermine the rational creature's free defection from the good.[26] Maritain proposes that God moves the will to the good by "shatterable motions" which the creature can freely refuse.[27]

Although I will not enter into the dispute about predestination and the divine permission of sin here, I bring it up because the idea of divine motions "shattered" by a human being's free refusal lies in the background of Mari-

---

25. Jacques Maritain, *St. Thomas and the Problem of Evil* (Milwaukee: Marquette University Press, 1942), 23. For a defense of St. Thomas's position on this matter, see Steven J. Jensen, "Aquinas's Original Discovery: A Reply to Barnwell," *American Catholic Philosophical Quarterly* 92, no. 1 (2018): 73–95.

26. For an overview of Maritain's positions concerning the divine permission of sin, see Taylor Patrick O'Neill, *Grace, Predestination, and the Permission of Sin* (Washington, DC: The Catholic University of America Press, 2019), 201–30.

27. See, for example, Jacques Maritain, *Existence and the Existent*, trans. Lewis Galantiere and Gerald B. Phelan (New York: Paulist Press, 2015), 79–80; Maritain, *God and the Permission of Evil*, trans. Joseph W. Evans (Milwaukee: Bruce Publishing Company, 1966), 38.

tain's reflections on the unnamable exemplar of noble suffering that he thinks we must posit within the divine: Maritain speaks of the divine permission of sin as God's acceptance of something unacceptable to him, and as—speaking metaphorically, he qualifies—God's being "deprived of a joy . . . that was due to Him."[28] That God wills to accept such a deprivation and seizes it as the opportunity to bring about a much greater good through it bespeaks a "mysterious divine perfection" that is "in God the unnamed exemplar for our suffering."[29] For the notion of an unnamed perfection, Maritain first appeals to Aristotle's assertion that some of the virtues and vices that must be distinguished by the philosopher sometimes have no name in ordinary language,[30] such as, for example, the vice of deficiency opposed to temperance has no name in Greek.[31] In this case, though, having conceptually distinguished this vice of deficiency, the philosopher can coin a term for it; in the case of the divine perfections of which Maritain wishes to speak, he asserts that they must be not only unnamed but also unnamable.[32]

Maritain motivates his discussion of this unnamable exemplar for our suffering by expressing some dissatisfaction on his part with St. Thomas's treatment of mercy as a divine name in *Summa theologiae* 1.21.3, in which Thomas asserts that mercy (*misericordia*) is attributed to God "according to its effect" (*secundum effectum*), which is the dispelling of the misery of another, but not "according to the affect of passion" (*non secundum passionis affectum*), which is the sorrow or grief over another's misery experienced by a human being taking pity on another. Maritain agrees that sorrow and grief imply dependence and imperfection that cannot be attributed to God, but he is concerned that all of this "leaves the mind dissatisfied," in light of scripture's frequent attestations of the divine mercy.[33] If love, "to which mercy is so near," is not

---

28. Maritain, "Quelques réflexions sur le savoir théologique," 19: "Chaque fois que pèche une creature (alors c'est elle qui a la première initiative, initiative de néant), Dieu est privé d'une joie ('de surplus,' selon notre manière de voir) qui lui était due par un autre et que cet autre ne lui donne pas, et quelque chose d'inadmissible à Dieu est produit dans le monde." Cf. Maritain, *St. Thomas and the Problem of Evil*, 12, in which Maritain speaks of human sin as a "wounding of God."

29. Maritain, "Quelques réflexions sur le savoir théologique," 21–22.

30. Maritain, "Quelques réflexions sur le savoir théologique," 15; Aristotle, *Nicomachean Ethics* 2.7.

31. Aristotle, *Nicomachean Ethics* 3.11.

32. Maritain also proposes that it is easy to imagine a case in which there simply isn't a word for a certain pure perfection in a given language, as, for example, if all the words for love in a given language included the notion of sexual desire. In that case, one would not be able to speak of God properly using that impoverished language's words for love. See Maritain, "Quelques réflexions sur le savoir théologique," 16.

33. Maritain, "Quelques réflexions sur le savoir théologique," 16–17.

attributed to God only *secundum effectum* but as properly naming God in himself according to what love is, then Maritain asks why we shouldn't say that "mercy is found in God according to what it is, and not only according to what it does, albeit in a state of perfection for which there is no name."[34]

Gilles Emery, while expressing respect for the profundity of Maritain's reflections, offers the criticism that, in the end, it is unclear whether the "unnamable perfection" posited by Maritain can be anything other than the divine love, once we have stripped everything of privation and defect away from the notion of "love which suffers in order to overcome suffering."[35] Although I am in fundamental agreement with Emery's criticism, as I will explain in the following, I will also suggest that there are resources in St. Thomas's writings on divine sorrow and mercy—both within and outside of *Summa theologiae* 1.21—that might help to address some of the dissatisfaction with St. Thomas's treatment of mercy motivating Maritain's account.

It is necessary to begin with St. Thomas's account of proper, analogical naming and metaphorical naming. In what follows, I will take a parallel case, that of divine knowledge (*scientia*), a divine name taken from human scientific knowledge—science as an intellectual virtue in the Aristotelian sense. How does *scientia* enter into divine predication? St. Thomas distinguishes those perfections/actualities found in creatures that can enter properly (*proprie*) into divine predication and those that do so metaphorically. A perfection/actuality falls into the latter category insofar as in its very notion (*ratio*) there is contained some element of materiality or defect. In his *Sentences* commentary, St. Thomas tells us that while the terms *cognitio* and *scientia* can be predicated properly of God, *sensus* cannot be; the former terms signify perfections in creatures that are exemplified absolutely (*simpliciter*) by God, while the latter term includes in its very signification the mode of cognition peculiar to a power conjoined to a bodily organ.[36] In a more expansive statement he offers about which names can only be predicated of God metaphorically, St. Thomas asserts in *De pot.* 7.5 ad 8 that any name that includes within its intelligible content (*ratio*) anything of potentality, privation, motion, "or anything similar" can only be predicated metaphorically of God.[37] In a parallel text from

---

34. Maritain, "Quelques réflexions sur le savoir théologique," 17.

35. Gilles Emery, "The Immutability of the God of Love and the Problem of Language Concerning the 'Suffering of God,'" in *Divine Impassibility and the Mystery of Human Suffering*, ed. James F. Keating and Thomas Joseph White (Grand Rapids, MI: William B. Eerdmans, 2009), 58. Cf. his similar criticism of Journet's position in "The Question of Evil and the Mystery of God in Charles Journet," in *Trinity, Church, and the Human Person* (Ave Maria, FL: Sapientia Press, 2007), 260–61.

36. *Super Sent.* 1.22.1.2 [Mand. 1.535].

37. *De pot.* 7.5 ad 8.

the *Summa theologiae*, Thomas clarifies that although names like being, goodness, and knowledge signify perfections that are first known to us as they exist in creatures, nevertheless these perfections "exist in God according to a more eminent mode than [that mode in which they exist] in creatures."[38] As a consequence, there are always features of the mode in which these absolute, unqualified perfections exist in creatures that will need to be denied when they "enter into divine predication," when we affirm that these perfections exist in God in a more eminent mode.

In his treatment of *scientia* as a divine attribute in *Summa theologiae* 1.14.1, St. Thomas responds to three objections against attributing *scientia* to God; the first two are especially instructive. The first objection is that *scientia* cannot be attributed to God because *scientia* is a habit that cannot belong to God, as it falls short of pure act. The second objection is that *scientia* is knowledge of conclusions caused by knowledge of first principles: nothing in God is caused, however, and so *scientia* cannot be attributed to God.

To the first objection, St. Thomas replies that whenever we attribute a perfection to God, "there is excluded from its signification everything that pertains to the imperfect mode which belongs to the creature. Whence *scientia* is not a quality in God, or a habit, but substance and pure act."[39] There are thus elements of the intelligible content (*ratio*) or definition of *scientia*— the genera that are the category of quality and its species, habit—that do not belong to God. I will return to this point in a moment.

St. Thomas replies to the second objection (that *scientia* is caused knowledge of conclusions) with the following:

> Those things which exist dividedly and multiply in creatures are in God simply and unitedly, as was said above. But man has diverse sorts of cognition, according to diverse cognized [objects]. For insofar as [man] knows principles, he is said to have understanding; but [he has] *scientia* insofar as he knows conclusions; [he has wisdom], insofar as he knows the highest cause; counsel or prudence, insofar as he knows [the things] to be done. But all these God knows by one, simple cognition, as will be shown below. Whence God's simple cognition can be named by all these names, yet so that from each of them there is excluded whatever is of imperfection and there is retained whatever is of perfection, insofar as they enter into divine predication.[40]

With respect to all of the names of cognitive perfections mentioned in this reply, St. Thomas makes clear that in each case, what is affirmed of God is

---

38. *ST* 1.13.3.
39. *ST* 1.14.1 ad 1.
40. *ST* 1.14.1 ad 2.

that he cognizes the object of that sort of cognition, not that he cognizes it in the way in which a human being knows it. So we can properly say that divine *scientia* is cognition of conclusions, which is just to say that God knows without discursion all the truths that for us are conclusions known through discursion from principles.[41] What is important is that Thomas wants to maintain that all of these names enter properly into divine predication, insofar as they signify God's simple *cognitio* or *intelligere* according to the *rationes* of what are distinct perfections/acts in our intellectual cognition, even though various elements of their imperfect mode of existence in creatures must be excluded from God.

For St. Thomas, it turns out, quite a bit can be excluded from what one understands concerning a created perfection like *scientia* when one regards it as an absolute perfection that can be properly attributed to God. He excludes the genera of this *ratio*, insofar as they imply composition and potentiality; he excludes notions like "being caused" and the discursive element in human *scientia* because these are inconsistent with divine simplicity and perfection. Given that a definition for St. Thomas is made up of genus and difference, the fact that he says that we attribute *scientia* to God while denying that the genera of this notion pertain to God suggests that it is the *differentia* of this notion that is attributed to God. This is, in fact, a point that Aquinas makes explicit in parallel texts throughout his career, that "*scientia* is not predicated of God according to the *ratio* of [its] genus, but according to [its] proper difference, which completes its *ratio*."[42] He tells us in *De pot.* 7.4 ad 2 that names like wisdom and justice are not denominated from the genus of quality, which signifies being inherent in a subject, "but rather from some perfection or some act, whence they enter into divine predication according to the *ratio* of their difference and not according to the *ratio* of their genus."[43] This clarification is key: that from which the divine name is derived (the *a quo nomen imponitur*), in the case of created perfections like wisdom and justice, is not the genus of quality or habit; it is rather the corresponding act or ultimate perfection. The perfection "from which wisdom and justice are [themselves] denominated" is not the genus of quality but rather wise and just acts. In the cases of

---

41. This could provide the foundation for a response to Davies's denial that moral agency and moral goodness can be properly attributed to God. Even if there are numerous features and conditions of human moral agency and goodness—our subjection to moral rules, the defectibility of our wills, our subjection to moral evaluation and judgment—that cannot be attributed to God, it might still be the case these notions can enter properly into divine predication, in the same way that much is excluded from our understanding of created *scientia* when we properly attribute this perfection to God.

42. *Super Sent.* 1.8.4.3 ad 1. Cf. *Super Sent.* 1.35.1.4 ad 7; *De pot.* 7.4 ad 2, ad 3.

43. *De pot.* 7.4 ad 2.

both metaphorical and proper, analogical predications, there can be elements of the very *ratio* of the created perfection that must be denied concerning God. In the case of names that are predicated metaphorically, such as *sentire*, it is what *specifically differentiates* this sort of cognition—that it is cognition that occurs through a bodily organ—that cannot be attributed to God. But in the case of any specific terms that enter properly into divine predication, it is the specifying act/perfection from which these specific qualities are denominated, rather than the genera of quality and habit, that is affirmed of God.

Since St. Thomas distinguishes a term like *scientia*, which contains nothing of imperfection or defect in its differentiating *ratio*, even if the genus of *scientia* and many aspects of human *scientia* must be denied of God, from a term like *sensus*, which contains something of materiality in its very *ratio* and so cannot be attributed properly to God, any attribution of sensation to God—as when we say that God hears our prayers—is metaphorical in character: the perfection in God signified by "hearing" is properly signified by a term like *cognitio* or *scientia*. As Maritain and Emery both note, however, it is essential to St. Thomas's account of the divine names said properly of God that such names, although they signify the divine essence, nevertheless "leave the reality signified as uncomprehended and as exceeding the signification of the name."[44] This is so, St. Thomas explains, because we know that whenever we signify God by a name like wisdom, "we do not intend to signify something distinct from His essence or power or *esse*."[45] The "propriety" of naming God by certain names derived from his creatures should never be mistaken for univocity, because we know that the simple divine reality infinitely exceeds the signification of any name. Since "those things found in a divided and multiplied way in creatures are in God in a simple and unified way," even when it comes to one divine attribute like *scientia*, St. Thomas treats a set of names said properly of God as all signifying the divine *scientia* under different aspects: all of the things that man knows in diverse ways, through the distinct perfections of *intelligentia*, *scientia*, *sapientia*, *consilium*, and *prudentia*, "God knows by a unified and simple cognition . . . whence the simple cognition of God can be named by all these names, but such that from each of them there is excluded anything of imperfection and there is retained anything of perfection, insofar as they enter into divine predication."[46] So although St. Thomas selects *scientia* among these names as the one given top billing in *ST* 1.14, he readily acknowledges that the term *scientia* does not convey on its own everything that must be said about God's knowledge.

----

44. *ST* 1.13.5.
45. *ST* 1.13.5.
46. *ST* 1.14.1 ad 2.

Furthermore, I would note that for St. Thomas in the case of *scientia* and *sensus*, there is a perfection that must be attributed to God—knowledge of material singulars—that is possible for us only through our *sensus* rather than directly through our intellectual *scientia*.[47] When living material creatures participate in a likeness of the divine *scientia* (which infinitely exceeds what the word *scientia* signifies), they do so, when it comes to the knowledge of material singulars, through *sensus*. Thus, although *sensus* and its various species can be predicated of God only metaphorically, there is nevertheless something of the perfection of God's knowledge that is found specifically in human sensation. Sensation is, in part, precisely how the united and simple perfection of divine knowledge is received in a divided and multiplied fashion in material creation. In this case, it is not necessary to say that there is some unnamable exemplar of the perfection of sensation in God; it is necessary only to say that even the best words we have for properly signifying the divine knowledge cannot fully capture its perfection, because the creaturely perfections from which those proper names are derived all fall short of the perfection and simplicity of the divine knowledge.

So, metaphorical divine names may "signify the perfections proceeding from God into created things in such a way that the imperfect mode in which the divine perfection is participated by the creature is included in the signification of the name," but something of the divine perfection might be found, in a given creature, precisely only in this imperfect mode.[48] I would suggest, then, that there is a legitimate need for metaphorical naming to complement proper naming, even if metaphorical naming must also be explicated and clarified in terms of proper naming. Even if mercy can be said only metaphorically of God—although I will show in a moment that this matter is more complicated in St. Thomas's thought than one might think—we still can, and should, say that something of the perfection of the divine love and goodness is participated, in material creation, only in the human heart that is prompted by sorrow for another's misery to dispel that misery as if it were one's own.

Before proceeding into a treatment of St. Thomas on divine mercy, it might be objected that in responding to Maritain, I need to address not only the attribution of mercy to God but also the attribution of sorrow or suffering. After all, although Maritain's account is motivated by his dissatisfaction with St. Thomas's treatment of divine mercy, he is ultimately concerned to find in God the exemplar of our suffering. So, what of divine sorrow? When St. Thomas discusses the metaphorical attribution of sorrow to God in the chapter on divine love in the *Contra Gentiles*, he distinguishes between the way in

---

47. For the attribution of knowledge of material singulars to God, see *ST* 1.14.11.
48. *ST* 1.13.3 ad 1.

which a passion like *misericordia* is attributed to God *secundum effectum* and a different sort of metaphorical predication "on account of the likeness of a preceding affection" (*propter similitudinem affectionis praecedentis*). In line with his theory of the passions, he explains that love (*amor*) and joy (*gaudium*) are the principles of all other affections, as moving principle and final cause. "God is said to sorrow, therefore, insofar as certain things happen contrary to those which He loves and approves, as in us too there is sadness about those things that have occurred against our will."[49] In us, our love is the principle of our sorrow, and love that does not sorrow over loss—given that we can suffer loss—is not love. And in so naming the divine love, we attribute sorrow to God. I will return to divine sorrow in my concluding remarks.

When treating divine mercy in *ST* 1.21, the text that Maritain finds less than satisfying, St. Thomas begins by claiming that mercy is supremely (*maxime*) attributed to God, putting mercy in some fashion in the company of such divine names as unity,[50] goodness,[51] and *qui est*.[52] He proceeds to treat mercy alongside several other divine names in a manner that parallels how he treats the set of names that can signify the divine knowledge, characterizing goodness, justice, liberality, and mercy as complementary names for signifying God as the one who bestows perfections on all things, even if "the communication of perfections, absolutely considered, pertains to goodness."[53] Unlike the treatment of divine knowledge in *ST* 1.14.1, however, here St. Thomas includes a divine name said *secundum effectum* (and so metaphorically) among the names complementary to goodness, alongside two names (justice and liberality) that are attributed properly to God: this would be as if St. Thomas had explicitly included *sensus* alongside *intelligentia*, *scientia*, and *sapientia* in *ST* 1.14.1. So again, even if mercy is said metaphorically of God, it can nevertheless uniquely complement names that properly signify the divine goodness, such that St. Thomas can go on to say that "mercy is the fullness of justice,"[54] that "the work of divine justice always presupposes and is founded upon the work of mercy,"[55] and that in the very act of creation there is found "in some way the character of mercy."[56]

---

49. *SCG* 1.91.

50. See *ST* 1.11.4 for the claim that God is *maxime unum*.

51. See *ST* 1.13.11 ad 2 for the claim that good is the *maxime proprium nomen Dei* insofar as God is named as the cause of all things.

52. See *ST* 1.13.11 for the claim that *qui est*, which signifies *ipsum esse*, is the *maxime proprium nomen Dei*, absolutely considered.

53. *ST* 1.21.3.

54. *ST* 1.21.3 ad 2.

55. *ST* 1.21.4.

56. *ST* 1.21.4 ad 4.

The *a quo nomen imponitur* of mercy as a divine name in *ST* 1.21.3 is certainly the passion of mercy as a species of sorrow,[57] and it is for this reason that St. Thomas says that mercy must be attributed to God metaphorically rather than properly. This is in line with his treatment of divine mercy in *SCG* 1.91, in which it is plainly asserted that mercy is attributed to God metaphorically "according to a likeness of effects."[58] Matters are somewhat complicated, however, by St. Thomas's treatment of mercy as a virtue in *ST* 2–2.30. In a. 3 of this question, Thomas distinguishes between (a) the passion of mercy, a movement of the sense appetite; (b) a movement of the intellectual appetite, insofar as the evil suffered by another can be displeasing to the will; and (c) the regulation by reason of this latter volitional movement, such that the passion of mercy is also regulated.[59] It is insofar as the movement of the intellectual appetite is ruled by reason so as to regulate the passion of mercy that mercy can be classed as a virtue. In accordance with this account, St. Thomas characterizes mercy as a moral virtue concerned with the passions.[60] Precisely as a moral virtue concerned with the passions, mercy still cannot be properly attributed to God.[61]

Nevertheless, references to divine mercy or pity (which I will use as the verb corresponding to *misericordia*) recur throughout *ST* 2–2.30. First, in an article devoted to the claim that the reason for pitying (*ratio miserendi*) is always a defect in the one pitying—which might seem to exclude absolutely the attribution of pity to God, as the first objection notes—St. Thomas notes that mercy (*misericordia*) is a sorrow over the misery of another, insofar as one apprehends the misery of the other as one's own. He distinguishes between two ways in which this apprehension of the misery of another as one's own might occur: (1) by a union of affection through love, and (2) by a real union between the suffering of the other and one's own suffering, insofar as one might see the suffering of another as likely to pass to oneself, which is why human beings tend to pity other people like themselves. Consequently, St. Thomas concludes that a defect is always the reason for pitying (*ratio miserendi*), either insofar as one regards the defect of another as one's own because of a union of love, or because of the possibility of suffering in a similar way oneself.[62] In replying to the first objection, which had claimed that "to pity (*misereri*) is proper to God," he asserts that "God does not pity (*misere-*

---

57. See *ST* 1–2.35.8 for the classification of mercy as a species of sorrow.

58. *SCG* 1.91.

59. *ST* 2–2.30.3.

60. *ST* 2–2.30.3 ad 4.

61. See *SCG* 1.92 for the claim that moral virtues concerning passions cannot be properly attributed to God.

62. *ST* 2–2.30.2.

tur) except on account of love, insofar as He loves us as His own."[63] Far from denying that God pities, St. Thomas clarifies that God's pity is only on account of love, rather than on account of the fear that motivates much human pity.

Most importantly, in *ST* 2–2.30.4, St. Thomas asks whether mercy (*misericordia*) is the greatest of virtues (*maxima virtutum*), and he responds as follows:

> In itself, mercy is the greatest, for it pertains to mercy that one should pour out (*effundat*) [goods] upon others and, what is more, that one should alleviate (*sublevet*) the defects of others, and this is supremely [the virtue] of one who is superior. Whence to pity (*misereri*) is also held to be proper to God, and in this His omnipotence is said to be supremely manifested.[64]

Despite consistently characterizing *misericordia* as said *secundum effectum* of God, here St. Thomas reports that to pity (*misereri*) is held to be proper to God and is the supreme manifestation of his omnipotence.[65] Two possibilities confront us: (1) perhaps St. Thomas is willing to use the verb *misereri* to designate properly the loving act of will by which God pours out goods upon others and alleviates their defects.[66] In this case, one might understand the *secundum effectum* attribution of *misericordia* such that the "effect" of the passion of mercy attributed to God is not just the curing of defects in creatures but the very act of *misereri*, as the loving act by which God heals wounds that he regards as his own. This reading would also be in accordance with the claim seen above that in the case of properly naming God as just or wise, we are attributing to God just and wise acts rather than habits; or, (2) perhaps St. Thomas is using the language of being "proper to God" not in opposition to metaphorical signification *secundum effectum* but in the sense of designating what belongs to God more than to anything else. In either case, it would seem that he can provide a serious reply to the concern motivating Maritain. On the former reading, *misereri* is, in fact, attributed properly to God, by properly signifying the loving act by which God treats our defects as his own, even though

---

63. *ST* 2–2.30.2 ad 1.

64. *ST* 2–2.30.4.

65. Elsewhere, explaining that presumption is a less grave sin than despair, St. Thomas notes that "on account of His infinite goodness, it is more proper to God to pity and to spare (*parcere*) than to punish; for the former belongs to God according to Himself, but the latter [belongs to Him] on account of our sins." See *ST* 2–2.21.2; cf. *Super Sent.* 4.46.2.2 qc. 3 s.c. 2.

66. Cf. *Super Sent.* 4.46.2.1.1, in which St. Thomas asserts that mercy motivated by the union of love is in God not as a passion but *secundum effectum*, but that this effect "proceeds from an affect of the will, which is not a passion but a simple act of the will."

he is free of all sorrow or defect in himself. On the latter reading, despite *misericordia* and *misereri* having the status of metaphorical names signifying *secundum effectum*, nevertheless *misericordia* is absolutely considered the greatest virtue, because the ultimate effect of *misericordia* is supremely produced by God and is the greatest manifestation of his omnipotence: the effects of the divine mercy disclose to us the nature of God. In the case of mercy, we would have a metaphorical divine name that is nevertheless especially privileged. In either case, as indicated above, the divine names *misericordia* and *misereri* complement in a critically important way what is said about God through other names, insofar as the divine love and goodness are participated by the human creature in a special way through mercy, so that in us, too, "among all the virtues which pertain to [our] neighbor, the most powerful is mercy."[67]

Concluding Remarks

For St. Thomas, speaking of God as merciful and pitying—whether this be entirely metaphorical or somehow proper—is indispensable for naming the one who out of superabundant love regards as his own the sufferings of creatures. Just as we need not say that there is an unnamable exemplar of *sensus* in the divine—for we can speak of God's knowledge, while understanding that the infinite perfection of God's knowledge is in one way participated in what we do through sensation—so, too, in the case of mercy, we need not say there is some unnamable exemplar of our suffering in love. Just as something of the infinite perfection of the divine knowledge is found only in us in our sensation, even with its materiality and privation, so, too, something of the infinite perfection of the divine love is participated, in us, in the virtuously sorrowful heart. This is the truth at issue when we speak of God as merciful, even if this is a metaphor *secundum effectum*. It is also the truth at issue when we speak of God as sorrowful, *secundum similitudinem affectionis praecedentis*.

We have seen that in his treatment of divine knowledge and the various terms used to designate it, St. Thomas notes that the simple perfection of the divine knowledge is participated by a multiplicity of perfections found in us. This is a particular application of what is for St. Thomas a more general truth, that the multiplicity of the divine attributes and the necessity of naming God through many names is because the infinite fullness of the divine perfection cannot be received in any one creature.[68] We have also seen that St. Thomas holds that the perfection of the universe requires the creation of defectible beings, that there be creatures subject to privation and suffering. I would suggest that these are two closely related truths, if it is recognized that something

---

67. *ST* 2–2.30.4.

68. See, for example, *Super Sent.* 1.2.1.3; *De pot.* 7.6; and *Resp.* 108 pr., 1–3.

of the divine perfection is uniquely participated by the suffering heart. For those *in via*, our imperfect imitation of the divine love involves a sorrow that cannot be properly attributed to the God who suffers no privation of the good: but what divine love alone is, our sorrow for the sake of love imitates better than our love alone. And so it is that in the vision of God in the life to come, "His name will be one,"[69] and "He will wipe away every tear."[70]

BIBLIOGRAPHY

Aristotle. *Nicomachean Ethics*. Edited by R. McKeon. The Basic Works of Aristotle. New York: Random House, 1941.

Brotherton, Joshua. "God's Relation to Evil: Maritain and Balthasar on Divine Impassibility." *Irish Theological Quarterly* 80, no. 3 (2015): 191–211.

———. *One of the Trinity has Suffered: Balthasar's Theology of Divine Suffering in Dialogue*. Steubenville, Ohio: Emmaus Academic 2019.

Carl, Brian T. "The Transcendentals and the Divine Names in Thomas Aquinas." *American Catholic Philosophical Quarterly* 92, no. 2 (2018): 236–42.

Davies, Brian. *The Reality of God and the Problem of Evil*. New York: Continuum, 2006.

———. *Thomas Aquinas on God and Evil*. Oxford: Oxford University Press, 2011.

Emery, Gilles. "The Immutability of the God of Love and the Problem of Language Concerning the 'Suffering of God.'" In *Divine Impassibility and the Mystery of Human Suffering*, edited by J. F. Keating and T. J. White, 27–77. Grand Rapids, MI: William B. Eerdmans, 2009.

———. "The Question of Evil and the Mystery of God in Charles Journet." In *Trinity, Church, and the Human Person*, 249–51. Ave Maria, FL: Sapientia Press, 2007.

Jensen, Steven J. "Aquinas's Original Discovery: A Reply to Barnwell." *American Catholic Philosophical Quarterly* 92, no. 1 (2018): 732–95.

Journet, Charles. *The Meaning of Evil*. Translated by Michael Barry. New York: P. J. Kennedy, 1963.

Knasas, John F. X. *Aquinas and the Cry of Rachel*. Washington, DC: The Catholic University of America Press, 2013.

Legge, Dominic. *The Trinitarian Christology of St. Thomas Aquinas*. New York: Oxford University Press, 2017.

Maritain, Jacques. *Existence and the Existent*. Translated by Lewis Galantiere and Gerald B. Phelan. New York: Paulist Press, 2015.

---

69. Zach 14:9 is cited by St. Thomas as a promise about the unified character of the beatific vision, in contrast to the multiplicity involved in knowing and naming God *in statu viae*. See, for example, *Super Sent.* 1.2.1.3; *SCG* 1.31; *Comp. theol.* 1.24; *Super Rom.* 1.6; and *De pot.* 7.6.

70. Revelation 21:4.

———. *God and the Permission of Evil*. Translated by Joseph W. Evans. Milwaukee: The Bruce Publishing Company, 1966.

———. "Quelques réflexions sur le savoir théologique." *Revue Thomiste* 69 (1969): 5–27.

———. *St. Thomas and the Problem of Evil*. Milwaukee: Marquette University Press, 1942.

Nicolas, Jean-Hervé. "La permission du péché." *Revue Thomiste* 60 (1960): 538–44.

O'Neill, Taylor Patrick. *Grace, Predestination, and the Permission of Sin*. Washington, DC: The Catholic University of America Press, 2019.

Shanley, Brian. *The Thomist Tradition*. London: Kluwer Academic Publishers, 2002.

Stump, Eleonore. "Aquinas on the Sufferings of Job." In *The Evidential Argument from Evil*, edited by D. Howard-Snyder, 51–52. Bloomington: Indiana University Press, 1996.

———. *Atonement*. Oxford: Oxford University Press, 2018.

——— *Wandering in Darkness*. Oxford: Oxford University Press, 2010.

Wippel, John F. "Metaphysical Themes in *De malo*, I." In *Aquinas's Disputed Questions on Evil: A Critical Guide*, edited by M. V. Dougherty, 12–33. Cambridge: Cambridge University Press, 2016.

White, Thomas Joseph. "Von Balthasar and Journet on the Universal Possibility of Salvation and the Twofold Will of God." *Nova et Vetera* 4 (2006): 633–66.

CHAPTER 10

Theodicy and Drama in
Hans Urs von Balthasar

KRISTEN DRAHOS

THEODICY AS A FUNDAMENTAL CONCERN OF THE
THEO-DRAMA

TO RAISE THE ISSUE OF THEODICY is to raise the question of the nature of history, or more specifically, of how history manifests as drama in such a way that it allows for, yet is not overrun by, evil. To try to see history as drama might not be intuitive for many today, when time seems quantifiable by increments meant to measure its duration rather than explore the dynamic of its formation. Hours and minutes delineate our days; holidays mark the passage of yet another calendar year; recounting stories chronicles the passage of time already "gone by." Time and history are atomized and catalogued. Drama as a mode of time, however, reinvests dynamic vitality and meaning's weight to the world's temporal finitude. The past, present, and future are inherently linked even as the diversity of history's events unfold and impact the story history weaves. Meaning unfolds in and through time. Without drama as the ground for a dynamic interaction between the world's finitude and God's infinite goodness and perfection, theodicy—like history itself—loses its vitality and reduces to a mere game of theological calculus and dogmatic hermeneutics. Just as drama claims there is more to time than its recorded measurement, so, too, does it demand an enlivened debate about divinity where the "who" of God is anything but a static "what" of determined outcomes.

Hans Urs von Balthasar positions philosophy as the primary inhibitor of dramatic vitality where two conflicting types—tragedies and epics—bookend a monolithic 'static problem.'[1] Ostensibly dramatic categories, tragedies and epics offer ersatz presentations of drama's dynamism through philosophic reconfiguration. On the one hand, tragedy surrenders the world to perpetual desolation that cannot be overcome, and the struggles of individuals or communities to

---

1. TD 2, 18.

205

fight fate is futile. Whether singularly scripted or multitudinous as perpetual fragmenting, both styles of this genre ultimately conform to the same end from which there is no rescue.[2] Epic narrations, on the other, measure everything by their conclusion's realization. All that conforms to and helps bring it about matters, and all that does not is rendered meaningless. In the end, the contrast between tragic desolation and epic incarnation ultimately showcases the same thing. Both tragedies and epics write the story of history from the vantage of their respective ends. Here Hegel and his epic, lyric, and dramatic categorizations of history loom large. At the outset, Hegel's philosophy initiates a rescue of drama from the grips of post-Kantian rationality. Hegel's scope is total such that all of history has a role to play in the story of Spirit's drama. However, like a wolf in sheep's clothing, Spirit ultimately evinces a winner-take-all scenario that devastates the recovered category altogether. The epic energy of Hegelian *Geist* cannot be contained, and the tension of otherness—aesthetic, religious, and political—ultimately gives way to concrete singularity.

For Balthasar to productively use the idea of drama, not only must he stave off the solidity of tragedies and epics; he must also recover drama's recast from Hegel's all-consuming grasp. The more Balthasar takes on Hegel, however, the more ground he gives for a category that Hegel's narration both justified and eliminated as part of Spirit's self-becoming—namely, evil as a dramatic problem. For Hegel, whatever destruction ensues during Spirit's becoming in and through time becomes a necessary casualty, and the need to stand against evil, or to assign moral weight and significance to it, slips away. The more that Balthasar presses against Hegel's totality, as well as the finality of epic and tragic narration, the more ground he gives for evil's presence and significance in drama itself. Freed from predetermined conclusions, evil appears as an increasingly powerful force, and what saved drama from Hegel's domestication now appears to threaten every aspect of the world. It integrates with and leaves lasting impressions upon the horizontal configuration of history through various distortions of finite freedom, a parody of the infinite power of divine freedom.

In answer, Balthasar relies on the interconnection of God with history. He anchors this idea both through the divine offering that undergirds existence as such and in the free gift of relationship that occurs throughout his-

---

2. Balthasar has his eye on a twofold problem with the tragic. Not only do classic tragedies concern him, but so, too, the modern and ongoing inheritance of the baroque's fractured dramatics. In this second sense Walter Benjamin's work is of primary concern. Ultimately for Balthasar, Benjamin's resistance to Hegelian totality gives way to the similar result of tragic conclusions. The permanent lack of resolution in the German *Trauerspiele* is an ersatz form of true drama. Like tragedy, it, too, has a foregone conclusion, and despite its energy it betrays a meaning-laden end.

tory. In every way, this horizontal and vertical interplay reveals the heart of what drama means. What is so necessary about the idea of drama as a form, writes Francesca Murphy, is how

> Drama is open to breaks in the sequence, abrupt "vertical" alterations of direction. The notion of story gives us a nice, rounded sense of an ending, of completion or closure. Stories and drama can be equally eventful, but nothing happens in a story which is not explained by something within the story. Whereas the events in drama hover on the edge of mystery, a story is entirely explicable on its own terms.[3]

Not only does this sense of vertical interruption challenge Hegel: it also opens avenues of hope that evil and its empirical trail of casualties are not the only option for a world that is, at heart, dramatic. Such a perspective, however, is far from assured. Murphy further reminds readers of the philosophical temptations that view evil from inductive and deductive logic, where the former approaches the question of evil empirically by weighing the amount of evil in the events of world history and human decisions against the goodness that accompanies it, while the latter considers whether the possibility of an infinite and loving God is *de facto* compatible with the existence of evil.[4] Both of these approaches, she points out, miss the difference that drama as a category brings to the conversation, namely, that God's interaction with the world is completely unlike any other relation on the horizontal plane of finite existence, and its logic is quite other than the natural human tendencies to quantify through inductive and deductive processes.[5] To think of this relationality, and

---

3. Francesca Aran Murphy, "Desacralized Time and Progress," *Second Spring* 2 (2002): 50–51. As quoted in Aidan Nichols, *A Key to Balthasar: Hans Urs von Balthasar on Beauty, Goodness, and Truth* (Grand Rapids, MI: Baker Academic, 2011), 58.

4. Francesca Aran Murphy, *God Is Not a Story: Realism Revisited* (Oxford: Oxford University Press, 2002), 132–35.

5. Both Brian Hebblethwaite and Jacob H. Friesenhahn bring Balthasar into conversation within the inductive and deductive debates of evil in analytic philosophy. Hebblewaite's approach remains deductive, as he places Balthasar's vision of finite freedom grounded upon infinite freedom alongside Austin Farrer's lectures, *The Freedom of the Will*. Friesenhahn, however, offers greater novelty in his recontextualization of not only Balthasar's immanent Trinitarian theology but also some of his economic ramifications in the analytic discussion. Friesenhahn's work suggests a hopeful avenue for conversation between a deeper study of Balthasar's dramatics and the analytic logic of contemporary discussions of theodicy. See Jacob H. Friesenhahn, *The Trinity and Theodicy: The Trinitarian Theology of von Balthasar and the Problem of Evil* (Burlington, VT: Ashgate Publishing Company, 2011); Brian Hebblethwaite, "Finite and Infinite Freedom in Farrer and von Balthasar," in *Human and Divine Agency: Anglican, Catholic, and Lutheran Perspectives*, ed. F. Michael McLain and W. Mark Richardson (New York: University Press of America, Inc., 1999), 83–96.

to properly think about the problem of evil, requires another kind of logic—a narrative logic—which offers a theological resource for rediscovering the "curves" of God's interaction with the world apart from the "right angles" that philosophy and theology have forced God into.[6]

Like Murphy, Balthasar wrestles with the curved logic of narrative, drama, and evil. To be sure, evil impacts every aspect of the world, from the building of individuals as 'genuine human figure[s]' over the course of a lifetime to the broad dimensions that color salvation history. However, Balthasar cannot ignore Christian revelation that places the cross of Christ as a mark of victory over sin and the world's brokenness and leaves the Lamb from Revelation as the perpetual, vivid imprint of a drama that refuses to succumb to tragedy. It is to Christ that he turns as the guarantor of history's dynamism and ultimate meaning. The Lamb's pascal mystery is and remains an apocalyptic point of dramatic transfiguration for the world, and the church stands as the ongoing mediator of the cross's power as Christ's body active within history until the end of time. There is an urgency to this task: the statement "The Christian revelation can only appear in its full stature—if it is presented as being dramatic *at its very core*" (emphasis Balthasar's) mirrors the imperative mood he finds in Rilke that he uses to open the second part of his trilogy.[7] The challenge facing Balthasar is that of creating a space for real and meaningful decision-making—including decisions that bring forth evil—within the horizontal aspect of creation, without reducing or negating God's mysterious love that elects to save the realities of history. Evil, in some mysterious way, must not be beyond the glory of God's grace and the drama of salvation.

EVIL'S ASPECTS: INDIVIDUAL AND HISTORICAL

Balthasar's view of evil moves between two fundamental poles—individual evil and evil in history—although the former informs and mediates the second. To understand evil means understanding where it originates and of what it

---

6. Murphy, *God Is Not a Story: Realism Revisited*, 1–10. It is worth noting that Aidan Nichols points to Schelling as a final coordinate for understanding Balthasar's agenda and orientation in the *Theo-Drama*. As Schelling explains, drama presents a synthesis of the subjectivity of lyrical self-expression with the necessary objectivity of the epic. The complexity of individual becoming is part and parcel of "an overall effect of complete objectivity" (Nichols, *A Key to Balthasar: Hans Urs von Balthasar on Beauty, Goodness, and Truth*, 58–59). Nichols sees shades of Schelling in the individuality that Balthasar develops in the significance of individual human existence for the idea of drama, as well as the desire for unity that refuses to capitulate to Hegel's all-consuming concept. While this point is relevant overall, it has less relevance on the particular problem of evil, since here Balthasar's main opponent is Hegel rather than Schelling.

7. *TD* 2, 51.

consists.[8] Finite freedom, as a result, becomes a critical component of Balthasar's discussion. On an individual level, freedom offers humans meaningful parts in the drama of history where they can be held responsible for the decisions they make, be they praiseworthy or blameworthy.[9] For Balthasar, the events of the world's ongoing drama can never erase the significance of individual actors or their decisions in the drama, and even those who appear inconsequential have roles that are vital for the performance. Likewise, theodicy cannot be thought apart from a serious consideration of finite freedom as enacted by individuals throughout history. No one is prescripted to commit evil actions. Adam and Eve cannot be used as a scapegoat that determines the fate of the world. On the one hand, this idea is liberating: humans are free and responsible agents. but on the other, it is daunting: why do people continuously commit evil actions if not on account of primordial fault? Balthasar turns to theological anthropology to address this issue.[10]

Humans, he claims, are a mixture of two poles that oppose and inform one another. First, they cannot but be the finite beings bound by space, matter, and their historical context. However, they also manifest not only a desire but a need to move into the infinite. This polarity comes to a head in their exercise of freedom, when they actualize concrete decisions that press toward not only an infinity of possible decisions but the attempted realization of infinite choice itself. Balthasar stresses that the infinity that humans reach toward as they navigate the polarity of their nature is not sinful. On the contrary, it fundamentally flows from, albeit in a limited way, the infinite freedom of God.[11] Problems

---

8. See also Hebblethwaite, "Finite and Infinite Freedom in Farrer and von Balthasar." While Hebblethwaite touches on finite freedom's relation to evil, the majority of his efforts concern volition as a capacity as such, primarily securing space for human freedom as undetermined in the context of divine freedom that grounds it, as well as has the capacity to redeem it through noncoercive grace.

9. This is a fundamental concern for Hebblethwaite, who follows analytic patterns of Alvin Plantiga and his free-will defense, although Hebblethwaite will focus his efforts on how humans can still be considered free in a final sense when aligned with communion with God and the saints in the beatific vision. This consideration of the final end of human freedom in God, unfortunately, lies outside the bounds of our current project.

10. Although he does not put it into the heart of his anthropology, Balthasar fully intends for his account to accord with revelation. He thus offers a robust history of theological reception of Genesis and the *imago Dei* at the end of his section on finite freedom. See *TD* 2, 316–34.

11. Balthasar writes, "if its progress toward self-realization is also to be free and not caught in the chains of some dialectical law, it needs to have an infinite freedom in and above itself, empowering it to realize itself as finite freedom. This infinite freedom must be sufficiently free (according to its nature) to allow finite freedom to operate freely within it; or rather, as we are talking about infinite freedom, actually to *impart* finite freedom in the first place." See *TD* 2, 200, 212.

arise, however, as humans make decisions ignorant of a fundamental feature of their freedom—namely, that their freedom is *given*, not self-created. To recognize this fact is to recognize the exteriority of infinity from the perspective of the creature, which as a result opens the meaning of one's own movement in infinity through another—God.[12]

Evil enters creation through human freedom acting out of balance with the polarity of its nature. Balthasar takes up Kierkegaard's diagnosis of various misinterpretations of the self in *Sickness Unto Death*, uniting them in a fundamental tendency toward the absolutizing of finitude at the expense of the infinite. At its most problematic, evil becomes finite choices that self-absolutize the finite as though it were the infinite itself.[13] This maximal misalignment of finitude as infinity occurs both on an individual and social level.[14] As individual wills clash with one another, so do they disrupt the dynamic interaction of finite beings within the history. Various versions of self-creation as universal truth war with one another.

Concrete ramifications of individual evil then continue developing in a twofold way. First, evil harms the individual in her personal, daily existence, which results in a fundamental misalignment toward others. Rather than knowing otherness by her very interior disposition toward infinite otherness, the world becomes recognizable only by her own limited perspective. What ought to give unlimited depth to her own self-understanding and unique, irreducible mystery to every other 'other' in the world reduces to what she can grasp of herself. The "absolute incommunicability of [her] own being . . . and the unlimited communicability of being as such' closes off."[15] What she sees is the mirror of her own creation, opening her to a host of concrete decisions that harm herself and others in her warped perspective. Second, as the will loses its connection to divine infinity, it loses the ability of full disinterest. Goodness, consequently, becomes a relative term. What is good turns into

---

12. Balthasar has a lengthy discussion that picks up the thought of Nicholas of Cusa in considering the way creation must, on the one hand, exist within God in order to be and be free, and yet also exist as distinct from God in order to remain distinct and vital as real. See *TD* 2, 193–96, 200–201, and 287. This point is particularly important as a moment wherein Balthasar aligns himself with modern notions of infinity and freedom—reminiscent of Kantian volition's relation to the sublime or the absolute sense of Spirit that is the fullness and limitlessness of Spirit's abstraction become real and concrete—as well as pushes against views of infinity that attempt to posit it absolutely within a created domain.

13. In this sense, the Cartesian absolute 'I' becomes the entirety of the cosmos. See *TD* 2, 2089.

14. Balthasar points to philosophy's positivistic tendencies in general and Sartre, Marx, and Nietzsche in particular as prime examples of this double-sided of self-absolutization. See *TD* 2, 268, and 286.

15. *TD* 2, 208.

what is good for the individual, since there is not ground of infinity outside of the self. This reduction to relativism sets individuals into competitive motion, where the gain and success of one individual's freedom clashes with the gain and success of others. Balthasar notes that there exist many attempts to join self-interest to a greater sense of otherness that might challenge this sense of conflict (he thinks of Kant here, in particular), but he also notes the principal challenge to all such systems as they play out in history—namely, there is nothing given beyond the self that it necessarily depends upon and is ordered by.[16]

This is not to say that evil can be separated from history and cordoned within the individual as such, or relegated to individual decisions alone. On the contrary, one of Balthasar's primary concerns in his writing on theodicy is a recognition of the historical tracks that evil makes within creation's ongoing drama. Evil marks history from the outset: Adam and Eve's decision is constitutive of this moment. It is important here for Balthasar to carefully consider how to engage the story of the fall. On the one hand, he takes care to eschew a prescripted narrative. Humans must remain free after the fall, even in the world is impacted by the primordial human decision. On the other, he must account for revelation without turning Adam and Eve into pure myth. He must show that their impact on history is real for drama to have value. Otherwise, human decisions might exist purely and abstractly apart from the context of time's ongoing course. The evil that Adam and Eve choose, therefore, marks the beginning of the problem of evil not just for individuals but for history itself. Evil's impact stretches beyond the individual actors of history's drama and into the setting and plot as well. The advantage of placing theodicy, at least in part, in the historic fabric of the world is the inability of individuals or communities to ignore or write out evil's scope in history. The disadvantage is, of course, what Walter Benjamin notes in his famous theses "On History": history bears witness to a seemingly endless pile of ruination.[17]

Balthasar offers three points by which to recognize historical evil and consider the severity of its presence. The first is evil's appearance in power. At the outset, Balthasar takes pains to defend power as such. To misconstrue power as evil would remove human responsibility for what arises within the world's drama. Power originates from infinite freedom and is given to finite freedom as gift—it is the very "'dynamism'. . . meant to point finite freedom in the direction of infinite freedom."[18] However, power appears as evil historically when it

---

16. *TD* 2, 210–12.

17. Walter Benjamin, "On the Concept of History," in *Walter Benjamin: Selected Writings*, vol. 4, *1938–1940*, ed. Howard Eiland and Michael W. Jennings (Cambridge, MA: The Belknap Press of Harvard University Press, 2006), 389–400.

18. *TD* 4, 163.

is severed from the good ground it comes from in God. When there is no longer a connection to infinite freedom's absolute aspect of goodness, giving and grounding finite freedom's energy, power loses its norm and direction. With only itself to turn to, finite freedom turns to itself as absolute, and the absolute enmeshes within the social order. Human freedom becomes consumptive as its drive toward infinity seeks to find its ground in collective social enterprises. Balthasar points to Nietzsche's "will to power" as the deepest manifestation of power severed from its norming good in infinite freedom.[19] In this case, finite freedom moves beyond any and all individuals who express it, itself determining good and evil in creative expressions of finitude. What creatively conquers becomes what is good; what is conquered becomes a casualty of this goodness. All that resists power is termed evil and ought to be destroyed.

This first point leads Balthasar to his second—namely, that evil's manifestation in history appears in the guise of deceit. It is "the lie" incarnate in matter. In the beginning of a discussion of freedom, evil, and power in his *Theo-Drama*, vol. 4, Balthasar writes "evil necessarily veils and misconstrues itself."[20] In delving deeper into finite power's attempt to absolutize itself, Balthasar points out that hiddenness acts as an essential part of evil's appearance in history: "Both things are always present and take effect: the act of concealment and its result. The contradiction is hidden, it is no longer visible. These two together show us that evil is *the lie*."[21] Hiddenness is important insofar as it gives evil an additional energy. Balthasar points out that although evil cannot erase the fundamental consciousness that finite freedom cannot ground itself, and that therefore its activities in trying to do so are permanently flawed, it must continuously work to cover up this fact. Therefore, evil grows in force not only on account of its initial absolutizing but it also constantly makes inroads to secure itself and deepen its hold. Uprooting evil from within history's drama becomes all the more difficult with this second entrenchment, since this deception works on the material as well as spiritual elements of finite freedom. History is replete with the battle lines of power's claims to self-absolutize, attempts to uproot what cannot help reveal itself to be a lie for freedom's fulfillment, and ever-new manifestations of self-absolutizing that appear under the guise of long-awaited liberation. As Balthasar notes, the lie never tires of taking on new and ever-shifting disguises in the attempt to maintain, for as long as possible, an illusion that it offers the answer to freedom's infinite needs.

Since the lie cannot be other than what it is, its power cannot be contained. This brings Balthasar to his third point in delineating historical evil's

---

19. *TD* 4, 163.
20. *TD* 4, 160–61.
21. TD 4, 164.

marks. It is, at its heart, all-consuming. For as long as time and freedom endure, evil fuels its operation through created finitude. Nothing is safe from its reach since its effects impact everything, from the interiority of human existence in freedom to the shape of history writ large. This idea pushes Balthasar into his final point about the dramatic appearance of evil in the vision of powers and principalities that Paul offers in the New Testament, which he sees mirrored in the book of Revelation. In the extreme positioning of this idea, he sees a symbolic expression of the lie built into concrete forms as individual actors, and the societies they construct, come to a head with the climax of God's journey with humanity. Presented in the concrete realities of history, evil is neither an abstract force operating in the world nor a divine nemesis able to contend with God. It is, in Nietzschian terms, the 'will to power' in all its forms, demanding 'another mask' at each new moment in history.

The Cross as Dramatic Answer to Theodicy

Balthasar turns to the Incarnation and the cross in order to address the various contours of theodicy within the dramatic form of history. On the one hand, this is not a novel approach. Balthasar aligns himself with Gregory of Nyssa, Augustine, Irenaeus, and Maximus the Confessor as he delineates his thinking about the meaning of Christ for the world. He turns to Matthew, John, and Revelation for scriptural warrants. However, his configuration of evil as a coordinate within the drama of history pushes Balthasar into new territory. God's free decision to intersect the human drama in a radical way through Christ prompts Balthasar to offer a particular, dramatic answer to the problem of evil itself. This perspective offers a horizon for interconnecting the idea of Christ's victory with history, neither surrendering to Hegel nor evacuating the space for finite freedom's meaningful interplay.

Throughout the trilogy, Balthasar's thought is heavily influenced by the relationship he establishes between the immanent and the economic Trinity.[22]

-----

22. Friesenhahn spends considerable time parsing the relationality between the immanent and economic Trinity in Balthasar's thought. In his book, he addresses the fundamental question of whether or not Christianity can offer a sustainable response to analytic concerns about the problem of evil that seem to rule out the possibility of Christian revelation as such. See, especially, Friesenhahn, *The Trinity and Theodicy*, 120–37. Friesenhahn uses Balthasar to navigate around the issue of Moltmann (a God involved in drama able to conquer evil but who ultimately becomes too attached to evil at the expense of divinity, making evil an intrinsic part of Godself and thus surrendering God as an answer to evil—evil, rather, becomes part of God's answer). Balthasar gives Friesenhahn an entrance to history and the drama of evil that maintains God's otherness while still allowing fundamental interaction between history and transcendence. Friesenhahn is, therefore, particularly useful for orienting Balthasar's work in relation to analytic concerns. The Christian God can, in theory,

Similar to other twentieth-century theologians, Balthasar acknowledges the fundamental interconnection between who God is *in se* and how God reveals Godself through action in the world. Although he is wary of Hegel, Balthasar is equally concerned about the Christian tendency toward idealism, where God's transcendence signifies a remote lack of involvement. Christianity must avoid both of these dangers. While God is not bound by the play of the world, he is intimately involved in it.[23] God's presence matters, from supporting the world's being in the grounding and ordering of finite freedom to offering time hope that its run is not meaninglessly prescripted by its end.

This makes the Incarnation central for Balthasar. All history leads to this climax of dramatic interaction between God and the world, and all history is ordered by its form. Without it, "we risk depriving the world/God relationship of all dramatic tension."[24] Before the Incarnation, God's journeying with the world is real but distant, claims Balthasar, be that in the shape of philosophy's natural search for understanding, other religions traditions, and even Israel's own election.[25] It is real in the sense that God interacts with and underlies the reality and freedom of the world's dramatic Being as such, but it is distant in the sense that God's infinite freedom remains separate from the world's finite interplay. The Incarnation, however, changes everything. As the Son becomes human without sacrifice to divinity, the form of finite and infinite interaction irrevocably

---

stand up to the problem of evil. The question of what this theory looks like within history's drama, though, is little explored within analytic philosophy—either by Friesenhahn or others. Fortunately, Balthasar is far from silent on this matter.

23. Although they are often pitted as rival thinkers, Balthasar and Rahner have a lot of overlap in this fundamental concern. A distinguishing feature between them has to do with who they consider more fundamental as a dialogue partner—Kant or Hegel. For Rahner, the challenges of Kant's idealist separation between noumenal and phenomenal can ultimately be reconceived in and through a sense of divine mystery. Rahner can thus prioritize economic speech without sacrifice to the mystery of Godself even as he puts forward his famous dictum, "the economic Trinity is the immanent, and vice versa." Balthasar, on the other hand, reclaims rather than repurposes Hegel's vision of drama. He must provide an account that allows drama to be fundamental to the world's Being, while only fundamentally mattering to God in the infinite freedom of divine love. This need creates a radically different agenda for Balthasar than for Rahner in terms of Trinity and God's relationship with history. See also *TD* 4, 273–81, 320–21.

24. *TD* 4, 76.

25. Balthasar's absolute Christocentrism allows him great latitude in (a) affirming all paths, of philosophical and religious, that lead toward Christ's ultimate invitation and transfiguration of finite freedom, and (b) offering special preference and a sense of dramatic providence to God's election of Israel. See *TD* 2, 77–89, 121–23, and 201; *TD* 4, 221–29. Still, Balthasar is careful to exclude any notion of 'progressive' motion toward Christ, as though the world's drama itself, rather than God's free initiative, brings forward the Incarnation. See *TD* 2, 87–94.

changes in the hypostatic union. Finitude is brought into direct contact with divinity. As the Father so fully emptied himself as to create the perfect Image in the second person of the Son before the world began, so too does the Son empty himself of divinity as he enters the created drama so that it might relate intimately with him. Thus, the Incarnation erases the distance between divinity and humanity, even if the latter never supplants the former: "The son's action is what history is for, his uniqueness sets it free to attain its proper character."[26]

History, though, is wrapped up in the contours of fallen freedom, and evil mars its drama. In the perfection of infinite freedom, which is bound and grounded by nothing other than God's own perfection, the Son assumes his mission to liberate the world from evil. Balthasar aligns his thinking with Bonaventure in putting the cross as the climax and center of the Incarnation's meaning. The cross is the definitive moment of and form for reconciliation and unification with God, and as such, it is the definitive answer to theodicy. As answer, though, the cross brings about a surprise. Rather than the *Christus Victor* model of Gregory of Nyssa or Augustine, or even Barth's divine "No" to the power of sin, Balthasar discusses the ramifications of the cross as a fully kenotic image. In this sense, the cross stands as the perfect dramatic expression of God's selfless love to the point that Christ "becomes sin" and journeys into the furthest reaches of hell. Because the Trinity's perfect self-giving cannot be surpassed, there is no danger that Christ might be lost in the utter generosity of his own gift on the cross.[27] Likewise, though, because the Son is the one who dies on the cross, the sacrifice offered goes into the deepest and most horrific spaces of finite evil. The forlorn cry on the cross is no facsimile. It is the cry of the only one who can reach the darkest abysses of humanity because he goes into them himself.[28] Thus, the way that Balthasar crafts the cross as a "No" to evil comes not in the shape of negation, but rather of transfiguration.[29] Balthasar articulates the activity of the cross as that which 'penetrates' the darkest moments of history to refashion them from within.

As a result, the world is remade as "radiant darkness" and recrafts the world internally. This idea is profoundly important for Balthasar. He takes up

---

26. *TH*, 62.

27. Balthasar's expressions here walk a razor's edge of orthodoxy in the attempt to show the depths that the cross reaches on Good Friday without succumbing to the Hegelian temptation of devastation to the Trinity. Adrienne von Speyr's visions are instrumental in this regard, giving Balthasar language that surpasses his expression even in *Mysterium Pascale*. See *TL* 1, 345–60.

28. Balthasar carefully constructs a "sin-bearer" who "becomes sin" yet ultimately recognizes "what separates him from the horror and yet connects him with it" is precisely "the form of the darkness of his mission in the darkness of the Father." In other words, "he is at once the farthest from hell and, as sin-bearer, the closest to it." See *TL* 2, 350–51.

29. *TD* 4, 334–35.

the image of the slain Lamb of God, who still bears the wounds of the world, from the book of Revelation as his focal point for the ongoing, dramatic meaning of Jesus' passion, death, and Resurrection. The Lamb in Revelation functions as a concrete symbol of the luminous, new life won through the sacrifice of the cross, but it also reveals the ongoing mission that the passion presents as the victorious Lamb continues to bleed on behalf of the world.[30] Balthasar does not employ this image to negate the efficacy of the historic event of Good Friday as the definitive moment of salvation history. On the contrary, he uses it to make the efficacy of Good Friday available to all from *within* the drama of history as such: "They interpenetrate, yet without cancelling out that highest dramatic quality."[31] Through the Lamb, resurrection's power joins the permanent mission of the cross in the kenosis of reaching into evil's darkest moments. The Lamb is not merely a final horizon that the world looks to, hoping to be saved from the marks of evil at the end of finite existence. It is, rather, the hope of the world in its current condition.

This point is critical for Balthasar as he configures the Lamb slain into a model of analogy that intersects with and transfigures finite freedom from within the idea of history as dramatic: "His wounds are not mere reminders of some past experience. Since this drama is experienced by the economic Trinity, which is one with the immanent Trinity, it is constantly actual."[32] The Lamb thus functions as an apocalyptic answer to evil as much as an eschatological horizon for the world. As apocalyptic, the Lamb penetrates every moment of world history, offering the power of the cross and the resurrection as the power of infinity that finite freedom requires. History receives redemption not through an undoing of the past but rather though an interior transfiguration and reorientation. God's freedom and action within the world stand as a historical event that creates a super-form (*Urform*) for the world in relation to God. Until the end of time, therefore, this ongoing drama—both of evil and of its transformation—remains.[33] In this sense, Balthasar stands at quite a distance from theologians like Barth. While Christ is certainly God's definitive "No" to sin, he becomes the embodiment of dramatic transfiguration. Salvation is not simply a rejection of sin but rather a change of history's deepest evil within drama itself. The Son plumbs the depths of sin in order to

---

30. Balthasar writes, "Jesus' agony lasts until the end of the world (Pascal); in fact, it goes right back to the world's beginning. His mortal wounds are eternally open (Bérulle)." Balthasar then conjugates these philosophers through the Carmelite tradition, showing how the Lamb is a permanent manifestation of "the dark night of the Cross" for the world. See *TD* 4, 134–35, 337.

31. *TD* 4, 462.

32. *TD* 4, 363.

33. *TD* 4, 318–19, 361–63.

make space every moment of history, no matter how broken, in the heart of the Trinity. Moreover, this intradramatic change opens space for the deepest sense of analogical freedom. Freedom that was grounded upon and opened toward divine infinity now receives its ground, function, and end directly from the Son. The immensity of this gift opens not only a response of praise but a dramatic form of communion. With and through the Son, humans are called to participate in the transfiguration of the world.

The Church and the Ongoing Drama of the Cross

This participation is fully voluntary, meaning that the love and hope offered to the world through the cross are noncoercive and can be rejected. In this sense, the cross as an answer to theodicy heightens the dramatic tension in the world.[34] Evil is unveiled for what it is, and the hope of finite freedom is offered to all. In truth, finite freedom is given its greatest gift and weightiest responsibility through the cross. Acceptance of the cross as freedom's form is acceptance of the fullest freedom that works with God in transfiguring the drama of history and drawing the world into God's love. Rejection of the cross is a rejection of freedom's ground, purpose, and end. While Balthasar leaves room for the hope of universal salvation—indeed, he dedicates an entire book to the question[35]—his analogical Christocentrism offers immense responsibility to humans in their own dramatic journey. Human freedom is meaningful in the dramatic unfolding of evil in the world as much as it is meaningful in the salvific transfiguration of history's fallenness through the cross.[36] While on the surface this idea might seem like an all-or-nothing approach that devalues created existence in time by focusing on the singularity of acceptance or rejection of the Lamb, Balthasar is careful to contextualize finite freedom's new prerogative in the living body of the church. Acceptance and rejection of the Lamb's offer is not the work of a moment but rather of a lifetime accomplished within the gathered and united body of the Lamb.

The church, therefore, acts both as the way for the drama of the individual to play out as each person must respond in freedom to the Lamb's invitation and the stage for the drama of the world to receive transfiguring grace. The church is Christ's body active within the drama of history until the end of time.[37] In a real and concrete way, each member finds that she has a particular

---

34. *TD* 4, 369.

35. *DWH*.

36. *TD* 4, 367–83.

37. Balthasar expresses this idea through the activity of Mary, whose 'yes' to God becomes a concrete and paradigmatic emblem of the church's 'yes' to the cross and Christ's redemptive mission. See *TD* 4, 351–61.

part to play in addressing evil in the world. On the one hand, the script of this drama has already been written. The Son's passion, death, and Resurrection are the salvation of the world. On the other, though, the world is saved through the intersection of God's love with the world's drama in the hypostatic union, which never destroys what it joins. History as drama continues to unfold, and the Lamb journeys with the world through the church. Through the Spirit, she acts as mediator of salvation and transfiguration.[38] Both sacramentally and through her living body—her many members—the church embraces world's drama to bring it into the heart of God.[39]

As the members of this body are joined to and ordered by the form of Christ as the Lamb, they enter into a new relation with evil and the suffering it engenders in history. Before the cross, evil's presence presented an unsolvable point of conflict. Finite freedom's rejection of God's infinite freedom set humanity at odds with God's love. The cross as the form of freedom that changes the course of this drama puts the members of the church in a challenging position. Fundamentally, it stands as a witness against evil and its many forms. Baptism is a permanent rejection of evil and its temptations. History and its drama, though, must also be redeemed—they are not abandoned because they are intertwined with evil. Thus, the members of Christ's body are tasked with the radical mission to go out and bring the love of the cross into every corner of the world. They are embodiment of the drama of the cross in history. Balthasar's attachment to the Carmelites as a lived witness of the church's missionary directive shows how seriously he takes this vision of dramatic activity.[40] To stand against evil is to love the world in the shape of the cross. It is to unite oneself with the slain Lamb's form and to be willing to walk into the 'depths of hell' on earth.

It might seem, in light of the Lamb and the mission of the church, that the problem of evil ought to shrink as time progresses. Are not Christians continually participating in the world's transfiguration to the effect that evil diminishes, that its marks are transfigured, and that the horizon of the world's drama draws increasingly close to its model and end in God's love? Balthasar cautions against this perspective. He worries that it speaks more to an epic vision of the world construed through a Hegelian lens of progress more than a Christian understanding of the dramatic operations of the cross. In *Theo-Drama*, vol. 4, Balthasar spends considerable time parsing the meaning of the book of Revelation not only as a central interpretative lens for the meaning

---

38. *TD* 4, 364–65.

39. Members are initiated into this mystery through baptism, or dying to sin, and Eucharist, or entering into the kenotic state of giving in a cruciform manner. See *TD* 4, 365–67.

40. See, especially, Balthasar's discussion of Therese of Lisieux in *TSiS*.

of the Incarnation and the cross but also in relation to its initial configuration as a text of 'end times' with respect to the church's function. For Balthasar, this apocalyptic book is instrumental in understanding the confrontation between the church and evil, the church's relation to evil's intensifying presence before the end of time, and the balance between endurance and martyrdom that the church embraces as the formal contours of her cruciform mission. This is not a text, he says, that Christians can ignore or sideline on account of the intensity or the style of its composition. It is and will remain a central cipher for interpreting history as dramatic and for understanding the role of the church in the world.

Two images are central for Balthasar in this respect: fire and "the race." They serve as guides to what he terms "The Confrontation," which marks the church's drama in the world after Christ's Incarnation and passion and lasts until the end of time. Fire, he writes, "provides us with a final, perpendicular excerpts of the last stages of dramatic action between heaven and earth, God and his creation."[41] This book's view of end times points not to a final period of days, as though predicting an ultimate fiery conflagration, but rather its images of flame and lightning point to the inbreaking of the cross within time. Fire reveals that "all subsequent events in the dimension of time, subject to this end-Word and within the embrace of the end-time, can only be a 'theology of history.'"[42] Although Christ stands as the pinnacle and center of the world's drama, he does not erase its dramatic form. On the contrary, the fullness of drama emerges as God's revealed love in the Son directly confronts human attempts self-absolutizing. Drama, in other words, does not abate. On the contrary, as the book of Revelation shows, it increases as time proceeds, and what stands against God's love entrenches itself all the more fully.

This is not to say that evil becomes a force as powerful as the cross. Rather, Revelation's fire balances between two poles. On one end, it is historical, bringing a vertical apocalyptic presence to history. On the other, it is tethered to finite freedom. "This fire is dramatic in a heightened sense: God no longer deals with man from without but—by becoming man—from within man and at man's innermost level."[43] This second element of relating fire to finite freedom ensures that the drama of the world never erases the individual actors. There is no risk of history becoming an apocalyptic battle between a collectively formed evil and God's love. In addition, this second pole draws creation into the most intimate relationship with cruciform love. Fire burns not externally but "at man's innermost level."[44] It is not the individual who

---

41. *TD* 4, 59.
42. *TD* 4, 60.
43. *TD* 4, 60.
44. *TD* 4, 60.

is subsumed by history's drama but rather history's drama that is transformed through the individual. Jesus baptizes "no longer with water" but rather the Spirit and fire. Each individual must face the dramatic challenge of response to this love—will he love "'as I have loved you,' with that unsurpassable love of him 'who gives his life for his friends' (Jn 15:12f)?"[45]

Individuals are essential in the unfolding drama, but Balthasar makes no mistake—this is a single drama with a focused center at the cross.[46] This centrality gives rise to his second image, the race. In this instance, the book of Revelation heightens Paul's words regarding his own journey and end. What begins as a recommendation given to all believers turns into a symbol of the world's dynamic interaction between its horizontal experience of time and its vertical interaction with the cross. In "the race," Balthasar sees the "mutual embrace of the Adam principle and the Christ principle as they march through history."[47] Turning back toward the horizon of history, Balthasar affirms that humanity's perspective is not negated by the cross or Christ's victory. There is still work to be done as finite freedom unites to the fire of the cross and embraces the world. The gift that the cross gives humanity is twofold. It is the total and absolute victory over evil through transfiguration in infinite freedom that only the cross can provide. It is also that which gives finite freedom its purpose, courage, and motivation. Finite freedom, too, has a role to play in saving the world. It receives its mission precisely in uniting itself with the love of the cross and boldly reclaiming each moment of time through the love of the Lamb.

CONCLUSION

Drama stands at the heart of Balthasar's discussion of theodicy. The cross presents a vital moment of intersection and reconfiguration for the world, and the church carries on the mission of the Lamb. For Balthasar, the shadow of Hegel and the threat of a static configuration of world history, either in epic or tragic domains, cut the world off from the vitality of Christian revelation and the operation of the cross within the world. Addressing evil in all its forms requires a dramatic presentation of the gospel message. To rightly see evil—enmeshed in finite freedom enacted within the social and historical matrix of existence—is no easy task. Neither is offering a wounded and scarred world

---

45. *TD* 4, 61.

46. He writes, the multiplicity of individual actors "do not create a multiplicity of independent dramas but are yoked together in a single, total drama that encompasses all the individual interactions. . . . This is because all encounters between man and God are included in the drama of Christ" (*TD* 4, 62).

47. *TD* 4, 67.

salvific hope that works within, rather than against, the very nature of creation itself. Balthasar is all too aware that the modern world, rationally compartmentalized and historically confined to static horizons, is in desperate need of the dramatic hope of the cross. His battle is to show the way Christianity and the church offers the very vitality for which the world longs. The question for theology today is whether or not it will pick up where Balthasar leaves off, continuing to develop and share the importance of theological drama as a critical answer to the problem of theodicy.

BIBLIOGRAPHY

Benjamin, Walter. "On the Concept of History." In *Walter Benjamin: Selected Writings*, vol. 4, *1938–1940*, edited by Howard Eiland and Michael W. Jennings, 389–400. Cambridge, MA: Belknap Press of Harvard University Press, 2006.

Friesenhahn, Jacob H. *The Trinity and Theodicy: The Trinitarian Theology of von Balthasar and the Problem of Evil*. Burlington, VT: Ashgate Publishing Company, 2011.

Hebblethwaite, Brian. "Finite and Infinite Freedom in Farrer and von Balthasar." In *Human and Divine Agency: Anglican, Catholic, and Lutheran Perspectives*, edited by F. Michael McLain and W. Mark Richardson, 83–96. New York: University Press of America, Inc., 1999.

Murphy, Francesca Aran. "Desacralized Time and Progress." *Second Spring* 2 (2002): 50–51.

———. *God Is Not a Story: Realism Revisited*. Oxford: Oxford University Press, 2002.

Nichols, Aidan. *A Key to Balthasar: Hans Urs von Balthasar on Beauty, Goodness, and Truth*. Grand Rapids, MI: Baker Academic, 2011.

Theological Anthropology

CHAPTER 11

Trinitarian Contemplation as the Perfection of the Cosmos

Aquinas on Analogy, Appropriation, and Dionysian Ascent

JACOB W. WOOD

ALTHOUGH THE "NATURE/GRACE DEBATE" in contemporary Catholic theology focused at the beginning of the third millennium on the work of Henri de Lubac and the question of human nature's end, an important extension of that debate concerns the work of Hans Urs von Balthasar and the question of how human nature may be known. The polemics on this topic began most recently with the work of Steven A. Long.[1] According to Long, Balthasar's idea of nature as a "limit concept," which can only be known negatively in the light of Christian Revelation, "implies an epistemic denial of the efficacy of abstraction in cognizing proportionate natural order, and that this denial is incompatible both with the teaching of Aquinas and with the requisites of metaphysical realism."[2] Long levies against Balthasar's anthropology the same critique as he levies against de Lubac's: by denying that humanity outside the sphere of Revelation and faith possesses the ability to arrive at a knowledge of human nature *precisely because* it cannot identify human nature's end apart from grace, Long alleges that Balthasar compromises the integrity of human nature, of the natural law, and of a political order founded upon the natural law.[3]

Even if not every Thomist may agree with Long's assessment of Balthasar's anthropology, there is something understandably Thomistic about

---

1. See Steven A. Long, "On the Loss, and the Recovery, of Nature as a Theonomic Principle: Reflections on the Nature/Grace Controversy," *Nova et Vetera* (English edition) 5, no. 1 (2007): 133–83. Subsequently, Long developed his thinking in *Natura Pura: On the Recovery of Nature in the Doctrine of Grace* (New York: Fordham University Press, 2010). The earlier essay is reprinted as chap. 1. The response to Balthasar appears as chap. 2.

2. Long, *Natura Pura*, 54.

3. Long, *Natura Pura*, 43–44. The object of Long's critique is *KB*, especially on pp. 267–325.

225

Long's approach. Aquinas observes in the *Summa Contra Gentiles* that when two people cannot agree on a theological starting point, recourse can always be had to natural reason "to which all are bound to assent,"[4] in view of the fact that—whatever human nature and its end may be—we all share that nature and the principles of reason with which it has been illumined. But what if we enter a context in which disputants who share the Christian faith do not agree on where reason ends and where faith begins (for the Thomist) or where faith ends and reason begins (for the Balthasarian)? In these circumstances, D. Stephen Long points out that a direct, philosophical critique of the sort that Steven A. Long undertakes leaves only two options: "surrender, or perhaps a return to polemics,"[5] neither of which is likely to lead to an irenic resolution of the question at hand.

Thomas Joseph White has suggested an alternative approach. If the disputants cannot agree on where natural reason begins, but they can agree that human knowing can be investigated from within the sphere of Revelation and faith, why not step back from epistemology and metaphysics and ask whether Aquinas offers any *theological* reasons why it would be important for human reason to be able to know created nature, including human nature, outside the sphere of Revelation and faith. In line with Balthasar's Christological orientation, White argues from the necessary preconditions for the possibility of a person knowing and accepting the Revelation of the divinity of Jesus Christ. Simply put: without the antecedent capacity to know nature and nature's God prior to the reception of grace—however fettered that capacity may be by sin—human reason would be incapable of making sense of the claim that Jesus Christ *is God*, even under the influence of grace.[6]

Notwithstanding the irenic intent of White's methodology, D. Stephen Long thinks that White begs the question.[7] White may have made a theo-

---

4. *SCG* 1.2.: "Unde necesse est ad naturalem rationem recurrere, cui omnes assentire coguntur."

5. D. Stephen Long, review of *Natura Pura: On the Recovery of Nature in the Doctrine of Grace* by Steven A. Long, *Modern Theology* 27, no. 1 (2011): 698. See also the more developed response in *Saving Karl Barth: Hans Urs von Balthasar's Preoccupation* (Minneapolis, MN: Fortress Press, 2014), 94–99. I do not intend to suggest that Long's reading of Balthasar on the natural knowledge of created natures is the only possible reading of Balthasar on this question, only that Long offers a common reading that any dialogue between Thomists and Balthasarians must take into account.

6. Thomas Joseph White, "'Through him all things were made' (John 1:3): The Analogy of the Word Incarnate according to St. Thomas Aquinas and Its Ontological Presuppositions," in *The Analogy of Being*, 246–79; reprinted in White, *The Incarnate Lord*: 203–22. See also White, "Classical Christology after Schleiermacher and Barth: A Thomist Perspective," *Pro Ecclesia* 20, no. 3 (2011): 229–63, especially 256–62.

7. Long, *Saving Karl Barth*, 94.

logical event (the Incarnation) the object of philosophical reflection, but his epistemic approach to that event allegedly relies upon the very metaphysical presuppositions about God, man, and the world, which a Christological framework was supposed to avoid.[8] For Long, the consequences are severe:

> If metaphysics (the analogy of being) *conditions* revelation, then . . . it straightjackets theology and overlooks the historical reality of Christian faith. . . . Does metaphysics not do violence to its object if it *conditions* what revelation can say in this strong sense? Any answer depends on what we mean by "conditions." It could mean nothing more than this: if God is incarnate in Jesus Christ, uniting humanity and divinity in one, then after the fact we know one of the conditions for it is that "humanity" and "divinity" exist, and are at least in part, intelligible. . . . If this were all that the Ressourcement Thomists claimed, it should neither cause controversy, nor be church dividing. But they appear to say more. At the least, they suggest that the *analogia entis* is the *epistemological* condition rendering our knowledge of the incarnation intelligible. At the most they assert the *analogia entis* is the *metaphysical* condition rendering the incarnation possible. . . . If it is the latter, how does it not lack humility in the face of God's mystery? . . . Could Aquinas affirm this?[9]

With White and D. Stephen Long, then, the question of how we know human nature specifically, with which the recent debate began, is thus completely subsumed under the larger question of how we know creation in general, as well as how we know God through it. Can human reason know created natures—including human nature—outside the sphere of Revelation and faith? If so, how does one avoid the critique that such knowledge would impose conditions on God's activity in the world? Any attempt to arrive at an irenic consensus between Thomists and Balthasarians on the knowability of human nature must first grapple with these more general questions before a consensus on theological anthropology can emerge. For only after offering an adequate account of the knowability of created nature in general will it be possible to offer an adequate account of the knowability of human nature in specific. The task of working toward an irenic consensus in theological anthropology thus demands that we shift our focus from the specific question of how human nature is known to the broader question of how created nature is known at all.

Matthew Levering thinks that what White proposes regarding the knowability of created nature in general need not be seen as imposing limitations

---

8. Long, *Saving Karl Barth*, 94.
9. Long, *Saving Karl Barth*, 167.

on God's activity in the world. Creation itself is "theophanic."[10] If God has, in fact, chosen to give himself to be known by natural reason through creation, then human reason's ability to know created natures—and to know God through them—can be seen as an *effect* of God's free decision to structure creation in a particular way, rather than an attempt to impose limitations on God's freedom. This analysis opens up another pathway toward an irenic consensus between Balthasarians and Thomists. If for the sake of finding common ground we want to be able to approach the knowability of created nature from within theology, why not start with the Doctrine of Creation instead of Christology and ask whether St. Thomas Aquinas offers any theological reasons from within this doctrine as to why God would want human reason to be able to know created natures and to know God through them? That is the question I intend to take up here. I shall argue that from Hugh of St. Victor in the twelfth century to Thomas Aquinas in the thirteenth, it was commonly believed that human reason's ability to know created natures was part of God's freely chosen plan for the perfection of the cosmos. Not only did God create human nature so that human persons might participate in knowledge and love of the Trinitarian persons; God also called each and every one of us to confer a participation of that knowledge and love upon the entire exterior world around us by drawing up our natural knowledge of creation into Trinitarian contemplation by connecting the knowledge of the divine being through analogy with contemplation of the Trinitarian persons through appropriation. In this context, Aquinas's belief that human reason can know created natures outside the sphere of Revelation and faith, and his particular use of the theory of Aristotelian abstraction to explain how that knowledge is attained, served not only as an important step in his understanding of how humanity can ascend to the contemplation of the Triune God by grace but also, especially, of how humanity can gather the whole of the cosmos into that ascent and so bring God's purpose for creation as a whole to its ultimate fulfillment. I will conclude by suggesting that though the contemporary debate between Thomists and Balthasarians about the natural knowability of human nature may seem intractable, an irenic recovery of the theological context of Aquinas's understanding of the knowability of created nature in general can clear the path for future studies to achieve consensus on the knowability of human nature in specific, even as it brings to light an overlooked dimension of Aquinas's own theological anthropology: the centrality of human nature in the ascent of Creation to the Triune God.

---

10. Matthew Levering, *Engaging the Doctrine of Creation* (Grand Rapids, MI: Eerdmans, 2017), 114n12.

Background to the Thirteenth Century:
Hugh of St. Victor and Peter Lombard

In order to understand how Aquinas arrived at his understanding of the role of human reason within God's purpose for creation, it is necessary to put his thought in context. The mid-thirteenth-century conversation about the relationship between human reason and creation was principally concerned with ideas drawn from two figures in the twelfth century: Hugh of St. Victor (c. 1096–1141) and Peter Lombard (c. 1100–1160).[11] Both of these figures agree on what we might call the "*ratio creationis*" (God's "purpose for creation"): God chose to create out of his goodness so that others might come to share in his happiness.[12] Since the only creatures capable of sharing in God's happiness are rational creatures, God structured the whole of creation into two tiers. Rational creatures (human beings and angels) fulfill the *ratio creationis* directly by taking delight in the service of God. Since human beings are partly corporeal, however, God created the physical universe to serve humanity so that we might have all that we need to find happiness in God.[13] For these medievals, the "service" that the exterior world renders to humanity is primarily noetic rather than utilitarian: while the exterior world may happen to provide for the satisfaction of our corporeal needs, its primary function is to assist us through our knowledge of it in the contemplation of God.[14]

Hugh and Peter differ on how precisely the exterior world performs its noetic service to humanity. For Hugh, as we contemplate the world around us, every creaturely perfection we encounter is reduced to a triad, which then points us toward an interior triad in the soul; the interior triad in the soul, in

---

11. For introductions to the life and work of Hugh, see Boyd Taylor Coolman, *The Theology of Hugh of St. Victor: An Interpretation* (New York: Cambridge University Press, 2010); Paul Rorem, *Hugh of Saint Victor* (New York: Oxford University Press, 2009). On Peter Lombard's life and work, see Marcia Colish, *Peter Lombard*, 2 vols. (Leiden: Brill 1994); Philipp Rosemann, *Peter Lombard* (New York: Oxford University Press, 2004).

12. Hugh of St. Victor, *De sacramentis* 1.2.4 (*PL* 176:208A); Peter Lombard, *Sententiae in IV libris distinctae* 2.1.3.5, 2 vols., ed. Ignatius Brady (Grotteferrata: Collegii S. Bonaventurae ad Claras Aquas, 1971–1981), 1:332.

13. Hugh of St. Victor, *De sacramentis* 1.2.4 (*PL* 176:208A); Peter Lombard, *Sent.* 2.1.4.1–2 (Brady 1:332); and Colish, *Peter Lombard*, 1:338.

14. Wanda Cizewski, "Reading the World as Scripture: Hugh of St. Victor's *De tribus diebus*," *Florilegium* 9 (1987): 76; Boyd Coolman, "'In Whom I am Well Pleased': Hugh of St. Victor's Trinitarian Aesthetics," *Pro Ecclesia* (2014): 331–54, at 342. Both explore the aesthetic dimension of Hugh's contemplative cosmology in the *De tribus diebus*, in relation to the existence of creatures that serve no practical purpose for human beings at all. See Peter Lombard, *Sent.* 2.1.4.6 (Brady 1:333).

turn, points us toward the Triune God.[15] More specifically, the immensity (*immensitas*) of the universe is a sign of the soul's power (*potentia*); the beauty (*pulchritudo*) of the universe is a sign of the soul's wisdom (*sapientia*); and the usefulness (*utilitas*) of the universe is a sign of the soul's goodness (*bonitas*) or love (*amor*). When we contemplate the soul's inner triad of *potentia, sapientia*, and *bonitas* under the light of faith, it leads us to the contemplation of the Father, the Son, and the Holy Spirit through the appropriation of each member of the inner triad to a specific Trinitarian person.[16]

There are two different ways in which Hugh thinks that appropriation takes place. The first is what we might call "accommodative." The accommodative sense of appropriation is an apophatic sense in which the perfections we appropriate to individual Trinitarian persons correct defects in our ordinary human understanding of their names: *potentia* helps us to avoid attributing the infirmities of old age to the Father, *sapientia* helps us avoid attributing the immaturity of youth to the Son, and *bonitas* helps us avoid attributing the malignancy of evil spirits to the Spirit.[17] The second sense of appropriation is what we might call "objective." The objective sense is a cataphatic sense in which the relationships among created perfections bear a similarity to the relationships among the Trinitarian persons: the power of the mind generates wisdom in the understanding like the Father generates the Son. Love in the will proceeds from the power of the mind and the wisdom of the understanding like the Holy Spirit proceeds from the Father and the Son.[18] Because the

---

15. Hugh of St. Victor, *De sacramentis* 1.3.29 (*PL* 176:231A–C). On antecedents to the treatment of creation and the Trinity in Hugh's earlier work, see Dominique Poirel, *Livre de la nature et débat trinitaire au XIIe siècle: Le "De Tribus Diebus" de Hugues de Saint-Victor* (Turnhout: Brepols, 2002), 315–420. We are focusing on the *De sacramentis* rather than the *De tribus diebus* or other, earlier works because *De sacramentis* was the most common source of Hugh's ideas for thirteenth-century authors.

16. Hugh of St. Victor, *De sacramentis* 1.3.28 (*PL* 176:230C–230D). Dominique Poirel, in *Livre de la nature*, 315–17, points out the flexibility of the members of this triad in Hugh's thought, especially the third, which appears variably in the *De sacramentis* as *benignitas, dilectio*, and *voluntas*, in addition to *bonitas* and *amor*. *Bonitas* and *amor* have been selected here because they occur at the point in Hugh's argument most relevant to the present purposes.

There is a debate as to whether Hugh or Abelard was the first to make significant use of the triad of *potentia, sapientia, bonitas/benignitas*. In *Livre de la nature*, 261–420, Poirel argues for the priority of Hugh, while Matthias Perkams, in "The origins of the Trinitarian attributes *potentia, sapientia, benignitas*," *Archa Verbi* 1 (2005): 23–29, argues for the priority of Abelard.

Colish, *Peter Lombard*, 1:232–33, is critical of Hugh here for what she perceives as a variety of inconsistencies and omissions in his handling of the Augustinian source material for his triads.

17. Hugh of St. Victor, *De sacramentis* 1.3.27 (*PL* 176:229C–D).

18. Hugh of St. Victor, *De sacramentis* 1.3.27 (*PL* 176:229A-C).

human soul can observe only these kinds of relationships in the created order among these specific perfections, the comparison between them and God obtains a level of objectivity, without therefore allowing us to apprehend the Trinitarian persons by purely natural reason.

In assessing Hugh's understanding of Trinitarian contemplation, Peter Lombard had to take into account the thought of Gilbert of Poitiers, a controversy over whose thought raged in the years after Hugh's death in 1141.[19] Gilbert had proposed a distinction between being (*Deus*) and essence (*Deitas*) in God, as well as a distinction between the divine persons, who he thought we distinguish numerically, and the divine essence, which he thought we identify on the basis of causality.[20] Reacting against Gilbert, Peter strictly emphasizes the identity of being and essence in God, as well as the essential identity of each person with the divine essence.[21] Since being and essence are identical in God, we should reject of any strong association between specific attributes and individual divine persons.[22] Peter will admit that *potentia, sapientia*, and *bonitas* can be appropriated to the Father, the Son, and the Holy Spirit respectively, but only in Hugh's accommodative sense, not in Hugh's objective sense.[23] Peter is emphatic on this point: "those things which are spoken of God by way of substance apply to the three persons equally."[24] Peter's emphasis on divine unity against Gilbert thus caused a twofold breakdown in Hugh's understanding of Trinitarian contemplation: 1) Peter makes the universe theophanic only

---

19. Colish, *Peter Lombard*, 1:133, observes that Gilbert completed his commentaries on the *Opuscula Sacra* of Boethius in 1142, the year after Hugh died. For the text of Gilbert's work, see Gilbert of Poitiers, *The Commentaries of Gilbert of Poitiers on Boethius*, ed. Nikolaus Häring (Toronto: Pontifical Institute of Mediaeval Studies, 1956). For other texts of Gilbert on the subject, see Nikolaus Häring, "A Commentary on the Pseudo-Athanasian Creed by Gilbert of Poitiers," *Mediaeval Studies* 27 (1965): 23–53; Häring, "A Treatise on the Trinity by Gilbert of Poitiers," *Recherches de théologie ancienne et médiévale* 39 (1972): 14–50.

20. For discussions of Gilbert's understanding of these distinctions and its significance for subsequent theology, see Michael Williams, *The Teaching of Gilbert Porreta as Found in his Commentaries on Boethius* (Rome: Apud Aedes Universitatis Gregoriensis, 1951); Lauge Olaf Nielsen, *Theology and Philosophy in the Twelfth Century: A Study of Gilbert Porreta's Thinking and the Theological Expositions of the Doctrine of the Incarnation during the Period 1130–1180* (Leiden: Brill, 1982).

21. Peter Lombard, *Sent.* 1.34.1 (Brady 246–51).

22. Peter was inspired in part here by Walter of Mortagne's and the *Summa Sententiarum*'s earlier critiques of Abelard. See Colish, *Peter Lombard*, 1:113–14.

23. Peter Lombard, *Sent.* 1.3.4 (Brady 76–77). This passage is drawn from Hugh of St. Victor, but notably it has been stripped of any reference to objectivity concerning the *vestigia*.

24. Peter Lombard, *Sent.* 1.34.3 (Brady 252): "Quae autem secundum substantiam de Deo dicuntur, tribus personis pariter conveniunt." See Colish, *Peter Lombard*, 1:247.

of God's unity, and 2) Peter makes the exterior world directly theophanic in itself, removing Hugh's requirement that the contemplation of God in the universe be funneled through the contemplation of God in the soul.[25]

One difficult question about Peter's understanding of divine simplicity that he initially avoided was the question of how we can distinguish the divine attributes from one another if we cannot reduce them to a contemplative triad.[26] But toward the end of the *Book of Sentences*, he at length proposes an answer when speaking of God's justice and mercy. Although all of the divine attributes signify the divine essence, they are distinguished from one another based upon the different "connoted effects," which the divine essence produces among creatures.[27] Since each of these effects signifies the whole divine essence equally, we may happen to find aids to our faith by seeking out *vestigia* among the things that God has made—particularly within the soul[28]—but these aids remain accommodative, not objective.

ALBERT THE GREAT

In the mid-thirteenth century, we can trace the influence of Hugh's triadic contemplation on the secular master, Philip the Chancellor, as well as on the early Franciscans, Alexander of Hales and Bonaventure of Bagnoregio. Under Hugh's inspiration, these theologians sought to identify ever-increasing levels of *vestigia* throughout the created order, pointing to such triads as formal, efficient, and final causality; one, true, and good; mode, species, and order (*modo, species, ordo*); and measure, weight, and number (*mensura, pondus, numerus*).[29] By contrast, we can trace the influence of Peter's under-

---

25. On this second point, see Peter Lombard, *Sent.* 1.3.1.1 (Brady 68–69), 1.3.1.6 (Brady 69); Colish, *Peter Lombard*, 1:238–42.

26. Louisa Valente, *Logique et théologie: Les écoles parisiennes entre 1150 et 1220* (Paris: J. Vrin, 2008), 173–77, points out that although Peter distinguishes different divine attributes throughout *Sent.* 1.3, 1.8, 1.22, and 1.34, he fails to offer a rationale for that distinction anywhere in book 1.

27. Peter Lombard, *Sent.* 4.46.3.3 (Brady 533–34). The appeal to Origen, together with Brady's notes on its source, can be found at *Sent.* 4.46.3.5 (Brady 534).

28. Peter offers an extended and nuanced discussion of Augustine on the psychological analogy in *Sent.* 1.3.3 (Brady 74–76).

29. On the relationship between Philip the Chancellor and the Franciscans, see Michael Robson, "Sermons Preached to the Friars Minor in the Thirteenth Century," in *Franciscans and Preaching: Every Miracle from the Beginning of the World Came about through Words*, 284 (Boston: Brill, 2012).

In Philip the Chancellor, *Summa de bono, De bono nature quod est diminuibile per malum culpe* 2.1, ed. Nicolai Wicki (Berne: Francke, 1985), 315–16, Philip unites efficient causality and "one" with "power" and the Father; exemplar causality and "true" with "wisdom" and the Son; and final causality and "good" with "goodness" and the Spirit.

standing of contemplation on the secular masters Stephen Langton and William of Auxerre,[30] and through William on the early theologians of the Dominican Order, including Hugh of Saint-Cher, Roland of Cremona, and Guerric of Saint-Quentin.[31] From there, Peter's thought exercised a particularly marked influence on the early work of Albert the Great (c. 1200–1280), the future teacher of Thomas Aquinas, to whose understanding of creation Aquinas was deeply indebted. Although, as we shall see in a moment, Hugh's triadic view of contemplation was never far from view.

Albert's early work on creation (c. 1241–1252) is open to certain aspects of the Victorine approach. For example, Albert appreciates and affirms an association between efficient causality and *potentia*; exemplar causality and *sapientia*; and final causality and *bonitas*.[32] But he does not hesitate to empha-

---

The triad of *modus, species, ordo* has a subordinate role in Philip the Chancellor, *Summa de bono, De bono nature quod est diminuibile per malum culpe* 2.2 (Wicki 322) but becomes the architectonic triad through which Alexander of Hales expounds the Victorine centrality of the soul in his *Quaestiones disputatae postquam fuit frater*. See Alexander of Hales, *De modo, specie, et ordine* m. 1, redactio 2, sol., in *Quaestiones disputatae quae ad rerum universitatem pertinent*, ed. H. M. Wierzbicki (Grottaferrata: Collegii S. Bonaventurae ad Claras Aquas, 2013), 387. See also *Summa Halensis*, Ia-Iae, nn. 111–15, in *Summa theologica [Summa fratris Alexandri]*, 4 vols. (Quaracchi: Collegium S. Bonaventurae, 1924-48), 1:173–82.

The triad of *mensura, pondus, numerus* receives significant attention in William of Auxerre's *Summa aurea* 2.8.2.9, ed. Jean Ribaillier, 7 vols. (Grottaferrata: Editiones Collegii S. Bonaventurae ad Claras Aquas, 1980–1987), 3:212–27, and comparatively little in Philip the Chancellor. It receives greater attention in *Summa Halensis*, Ia-IIae, nn. 27–33 (Quaracchi 2:38–44) and Bonaventure. On the use of the triad in Bonaventure, see Alexander Schaeffer, "The Position and Function of Man in the Created World according to Saint Bonaventure," *Franciscan Studies* 20, no. 3/4 (1960): 261–316, and 21, no. 1/2 (1961): 233–382; Esther Woo, "Theophanic Cosmic Order in Saint Bonaventure," *Franciscan Studies* 32 (1972): 306–30; and Leonard Bowman, "The Cosmic Exemplarism of Bonaventure," *The Journal of Religion* 55, no. 2 (1975): 181–98.

30. Regarding Stephen Langton's approach to theological language and its relationship to Peter Lombard, see Valente, *Logique et théologie*, 257–66. On William of Auxerre's understanding of theological language, see 266–72.

31. A detailed discussion of the theory of divine naming in these figures remains an important *desideratum*. In the meantime, see John Fisher, "Hugh of St. Cher and the Development of Medieval Theology," *Speculum* 31, no. 1 (1956): 57–69; Christian Trottmann, *Théologie et noétique au XIIIe siècle: à la recherche d'un statut* (Paris: J. Vrin, 1999), 94–102. Trottmann (97) notes that the early Dominicans were marked by the influence of William of Auxerre and Praepositinus of Cremona.

32. On efficient and exemplar causality, see Albert the Great, *De IV coaequevis*, 1.1.7, in *Opera Omnia*, ed. Auguste Borgnet et al., 38 vols. (Paris: Vivès, 1890–1899), 34:317. Albert differs from the earlier tradition in that he sees *potentia* not in the *immensitas* of creation but in the fact that God brought it to be out of nothing. On final causality, see Albert the Great, *De IV coaequevis* 3.18.2.1 sol. (Borgnet 34:451).

size the distance involved in any attempt to identify an objectively triadic structure for our contemplation of God in the exterior world:[33] God's power as efficient cause so infinitely exceeds creatures that we cannot arrive at anything more than the knowledge that God exists and that there is only one God by reasoning from efficient causality.[34] We cannot apprehend God's other attributes by natural reason except with probability,[35] and even then, we can only distinguish them—as Peter Lombard had done—based upon the effects that they connote in creatures.[36]

At the very start of his Parisian career (c. 1241–1243), and prior to book 1 of his *Commentary on the Sentences*,[37] his criticism of Philip the Chancellor and the early Franciscans is unusually harsh:

> From this it is clear that the work of some people, who want to reduce all these [triads] to one, is pointless, because it is not possible to adapt any one of them perfectly [to the Trinity], and also because if you ask them why different Christian authors offer different formulations [of triads], they cannot tell you.[38]

It is not that Albert denies the importance or usefulness of the triadic contemplation of the exterior world. It is just that he thinks that it is based on such an "obscure similarity" between God and creatures that there is no way for us to establish objectively whether to appropriate a given divine attribute to one person or another.[39] Perhaps for this reason Albert tends to frame his discussion

---

33. Jan Aertsen, *Medieval Philosophy as Transcendental Thought: From Philip the Chancellor, ca. 1225 to Francisco Suárez* (Boston: Brill, 2012), 183.

34. Albert the Great, *Super Sent.* 1.3.2 ad 1 (Borgnet 25:93).

35. On the limitation of certitude to God's being and unity, see Albert the Great, *Super Sent.* 1.3.1 ad 1–3 (Borgnet 25:92–93); on the probable nature of natural knowledge of other divine attributes, see 1.3.2 sol. (Borgnet 25:93).

36. Albert the Great, *Super Sent.* 1.3.4 sol. (Borgnet 25:95).

37. On the difficult questions surrounding the dating of book 1 of Albert's *Commentary on the Sentences* with respect to the *De IV coaequevis,* the *De homine,* and the *De bono,* see Bernhard Geyer, Praefatio to Albert the Great, *De bono,* in *Opera Omnia,* vol. 28 (Munich: Aschendorff, 1951), XII–XIII.

38. Albert the Great, *De bono* 2.2, in *Opera Omnia,* 41 vols. (Munich, Aschendorff, 1951–Present), 28:26: "Et ex hoc etiam patet, quod inutilis est labor quorundam, qui omnia haec volunt reducere ad unum, eo quod impossibilis est adaptatio propria et etiam ideo, quia si quaeratur ab eis ratio diversitatis enumerationis habitae a sanctis, non possunt assignare." This edition of Albert's *Opera Omnia* will hereafter be abbreviated "Col." for "Cologne."

39. Albert the Great, *De bono* 2.3 sol. (Col. 28:27–28): "However, we call it a 'footprint' (*vestigium*), because there is an obscure similarity with God in the paths that he has trod." ("Vestigium autem dicitur, eo quod est obscura similitudo dei in viis eius."

of the *ratio creationis* in his early work in terms of the "completion" (*perfectio*) of the universe as such, rather than in terms of its manifestation of God.[40]

In book 1 of his *Commentary on the Sentences* (c. 1243), Albert develops a slightly more receptive approach to the Victorine tradition. He does so by revisiting Peter Lombard's response to Gilbert of Poitiers. If the only act of reasoning we engage in when naming God from the exterior world is one based upon connoted effects, as Peter argues, then we can only ever attain to the knowledge of God insofar as he is a cause (*causa ut causa*), never to the knowledge of God in himself.[41] Yet the theologian has to do more than speak of God insofar as he is a cause. For God would possess all of his attributes whether or not he had ever created anything at all. If all we ever do is speak of God insofar as a cause, we have not yet said anything properly about God himself.[42]

Reworking Peter's response to Gilbert, Albert argues that as long as we first distinguish the meaning of a perfection from its concrete existence in a particular subject, we can ultimately apply each of the perfections we encounter among creatures to God in himself.[43] If we consider a perfection solely in terms of its meaning, then each perfection has a distinct *ratio*: for example, *wisdom signifies one thing, and goodness another*. If we consider a perfection solely insofar as it is as present in God, then all perfections are "one and the same" (*unum et idem*) with the divine essence on account of divine simplicity: for example, *God's wisdom is his goodness*. This is as far as Albert thought that Peter Lombard had gotten. But if we combine these two ways of naming God in the form of a single proposition, then Albert thinks we can signify something in our minds with composition that exists in reality without composition.[44] In God, each perfection has a different *ratio* but exists in a mode characterized by simplicity. We can thus distinguish the names with reference to the creatures from which they are taken (wisdom and goodness have a different *ratio*) but recognize that both *rationes* are to be found in God

---

40. Albert the Great, *De IV coaequevis*, 4.71.3 co. (Borgnet 34:730); 4.72.1 ad 6 (Borgnet 34:740); 4.73.9 co. and ad 4 (Borgnet 34:760). Albert does, of course, acknowledge that the universe is ordered toward God as an exterior end. See Albert the Great, *De IV coaequevis* 3.18.2.1 sol. (Borgnet 34:451). In 3.18.2.2 sol. (Borgnet 34:452), he expresses a distinction between the *finis ut terminus*, which is a proximate end, and the *finis ut finis*, which is a remote end.

41. Ruello, *Les "noms divins,"* 47.

42. Ruello, *Les "noms divins,"* 46. See Albert the Great, *Super Sent.* 1.8.3 s.c. 2 (Borgnet 25:224). The *quidam voluerunt dicere* ("some people wanted to say") here is an obvious allusion to Peter Lombard and those who followed him on this matter.

43. Albert the Great, *Super Sent.* 1.8.3 co. (Borgnet 25:224), 1.8.4 co. (Borgnet 25:225–26).

44. Ruello, *Les "noms divins,"* 48–49.

(God's wisdom is his goodness). This enables us to arrive at the conclusion: *God is wise and good.*[45]

Notwithstanding Albert's earlier criticism of Philip the Chancellor and the Franciscans, Albert's new way of understanding the *rationes* of divine attributes opened to him the possibility of engaging in a limited version of triadic contemplation through objective appropriation: we can appropriate a given perfection to a specific divine person when we identify an objective similarity between the *ratio* of that perfection and that divine person. Albert gives two examples of how this can work. The first is of his own invention: *potentia* includes "principle" (*principium*) in its *ratio*; *principium* applies more to the Father as a principle from no principle than to the Son as a principle from a principle. The second he borrows directly from Hugh: *potentia* relates to *sapientia* and *bonitas* as the Father does to the Son and the Spirit.[46] *Nota bene*: Albert's objective sense of appropriation has strict apophatic limits. At this point in the development of his thought, his understanding of the *rationes* of perfections in God is colored by a supereminence that so far transcends our cognition that it leaves us in the dark concerning the precise meaning of a *ratio* in God.[47] We can make a judgment that something corresponding to the *ratio* of a created perfection exists in God, but in that very act of judgment, we lose a sense of what exactly the *ratio* is like in God.[48]

---

45. Albert the Great, *Super Sent.* 1.8.4 co. (Borgnet 25:229).

46. Albert the Great, *Super Sent.* 1.34.5 (Borgnet 26:171); Gilles Emery, *The Trinitarian Theology of Saint Thomas Aquinas*, trans. Francesca Murphy (New York: Oxford University Press, 2010), 320. See also Albert's discussion of "eternal" (*aeternus*) in Albert the Great, *Super Sent.* 1.31.5 (Borgnet 26:107).

47. Bernard Blankenhorn, *The Mystery of Union with God: Dionysian Mysticism in Albert the Great and Thomas Aquinas* (Washington, DC: The Catholic University of America Press, 2016), 118.

48. Albert the Great, *Super Sent.* 1.3.10 (Borgnet 25:99). Blankenhorn, *The Mystery of Union with God*, 118, sees in this distinction a deployment of the distinction between the *res significata* and *modus significandi*, although the terms do not appear here as explicitly as they will later in Albert's *Commentary on the Divine Names*, concerning which, see below.

49. On the reception of Gallus's *Extractio*, see Blankenhorn, *The Mystery of Union with God*, 44. On the date of Gallus's *Explanatio*, see Boyd Coolman, *Knowledge, Love, and Ecstasy in the Theology of Thomas Gallus* (New York: Oxford University Press), 8. On the date of Albert's *Commentary on the Divine Names*, see Blankenhorn, *The Mystery of Union with God*, 51, 123–24.

One piece of evidence that may support the influence of the *Explanatio* as distinct from the *Extractio* is the connection between Trinitarian theology and the *ratio creationis* in both Gallus's and Albert's respective discussions of love. The *Extractio* does not make this connection in its treatment of love. See Thomas Gallus, *Extractio in libros Dionysii, De divinis nominibus* 4, in Denys the Carthusian, *Commentaria in Opera S, Dionysii* (Cologne 1556), 521. However, such a connection can be found in Gallus's *Explanatio in libros*

In his *Commentary on the Divine Names,* which Albert lectured after he left Paris for Cologne in 1248, and which formed the immediate basis of Thomas Aquinas's discussion of creation and theophany at the start of his own theological career, Albert used his theory of *rationes* from his *Commentary on the Sentences* to rework his earlier understanding of the *ratio creationis.* He appears to have been inspired in this work by the Victorine, Thomas Gallus, whose *Extractio* on the *Divine Names* Albert would certainly have known in Paris, and whose larger *Explanatio* on the *Divine Names* was completed by 1245.[49] Similar to Gallus,[50] Albert distinguishes two ways in which a thing can relate to the good as its end: by desire (*desiderium*), in the case of a good which is not yet possessed or is incompletely possessed, or by love (*amor*) in the case of a good that is completely possessed.[51] Since God is the *Summum bonum,* it is not proper to speak of desire in God but only of love, because God possesses the fullness of goodness in himself completely.[52] God's superabundant goodness, which is also superabundant love, moves him to share his goodness and his love with others by creation.[53]

When God communicates a share of his goodness to a creature by love, this communication creates an analogical similarity between that creature and God through exemplar causality. Albert explains the nature of this similarity in two ways. First, he explains it in relation to the divine ideas. Associating Plato's separated forms with the divine ideas, as Gallus had done,[54] Albert argues that every creature is related to God by participating in a divine idea, in a manner analogous to that in which Plato thought that each creature participates in its ideal form.[55] Albert also allows for a second way in which divine exemplarity functions by emphasizing with Gallus the fact that the relationship

---

Dionysii, De divinis nominibus 4 (*CCCM* 223:182, 209, 230, 242, 267). It can also be found in Albert the Great, *Super De div. nom.* 4.119 ad 3–6 (Col. 37.1:215).

Gallus's *Extractio* on the *Divine Names* will hereafter be abbreviated *Ext. De div. nom.*; Gallus's *Explanatio* on the *Divine Names* will hereafter be abbreviated *Exp. De div. nom.* The Cologne edition of the *Extractio* is the source for the edition of the *Extractio* later reprinted in *Dionysiaca,* vol. 1, ed. Philippe Chevallier (Paris: Desclée de Brouwer, 1937).

50. See Gallus, *Ext. De div. nom.* (Col. 521–23); Gallus, *Exp. De div. nom.* 4 (*CCCM* 223:182, 187–88, 209, 230, 242, 267, 318); and Coolman, *Knowledge, Love, and Ecstasy,* 61.

51. On the nature of the good, see Albert the Great, *Super De div. nom.* 4 (Col. 37.1:116). On the distinction between *desiderium* and *amor,* see Albert the Great, *Super De div. nom.* 4 (Col. 37.1:212).

52. Albert the Great, *Super De div. nom.* 4.132 (Col. 37.1:223). See Gallus, *Ext. De div. nom.* 4 (Col. 519).

53. Albert the Great, *Super De div. nom.* 4 (Col. 37.1:214).

54. Gallus, *Ext. De div. nom.* 5 (Col. 545–46); Gallus, *Exp. De div. nom.* 5 (*CCCM* 223:325, 352).

55. Albert the Great, *Super De div. nom.* 4.143 ad 2 (Col. 37.1:231).

of creatures to God as exemplar cause is inseparable from the relationship of creatures to God as efficient cause,[56] so much so that at one point, Albert now refers to God as the "efficient exemplar" cause of creatures.[57] The acknowledgement of a close relationship between efficient and exemplar causality allows Albert to say that the exemplar causes of creaturely perfections are found not only in the divine ideas, as Gallus would have it,[58] but also and especially in the divine essence.[59]

In his discussion of humanity, Albert now argues that it is on account of God's greater love for rational creatures that he created them in his image. Because they are made in his image, they can perceive the imitations of God present in the things that he has made.[60] Developing Gallus,[61] and thereby giving a greater level of nuance to his own earlier formulations, Albert suggests that we perceive the connection between creaturely imitations and God by distinguishing between two aspects of any name that we want to attribute to God on the basis of a perfection we find among creatures in the exterior world. On the one hand, there is the "substance" of the name: the "thing signified" (*res significata*) or "that on which the name is imposed" (*id cui nomen imponitur*). On the other, there is the name's "quality": its "mode of signifying" (*modus significandi*) or "that by which the name is imposed" (*id quo nomen imponitur*).[62] In order to apply the name of a perfection to God, we maintain the substance of the name but deny any creaturely quality associated with it.[63] Since we do not know what it is like for a perfection to exist in God, Albert agrees with Gallus that we cannot say that we know "what it is" (*quid est*) to predicate a given perfection of God. As in Albert's *Commentary on the Sentences*, however, he does at least think that we can know "that there is" (*quia est*) something in the divine essence corresponding in substance to the exterior perfections we behold in the world around us.[64]

---

56. Gallus, *Ext. De div. nom.* 1 (Col. 408–9); Gallus, *Exp. De div. nom.* 4 (*CCCM* 223:213), 5 (*CCCM* 223:338, 355); and Albert the Great, *Super De div. nom.* 5.10 sol. (Col. 37.1:309).

57. Albert the Great, *Super De div. nom.* 5.17 (Col. 37.1:312).

58. Gallus, *Ext. De div. nom.* 5 (Col. 545–46); *Exp. De div. nom.* 4 (*CCCM* 223:185), 5 (*CCCM* 223:325).

59. Albert the Great, *Super De div. nom.* 4.73 ad 1 (Col. 37.1:184).

60. Albert the Great, *Super De div. nom.* 4.131 sol. (Col. 37.1:222).

61. See Gallus, *Exp. De div. nom.* 4 (*CCCM* 223:231).

62. Albert the Great, *Super De div. nom.* 1.43 sol. (Col. 37.1:25).

63. See Albert the Great, *Super De div. nom.* 1.3 sol. (Col. 37.1:2), 1.4 sol. (Col. 37.1:3).

64. Albert the Great, *Super De div. nom.* 2.55 sol. (Col. 37.1:80). On the apophatic implications of this theory of divine naming, see Blankenhorn, *The Mystery of Union with God*, 153–56.

Thomas Aquinas

Thomas Aquinas (ca. c. 1225–1274) was well familiar with Albert's work on contemplation, attribution, and appropriation. When Aquinas arrived in Paris in 1246, Albert had already completed book 1 of his *Commentary on the Sentences*. Aquinas subsequently accompanied Albert to Cologne in 1248 and served as Albert's personal assistant (*socius*). His duties included taking down a transcript (*reportatio*) of Albert's oral lectures on the *Divine Names*, a copy of which still survives in Aquinas's famously illegible handwriting.[65] Not surprisingly, then, when Aquinas left Albert's *studium* in Cologne in 1252 to begin his scholarly career as a bachelor of the *Sentences* at the University of Paris, it was to Albert's work that he turned for inspiration.

Aquinas's discussion of the *ratio creationis* in his *Commentary on the Sentences* repeats a great deal of what we find in Albert's *Commentary on the Divine Names*. Citing the same passage of Dionysius's *Divine Names* that Albert uses to identify the *ratio creationis* as love, Aquinas rehearses Albert's distinction between love and desire, associates love with divine goodness as Albert had done, and argues with Albert that God's love of his own goodness causes him to share that goodness with others to the extent that it is possible for them to receive it.[66] Yet Aquinas does not content himself with a mere restatement of Albert's ideas. He also tries to map what he found in the later Albert onto what he read in Peter Lombard's text, with the result that— whether purposefully or inadvertently—Aquinas's work may represent the first attempt at integrating the Dionysian ideas that Albert developed in Cologne with the established Parisian theological tradition.

In order to achieve this integration, Aquinas distinguished between two ways in which we can consider the *ratio creationis*: the "end that the agent has in mind" (the *finis operantis*) and the "end of the work which the agent makes" (the *finis operis*).[67] Strictly speaking, God's purpose in creation (the *finis operantis*) is to love his own goodness, but the purpose built into the things God makes (the *finis operis*) is to participate in that goodness as much as possible.[68] Since no creature is "proportioned" to God, no creature can receive a complete sharing in God's goodness. Instead, every creature receives

---

65. See Jean-Pierre Torrell, *Initiation à Saint Thomas d'Aquin*, 2nd ed. (Paris: Cerf, 2015), 47–48.

66. See Thomas Aquinas, *Super Sent.* 2.1.2.1 co., in *Scriptum super libros Sententiarum Magistri Petri Lombardi Episcopi Parisiensis*, 4 vols., ed. Pierre Mandonnet and Fabien Moos (Paris: Lethielleux, 1929–1947) 2:46. See Albert the Great, *Super De div. nom.* 4.118 (Col. 37:214).

67. *Super Sent.* 2.1.2.1 co. (Mandonnet 2:45–46).

68. *Super Sent.* 2.1.2.1 co. (Mandonnet 2:45–46).

a limited similarity with God's goodness in virtue of its form and tends over the course of its existence toward perfecting its form in the greatest possible likeness to God's goodness.[69] Rational creatures thus stand at the height of the *finis operis* of creation, because rational creatures alone have the capacity to attain to the divine essence by seeing and loving God in glory.[70]

Although Albert does not devote a significant amount of attention to the relationship between other creatures and humanity in his *Commentary on the Divine Names*, Aquinas uses the distinction between the *finis operantis* and the *finis operis* to revisit this relationship and thereby expand upon the cosmological implications of Albert's thought. He does so by distinguishing between a twofold order of the universe based upon God's twofold intention for creation.[71] The primary order of the universe is derived from the *finis operantis*, by which all things are ordered toward divine goodness. A secondary order of the universe is derived from the *finis operis*, "according to which one thing assists another in arriving at a likeness to God."[72] For Aquinas, this mutually assisted ascent happens on two levels: rational creatures assist one another in the movement toward seeing and loving God directly, while "every corporeal creature," which cannot see and love God directly, seeks likeness to God *through* rational creatures, by "tend[ing] towards becoming like an intellectual creature as much as it can. . . . For this reason the human form, that is the rational soul, is also said to be the ultimate end intended by inferior natures."[73]

Although Aquinas acknowledges that his idea of a mutually assisted ascent is taken from Dionysius, his understanding of Dionysian reciprocity is admittedly thin at this point in his career. He basically reduces it to Aristotle's understanding of hierarchical governance.[74] But in the *De veritate* (1256–1259), which Aquinas disputed as a young master of the sacred page after he had finished his *Commentary on the Sentences*, he arrived at a deeper understanding of Dionysian ascent through reflection upon the Aristotelian theory of intellectual abstraction. Aquinas's understanding of abstraction is subject

---

69. *Super Sent.* 2.1.2.2 co. (Mandonnet 2:48).

70. *Super Sent.* 2.1.2.2 co. (Mandonnet 2:48).

71. See *Super Sent.* 2.1.2.3 co. (Mandonnet 2:50).

72. *Super Sent.* 2.1.2.3 co. (Mandonnet 2:50): "[ordo] secundarius est secundum quod una juvat aliam in perveniendo ad similitudinem divinam."

73. *Super Sent.* 2.1.2.3 co. (Mandonnet 2:51): "Sed quia optimo assimilatur aliquid per hoc quod simile fit meliori se, ideo omnis creatura corporalis tendit in assimilationem creaturae intellectualis quantum potest . . . et propter hoc etiam forma humana, scilicet anima rationalis, dicitur esse finis ultimus intentus a natura inferiori."

74. In *Super Sent.* 2.1.2.3 co. (Mandonnet 2:50), he cites Aristotle, *Metaphysics* 12.10 (1075a11–23). In *Super Sent.* 2.1.2.3 ad 3, the example he gives is that of a peasant who participates in the peace of the king's life because he himself lives a peaceful life on account of the king's laws.

to significant dispute among Thomists, but Therese Cory has provided some helpful clarification to current debates by placing Aquinas's epistemology in its thirteenth-century context. Not only does Cory's clarification align very carefully with the text of *De veritate*,[75] but it can also help us to see why the theory of abstraction helped Aquinas to develop a contemplative cosmology of his own, based upon a Dionysian ascent to the Triune God, which begins in God's theophanic presence in creation.

In Aquinas's day, the theory of abstraction was bound up with the discussion of light. Aquinas's contemporaries thought that light causes that which can potentially be seen to actually be seen; similarly, they asked how the active power in our intellect (which Aquinas called the "agent" intellect) can make those things that can potentially be understood to be actually understood (in what Aquinas called the "possible intellect").[76] In thinking through this question, Aquinas and his contemporaries had at their disposal two principal theories from within the Aristotelian tradition: those of Arabic Aristotelians Avicenna (Ibn-Sīnā; c. 980–1037) and Averroes (Ibn Rushd; d. 1198). Avicenna held that light communicates color to the objects in the room, thus enabling them to be seen; Averroes thought that the objects always have color, but that light communicates to the air and to the eye the ability for the color in the objects to pass from the objects in which it resides to the eye.[77] According to Cory, Aquinas drew upon Avicenna and Averroes to develop his own account of intellectual knowledge. It begins when the agent intellect illuminates the image that we form of that object in our imagination (which Aquinas calls a "phantasm") with intelligible light. This illumination does not communicate a new form to the phantasm (*pace* Averroes) or to the object (*pace* Avicenna); rather, it actualizes the potential of the object for intelligibility by actualizing the potential of its phantasm to become immaterial in the form of an "intelligible species."[78] When the intellect actualizes a phantasm's potential for intelligibility, it actually confers a perfection upon the object of its thought which—in the case of corporeal creatures—the object of its thought cannot confer upon itself: it allows it to exist in a higher mode of being by sharing in the intellect's own immateriality and intelligibility.

---

75. See *De ver.* 10.6 co., in *Opera Omnia*, 50 vols. (Rome: Commissio Leonina, 1882–), 22:311–13.

76. Therese Scarpelli Cory, "Rethinking Abstractionism: Aquinas's Intellectual Light and Some Arabic Sources," *Journal of the History of Philosophy* 53, no. 4 (2015): 613. Cory's article provides an overview of contemporary views of abstraction on pp. 609–14.

77. Cory, "Rethinking Abstractionism," 613–15. For a more detailed discussion of Aquinas specifically in relation to Averroes, see Cory, "Averroes and Aquinas on the Agent Intellect's Causation of the Intelligible," *Recherches de théologie et philosophie médiévales* 82, no. 1 (2015): 1–60.

78. Cory, "Rethinking Abstractionism," 618–21, 626.

For Aquinas, the "gift" of immateriality and intelligibility, which the intellect confers upon its natural objects, is an important stage in the universe's Dionysian ascent to God. As Aquinas understands it, this ascent has three stages, corresponding with three divisions from divine unity to which corporeal creatures are subject.[79] The first division is the division of individual members of a species from one another, which happens through their matter; when a human being has a sensory encounter with a material creature, the apprehension of that creature's nature through the abstraction of an intelligible species from the phantasm of it causes the removal of this division by allowing the creature's nature to exist as immaterial and unified in the possible intellect, rather than as distributed among the material individuals that participate in that nature. The second division is the division of different species from one another; when that same human being arrives at knowledge of the creature's nature through acts of judgment, which distinguish that nature from other, similar natures, the intellect's consideration of the various species it knows causes the removal of this division by allowing those species to exist in an ordered harmony. In this way, the human intellect not only sits at the height of the perfection of the cosmos; it is also in some sense the *place* in which the unity of the cosmos is achieved. There is one further step in the Dionysian ascent of the universe through the human intellect. In the *Commentary on the Sentences* and the *De veritate*, Aquinas does not yet go a step further in this context and say, as he later will, that there exists a third division—the division of creatures from God—whose removal is accomplished when we know and love God through our knowledge of material creatures.[80] The implication is certainly present, however, and it is drawn out more explicitly in Aquinas's discussion of appropriation.

Aquinas's understanding of appropriation underwent rapid development during the years 1252–1257, while he was writing his *Commentary on the Sentences* and beginning his *De veritate*.[81] Initially, in *Super Sent.* 1.2.1.2 (ca. 1252), Aquinas followed closely what he found in Albert's *Commentary on the Divine Names*,[82] but his adherence to Albert's thought on this topic did not last long. By about 1256, a controversy erupted regarding the way in

---

79. For what follows in this paragraph, see *De ver.* 2.2 co. (Leon. 22:44–45), as well as Oliva Blanchette, *The Perfection of the Universe According to St. Thomas Aquinas: A Teleological Cosmology* (University Park: Pennsylvania State University Press, 1992), 295–300.

80. *ST* 1.65.2 co. (Leon. 5:149–50).

81. On the general chronology of Aquinas's works, see Torrell, *Initiation à Saint Thomas d'Aquin*, 421–34. On the particular chronology of the controversy over the divine attributes, see Adriano Oliva, *Les débuts de l'enseignement de Thomas d'Aquin et sa conception de la* sacra doctrina, *avec l'édition du prologue de son Commentaire des* Sentences (Paris: J. Vrin, 2006), 109–23, 130–39, and 160–63.

82. *Super Sent.* 1.2.1.2 (Mandonnet 1:61–63).

which creatures are theophanic. In the midst of this controversy, Aquinas developed a significantly more cataphatic—and in some senses Victorine—view of human reason and contemplation.

The controversy centered around the work of another Dominican, Peter of Tarentaise (later Bl. Pope Innocent V; c. 1224–1276), who studied as a bachelor of the *Sentences* in Paris around the same time as Aquinas, although perhaps a year or two behind.[83] Tarentaise attempted to steer Albert's theory of *rationes* in a radically cataphatic direction by drawing upon Bonaventure's theory of divine unity. Bonaventure had argued, by drawing upon Albert's distinction between our way of understanding and the reality of things in God, that in the special case of divine unity, we can use a negative judgment ("God is not divided") to signify a positive reality ("God is one," possessing the fullness of perfection).[84] Tarentaise agreed with the form of Bonaventure's argument. But if Bonaventure was right in utilizing Albert's theory of divine naming to achieve this positive result in the case of *one* attribute, and if Albert had applied the same theory of divine naming to the *ratio* of every *other* divine attribute, why would we not draw a similarly positive conclusion about our knowledge of *every* divine attribute?[85] Tarentaise's argument caused a significant stir among his confrères and colleagues. Was Tarentaise merely pointing out the inevitable cataphatic implications of Albert's reworking of Peter Lombard? Or had Tarentaise distorted the Lombardian tradition by pushing it in what was effectively an Abelardian direction?

In the contentious atmosphere that arose over Tarentaise's work, Aquinas had to make a decision about whether to repudiate it or defend it.[86] Perhaps surprisingly, he chose to defend it. As a result, he decided to revise his *Commentary on the Sentences* and to replace *Super Sent.* 1.2.1.2 with an updated text that defended Tarentaise's work as the legitimate extension of the Lombardian tradition. Unfortunately for Aquinas, though perhaps fortunately for

---

83. H.-F. Dondaine, Préface to *Resp.* 108 (Leon. 42:264) places Tarentaise as a bachelor of the *Sentences* at Paris from 1256 to 1258. Oliva, *Les debuts de l'enseignement*, 119, describes him as a contemporary of Aquinas and, while recognizing Aquinas's influence on Tarentaise, points out on p. 160 that Tarentaise must have influenced the composition of *Super Sent.* 1.2.1.3 prior to the composition of *De ver.* 4 in 1256–1257. This may place Tarentaise's period as a bachelor of the *Sentences* slightly earlier.

84. Bonaventure, *Super Sent.* 1.24.1.1 co., in *Opera Omnia*, 10 vols. (Grottaferrata: Collegii S. Bonaventurae ad Claras Aquinas, 1882–1901), 1:421.

85. Peter of Tarentaise, *Super Sent.* 1.2.1.3 co., in *In IV libros Sententiarum Commentaria*, 2 vols. (Toulouse: Apud Arnaldum Colomerium, 1652), 1:20.

86. Aquinas was later called upon to render a formal, albeit private, judgment on 108 propositions drawn from Tarentaise's work, a text that has come down to us as the *Responsio ad magistrum Iohannem de Vercellis de 108 articulis* (Leon. 42:259–94). On the divine attributes, see aa. 1–3 (Leon. 42:279–80) and a. 51 (Leon. 42:287).

us, that attempted replacement was a codicological failure. Both the original and the revised text were preserved for posterity: Aquinas's original text remained as *Super Sent.* 1.2.1.2; his revised text now became *Super Sent.* 1.2.1.3.[87]

Super Sent. 1.2.1.3 gets right to the heart of the debate. Instead of merely asking "whether there is a plurality of attributes in the divine essence?" (*utrum in divina essentia sit pluralitas attributorum*),[88] as 1.2.1.2 does, Aquinas now asks "whether the plurality of *rationes* according to which the attributes differ is in God, or only in the intellect of the one thinking?" (*utrum pluralitas rationum secundum quas attributa differunt sit in Deo, vel tantum in intellectu ratiocinantis?*).[89] The most important aspect of Aquinas's response for the present purposes is his discussion of the distinction between "that on which a name is imposed" (*id cui nomen imponitur*) and "that from which a name is imposed" (*id a quo nomen imponitur*). Albert had preserved a level of apophaticism in his doctrine of analogy by arguing that when we name God (that is, when God is *ille cui nomen imponitur*), a creature is still the *id a quo nomen imponitur*.[90] But Aquinas sees this as inconsistent. If we want to say that the *rationes* of names exist in God, as Albert does, then it is not enough to make that claim solely on the basis of creaturely perfections. There has to be some sense in which our saying that "God is good" means not just that God is good *in a way that creatures are not*, because God is the cause of creaturely goodness; it also has to mean that God is good *in the most perfect way*. Otherwise, "God is good" means nothing more to us than "God is, and a creature is good," the very conclusion that Albert developed his theory of *rationes* to avoid. On the contrary, if it means anything at all for us to say that "God is good," indeed if we can speak meaningfully of God at all, the *id a quo nomen imponitur* has to be divine when a word is predicated of God, not just the *id cui nomen imponitur*.[91] Otherwise, the entire theological enterprise

---

87. See the notes on the manuscript tradition in Oliva, *Les debuts de l'enseignement*, 109–17.

88. *Super Sent.* 1.2.1.2 arg. 1 (Mandonnet 1:61). I have constructed the title of the article from Aquinas's own words at the beginning of the first argument rather than Mandonnet's heading, which is more generic.

89. *Super Sent.* 1.2.1.3 arg. 1 (Mandonnet 1:63). Again, I have constructed the title from Aquinas's own words.

90. Albert the Great, *Super De div. nom.* 1.43 sol. (Col. 37.1:25). In this text, Albert does not explicitly use the language *id a quo nomen imponitur* in association with the *ratio nominis*, but he does employ this language elsewhere for the same purpose. See, for example, Albert the Great, *Super De div. nom.* 13.4 ad 1 (Col. 37.1:434).

91. *Super Sent.* 1.2.1.3 co. (Mandonnet 1:69): "Therefore, in this way a third point is clear: that the *rationes* of attributes are truly in God, because the *ratio* of a name has a greater dependence on that from which the name is imposed, than that on which it is

not only falls to pieces in the absence of the ability speak of God, but even more significantly, God's purpose of creation will be frustrated. For if the *finis operis* of creation is achieved through lower creatures being drawn up *through our knowing them* into the praise, service, and enjoyment of God, then a failure at the level of divine attribution not only prevents us from knowing and naming God, but also prevents the exterior world from ascending to the Trinitarian persons through our acts of appropriation.

Aquinas's embrace of Tarentaise's cataphatic understanding of attribution had a correspondingly cataphatic effect on his understanding of appropriation. In his early work, Aquinas frames his understanding of appropriation in terms of a distinction between two ways in which we can consider the *ratio* of a divine attribute: we can either consider the *ratio* as it is found in creatures, or we can consider the *ratio* as it is found in the divine essence.[92] If we consider the *ratio* as it is found in creatures, then we have to engage in appropriation by negation. This leads us to Hugh's accommodative sense, in which *potentia* helps us to avoid attributing the infirmities of age to the Father, *sapientia* the inexperience of youth to the Son, and *bonitas* the malignancy of evil spirits to the Spirit. If we consider the *ratio* of a name as it is found in the divine essence, however, there is opened to us a pathway to Albert's objective sense:

> But if the *rationes* of names are taken as they exist in God, then in this way also can [appropriation] be undertaken, albeit by an assimilation to the personal properties: as *potentia*, which includes "principle" in its *ratio*, is ascribed to the Father, who is the fontal principle of the whole divinity (for *potentia* is the principle of transmutation, as is said in *Metaphysics* 5, text 17); and since the Son proceeds by way of intellect, which is perfected by wisdom, wisdom is attributed to him; and since the Holy Spirit proceeds by way of will, whose object is *bonitas*, therefore *bonitas* is appropriated to him.[93]

---

imposed" ("Sic ergo patet tertium, scilicet quod rationes attributorum sunt vere in Deo quia ratio nominis magis se tenet ex parte ejus a quo imponitur nomen, quam ex parte ejus cui imponitur").

Thomas's text here raises the question of how we should consider the divine attributes as exemplar causes in relation to the divine ideas, concerning which see Gregory Doolan, *Aquinas on the Divine Ideas as Exemplar Causes* (Washington, DC: The Catholic University of America Press, 2008), 77–78, 219–42.

92. *Super Sent.* 1.31.2.1 co. (Mandonnet 1:721).

93. *Super Sent.* 1.34.2 co. (Mandonnet 1:794): "Si autem accipiantur rationes nominum prout in divinis sunt, sic etiam poterit fieri [appropriatio] per assimilationem ad propria, ut Patri, qui est fontale principium totius divinitatis, potentia ascribatur, quae in ratione sua principium includit: est enim potentia principium transmutationis, ut in V *Metaph.*, text. 17, dicitur; et quia Filius procedit per modum intellectus, qui sapientia perficitur, attribuitur sibi sapientia; et quia Spiritus sanctus procedit per modum voluntatis,

To be sure, Aquinas does not thereby think that *potentia, sapientia,* and *bonitas* can be appropriated to Trinitarian persons *only* in this way: "The essential attributes are common to the three [persons],"[94] and so all appropriation is only achieved by way of "fittingness" (*convenientia*). However, *convenientia* here does not preclude objectivity: "the similarity between what is appropriated and a personal property causes objective fittingness [*convenientia ex parte rei*], which would exist even if we did not; while its subsequent helpfulness causes subjective fittingness [*convenientia ex parte nostra*]."[95]

Were it not for Aquinas's subsequent embrace of Tarentaise, we would be justified in concluding that Aquinas was merely repeating here what he found in Albert, together with Albert's apophatic limits on objective appropriation. Indeed, assuming this text predates the composition of *Super Sent.* 1.2.1.3, this was very likely Aquinas's original intention. However, given that Aquinas did not attempt to alter his understanding of objective appropriation after his embrace of Tarentaise—indeed, he continued to hold it all the way into the *Prima Pars* of the *Summa theologiae* (1265–1268)[96]—we must conclude that at some point, Aquinas intended his more cataphatic understanding of Albert's *rationes* to be incorporated into his objective sense of appropriation. Only in this way could Aquinas later say, as indicated, that our knowledge of God through creatures helps to remove the division between those creatures and God.[97] For it is only in this way that human reason can assist creatures in a Dionysian ascent through attribution and appropriation to a participation in the highest perfection available to any creature: the knowledge and love of the Father, the Son, and the Holy Spirit.

Conclusion

Placed in its medieval context, Aquinas's understanding of God's purpose for creation can offer a pathway toward irenic consensus between Balthasarians

---

cujus objectum est bonitas, ideo sibi appropriatur bonitas." The language of "fontal" principle, as applied to the Father, comes ultimately from Gallus. See Coolman, *Knowledge, Love, and Ecstasy,* 58.

94. *Super Sent.* 1.31.1.2 co. (Mandonnet 1:721): "attributa essentialia communia sint tribus."

95. *Super Sent.* 1.31.1.2 co. (Mandonnet 1:721): "similitudo appropriati ad proprium personae, facit convenientiam appropriationis ex parte rei, quae esset etiam si nos non essemus; sed ex parte nostra facit convenientiam utilitas consequens."

96. Aquinas continues to use Hugh's twofold distinction in appropriation later in his career. See *ST* 1.39.7 co. and ad 1 (Leon. 4:407). However, as Emery, *The Trinitarian Theology of Saint Thomas Aquinas,* 328–29, observes, Aquinas gives increasingly more emphasis to the subjective side of the distinction in his later work.

97. *ST* 1.65.2 co. (Leon. 5:149–50).

and Thomists on the question of human reason's ability to know created natures in general and so points the way toward a consensus of human reason's ability to know human nature in specific. Rather than focusing on what human reason *ought to be able to do* in view of the metaphysical principles undergirding our understanding of its operation, or focusing on what human reason *ought not to be able to do* in view of the theological principles undergirding our understanding of divine freedom, we can place the scope and purpose of human reason within the sphere of divine freedom and ask: what ought human reason be able to do in view of the place that God has freely chosen for it within his plan for creation? Aquinas's answer is that God chose to place human reason at the center of the universe's ascending *reditus* to himself. In its contemplation of the exterior world, human reason confers a series of gifts upon the created world, which God intends for the created world to receive through humanity: first the gifts of immateriality and intelligibility, and ultimately the gift of participation in the praise, service, and enjoyment of the Triune God.

An irenic recovery of the theological context of Aquinas's understanding of analogy is a first, though necessary step toward a consensus between Thomists and Balthasarians on the knowability of human nature. It will remain the work of future studies to show how Aquinas's theological understanding of human reason's knowledge of created nature in general can be applied to the question of human reason's knowledge of human nature in specific. On that, consensus may be more difficult to achieve, in view of the complex relationship between nature and grace,[98] but that does not mean that consensus is impossible. For if it belongs to a rational creature to be "subject to divine providence in a more excellent way" than other creatures, because "it participates in providence by *governing itself* and others,"[99] then the same theological principles which apply to our knowledge of the exterior world can potentially be applied to ourselves, in the cooperative ascent by which we become ever-more "partakers of the divine nature" (2 Pet 1:4).

Regardless of how that future conversation may proceed, the study of how we know created nature in general is not without importance for theological anthropology. As we have seen, Aquinas's understanding of how human reason knows created nature was united in his own mind to the role

---

98. For a discussion of the history of that controversy in view of an irenic resolution, see Jacob Wood, *To Stir a Restless Heart: Thomas Aquinas and Henri de Lubac on Nature, Grace, and the Desire for God* (Washington, DC: The Catholic University of America Press, 2019).

99. *ST* 1–2.91.2 co. (Leon. 7:154) (emphasis added): "Inter cetera autem, rationalis creatura excellentiori quodam modo divinae providentiae subiacet, inquantum et ipsa fit providentiae particeps, *sibi ipsi* et aliis *providens*."

that human reason—and human nature—play in God's plan for the perfection for universe. Through the natural knowledge of the creatures around us, we confer upon them the gifts of immateriality and intelligibility; by knowing God analogically through their perfections, we confer upon those creatures a participation in the knowledge of the divine being; and by connecting those perfections with the Trinitarian processions through appropriation, we confer upon them the highest perfection that God intends for them: a participation in the praise, service, and enjoyment of God. This overlooked element of Aquinas's theological anthropology has important spiritual consequences that will be of interest to any sapiential theologian, Thomist or Balthasarian. For if the human contribution to the perfection of the cosmos depends upon our knowledge of the things we encounter, then in each encounter with one of God's creatures—indeed, even alone with the Alone in the deepest recesses of our hearts—we cannot but find ourselves at every moment on the precipice of Balthasar's *Ernstfall*: the decisive moment in which to choose whether to offer ourselves and the whole of what we encounter to the Father, through the Son, in the Spirit, or whether to shrink—through fear, desire, distraction, or any number of other temptations—from the majesty, the sacrifice, and ultimately the impenetrable love that God has for us and for the world. And unless Thomists and Balthasarians together embrace that calling and pursue it together with courage to the end, it will be significantly more difficult to attune the ears of the world to hear it and to incline the hearts of the world to answer it.

Bibliography

Aertsen, Jan. *Medieval Philosophy as Transcendental Thought: From Philip the Chancellor, ca. 1225 to Francisco Suárez.* Boston: Brill, 2012.

Blanchette, Oliva. *The Perfection of the Universe according to St. Thomas Aquinas: A Teleological Cosmology.* University Park: Pennsylvania State University Press, 1992.

Blankenhorn, Bernard. *The Mystery of Union with God: Dionysian Mysticism in Albert the Great and Thomas Aquinas.* Washington, DC: The Catholic University of America Press, 2016.

Cizewski, Wanda. "Reading the World as Scripture: Hugh of St. Victor's *De tribus diebus*." *Florilegium* 9 (1987): 65–88.

Colish, Marcia. *Peter Lombard.* 2 vols. Leiden: Brill 1994.

Coolman, Boyd. *Knowledge, Love, and Ecstasy in the Theology of Thomas Gallus.* New York: Oxford University Press, 2017.

———. *The Theology of Hugh of St. Victor: An Interpretation.* New York: Cambridge University Press, 2010.

———. "'In Whom I Am Well Pleased': Hugh of St. Victor's Trinitarian Aesthetics." *Pro Ecclesia* (2014): 331–54.

Cory, Therese Scarpelli. "Rethinking Abstractionism: Aquinas's Intellectual Light and Some Arabic Sources." *Journal of the History of Philosophy* 53, no. 4 (2015): 613.

Doolan, Gregory. *Aquinas on the Divine Ideas as Exemplar Causes.* Washington, DC: The Catholic University of America Press, 2008.

Emery, Gilles. *The Trinitarian Theology of Saint Thomas Aquinas.* Translated by Francesca Murphy. New York: Oxford University Press, 2010.

Fisher, John. "Hugh of St. Cher and the Development of Medieval Theology." *Speculum* 31, no. 1 (1956): 57–69.

Gilbert of Poitiers. *The Commentaries of Gilbert of Poitiers on Boethius.* Edited by Nikolaus Häring. Toronto: Pontifical Institute of Mediaeval Studies, 1956.

Häring, Nikolaus. "A Commentary on the Pseudo-Athanasian Creed by Gilbert of Poitiers." *Mediaeval Studies* 27 (1965): 23–53.

———. "A Treatise on the Trinity by Gilbert of Poitiers." *Recherches de théologie ancienne et médiévale* 39 (1972): 14–50.

Hugh of St. Victor. *De sacramentis. PL* 176: 172–618.

Levering, Matthew. *Engaging the Doctrine of Creation.* Grand Rapids, MI: Eerdmans, 2017.

Long, D. Stephen. Review of *Natura Pura: On the Recovery of Nature in the Doctrine of Grace* by Steven A. Long. *Modern Theology* 27, no. 1 (2011): 695–698.

———. *Saving Karl Barth: Hans Urs von Balthasar's Preoccupation.* Minneapolis, MN: Fortress Press, 2014.

Long, Steven A. "On the Loss, and the Recovery, of Nature as a Theonomic Principle: Reflections on the Nature/Grace Controversy." *Nova et Vetera* (English edition) 5, no. 1 (2007): 133–83.

———. *Natura Pura: On the Recovery of Nature in the Doctrine of Grace.* New York: Fordham University Press, 2010.

Nielsen, Lauge Olaf. *Theology and Philosophy in the Twelfth Century: A Study of Gilbert Porreta's Thinking and the Theological Expositions of the Doctrine of the Incarnation during the Period 1130–1180.* Leiden: Brill, 1982.

Oliva, Adriano. *Les débuts de l'enseignement de Thomas d'Aquin et sa conception de la* sacra doctrina, *avec l'édition du prologue de son Commentaire des* Sentences. Paris: J. Vrin, 2006.

Perkams, Matthias. "The origins of the Trinitarian attributes *potentia, sapientia, benignitas.*" *Archa Verbi* 1 (2005): 23–29.

Peter Lombard. *Sententiae in IV libris distinctae.* 2 vols. Edited by Ignatius Brady. Grotteferrata: Collegii S. Bonaventurae ad Claras Aquas, 1971–1981.

Peter of Tarentaise. *In IV libros Sententiarum Commentaria.* 2 vols. Toulouse: Apud Arnaldum Colomerium, 1652.

Poirel, Dominique. *Livre de la nature et débat trinitaire au XIIe siècle: Le "De Tribus Diebus" de Hugues de Saint-Victor.* Turnhout: Brepols, 2002.

Robson, Michael. "Sermons Preached to the Friars Minor in the Thirteenth Century." In *Franciscans and Preaching: Every Miracle from the Beginning of the World Came about through Words,* 273–96. Boston: Brill, 2012.

Rorem, Paul. *Hugh of Saint Victor*. New York: Oxford University Press, 2009.

Rosemann, Philipp. *Peter Lombard*. New York: Oxford University Press, 2004.

Ruello Francis. *Les "Noms Divins" et leurs "raisons" selon saint Albert Le Grand commentateur du "De divinis nominibus."* Paris: Librairie Philosophique J. Vrin, 1963.

Thomas Gallus. *Extractio in libros Dionysii*. In Denys the Carthusian, *Commentaria in Opera S, Dionysii*. Cologne, 1556.

———. *Thomae Galli Explanatio in Libros Dionysii*. Edited by Declan Anthony Lawell. Turnhout: Brepols, 2011.

Torrell, Jean-Pierre. *Initiation à Saint Thomas d'Aquin*. 2nd ed. Paris: Cerf, 2015.

Trottmann, Christian. *Théologie et noétique au XIIIe siècle: à la recherche d'un statut*. Paris: J. Vrin, 1999.

Valente, Louisa. *Logique et théologie: Les écoles parisiennes entre 1150 et 1220*. Paris: J. Vrin, 2008.

White, Thomas Joseph. "Classical Christology after Schleiermacher and Barth: A Thomist Perspective." *Pro Ecclesia* 20, no. 3 (2011): 229–63.

———. "'Through him all things were made' (John 1:3): The Analogy of the Word Incarnate according to St. Thomas Aquinas and Its Ontological Presuppositions." In *The Analogy of Being*, 246–79. Grand Rapids, MI: Eerdmans, 2011.

Williams, Michael. *The Teaching of Gilbert Porreta as Found in his Commentaries on Boethius*. Rome: Apud Aedes Universitatis Gregoriensis, 1951.

Wood, Jacob. *To Stir a Restless Heart: Thomas Aquinas and Henri de Lubac on Nature, Grace, and the Desire for God*. Washington, DC: The Catholic University of America Press, 2019.

CHAPTER 12

Freedom and the *Analogia Entis* in the Theological Anthropology of Hans Urs von Balthasar

MICHAEL ALTENBURGER

THE AIM OF THIS CHAPTER is to offer a brief elucidation of arguably the most powerful philosophical and theological tool in Hans Urs von Balthasar's arsenal—the *analogia entis*—as it relates to Balthasar's anthropology. Balthasar himself states that the "concrete thrust" of the *analogia entis* is the question of human freedom, which sits at the core of his anthropological reflections.[1] As such, his theo-drama is where the question of freedom emerges most prominently and is the central locus where anthropological answers are found. Even so, it should also be said that all volumes of Balthasar's great trilogy are anthropologically inflected. The theological aesthetics is not restricted to the possibility of metaphysical disclosure or God's visibility but about how humans *see* the form, more specifically, about how the human person in faith can be said to see the revelation of God in creation. The theo-drama and theo-logic have similar anthropologically grounded approaches, focusing on how the human person can act in God and think with God, respectively.

It would be unsustainable to claim that Balthasar offers an explicit, comprehensive treatment of anthropology,[2] but what is so provocative about his approach is the same reason why it is so frustrating: Balthasar deploys the *analogia entis* to humble systems that have presumed and dominated too much in order to open up new avenues of approach and to find new ways to see how God's love is active in the world. The view is never panoramic nor complete, but the animating conviction is that the human person can see, act, and think such that the fragments of God's action in the world can be con-

---

1. *TD* 2, 123.

2. The volume *A Theological Anthropology* is a misleading title, as the original German was *Das Ganze im Fragment*, which would be more literally translated as "the whole (or total) in the fragment." The book is, in many ways, an excellent summary of some of Balthasar's positions, but he does not fully unpack the anthropological foundations. See *TA*.

tinually constellated in a way that points to an ever-greater fullness and reality. Humans have a real freedom and agency—when empowered and uplifted by grace—to participate in the revelation of God in Christ. That is the central focus of this chapter: to explore how the *analogia entis* destabilizes in order to offer a dynamic synthesis of the cooperation of human freedom with God's action in the world.

That is the "what" of the chapter, but a preliminary word should be said about the "why." The central question here is how to connect Christian seeing, acting, and thinking with divine revelation disclosed in and through all of history's contingency. Balthasar presents a unique means to bridge the eternal and the historical by harmonizing the metaphysical, universal principle of the *analogia entis* with the particularity of the revelation of the Trinity in Christ. In doing so, he also opens up the possibility of a tremendous plurality of understandings that can nevertheless find a harmony and fulfillment in Christian faith. In other words, because Balthasar is positing fundamental polarities of human flourishing as rooted in the Trinitarian God (namely, the human person as rooted in the cosmos, spirit and body, man and woman, individual and community), he can thereby assert nonnegotiable aspects of any anthropology that claims to be Christian even as he opens up the possible expressions of such anthropological tensions across cultures and traditions.[3]

I will argue that a proper understanding of the *analogia entis* is fundamental for Balthasar's anthropology and his understanding of "personhood."[4] I will then demonstrate why that understanding of the *analogia entis* is so important for the key second volume of the *Theo-Drama*, subtitled *Dramatis Personae: Man in God*, which is an extended treatment of divine and human freedom. Indeed, I follow Michelle Schumacher when she writes, "In fact, it is precisely this notion of freedom which is foundational with respect to the transcendentals at the heart of his fifteen-volume trilogy."[5] It is surprising how

---

3. *KB*, 257.

4. This last point deserves one final qualification. Balthasar makes a distinction between anthropology and person. In fact, he is quite clear that what he means by "person" is simply "mission," but it takes a bit of work to understand what that means. While others have excellently exegeted Balthasar's anthropology from the "top down," so to speak, my aim here is to approach more from the "bottom up." I hope to demonstrate the foundations of Balthasar's position and some of the reasoning for why he makes certain decisions. My approach highlights Balthasar's reasoning but stands in a certain tension with his own, since he does not want to construct a "theo-drama from below." Nevertheless, this approach provides clarity about how very compelling and rich his insights are.

5. Michele Schumacher, *A Trinitarian Anthropology: Adrienne von Speyr & Hans Urs von Balthasar in Dialogue with Thomas Aquinas* (Washington, DC: The Catholic University of America Press, 2014), 116–17. Schumacher's book is an ambitious and impressive synthesis of St. Thomas Aquinas, Balthasar, and Balthasar's longtime friend and inspiration,

the issue of freedom in Balthasar's work is much more often talked about or around rather than addressed directly.[6] I aim to begin to ameliorate that here by examining how the fundamental issue of freedom is expressed across the dynamic polarities of the cosmos or nature, spirit and body, man and woman, and individual and community.

ANALOGIA ENTIS

The *analogia entis* is a series of claims advanced most famously by the Jesuit philosopher-theologian Erich Przywara over the course of the early to mid-twentieth century. Whatever one may think of Przywara's arguments, there can be little doubt that the man possessed staggering intellectual gifts, erudition, and productivity.[7] This vast command of philosophy and theology culminates in the *analogia entis*, which he claims to be *the* foundational principle of Catholic theology and philosophy. Balthasar was a student of Przywara and continued to engage with him for the rest of his life, making the *analogia entis* a core of his own theological vision.

There are important features of Przywara's *analogia entis* that can be identified to help make sense of the many anthropological claims that Balthasar would later advance. The first is that the *analogia entis* is not a metaphysical system. Przywara's position is both more and less than that. He aims for something *more* in claiming to be unpacking the fundamental Catholic position that relativizes *any* metaphysical system through the deceptively simple claim that God is in-and-beyond any system of thinking. He is clearly attempting something *less* because he is not offering his own complete system but using the *analogia entis* to amplify insights that have been underappreciated for their explanatory power and dampen others that presume too much.

---

the mystic Adrienne von Speyr. Schumacher's approach is primarily "katalogical," meaning that she follows Balthasar and Speyr in extrapolating what human personhood means from Jesus Christ and the Trinity. My approach does not pretend to compete with Schumacher's achievement but rather attempts something of a complement in exploring the metaphysical basis for Balthasar's claims.

6. Notable exceptions in this regard are Thomas G. Dalzell's *The Dramatic Encounter of Divine and Human Freedom in the Theology of Hans Urs von Balthasar* (Bern, Switzerland: Peter Lang AG, Internationaler Verlag der Wissenschaften, 1997) and Jacques Servais, "Freedom as Christ's Gift to Man in the Thought of Hans Urs von Balthasar," *Communio* 29, no. 3 (2002). The latter, however, is more nearly Christology than anthropology, which indicates how deeply Balthasar has harmonized the two.

7. In one ten-year period, he produced 230 articles and reviews, 237 lectures, and seventeen books. See Erich Przywara, *Analogia Entis: Metaphysics: Original Structure and Universal Rhythm,* trans. John Betz and David Bentley Hart (Grand Rapids, MI: Eerdmans, 2014), 15.

Because the *analogia entis* is such a powerful tool, it is capable of enlivening philosophical and theological systems by inviting them to imagine ever-new ways to conceptualize the dynamic between revelation and metaphysics.

What lies behind this is the keenest sense of the overwhelming awe and glory of God. Pryzwara's *analogia entis* has an Ignatian inflection in that Przywara lived the spirituality of the Jesuit order and its emphasis on the "ever greater glory of God." While St. Ignatius inflected this in his own way, this spiritual reality is expressed throughout the biblical text and other Christian spiritualities. The *Deus semper maior* lives in the rhythm between an "ever-greater" that humbles any system of thought and yet glories in God's action and revelation in history and time. It exalts the good of creation even as it limits what it can claim to achieve. It is rooted in divine revelation and yet looks outward to discern the fragments of that revelation throughout all of human history. This is the key point that should color any claim that follows—the *analogia entis* humbles any system of thought only in order to give greater glory to God. It valorizes the good of creation and the fragments of God's truth spread throughout in order to create the structure for tantalizing pointers to the infinite fullness of God. In this sense, it is highly constructive. However, it also is fundamentally about the incompleteness and the striving for fulfillment of material creation. It disallows any system that claims to achieve that in this life. In this sense, it is deeply deconstructive but only in order to hold open the reality of the ever-greater.

Having thereby established this rather grandiose first point, we can now turn to what the *analogia entis* means a bit more concretely. First, analogy and how it frames an understanding of language's relation to reality has several traps that have to be carefully avoided to clarify what Przywara means by the term. The use of analogical language itself navigates between the assertion that human language somehow perfectly maps onto metaphysical truth and a kind of despair of language saying anything meaningful about the transcendent. The language of analogy, as both a comparison in the strict sense of the word (a:b::c:d) and a way of expressing the relationship between different things, mediates between these two extremes. Analogy says something real, but it does so by acknowledging its limitations as rooted in comparison/relationship, not something capable of maintaining a one-to-one correspondence.

The second linguistic and conceptual clarification has to do with the two kinds of analogy: proportion and attribution. Proportion is the more straightforward, as it leans into analogy as a comparison. The analogy of proportion is an analogy that recognizes a difference in degree between the compared terms. To say that a human is "good" like God is "good" recognizes that some degree of similarity obtains and that this similarity is stable enough to be saying something true. Analogy of attribution compares two things as well but as related or directed to a third. Here the famous example is with "health," where two very dissimilar things, urine and medicine, are related to the human person, who is the primary analogate of what "healthy" means in this regard. Both forms of analogy are important, but the former analogy of proportionality emphasizes more the dissimilarity between the things compared and, in the God/world relation, is helpful in that regard. However, Przywara understood both forms of analogy to be in play with the *analogia entis* and that both were needed to balance the other out.[8]

This rather granular detail is important because it sets the stage for what follows next. Przywara's *analogia entis*, for all its complexity, is fundamentally a metaphysical principle that undercuts any and all metaphysical and/or ontological systems that self-enclose through absolute claims. These clarifications of analogy as steering between both presumption/agnosticism and proportion/attribution already highlights the metaphysical balancing act that Przywara will perform and that Balthasar will follow with his own claims. Whatever comparisons an analogy might successfully achieve, especially in regard to God, they must always be understood within the famously articulated principle of the Fourth Lateran Council: "One cannot note any similarity between Creator and creature, however great, without being compelled to note an even greater dissimilarity between them."[9] There is an absolute distinction between God and world that conditions any comparison even as it creates the distance to allow a real analogy. This absolute distinction would include, importantly, the refusal of any idea of "Being" that becomes a third term between God and the world, where each can be understood to participate but merely in different degrees of intensity.

In positing such fundamental claims, Przywara also begins with the fundamentals of metaphysics itself—existence and essence. To anticipate what will follow, it should be noted here that the *analogia entis* is a somewhat misleading term. In fact, Przywara's concept of analogy is twofold and can be referred to more aptly as an "analogous analogy."[10] The first analogy rests

---

8. Przywara, *Analogia Entis: Metaphysics: Original Structure and Universal Rhythm*, 39n111.

9. *"Inter creatorem et creaturam non potest tanta similitude notari, quin inter eos non sit maior dissimilitudo notanda"* (*DH*, 806).

10. The *analogia entis*, as a theological principle, is protected from accusations of direct access to God by a *double* analogy: "However much philosophy can dimly grasp the origins of finite being in the Absolute, only theology knows that finite being is the subject of a freely offered revelation. It follows, therefore, that theology renders the philosophical analogy of being analogous. The analogy of being can be seen as a moment subsisting within the analogy of faith, which reveals the inner nature of the Absolute and the ultimate purpose of the finite order. The nature of the first is lovingly to save and that of the second is freely to be saved. . . . This double level of dissimilarity so attenuates any similarity between God and the world that at once it affirms the radical contingency of the finite order while it

upon the classic metaphysical distinction between existence and essence, between particular beings and the infinite ground of Being out of which they spring. The contingency of each particular being points toward the Absolute Being that is the always greater, more mysterious ground of particular being. That is how contingency is structured into existence itself, but there is also an additional destabilization that Przywara pushes in regard to essence. That a thing exists in a particular essence of rock, bird, or human, for example, is stable enough to preserve the continuity of "whatness" of the thing but is also fundamentally involved in becoming. As beings in time and history, the very essence of a thing, no matter its particularity, is nevertheless involved in becoming toward something else. David Bentley Hart writes:

> Becoming is an ecstasy, and nothing besides; it is indeed a constant tension—between what a thing is and what it is not, between its past and its future, between interior and exterior, and so on—but it is not originally a violent departure from the stability of an original essence. Our being is simply the rapture of arrival, and while its contours are always necessarily defined by the shadows of the 'no longer' and the 'not yet,' it is only secondarily, because of sin, that these become for us sources of a tragic anxiety (mourning for the lost, lust for the unattained) rather than faith, hope, and love ('remembrance' of our true end, eros for God's infinity, the love of all things in God).[11]

This instability, contingency, and incompleteness that are structural features of the *analogia entis* are not because of some primordial punishment but the grounds for an infinite possibility of decision and becoming. Hart provides the additional inflection about the gratuity and goodness of creation that is also a structural feature of Przywara's position. In short, the very mystery of becoming and contingency always aims toward something but never reaches it, and that is at the core of essence and existence, all of which suggests a still greater mystery of fulfillment.

This first analogy, between individual beings and the being out of which they spring and some fullness toward which they strive but cannot attain, is limitedly perceivable by human thought. However, according to Przywara, the human mind can never attain a contemplation of either pure Being (meta-ontics) or pure Thought (meta-noetics); instead, it oscillates (*schwingen*) between thought and being, between particular beings and their constant opening up

---

establishes a basis for a novel revelation that can challenge the hegemony of intramundane aesthetics." See Stephen Fields, "The Beauty of the Ugly: Balthasar, the Crucifixion, Analogy, and God," *International Journal of Systematic Theology* 9.2 (2007): 178.

11. David Bentley Hart, *The Beauty of the Infinite: The Aesthetics of Christian Truth* (Grand Rapids, MI: Eerdmans, 2003), 244.

and pointing beyond themselves to the mysterious ground of absolute Being.[12] For Przywara, God cannot be domesticated or relativized against some other purportedly pure philosophical ground—the systems must be theocentric:

> On the one hand, my writings present a theory that (in contrast to the *individuum de ratione materiae of scholastic Thomism*) seeks to comprehend the individually diversified fullness of things: a *differentiated universalism* of the "unity-in-tension between individual and community"; on the other hand, however, they present a theory that intends (over against a humanistic rationalism that goes all the way up to neo-scholasticism) a radical humbling of every (ontic) end-in-itself of self and community and of every rounded (noetic) calculation under the sovereignty of God: a *theocentrism—relativizing* all things human—of God in Christ in the church.[13]

The swipe at scholasticism here should not obscure Przywara's robust reliance on Thomas nor his appreciation for rigor and method. However, he is concerned with shaking things up—polarity, oscillation, and tension rule Przywara's *analogia entis.*

This primary analogy serves as the first wall of defense. Existence and essence and their emergence in the play of being serves (and this is difficult to overemphasize) as only the first analogy, which then must be understood within the context of the second analogy between creation and God. All sensible particulars can only point through analogy to the fullness of being, and this analogy, discovered in the *schwingen* between thought and being and existence and essence, relies upon the more primary analogy in which God is revealed as the creator and source of being:

> In other words, whereas the first analogy emphasizes a participatory "sharing," even "taking" (*teil-nehmend*), of creaturely being in the divine (and thus accords with a strictly Platonic understanding of analogy), the second analogy emphasizes that being "is" only *as* the "im-parting" of a gift, moreover, that the creature only "is" insofar as it is between nothing and the "Creator *ex nihilo.*" Accordingly, for Przywara, the full form of the *analogia entis* must be understood in terms of the intersection of these *two* analogies—the latter of which fills out the former with its properly theological heights and depth—and thus, by implication, in terms of an intersection of philosophy and theology.[14]

---

12. John Betz, "After Barth: A New Introduction to Erich Przywara's *Analogia Entis*," in *The Analogy of Being: Invention of the Antichrist or the Wisdom of God?* ed. Joseph White, OP (Grand Rapids, MI: Eerdmans, 2011), 60.

13. Przywara, *Analogia Entis: Metaphysics: Original Structure and Universal Rhythm*, xxi.

14. Betz, "After Barth," 64.

While reason might attain some notion of the first analogy, revelation alone is capable of disclosing the truth of faith—the Trinity is gratuitous love and source of all being. The *analogia entis*, which Przywara acknowledges to be a primarily theological principle, functions philosophically to open up to the theological.[15]

We can now see how radically the *analogia entis* functions as the destructor of philosophical idols that seek a pure ground on which to build systems that either exclude or domesticate God. Destructively, the *analogia entis* invalidates any philosophy predicated on some conception of pure thought or being that would seek to confine God to systemization, irrelevancy, or nonexistence. Constructively, the *analogia entis* imbues profound dynamism to cause and effect, existence and essence insofar as the radical becoming of existents from the mysterious and infinitely fruitful ground of being analogously corresponds, in ever greater dissimilarity, to the pure unity of existence and essence in the Trinity.

The contingency of existence is amplified in the *analogia entis*, but even more, essence is disrupted. Przywara is making a bold move here to emphasize that everything, especially the human person, is *perpetually in becoming*.[16] For all of Przywara's "in-and-beyond" language and the diversity of references that it can include, it primarily refers back to the dynamism and becoming of being as expressed in the *analogia entis*. On the philosophical level, this can be as simple as charting the middle course between Heraclitus (all is flux) and Parmenides (all is one). But in modernity, Przywara (and Balthasar with him) is particularly strident in his criticisms of philosophical systems that tend so regularly to absolutize into something, whether it is Hegel's Absolute Spirit, Marx's dialectical materialism, or Derrida's *différance*. This deep philosophical humbling of any system that postures to an absolutism of pure identity, ego, or nothingness is itself humbled by the mystery at the heart of creation, especially the heart of the human person, that is perpetually suspended both by

---

15. "But if the *analogia entis* is essentially a code word for our natural knowledge of God, this knowledge, as merely natural knowledge, is severely limited. Indeed, this is why natural theology, without the light of revelation, is always on the verge of idolatrously collapsing the distinction between Creator and creature that the *analogia entis* holds open. In other words, positively stated, it is only in the light of revelation that the full scope of the *analogia entis*, both the radical immanence and the transcendence of God, appears" (Betz, "After Barth," 52–53).

16. "For just as epistemology is without any firm footing, so too is the creature's fundamental being, since unlike God, whose essence is to exist, the essence of the creature is precisely *not* identical to existence. Rather, essence and existence are related in the creature in such a way that the essence of the creature is never fully given, i.e., never identical or reducible to its existence, but is always on the horizon of its existence as something to be attained" (Przywara, *Analogia Entis: Metaphysics: Original Structure and Universal Rhythm*, 63).

the contingency of existence itself and the dynamic becoming of everything.[17] The philosophical conditioning that makes space for that mystery opens itself more and more to the theological revelation of the God who is the source of being itself. Because we are suspended between the polarity of existence and essence (and the polarities of contingency and becoming even within that!), there is a philosophical cultivation of the stretching out, the *ekstases*, which finds its fulfillment in the revelation of God in Jesus Christ.

In no way does this mean that Przywara's explorations of the contingency and dynamism of existence and essence create a predetermined framework in which Christian revelation just "fits" in, nor does it, for that matter, place emphasis on the similarity of the analogy before the ever-greater dissimilarity. For Przywara, creation is a dynamic synthesis of things that can strive for but never arrive at a perfect unity, and *that* is a distant, incomplete analogy of the perfect unity of God. The twist is that the very thing that shows a similitude and unites us to God (the inseparability of essence and existence) is also that which can be the key to beginning to understand the radical difference between creature and God—that the tension between existence and essence endlessly strives toward a unity it can never attain. This has just as much a philosophical import as it does a theological, for it means that all systems, philosophical or theological, require a corrective lest they self-aggrandize into idolatry.

Here we strike at something that is at the heart of Balthasar's work—the "unsystematic" nature of his approach. Perhaps we can appreciate with more sympathy why, for a man who wrote so prolifically and comprehensively, he resisted overdetermining his theological insights. Balthasar understood this to be primarily theologically sanctioned by the ever-greater glory of God as expressed via the *analogia entis*. We can further understand how this impetus to avoid rigid systematization was further cultivated by all the titanic strivings of communism, Nazism, and different philosophies in his own day.

Balthasar very much is practicing what he preaches in his method, something that will become particularly obvious in his anthropology. Because of his reliance on the *analogia entis*, Balthasar establishes a series of anthropological polarities (body/spirit, man/woman, individual/community, freedom/obe-

---

17. "In fact, for Balthasar, once analogy is inserted into a system of thought or way of thinking that is purely objective, ready at hand, and *restlos* ('without rest'), then the principle ceases to reveal the dynamic rhythm of being itself. . . . Przywara's analogy, according to Balthasar, is likewise a moving image of the inner dynamic structure of every and all being created by God. The principle of analogy for Balthasar cannot be used as a means to evacuate created being of its mystery." See Peter Casarella, "Hans Urs von Balthasar, Erich Przywara's *Analogia Entis*, and the Problem of a Catholic *Denkform*" in *The Analogy of Being: Invention of the Antichrist or the Wisdom of God?* ed. Thomas Joseph White (Grand Rapids, MI: Eerdmans, 2011), 196.

dience, etc.) that are structurally oriented toward each other without achieving the perfect synthesis, and these features are the anthropological expression of that tension of infinite becoming and striving that is the beating heart of the *analogia entis.* Balthasar is not being obscurantist but rather is performing his truth—that the human person cannot sit still but must live into the reality of the mystery of becoming and ever-greater openness to God and neighbor.

FREEDOM

Balthasar does much to structure the *analogia entis* into his own thought, but this destabilization risks deleterious effects if it does not become balanced by a real possibility of participating in something transcendent. Given the power of the *analogia entis* to shift emphasis to *ekstases* and becoming, the anthropological expression of this emerges more and more clearly around the issue of freedom. Freedom becomes *the* anthropological issue for Balthasar because it is the means by which the radical gratuity of God and the contingency of human existence can coalesce in grace and mutual love:

> The basic presupposition for all understanding of existing things and of Being is the relationship between uncreated and created freedom; it is the creature's freedom that causes him to be termed the "image and likeness of God"—and this likewise is the concrete thrust of the "*analogia entis.*" On the other hand, the whole point of this distinction between the created and uncreated is that, in it, the glory of God shall fulfill itself "superabundantly" in the freedom of the creature. It follows, then, that the self-fulfilling Word of God, that is, his perfect self-giving, must elicit a perfect answer from and in the free creature; absolute freedom must not force or overpower the creature's freedom. In affirming this, we must maintain the whole span of tension.[18]

The foregrounding of the relationship between divine and human freedom through the *Theo-Drama,* therefore, is really just the logical outcome of the *analogia entis* and the stress it places on contingency and becoming. Given the instability of creaturely being as such, the agency of the human person to shape and direct that becoming becomes *the* key anthropological question. And given the work that Przywara and Balthasar both do to enfold human freedom and its limited sphere of agency within divine freedom, the question presses to the fore of how to orient and harmonize the two. Balthasar will argue that the human person has a real, albeit limited, capacity for agency that can cooperate with the divine, but he deploys polarities and various tensions in order to avoid the risk of falling back into something too programmed and structured.

---

18. *TD* 2, 123.

When we arrive at the second volume of the *Theo-Drama*, then, Balthasar's extended reflection on the "stage" as a fundamental piece of his larger theater analogy is not a whimsical aesthetic trope but a serious theological reflection. With the *analogia entis* in the background, Balthasar must carefully articulate how the "stage" of creation can operate within its own sphere of autonomy and agency even as he must correlate that with divine freedom in such a way that divine freedom undergirds and supports human freedom without supplanting it. It is no small task he has set for himself.

Among the first moves that he makes is to disregard the possibility for a "neutral" starting point: "In this play, all the spectators must eventually become fellow actors, whether they wish to or not."[19] The language and prioritizing of stage before looking at the actors is significant because it obviates any type of purported neutral place from which one can begin. Balthasar invokes biblical revelation to make this claim, but this approach does much to avoid any kind of scientific or objective middle ground where one can claim to be arguing from and then adjudicating other positions. In other words, for Balthasar, "to be" is to be involved in the drama. To claim that one is just being "objective" already renders the person up short because, from the beginning, the person is denying her role and its moral implications—that person is seeking a type of stability and neutrality that the *analogia entis* disallows. Balthasar has cut off such an approach and asserts that who the thinker is as a person and how she is directing her own becoming matters.

Balthasar accomplishes this synthesis of the personal and philosophical/theological both metaphysically with his extended analogy of the theo-drama, but he also more explicitly addresses contemporary theological issues in order to incorporate them into his argument. The first volume of *Theo-Drama* proceeds through nine trends of contemporary theology (event, history, orthopraxy, dialogue, political theology, futurism, function, role, and freedom and evil), and Balthasar determines that all of them point to and must be answered within the theo-drama he advances. Balthasar wants to show that his approach and its central questioning of how God answers the question of human freedom (as exercised both for and against God) remains in the person of Jesus Christ. All questions collapse, therefore, into this question of reconciling divine and human freedom in Jesus Christ, especially as they center on the difficulty of reconciling human sin with God's redemptive act.[20]

---

19. *TD* 2, 58.

20. "If there is to be drama, characters must face each other in freedom. If there is to be theo-drama, the first presupposition is that, 'beside' or 'within' the absolute, divine freedom, there is some other, nondivine, created freedom; a freedom that shares, in a true sense, something of the autonomy of the divine freedom, both in the decision for God and in the decision against him. The question of how such a dialogue is possible if God is the

We must stop here for a moment and consider this. There are three fundamental, interrelated tensions that Balthasar has identified and with which he must contend in this approach: the tensions of 1) the sin and violence in history that Christ confronts, 2) divine and human freedom, and 3) the *analogia entis* holding creation open in its instability to a greater fulfillment. Balthasar has to show how God is not extrinsically dealing with human sin and evil but entering into it in order to redeem it, is redeeming it in a way that does not mechanistically reprogram human freedom but allows it its own space, and is offering the intimation of comprehensive Christological form that can "reconcile all things" (Col 1:20). However, he must also do this in such a way that does not violate the grammar of the *analogia entis* by providing an absolutizing answer or solution but rather points toward it in such a way that can be grasped in faith.[21]

An anthropology that offers clearly articulated pathways of fulfillment, therefore, will not be countenanced by Balthasar because we stand beneath the shadow of the cross and in the *analogia entis*. The revelation of Christ on the cross is the fullest revelation of God's love for a fallen humanity. If the full dramatic quality of any anthropology is going to be explored, it must begin by creating the space for the extremity of this tension between God's offer of redemption and human freedom in becoming.[22] Philosophy and its attempts at a synthesis in answer to the riddle of human existence must be taken seriously, but, crucially, these attempts must be scrutinized by the *analogia entis*. The *analogia entis* both 1) demands an ever-greater difference between human and divine freedom so that the distinction is heightened and overcome by love, even as 2) God's immanence is also maintained as "the Other who is not other" (as the God who is not one being among other

---

Absolute and the 'All' (and nothing can drop out of the Absolute); and moreover of how, even presupposing the biblical view of God, creation can be 'good' and yet this created freedom can forfeit God and itself—this question forms the threshold of all that follows" (*TD* 2, 62–63).

21. From the rationalist perspective, John Henry Newman, for both Przywara and Balthasar, is particularly important here: "How does the totality become recognizable in the partial aspects? Newman's answer is: in the convergence of the indicators. However, not only must they exist objectively, they must also be subjectively discernible, and the organ for this is the 'illative sense'" (*TD* 2, 132).

22. "It follows from what we have just said that, in lifting the 'dramatis personae' out of the ongoing play, we cannot begin with a pure anthropology or a pure theology ('God in himself'). For a purely philosophical anthropology does not unveil finite freedom in its full dimensions, as—illuminated by the light of revelation—seems appropriate to man; and equally, a purely theological doctrine of God that did not arise out of a theology of God-made-man would fail to present the full dimensions of the divine freedom: it would not set forth the true relationship between God and created freedom" (*TD* 2, 196).

beings and therefore is neatly distinct from being but also transcends any and all conceptions of it).[23] Both the difference between God and humanity and how God overcomes human rebellion from within actual human freedom must be shown.

One very understandable reason to be frustrated by Balthasar is that he constantly posits tensions in order to avoid any easy and/or absolutizing answer to this challenge, which he does with the concept of freedom as a tension between self-possession and consent (I will treat extensively below four additional tensions).[24] But another way to understand this, especially given our deeper appreciation for the *analogia entis*, is to see how these tensions function as little engines that drive the dynamism and becoming of creation and do not allow it to rest in any absolutizing. When it comes to the question of human freedom, precisely such a tactic is also in play. Balthasar explores how human freedom is both 1) an autonomous motion and 2) consent. Freedom is autonomous motion because the human person is self-possessed and the agent of their own action but, additionally, freedom is also consent in that human freedom "comes up against other finite freedoms" and cannot force them into the self: "the freedom of the 'other' must disclose itself by opening up its own inner area."[25] Both the individual and the communal, the intellectual and the volitional, and the finite and the infinite are held in a productive tension that strives for a reconciliation beyond that which the anthropological is able to create for itself.

Given these tensions, Balthasar can now harmonize the anthropological features with how they find their fulfillment and transformation in Christian faith, specifically through the Trinitarian relations.[26] Precisely because the human person simply is the tension between self-possession (autonomous motion) and a kind of letting be of the other in freedom (consent), the Trinitarian relations become the supreme analogy by which human fulfillment can be understood:

> Thus, finally, it becomes clear why finite freedom can really fulfill itself in infinite freedom and in no other way. If *letting-be* belongs to the nature of infinite freedom—the Father *lets* the Son be consubstantial God, and so forth—there is no danger of finite freedom, which cannot fulfill itself on its own account (because it can neither go back and take possession of its origins nor can it attain its absolute goal by its own power), becom-

---

23. *TD* 2, 193–94.

24. I counted no less than twenty-five such tensions in less than half of *TD* 2.

25. *TD* 2, 228.

26. While the approach here has been to proceed from the "bottom up" to better track Balthasar's logic, it should be clear that Balthasar is consistent about the need for revelation and its control of his theological discourse.

ing alienated from itself in the realm of the Infinite. It can only be what it is, that is, an image of infinite freedom, imbued with a freedom of its own, by getting in tune with the (trinitarian) "law" of absolute freedom (of self-surrender): and this law is not foreign to it—for after all it is the "law" of absolute Being—but most authentically its own.[27]

This polarity of self-possession and letting-be is the source of the deepest promise and the greatest risk.[28] Positively, the self-possession and letting-be can analogously mirror Trinitarian relations where the Father is both distinct from and unified with the Son and Holy Spirit (real unity, real distinction) in an infinite interplay of love. Negatively, this striving for harmonious resolution between the polarity of self-possession and letting-be can absolutize for the human person in either direction: to a self-enclosure that treasures finite goods at the expense of the infinite and to an indifference to decision and personal/social responsibility.

It is at this point that we risk crossing over into Christology, where the God-man offers the path to eternal becoming in Trinitarian love and perfectly unites divine and human freedom in himself, but we are at least now in a position to understand the more obvious and straightforward anthropological features in Balthasar's work. Because Balthasar has so thoroughly structured the *analogia entis* into his anthropology and calibrated that anthropology against Trinitarian relations, the very mystery of the ever-greater God must find some analogue in the human person as well, who is made in God's image and likeness.[29] Balthasar finds this analogue primarily in the question of human freedom and its fundamental tension between self-possession and self-giving. This resistance to rigid definitions of the human person by Balthasar significantly conditions his thought, but he does arrive at four features that provide struc-

---

27. *TD* 2, 259.

28. "Wholeness streams and shines through the fragments. The more uninhibited this action is, the more conscious the fragments have of their fragmentariness. And there seems to be a strange relationship between the spirit of streaming, shining wholeness and the spirit of the abandonment of the fragment. It is as if to renounce all efforts to achieve wholeness is to precisely to practice wholeness itself, as if God is nowhere nearer than in the humility and poverty of indifference, in the openness to death, in the renunciation of every hold on or attempt to make certain of God" (*TA*, 110).

29. "In a 'negative anthropology' that takes its bearings purely from man, negativity is a critique that radically attacks every objectified picture of man; in Sartre it is the absolutizing of finite freedom, which eventually undermines every definition of being. In Christianity, however, negativity is oriented to the positive, to the God who is ever-greater, in such a way that we can never catch up with him. Accordingly, we who are his 'image and likeness' do not despair because of our inability to arrive at a definition; instead, we are aware of a comparative dimension: man is *more* than what can be included in a conceptually clear definition" (*TA*, 345).

tural tensions to his anthropology: the human person and human freedom as rooted in the cosmos or nature, spirit and body, man and woman, and individual and community. Each of these tensions is currently undergoing its own kind of deformation in modernity, which Balthasar analyzes to reveal the more fruitful tension at the core. We can address each in turn.

THE FOUR FEATURES OF BALTHASARIAN ANTHROPOLOGY

Balthasar begins his reflection on "man and nature" by exploring this theme and the following three themes through the lens of the "Pre-Christian." Convinced as he is that the revelation of Christ has transformed everything it touches, Balthasar must turn to the pre-Christian period in order to discern the fragments of truth that point toward Christ. Unsurprisingly, Balthasar finds that the pre-Christian person "lives in the awareness of a primal *analogia entis,*" wherein there is a natural awe of the divine world, however that is conceived across cultures. The pre-Christian person understood the need for a harmonizing of the natural and human orderings. The human person was a *microcosmos* of the *macrocosmos,* and this truth was primarily mediated to her through the *polis.* While Christianity revised and reformed these pre-Christian elements, they nevertheless persisted for centuries in a fruitful synthesis with Christian belief, wherein that mediating *polis* became the *ecclesia.* This tension between the *microcosmos* and *macrocosmos* is lost in modernity because the human person has denied any transcendent dimension to the material world (and hence has become "lost in the cosmos," to borrow Romano Guardini's phrase).[30] Because material creation no longer mediates the transcendent, the human person thinks herself more directly in relation to God and risks sublating herself with the divine. This has unleashed all kinds of damaging philosophical systems that fail to maintain the fruitful tension of the transcendent ordering of the material world and the capacity to participate in that ordering for human flourishing.

This breakdown of the harmony between the cosmos and its ordered relation brings into relief the remaining three features—spirit and body, man and woman, individual and community.[31] Because creation has lost its mediating function for humanity, these three features are forced to bear a weight that they cannot bear without the larger metaphysical contextualization. The development of the anthropological feature of spirit and body culminates in two

---

30. Romano Guardini, *The End of the Modern World* (Wilmington, DE: ISI Books, 2001).

31. In this regard, Balthasar acknowledges his debt to Przywara, who had already developed these three dimensions with his anthropological works of *Deus semper Major, Humanitas,* and *Mensch: typologische Anthropologie.*

competing positions. First, the human person is the "perfecter of the cosmos" and mediator because of her position between the spiritual and animal; she can perfect both because she has knowledge of both. The second position is the opposite—because of this mediator position, the human person struggles for a precise knowledge of either and so is forced to choose the pursuit of one over the other. Balthasar holds that St. Thomas Aquinas is the champion and best explicator of the first, while St. Gregory of Nyssa represents the second. Balthasar does not attempt any sort of synthesis here but concedes that, without the transforming grace of Christ, the human person is condemned to a bland kind of middle. Without Christ and the grace to realize spirit in body and body in spirit, an irresolvable ambiguity persists without resolution.

The tension between man and woman forms a kind of bridge between the two other features. The spiritual/bodily and individual/community integration that the human person seeks is acutely mirrored in the distinction between man and woman, who are always in communion but never in a perfect harmony. Interestingly, Balthasar refuses to correlate the spiritual/rational with the masculine and instead asserts that "no metaphysical polarity can be adduced to explain the differences of the sexes in mankind."[32] Instead, Balthasar again follows Przywara in noting the similarity of the two genders with God who is biblically revealed in fatherhood and motherhood (and the nuptial relationship with Israel), and the dissimilarity in that human sexuality is part of the animal sexuality of the created world.[33]

Finally, the tension of the individual and community is "the most subdued" in the pre-Christian period and yet deeply intensified with the advent of Christ. With the pre-Christian, there is a constant struggle between instantiating a harmony between the community and the cosmos and the threat of tyrants and utilitarianist threats that erase the individual. Balthasar continues beyond the pre-Christian to political reflections on Hegel and several others but finds a common fault in them all—they cannot sufficiently distinguish between God as the being-in-its-totality revealed in the cosmos and the true Christian God in-and-beyond-being, as indicated by the *analogia entis*. Because there is not a sufficient distinction, the ordering of the cosmos is fundamentally rent by death, and the human person is forced to prioritize the bodily or the spiritual over the other. Either too great an emphasis on community or the individual can do this, but the main tension to be upheld for

---

32. *TD* 2, 368.

33. After an extended exploration of the Christian tradition, Balthasar refuses to offer his own speculation on what prelapsarian erotic attraction might look like. More interestingly, however, Balthasar finds an analogous replication of God's "humiliation" in the creation of human freedom with the creation of each child, who is gifted with this same freedom yet by events initiated by his creatures. See *TD* 2, 372.

Balthasar is a deeper individual fruition that comes about in and through the community, for the betterment of both.[34] The poles of individual and community are heightened so as to achieve a greater synthesis.

These four tensions at the core of anthropology are transformed with Christ. The advent of Christianity and *creatio ex nihilo* announces both an intentionality to creation and a complete separation between God and his creation.[35] Creation is shown in all its contingency even as the revelation of the gratuity of that creation is revealed to be the intentionality of infinite love.[36] One might expect Balthasar here to offer Christian faith as a kind of resolution to these anthropological tensions, and yet he theo-dramatically heightens them. Whereas the anthropological tensions were significant primarily for a this-worldly ordering and against the backdrop of a more nebulous spiritual world in the pre-Christian period, now the offer of eternal life and participation with God becomes real: "For the present we are only concerned with the *heightening* of the creature's inner constitution, whose finitude is now explicitly stretched between the poles of nothing and infinity, or rather of 'nothingness' and 'God.'"[37] The tensions at the core of his anthropology are heightened because they are revealed to have a source in the intention of God's creation and a promised fulfillment through Christ. What this means is that these tensions are irresolvable even as they offer myriad forms of new correlating and harmonizing in grace to achieve expressions of the ever-greater love that is their source.

Because these anthropological tensions are heightened and transformed by Christianity, Balthasar sees an increasing antagonism from the world in the post-Christian period. Christianity's explanatory power does not brook competitors, and, as such, any system claiming to greater explanatory power will

---

34. *TD* 2, 415.

35. It should be said here too that Balthasar's sustained emphasis on kenosis in both the Trinitarian and Christological registers ultimately is the revelation of the kenosis that sustains the *analogia entis*. This kenosis is not a nothingness out of which creation is made; as if in some mythological protology there exists "nothing" which God somehow fashions creation out of. Instead, the "nothing" is even more literal—God does *not* create out of anything other than his own infinite freedom and love, which simultaneously creates a relative autonomy for that creation even as it is enfolded within the gift of being itself. Again, there is no third term here called "Being" where two things (God and creation) participate in different degrees. The "emptying" of kenosis into creation is not a depotentializing of God or some loss in himself but the gratuitous sharing of existence to creation which is given the space to participate in that fullness of becoming in its own manner. God, in a very specific way indicated by "kenosis," withdraws in order to allow his creation to stand forth for otherwise it would be outshone by the glory of himself.

36. *TD* 2, 400–401.

37. *TD* 2, 400.

necessarily provoke antagonism. Only Christianity has the tools to so thoroughly achieve a philosophical and theological synthesis that can absorb all the world's truth. Christianity does this by valorizing the integrity of the created order for all its explanatory and disclosive metaphysical fullness. The twist is that the universality of Christian truth has been transmuted in the post-Christian period into scientific laws that thereby supplant Christianity's claim to universality. The purported neutrality of a scientific method gains the objectivity of the neutral observer at the expense of relativizing all culture and spiritual systems of thought.[38] The Christian will face increasing antagonism in the contemporary context precisely because orthodox Christian belief, while capable of incorporating truth from everywhere, structurally cannot accept truth anywhere but from the God of Abraham, Isaac, and Jacob, who became incarnate in Jesus Christ. The conflict escalates to the apocalyptic because neither side can capitulate without compromising what it is. Only one will endure.

Conclusion

What Balthasar appears to be doing throughout his enormous body of work is constantly drawing the reader back to fundamental anthropological and existential questions of "Who are you? Who do you decide to be?" All the importance of rationality, reason, empirical sciences, and spirituality are incorporated into Balthasar's system. He quite readily pulls from the best and most interesting of Christian thinkers, most notably Thomas Aquinas, Gregory of Nyssa, and Maximus the Confessor, but the point of such fundamental importance for Balthasar and for his anthropology is that such systems of thought and sources of truth can become inhibitors of what is most fundamentally human—the openness to a grace that is greater than any human conception. Structuring his anthropology through the *analogia entis*, Balthasar opts for the anthropological feature of freedom and core fundamental tensions because Balthasar wants to ask if the human person can exercise agency and responsibility to live into these tensions such that, in accepting the limitations of one's particularity and humanity, one remains open to their transformation in grace. While there are myriad other philosophical systems that offer answers to these

---

38. "Here we see the truth of the theological statement that it must become ever more difficult to be a Christian in a world which is becoming unified. It is not because Christians themselves have difficulties in taking part in cultural work or in beginning at the level of dialogic reason in just as open and understanding intercourse as non-Christians. Rather, it is because secular reason as it links up cannot be other than tolerantly relativizing, and from its point of view must expect Christianity to understand itself as relatively as it is necessarily understood by others who are non-Christians. At this point the Christian's testimony to the truth is a testimony of life and blood (*martyrion*)" (*TA*, 191).

tensions through nihilism, escapism, or biological determinism, Balthasar is instead asking to embrace the tension of mission, the tension of accepting in obedience one's particularity with the openness that God wills that particularity and ordains it toward a greater wholeness, which only he can give.

There would be a kind of intellectual hypocrisy to Balthasar's commitment to the importance and relevance of the *analogia entis* if he were to commit, to the exclusion of all else, to a strictly Thomistic anthropology or one derived, say, from Gregory of Nyssa. Truth is too disclosive, too ever-greater to be corralled in such a manner. And herein lies the subtle irony of Balthasar's theology—it performs a provocation to the reader herself. There are many good reasons to be critical of Balthasar. His unsystematic and enormous body of work could have used a far firmer editing hand than his own, his imprecision in language is at best a result of faithful exuberance but at worst undisciplined, and his engagement with mysticism and Adrienne von Speyr, in particular, founds an entire theological system on grounds that require far more scrutiny. And yet herein lies the provocation: this is an orthodox Catholic theologian, resolutely committed to the Catholic Church and its hierarchical expression, asking the tradition to consider so many things in deeper ways than it has before. In such a questioning, Balthasar is performing in a way unmatched in Catholic theology in the twentieth century, if the reader will remain open to the possibility of the ever-greater.

The case is not such that Balthasar oversimplifies the human person but rather that Balthasar does not want to limit anthropological reflection. He therefore opens it up for as many and varied expressions as possible. In so doing, however, lhe also limits it by submitting it to the all-embracing revelation of Christ and the freedom of the human person. The fundamental question to any anthropological expression is this: no matter the situation or circumstance, does the human person exercise their agency in such a way that brings about a harmony with the will of Christ? To proceed any farther with Balthasar's anthropology would take us directly into the heart of his Christology. Indeed, a discussion of Balthasar's anthropology is difficult because of how thoroughly he has structured his approach into his Christological and Trinitarian reflections as well. The value of the *analogia entis* for the discussion here, however, is to reveal how deeply its dynamism is built into all of Balthasar's thought and how it becomes most concretely relevant in the question of human freedom.

BIBLIOGRAPHY

Betz, John. "After Barth: A New Introduction to Erich Przywara's *Analogia Entis*." In *The Analogy of Being: Invention of the Antichrist or the Wisdom of God?* edited by T. J. White, 35–87. Grand Rapids, MI: Eerdmans, 2011.

Casarella, Peter. "Hans Urs von Balthasar, Erich Przywara's *Analogia Entis*, and the Problem of a Catholic *Denkform*." In *The Analogy of Being: Invention of the Antichrist or the Wisdom of God?* edited by T. J. White, 192–206. Grand Rapids, MI: Eerdmans, 2011.

Dalzell, Thomas G. *The Dramatic Encounter of Divine and Human Freedom in the Theology of Hans Urs von Balthasar*. Bern: Peter Lang AG, Internationaler Verlag der Wissenschaften, 1997.

Fields, Stephen. "The Beauty of the Ugly: Balthasar, the Crucifixion, Analogy, and God." *International Journal of Systematic Theology* 9, no. 2 (2007): 178.

Guardini, Romano. *The End of the Modern World*. Wilmington, DE: ISI Books, 2001.

Hart, David Bentley. *The Beauty of the Infinite: The Aesthetics of Christian Truth*. Grand Rapids, MI: Eerdmans, 2003.

Przywara, Erich. *Analogia Entis: Metaphysics: Original Structure and Universal Rhythm*. Translated by John Betz and David Bentley Hart. Grand Rapids, MI: Eerdmans, 2014.

Schumacher, Michele. *A Trinitarian Anthropology: Adrienne von Speyr & Hans Urs von Balthasar in Dialogue with Thomas Aquinas*. Washington, DC: The Catholic University of America Press, 2014.

Servais, Jacques. "Freedom as Christ's Gift to Man in the Thought of Hans Urs von Balthasar." *Communio* 29, no. 3 (2002).

Eschatology

CHAPTER 13

Eschatology in Thomas Aquinas

Rev. Bryan Kromholtz, OP

St. Thomas's teachings concerning what today we call "eschatology" cover a sizeable number of interrelated topics over a wide range of works in his oeuvre.[1] For the most part, his positions on eschatology are those commonly held by Christians of his day, positions that have become classic, at least in the Catholic Church.[2] We can very briefly summarize them as follows. When Christ comes again to earth at the end, he will simultaneously raise from the dead all humans who have ever lived. They will all rise incorruptible and go either to glorious eternal life (for those conformed to the charity of

---

1. Only a limited number of those works are cited here: the editions consulted are listed below (with abbreviations given in parentheses). Thus, reference is made to his *Summa theologiae* (*ST*), 5 vols., ed. Institutum Studiorum Medievalium Ottaviensis (Ottawa: Studium Generale OP, 1945); *Scriptum super libros Sententiarum*, books I-IV (*Super Sent.* 1, etc.), in *Opera omnia*, vol. 7.2, *Commentum in quatuor libros sententiarum Magistri Petri Lombardi, volumen secundum, pars altera, Commentum in quartum librum sententiarum Magistri Petri Lombardi* (Petrus Fiaccadori: Parma, 1858), 872–1259. For references to his *Summa contra Gentiles* (*SCG*), *Compendium theologiae seu brevis compilatio theologiae ad fratrem Raynaldum* (*Comp. Theol.*), *Quaestiones disputatae de veritate* (*De ver.*), and *Quaestiones disputatae de anima* (*De an.*), see *Sancti Thomae de Aquino Opera omnia iussu Leonis XIII P. M. edita* (Rome–Paris: Leonine Commission, 1882–), vols. 13–15 (1918, 1926, and 1930); vol. 42 (1979), 83–205; vols. 22/1–3 (1970, 1972, and 1976); and vol. 24/1 (1996), respectively. For his *Super Primam epistolam ad Corinthios lectura* (*Super I Cor.*), *Super Secundam epistolam ad Corinthios lectura* (*Super II Cor.*), and *Super Epistolam ad Ephesios lectura* (*Super Eph.*), see *Super Epistolas S. Pauli lectura*, 2 vols., ed. Raphaelis Cai, 8th ed. (Rome: Marietti, 1953), vol. 1, 231–435, 437–561, and vol. 2, 1–87, respectively. See also his *Super Evangelium S. Ioannis lectura* (*Super Ioh.*), ed. R. Cai, 5th ed. (Taurini: Marietti, 1952); *Quaestiones disputatae de potentia* (*De pot.*), in *Quaestiones disputatae*, vol. 2, ed. P. Bazzi et al., 8th ed. (Rome: Marietti, 1949). References to Marietti editions will use the abbreviation *Mar.* followed by a paragraph number.

2. This is not to say that there was unanimity on these matters in Thomas's day. One oft-disputed eschatological topic was the saints' beatific vision, including its possibility, nature, and timing. See Christian Trottmann, *La vision béatifique: Des disputes scolastiques à sa définition par Benoît XII*, Bibliothèque des écoles françaises d'Athènes et de Rome, fascicule 289 (Rome: École Française de Rome, 1995).

273

Christ) or to eternal punishment (for the rest). At the same time as this general resurrection, the world's ordinary motion and time will cease, and the world itself will be transformed and renewed, as a fitting accompaniment to those raised to glory. Before that resurrection, at the death of each person, the soul of the deceased is separated from the body—with the just being brought to the beatific vision of God (either directly or after a period of purification) and the unjust being condemned to everlasting punishment.

Those who wish to explore the Common Doctor's teachings on such matters have some readily accessible options. While the *Summa theologiae* lacks its intended, final section on the end of all things—since it was left unfinished—the other three of St. Thomas's major theological syntheses all contain comprehensive treatments of his teaching on these matters, each in its own way.[3] Furthermore, secondary literature is not lacking. Over the past few decades, some studies offering summary treatments of the Angelic Doctor's eschatology, or offering considerable attention to his eschatology, have been published,[4] and many other works deal in a significant way with

---

3. See *Super Sent.* 4.43–50; *SCG* 4.79–97; and *Comp. Theol.* 1.151–84, 241–45. While the latter work, structured around the three theological virtues, also was left unfinished, its first part (on "Faith") was completed. The first of these works is still unavailable in English translation in its integrity, although nearly all of the section cited, along with much of the material on the Sacraments, forms (in rearranged order) the final part of the "Supplement" to the *Summa theologiae* available in most editions and translations.

4. Carlo Leget, "Eschatology," in *The Theology of Thomas Aquinas*, ed. Rik Van Nieuwenhove and Joseph Wawrykow (Notre Dame, IN: University of Notre Dame Press, 2005), 365–85; David Berger, "'. . . de fine immortalis vitae ad quem per ipsum resurgendo pervenimus' – Zur Eschatologie des Thomas von Aquin," *Angelicum* 83 (2006): 727–46; Matthew L. Lamb, "The Eschatology of St Thomas Aquinas," in *Aquinas on Doctrine: A Critical Introduction*, ed. Thomas G. Weinandy, Daniel A. Keating, and John P. Yocum (London: T&T Clark, 2004), 225–40; Leo J. Elders, "L'escatologia di San Tommaso d'Aquino," *Doctor Communis* 46 (1993): 207–20; Battista Mondin, "Risurrezione finale," in *Dizionario Enciclopedico del pensiero di San Tommaso d'Aquino* (Bologna: Edizioni Studio Domenicano, 1991), 530–33; and Otto Hermann Pesch, *Thomas von Aquin: Grenze und Größe mittelalterlicher Theologie; Eine Einführung* (Mainz: Matthias-Grünewald, 1988), 187–207. See also M. L. Lamb, "Wisdom Eschatology in Augustine and Aquinas," in *Aquinas the Augustinian*, ed. Michael Dauphinais, Barry David, and Matthew Levering (Washington, DC: The Catholic University of America Press, 2007), 258–75; Eleonore Stump, "Resurrection and the Separated Soul," in *The Oxford Handbook of Aquinas*, ed. Brian Davies and Eleonore Stump, reprint ed. (Oxford: Oxford University Press, 2014 [orig.: 2012]), 458–66; Carlo Leget, *Living with God: Thomas Aquinas on the Relation between Life on Earth and "Life" after Death*, Publications of the Thomas Instituut te Utrecht, New Series 5 (Leuven: Peeters, 1997); and Bryan Kromholtz, *On the Last Day: The Time of the Resurrection of the Dead according to Thomas Aquinas*, Studia Friburgensia 110 (Fribourg: Academic Press Fribourg, 2010), esp. 69–112.

St. Thomas's treatment of specific topics that fall under eschatology, too numerous to list here.[5]

This chapter does not aim to present the material of his teachings on eschatology, even in summary fashion. Rather, the purpose here is to consider the more programmatic, guiding commitments that underlie his overall approach to eschatology, commitments that give shape to the entirety of his teaching. We will focus on five areas in St. Thomas's work: (1) the place of "finality" in that work; (2) beatitude as the goal of humanity; (3) the bodily resurrection of the dead as the perfection of the whole person, including the person's (4) bodily activities or operations, finally, very briefly, we will also consider how St. Thomas's eschatology can be read in a way suggested by the approach of Hans Urs von Balthasar, namely, by considering (5) how the end is a participation the life of Christ, and thus in the life of the Trinity.

Finality: The End in View

When discussing matters of what we now call "eschatology," we might expect Thomas to label such matters "the last things" (*novissima*). However, this term is not one that he typically employed. Instead, he very often refers to the "final end" or simply "the end."[6] It is significant that Thomas uses the singular here, speaking of "the end" rather than merely "the last things." For Thomas, eschatology certainly concerns the temporal end of history: the human race and the entire world, as mentioned above, are in a state of waiting for a final transformation to come—a real end to time as we know it, divinely thought and wrought, at the coming of Christ to judge the living and the dead. But this "end" is not merely what happens to come last in a series of events; it is also that toward which all of creation has been directed.[7] In this way, the "end" is present in some way throughout Thomas's theology, since it is the purpose or goal of all creatures. In developing this theological conception of finality, he drew upon certain philosophical sources, adapting them for his purposes; thus, a very brief description of this appropriation of philosophy for his eschatology is in order.

It is well known that Thomas systematically employed philosophy in his theology, and, in particular, he is known for the degree and depth to which he appropriated Aristotle's philosophy for the task.[8] Those familiar with "the

---

5. At www.http://www.corpusthomisticum.org/bt/index3.html, accessed August 9, 2022, there is a searchable, considerably developed (though far from exhaustive) bibliography.

6. See, for example, *Super Sent.* 1 prolog.; *Super Sent.* 4.43 prolog.; *SCG* 4.1.11; *ST* 1.2 prolog.; and *ST* 3 prolog.

7. Lamb, "The Eschatology of St Thomas Aquinas," 225.

8. See Gilles Emery and Matthew Levering, eds., *Aristotle in Aquinas's Theology* (Oxford: Oxford University Press, 2015).

Philosopher," as Thomas called him, would know of the four causes (final, efficient, formal, and material) and their centrality to Aristotle's work. Thomas makes repeated use of those four causes (i.e., these four kinds of answers to the question, "Why?") as a kind of framework for analysis. For eschatology, unsurprisingly, *final* causality—a consideration of the purpose, goal, or end of something—is the concept by which Thomas considers the end theologically. He will note that we see that all things are ordered to some kind of end; for Thomas, the entirety of creation and redemption as revealed in the Old and New Testaments is such an ordering toward the ultimate end. The prologues of his four major works of theological synthesis (the *Commentary on the Sentences of Peter Lombard*, the *Summa Contra Gentiles*, the *Compendium of Theology*, and, of course, the *Summa theologiae*) all mention the final end as an orienting and indispensable element.[9] This end is what God intends for his creation; each human person may participate in that end through grace.[10]

The Aristotelian contribution to this conception is significant but not exclusive. St. Thomas also makes use of certain neo-Platonic sources for his theology, including Dionysius the Pseudo-Areopagite, in particular. The entire shape of Thomas's theology has been plausibly said to follow an adapted form of the Dionysian *exitus/reditus* pattern (although shorn of neo-Platonic emanationism), according to which all things have come forth from God (but according to his free act of creation), and all, in some way, have their end in him in that they are ordered toward his goodness (and

---

9. See *Super Sent.* 1 prolog.; *Super Sent.* 4 prolog.; *SCG* 4.1.1 and 11; *Comp. Theol.* 1.1–2, 2.2; *ST* 1.2 prolog.; and *ST* 3 prolog. See also Leget, "Eschatology," 370; Berger, "'. . . de fine immortalis vitae,'" 728.

10. The interpretation of St. Thomas's work on the grace/nature relation continues to be the focus of much scholarship, particularly with reference to the controversy and disputes surrounding the work by Henri de Lubac, *Surnaturel: Études historiques*, ed. and pref. by Michel Sales (Mesnil-sur-l'Estrée: Lethielleux/Groupe DDB, 2010 [orig.: 1945]). Much of the same material from *Surnaturel*, along with certain clarifications of and expansions upon it, is found in two later volumes: Henri de Lubac, *The Mystery of the Supernatural*, trans. Rosemary Sheed, introd. by David L. Schindler (New York: Crossroad, 1998 [orig. French: 1965]) and de Lubac, *Augustinianism and Modern Theology*, trans. Lancelot C. Sheppard, introd. by Louis Dupré (New York: Crossroad, 2000 [orig. French: 1965]). Among the vast amount of literature on the topic, just a few of the noteworthy works in English (particularly with respect to the interpretation of Aquinas's thought) include Lawrence Feingold, *The Natural Desire to See God according to St. Thomas Aquinas and His Interpreters*, 2nd ed. (Ave Maria, FL: Sapientia Press, 2010); Serge-Thomas Bonino, ed., *Surnaturel: A Controversy at the Heart of Twentieth-Century Thomistic Thought*, trans. Robert Williams, trans. rev. by Matthew Levering (Ave Maria, FL: Sapientia Press, 2009 [orig. French: 2001]); and Guy Mansini, "The Abiding Significance of De Lubac's Surnaturel," *The Thomist* 73 (2009): 593–619.

will be brought to their completion by him).[11] There is a kind of finality built into all of creation by God himself, with lower things ordered toward the higher. This Dionysian, hierarchical order of things in the hands of Thomas becomes a supporting explanation for how the contingent, salvation-historical divine deeds of the God of Israel are in fact a coherent story of the whole of creation's tending toward (or straying from)—and longing for (or dreading)—divine resolution.[12] There is more to say about this tendency toward fulfillment, since it has a particular shape and intensity for those creatures capable of consciously and freely pursuing goals. The particular end of knowing and loving him, reserved for intellectual creatures, is that act by which they receive their ultimate beatitude, the subject to which we now turn.

BEATITUDE: THE END OF HUMANITY

It is well-known that the concept of "beatitude" as the proper end of each person plays a major role in Thomas's teaching in the *Summa theologiae*, serving as the orienting theme of the *Secunda Pars*.[13] For Thomas, human beings, and all rational creatures, seek beatitude as their final end,[14] but they cannot

---

11. *Super Sent.* 2.1.2.2; *ST* 1.44.4, 1.65.2; and *Comp. Theol.* 1.100–101. The neo-Platonic *exitus/reditus* schema in St. Thomas's work was noticed by Marie-Dominique Chenu, "Le plan de la Somme théologique de saint Thomas," *Revue Thomiste* 47 (1939): 93–107. Subsequently, the use of neo-Platonic sources by Thomas, judiciously and critically appropriating them (e.g., leaving out any emanationism so as to safeguard conceptually the freedom of the living God), has been increasingly noted and studied. See, for example, Jean-Pierre Torrell, *Saint Thomas Aquinas*, vol. 1, *The Person and his Work*, trans. Robert Royal, rev. ed. (Washington, DC: The Catholic University of America Press, 2005), 127–29, and *Saint Thomas Aquinas*, vol. 2, *Spiritual Master*, trans. Robert Royal (Washington, DC: The Catholic University of America Press, 2003), 53–58; Fran O'Rourke, *Pseudo-Dionysius and the Metaphysics of Aquinas*, Studien und Texte zur Geistesgeschichte des Mittelalters, 32 (Leiden: E. J. Brill, 1992); and David Burrell and Isabelle Moulin, "Albert, Aquinas, and Dionysius," in *Re-thinking Dionysius the Areopagite*, ed. Sarah Coakley and Charles M. Stang, 103–19 (Chichester: Wiley-Blackwell, 2009).

12. See Torrell, *Saint Thomas Aquinas*, 1:150–56. This is not to say that for Thomas the end of creation is entirely given within creation, as if written into it. The end that God brings will fully bring creation to its fulfillment but will also elevate it beyond what it could naturally anticipate.

13. *ST* 1–2.1 prolog.; see Servais Pinckaers, *The Sources of Christian Ethics*, trans. Mary T. Noble (Washington, DC: The Catholic University of America Press, 1995), esp. 5–6, 222, 262–63.

14. *Super Sent.* 4.43.1.1.1 co., 49.1.3.1 co.; *SCG* 3.25.14; and *ST* 1.12.1, 1–2.1.7 s.c., 1–2.2 prolog.; see also *De ver.* 6.1 co., 23.2 co.

find their ultimate beatitude in other creatures.[15] Men cannot even find their ultimate beatitude in higher creatures (angels).[16] Of course, along with Aristotle, Thomas holds that there is a limited, imperfect kind of happiness, or beatitude, that humans may attain—that is, the happiness that they can attain by their own powers, the end that is proportioned to those powers (a life of contemplative and active virtue, with friends, health, and the bodily necessities).[17] This kind of happiness is imperfect, however, and even if it somehow could be perfected (*per impossibile*), it could never last forever. Perfect happiness—the perfect end of man—requires something beyond man's own power.

Indeed, Thomas holds that humans as well as all other creatures have their ultimate end in God, in some way. God himself, under the aspect of the divine "Goodness," is the end of all creatures, including all grades of being: angels, humans, animals, plants, and minerals.[18] But only rational creatures—human beings—can consciously and freely choose their end, which is to know and to love God, who is all wisdom and all goodness. For them, the act by which this is to happen is the vision of God's essence.[19] This beatific vision is an "operation," (*operatio*) or action of the soul, although one that requires a special, divine, interior assistance, the "light of glory."[20] It is not "vision" through the bodily eyes,

---

15. *Super Sent.* 4.49.1.1.1; *SCG* 3.32; and *ST* 1–2.2.5. For Thomas, earthly benefits such as riches, honors, fame, power, pleasure, goods of the body or soul, or any created good cannot bring ultimate happiness; see *ST* 1–2.2.1–8; *SCG* 3.27–32.

16. *SCG* 3.44; *ST* 1–2.3.7.

17. *ST* 1–2.3.2 ad 4; *ST* 1–2.4.7 co., 1–2.4.8 co., 1–2.5.3 co. On Thomas's view of the "imperfect beatitude" that is attainable by unassisted human nature, see Thomas Joseph White, "Imperfect Happiness and the Final End of Man: Thomas Aquinas and the Paradigm of Nature-Grace Orthodoxy," *The Thomist* 78 (2014): 247–89. It may be noted that Thomas sometimes uses the term "imperfect beatitude" for that not-yet-perfect participation in charity that can be ascribed to the faithful *in via*; see *ST* 1–2.69.3 co.; Jacob W. Wood, "The Study of Theology as a Foretaste of Heaven: The Influence of Albert the Great on Aquinas's Understanding of *Beatitudo Imperfecta*," *Nova et Vetera* (English edition) 16, no. 4 (2018): 1103–134., esp. 1131–133.

18. *Super Sent.* 2.1.2.2; *ST* 1.44.4, 1.65.2; and *Comp. Theol.* 1.100–101; see also *Super Sent.* 4.48.2.3 ad 6; *SCG* 3.17.2; *De ver.* 5.9 ad 13, 22.2; *De pot.* 5.4 co.; and *ST* 1–2.1.8 co. On the notion that even mineral things, such as stones, love God in their own way, see *ST* 1–2.26.3, co.; see also *ST* 1–2.109.3 co.

19. *Super Sent.* 4.49.1.2.3 s.c. 2 and co., 49.2.1; *SCG* 3.37, 3.48–54, 4.54.2; *De ver.* 18.1 co.; and *ST* 1–2.1.7 s.c., 1–2.2.8 co., and 1–2.3.8 co. In his early work on this topic, Thomas explicitly drew on the thought of Averroës in setting forth a philosophical justification for the Christian doctrine of beatitude; see Richard C. Taylor, "Arabic/Islamic Philosophy in Thomas Aquinas's Conception of the Beatific Vision *Super Sent.* 4., D. 49, Q. 2, A. 1," *The Thomist* 76 (2012): 509–50.

20. On operation, see *Super Sent.* 4.49.1.2.2 and *ST* 1–2.3.2; on the light of glory, see *ST* 1.12.2 and 5.

even after the resurrection.[21] Rather, it is an operation of the intellect (the speculative intellect) through which the soul loves the God it beholds (by a divinely-assisted act of the will).[22] This vision cannot be fully reached in this life but can only be reached after this life; once it is attained, it is definitive.[23]

So, it is not mere obedience to God that is the goal of human life, although God's commandments provide external assistance along the way in which we *viatores* go. It is not a mere stoic shunning of appetite or passion that is our goal, although our enjoyment of any pleasure or even intellectual joy can only be temporary and so should be treated as such.[24] Rather, we are fundamentally, positively, oriented toward final happiness, a goal that we can reach only at the end and that should relativize, without emptying of meaning, the highs and lows of this life.

Now, this vision of God is available even to the *disembodied* soul, yet the entire human person, both soul and *body*, is to be in beatitude after the resurrection.[25] And this beatitude should not be understood individualistically; it has a collective dimension, as well. Thus, there is to be a *communion* of saints in which the joy of each is shared as the joy of all, a communion of the blessed in communion with God the Father, Son, and Holy Spirit.[26] These are all aspects of the end that should be explored further, beginning with the resurrection of the dead.

---

21. *Super Sent.* 4.49.2.2; *SCG* 3.33; *ST* 1–2.3.3; see also *ST* 1.12.3. Of course, Christ will be seen bodily; see *Super Sent.* 4.48.2.1 co., 49.2.2 ad 6.

22. *Super Sent.* 4.49.1.1.2–3; *SCG* 3.26; and *ST* 1–2.3.4–5, 1–2.26.13.

23. *Super Sent.* 4.49.1.1.4, 49.2.7; *SCG* 3.38–40, 3.47–48; and *ST* 1–2.3.6, 1–2.5.3.

24. On the positive, integral role played by the passions in Aquinas's account of the human person, see Paul Gondreau, "The Passions and the Moral Life: Appreciating the Originality of Aquinas," *The Thomist* 71 (2007): 419–50; Nicholas E. Lombardo, *The Logic of Desire: Aquinas on Emotion* (Washington, DC: The Catholic University of America Press, 2011).

25. *Super Sent.* 4.43.1.1.1 co., 49.1.4.1, 49.2.5; *ST* 1–2.4.6. Recently, a debate has emerged, chiefly among philosophers, over whether it is better/more consistent to characterize as a "person" the human individual that continues after death, in Aquinas's view (or according to positions developed significantly from Aquinas's thought). The affirmative, "survivalist" position, held by a minority of scholars, is contrasted with the more standard "corruptionist" view. For some discussion and references, see Turner C. Nevitt, "Survivalism, Corruptionism, and Intermittent Existence in Aquinas," *History of Philosophy Quarterly* 31, no. 1 (2014): 1–19; Nevitt, "Aquinas on the Death of Christ: A New Argument for Corruptionism," *American Catholic Philosophical Quarterly* 90, no. 1 (2016): 77–99; Patrick Toner, "Personhood and Death in St. Thomas Aquinas," *History of Philosophy Quarterly* 26, no. 2 (2009): 121–38; and Toner, "St. Thomas Aquinas on Death and the Separated Soul," *Pacific Philosophical Quarterly* 91, no. 4 (2010): 587–99.

26. *Super Sent.* 4.49.1.2.5 co.; see also *Super Ioh.* 14.1 (*Mar.*, para. 1856); *SCG* 4.50.10; and *ST* 1–2.4.8.

Glory Perfects Nature

If the soul may enter beatitude through the *visio Dei*, it may be wondered whether or how bodily resurrection would add anything of significance to the blessed. Thus, some have wondered whether such a view of disembodied beatitude for the soul is mistaken, since it would make the resurrection of the dead merely a superfluous, or even an extraneous, addition to the end of human life.[27] After all, if beatitude—indeed, *perfect* beatitude—can be reached by the disembodied soul (through the beatific vision, as we have noted), what could the body possibly add to this?[28]

Given Thomas's commitment to this teaching regarding the perfect beatitude of a saint's soul, it is not altogether easy for him to explain how resurrection is needed for complete human fulfillment. He definitely holds, however, that the resurrection is needed for the complete human *person* to be in beatitude, for fundamental reasons that come from the heart of Thomas's entire philosophico-theological project.

First, Thomas recognizes bodily resurrection as a central, indispensable aspect of the revelation that Christians are to accept. Citing St. Paul's argu-

---

27. Over the past several decades, it has become a widespread belief that, in the mind of the typical Christian, hope had heretofore become overly focused on the fate of the soul rather than on bodily resurrection, where the full weight of biblical revelation truly lies. An influential expression along these lines came from Oscar Cullmann, *Immortality of the Soul or Resurrection of the Dead? The Witness of the New Testament* (London: Epworth Press, 1958). For discussion of this broader trend and some of the proposals developed from it, see Joseph Ratzinger, *Eschatology: Death and Eternal Life*, 2nd ed., trans. Michael Waldstein (Washington, DC: The Catholic University of America Press, 2006 [orig. German: 1977]), 104–12, as well as the "Forward to This Edition," xvii–xxii, from 2006 (by the author as Pope Benedict). For a recent (rather unconvincing) challenge specifically directed at St. Thomas's teaching on the *visio beatifica* as end, see, for example, Germain Grisez, "The True Ultimate End of Human Beings: The Kingdom, Not God Alone," *Theological Studies* 69, no. 1 (2008): 38–61, which proposes that Aquinas's teaching on the beatific vision does not leave sufficient room for bodily resurrection and the kingdom: "Thomas rightly holds that resurrection will make for the well-being of the beatitude of souls that enjoy the beatific vision. But to hold that truth coherently, he would have had to admit that the beatific vision leaves something more to be desired, which would have required a complete reconstruction of his treatise on beatitude." See the response by Ezra Sullivan, "Seek First the Kingdom: A Reply to Germain Grisez's Account of Man's Ultimate End," *Nova et Vetera* 8, no. 4 (2010): 959–95.

28. One recent article, drawing significantly but not exclusively from Aquinas's work, proposes "embodied worship" as a plausible way of coherently uniting the spiritual and bodily aspects of perfected Christian life. See Isaac Augustine Morales, "'With My Body I Thee Worship': New Creation, Beatific Vision, and the Liturgical Consummation of All Things," *Pro Ecclesia* 25, no. 3 (2016): 337–56.

ment, among others, that belief in the resurrection is essential to the Christian believer ("If for this life only" we have "hoped in Christ," we are "the most pitiable" of all human persons, 1 Cor 15:19), he places the general resurrection at the head of his section on "eschatology" in the *Summa Contra Gentiles*.[29] Indeed, for Thomas, bodily resurrection is of primary importance for the eschatology in each of his major theological works.[30] However, it is noteworthy that Thomas sometimes argues not only that a future, bodily resurrection for the human race is indisputably central to Christian revelation but also that even reason alone can arrive at probable arguments in favor of such a resurrection. Thomas contends that if the human soul is immortal, persisting after separation from its body, yet is naturally united to the body and is essentially the form of the body, it would be contrary to the nature of the soul to be without the body forever. Since nothing contrary to nature should go on forever, the soul must once again be united to the body. In this way, Thomas maintains that the very immortality of the soul presents a kind of demand for a future resurrection.[31]

This kind of argumentation, based on reflections and sources available to the unaided human intellect, points toward the second reason that resurrection is so central for Thomas's view of human finality, namely, his thoroughgoing and consistent conviction regarding the essential goodness of creation and the nature of the human person as part of that creation. That "God looked at everything he had made, and found it very good" (Gen 1:31) can, for St. Thomas, be enunciated as a corresponding, basic philosophical principle: created beings are essentially good, at the very least, insofar as they exist.[32] Though sin brings corruption, it does not bring total corruption. Jesus came to save human beings, not to destroy us or to replace us with some other kind of being.

For this reason, St. Thomas consistently affirms that in the justification and sanctification of man, human nature is not eliminated but elevated, that

---

29. *SCG* 4.79.4.

30. Namely, *Super Sent.*, *SCG*, and *Comp. Theol.*, particularly for the parts noted in n. 3 as well as *ST*. See Kromholtz, *On the Last Day*, 84–90; Brian V. Johnstone, "The Debate on the Structure of the *Summa Theologiae* of St. Thomas Aquinas: From Chenu (1939) to Metz (1998)," in *Aquinas as Authority: A Collection of Studies Presented at the Second Conference of the Thomas Instituut te Utrecht, December 14–16, 2000*, ed. Paul van Geest, Harm Goris, and Carlo Leget, Publications of the Thomas Instituut te Utrecht, New Series 7 (Leuven: Peeters, 2002), 187–200.

31. See *SCG* 4.79.10; see also *Super Sent.* 4.43.1.1.1 co.; *SCG* 4.79.11, 81.5–14, 82.5–9; and *Super I Cor.* 15.2 (*Mar.*, para. 924). In this, Thomas's teaching differs from that of many of his contemporaries, including, for example, Saints Bonaventure and Albert, who in the main hold that philosophy is unable to argue in favor of bodily resurrection; see Kromholtz, *On the Last Day*, 121n30.

32. See *ST* 1.74.3 ad 3.

is, "grace does not destroy nature but perfects it."[33] It is well known that this axiom, and the conviction about the redeemability of human nature behind it, is thoroughly present in Thomas's work as a kind of foundational principle. But it is less well-known—and certainly less often noted—that what he says about grace in this life he also says about *glory* in the next. Thus, Thomas also maintains that "glory perfects nature, and does not destroy it," expressing this principle in several ways.[34] This expectation that the human condition *in patria* involves no suppression of human nature, but its full flowering and perfection, is consistently upheld as a central tenet of his teaching about the life of glory to which human persons are called and which by grace they may attain after death. Thus, whatever Thomas may say about human nature should hold, in some way, for redeemed, raised, and renewed humanity in the resurrection. We can note just a few important aspects of his view of human nature—albeit, extremely briefly—in order to see how the principle that glory perfects nature plays a central role in Thomas's interpretations of the promise of resurrection of the dead and the life of the world to come.

Thomas's view of the human person is one in which soul and body are tightly united. The soul is the only form of the body, suffusing it entirely. Regarding the relation between soul and body, Thomas rejects "Plato's" understanding (common among Thomas's contemporaries and predecessors) by which the soul is regarded as a substance that inhabits the body and uses it as a kind of instrument.[35] Thomas's own view, involving a certain appropriation of Aristotelian thought, is that the soul is the only form of the body.[36] If the soul were a substance by itself, its union with the body would necessarily be merely an accidental union.[37] In Thomas's conception, there is only one form, the substantial form, for a given human person, and it is the body's form.[38] Thus, he says that a living

---

33. *ST* 1.1.8 ad 2, merely one of many examples that could be cited in Thomas's works.

34. *Super Sent.* 4.49.2.3 ad 8: *gloria perficit naturam, et non destruit.* See also *Super Sent.* 4.44.2.4.1 ad 3: *corporis gloria naturam non tollit, sed perficit* ("The glory of the body does not take away nature, but perfects it"); *Super Sent.* 4 4.44.2.1.4 ad 5: *gloria non tollit naturam* ("Glory does not take away nature"); *De ver.* 8.5 ad 3: *gloria non destruat naturam* ("Glory does not destroy nature"); and *ST* 1–2.26.13 s.c.: *natura non tollitur per gloriam, sed perficitur* ("Nature is not taken away by glory, but is perfected [by it]").

35. *SCG* 2.57; *ST* 1.75.4 s.c. and co. A "Platonistic" a view of the relation of soul and body may be found, for example, in the works by William of Auvergne, Bonaventure (with certain nuances), and in the *Summa Fratris Alexandri.* See Kromholtz, *On the Last Day,* 74n23 for references.

36. *ST* 1.76.1; *SCG* 2.58 and 68; and *Super Sent.* 2.31.2.1 co.

37. *ST* 1.76.8, 1.89.1 co.; *De pot.* 3.10 co.

38. *ST* 1.76.3–4; *Super Sent.* 2.18.1.2 co. Thomas's position here, positing the "unicity" of the human form—that is, that there is one and only one substantial form in the human body, and that the body does not have its own form that is distinct from the soul—

human person, with the soul informing the body, is a substance. In a human person, neither the soul alone, nor the body alone, is a man.[39] Only the composite, with the soul informing the body, is a human being complete in its nature.

It is necessary to consider this unified, soul-body composition of human nature in order to consider what happens when that composition breaks down. For Thomas, then, death, the "personal" end of all of us in the current world, is precisely such a breakdown: it consists of the separation of the soul from the body. After death, the soul continues to exist, but it is separated from the body. Its existence is not limited merely to being, for the separated soul is capable of a certain set of operations or actions: to exercise both intellect and will. Thus, it can think about what it knows or can choose to think about this or that.[40] Although death allows for the introduction to the beatific vision (at least for the just), this separation of the soul from the body, *per se*, is not a good thing for the soul, because it is natural to it to be united to a body as its form. In this way, the soul has a kind of natural "desire" to be united to the body, to inform the body.[41] A separated soul, then, exists in a peculiar condition: it is continuing to exist in a deficient manner, with a major gap in the composition to which it is to contribute, as it were.[42] This means that there is a kind of inclination toward resurrection in the separated soul. Before death, it had been united to its body; after death, it is still ordered toward being united once again to its body—through resurrection.[43]

---

was a minority position in his own time and one not readily regarded as an acceptable opinion. See, for example, Leget, *Living with God*, 74n18.

39. See *SCG* 2.89.17.

40. On thinking, see *Super Sent.* 4.50.1.1–3; *De ver.* 19.1–2; *SCG* 2.81.14; and *ST* 1.89.1–6. It should be noted that, for Thomas, since it is unnatural to the soul to know without being united to the body (and thus, without recourse to the phantasm), the separated soul's mode of knowing is deficient—it is merely "general" and "confused"; see *ST* 1.89.1 co., 1.89.3 co., and 1.89.4 co.; *De an.*18 co. and 20 co.; and Richard Schenk, "And Jesus Wept: Notes toward a Theology of Mourning," in *Soundings in the History of a Hope: New Studies on Thomas Aquinas* (Ave Maria, FL: Sapientia Press, 2016), 102–30, esp. 110–11. This explicit teaching regarding the deficiency of the separated soul does not seem to be found in Thomas's early works, suggesting a development of his thinking. However, it may also be pointed out that throughout Aquinas's career, he also teaches that separation from the body allows the soul's thinking to become less weighed down by bodily concerns through lacking a corporeal element, which is subject to corruption; see *SCG* 2.81.12–13; *De pot.* 5.10 ad 6; *ST* 1.89.2 ad 1; *Comp. Theol.* 1.163 and 167; *De an.* 15 co. and ad 13; and *De an.* 17 ad 1. On willing to think about successive objects, see *SCG* 4.95.6–7; see also *Comp. Theol.* 1.174; Simon Francis Gaine, *Will There Be Free Will in Heaven? Freedom, Impeccability and Beatitude* (London: T&T Clark, 2003).

41. See *ST* 1.76.1 ad 6.

42. See *ST* 1.89.1 co., 118.3 co.

43. See *Super Sent.* 4.43.1.1.1 ad 2; see also *ST* 1.76.1 obj. 6 and ad 6.

For Thomas's conception of the human person as a unity of body and soul, there is a certain difficulty in dealing with the separated soul's peculiar kind of existence after death, yet the soul's ongoing existence without the body makes for a kind of argument for the resurrection. As we have noted, he holds that the soul without the body is incomplete, for it does not have what is needed for the nature of which it is a kind of "part," and it would be unfitting for something to continue to exist in perpetuity without possibility of being completed in its nature. Thus, it is fitting that there should be a resurrection of the body for each soul, even if neither soul nor body are capable of rejoining themselves together. Thus, the very "unnaturalness" of the separated soul's kind of existence acts as a kind of tension that ought to be resolved. It is a condition that is temporary because its own nature indicates that it ought to inform its own body. Because the soul's nature is ordered toward being united with its own body, and informing it, resurrection is not merely a plausible aspect of humanity's end, but ultimately an essential one.

This is one illustration of the way that Thomas sees the goodness of human nature as integral to the work of salvation in the eschaton. The entire human nature—soul and body—ought to be preserved in the end. Indeed, this becomes a kind of argument for the resurrection. Now, there is no doubt that he holds that the general resurrection of the dead has been revealed, but this datum of revelation helps confirm what one might argue from the data of human nature—that it ought to be, at last, perfected in resurrection.

Risen Persons in Action

If human persons are finally to have a bodily existence that is imperishable and perfected in its nature, it may, of course, be pondered what such an existence might entail. So much of what we do in this life has to do with maintaining bodily integrity in the face of the "ravages of time": eating, drinking, and sleeping to preserve natural life, sexual intercourse for preserving the species. What possible things might *risen* persons *do*? Why should they do anything?

For Thomas, these questions are legitimate, since he holds that human nature will not be suppressed by the state of glory but perfected. Thus, he holds that there will certainly be bodily operations for those who are raised. However, there will *not* be those functions associated with generation and corruption. There will be no eating or drinking, because bodies will neither grow nor corrupt, and since no one will die anymore (1 Cor 15:26), there will be no sexual intercourse: there will be no need for reproduction.[44] But

---

44. *Super Sent.* 4.44.1.3.4; *SCG* 4.83; and *Comp. Theol.* 1.156. Yet, the bodily organs associated with digestion and reproduction will remain because they belong to the integrity

there will be many other operations for those raised up on the last day, and one of them is *sensing*. Thomas states in many texts that the bodily senses will operate after the resurrection.[45] Another operation is *movement* (or, local motion). Those raised to glory will be able to move by their own power from one place to another.[46] And they will be able to move quickly, at will.[47]

In Thomas's view, the human person should do all that is compatible with ongoing, incorruptible being because it is fitting for a given nature to exist to the full extent of its powers. In this, the risen human *person* will be *more* like God than the separated soul is, even though the soul is immaterial (as God is). This is because the human person, including all of its well-ordered inner workings and external actions, has *being* more perfectly than the soul alone has it. Indeed, the human person is a creature that is made to be in action or operation; as such, it is *more* perfect when in operation, just as a beating heart is more perfect than one that is not beating.[48]

Furthermore, these bodily actions or operations do not get in the way of the beatific vision or distract from it, nor does the beatific vision obscure the operations. Indeed, these operations themselves will even be enriched by the vision of God. Of course, those who will be glorified in their body will be most pleased to see Christ himself and God's creatures, all expressions of God's glory. In addition, for Thomas, a risen person who senses creatures can, through doing so, contemplate God himself. To illustrate, Thomas offers an analogous example from ordinary life:

> When one of two things is the type of the other, the attention of the soul to the one does not hinder or lessen its attention to the other: as a physician while looking at urine is not less able but more able to bear in mind the rules of his art concerning the colors of urine. And since God will be apprehended by the saints as the type of all things that will be done or known by them, their attention to perceiving sensibles, or to contem-

---

of the human body, as stated in *SCG* 4.88.1: "since the resurrection is to restore the deficiencies of nature, nothing that belongs to the perfection of nature will be denied to the bodies of the risen." See *SCG* 4.88.1–4; *Super Sent.* 4.44.1.3.1, 44.1.3.3; *Comp. Theol.* 1.157; and *Super Eph.* 4.4 (*Mar.*, para. 216).

45. *Super Sent.* 4.44.2.1.3–4, 49.2.2 co. and ad 6; *SCG* 4.86.4; see also *Comp. Theol.* 1.177; *ST* 1–2.3.3 co.; and *Super Sent.* 4.44.2.3.2. See also Rafael Hernández Urigüen, "Hacia la vision beatífica: Sugerencias para una estética teológica desde la escatología," *Scripta Theologica* 38 (2006/2): 855–79, esp. 868.

46. *Super Sent.* 4.44.2.3.2; *SCG* 4.83.1–8; and *Comp. Theol.* 1.171.

47. *Super Sent.* 4.44.2.3.1–3; *SCG* 4.86.3; see also *Comp. Theol.* 1.168.

48. *Super Sent.* 4.49.1.4.1 ad 1; see also *Super Sent.* 4.43.1.1.1 ad 4, 50.1.1 ad 5; *De pot.* 5.10 co. and ad 8.

plating or doing anything else, in no way hinders their divine contemplation, nor conversely.[49]

He says something similar of the saints' local motion: all the saints, who will have been raised up with glorified bodies, while sensing created things, doing things, or thinking about virtually anything, can also contemplate God, without difficulty, and their contemplation of God "in no way hinders" their various operations. In exercising their powers, "God's wisdom will shine forth eminently (*Dei sapientia eminenter relucebit*)."[50] The difference in metaphysical grade, as it were, between the vision of God and bodily operation is such that one operation does not compete with the other. Indeed, the exalted, divinely supplied operation of the vision of God truly *enhances* the natural, bodily operations of the human creature. This shows another way in which Thomas goes as far as he can to try to explain how human nature may be perfected in its entirety and integrity, as far as is consistent with a world without end. In human existence and operation, both spiritual and bodily, God is to be seen by the just, and in his creatures, he will be glorified.

The Christological Form of the End

Our study of Thomas's eschatology is intended to help us better grasp what has been revealed to us, to uncover illuminating insights into God's self-revelation and to let them shine in our own day. It is also hoped that, in another way, a kind of illumination may occur in the other direction: by looking at Thomas's works in light of more recent questions, or of classic questions posed in new ways, a different kind of light may be directed at them and so may reveal aspects of Thomas's thought that otherwise would remain hidden, or at least, would remain more obscure.

We will suggest that one such recent kind of light may include the overall approach of Hans Urs von Balthasar to eschatology and to all of theology. Briefly (perhaps too briefly), we may characterize that approach as the interpretation of revelation—all of salvation history—as undergirded by and inscribed within the life of the Persons of the Trinity as revealed in Jesus Christ.[51] We

---

49. *Super Sent.* 4.44.2.1.3 ad 4: *Quando unum duorum est ratio alterius, occupatio animae circa unum non impedit nec remittit occupationes ejus circa aliud; sicut medicus dum videt urinam, non minus potest considerare regulas artis de coloribus urinarum, sed magis; et quia Deus apprehendetur a sanctis ut ratio omnium quae ab eis agentur vel cognoscentur; ideo occupatio eorum circa sensibilia sentienda, vel quaecumque alia contemplanda aut agenda, in nullo impedit divinam contemplationem, nec e converso.*

50. *Super Sent.* 4.44.2.3.2 co.

51. This is especially true of his work on eschatology; as he puts it in *TD* 5: "The real 'last thing' is the triune life of God disclosed in Jesus Christ." See also Nicholas J. Healy,

should not expect to find an entirely equivalent mode of theological exploration and expression to be undertaken by Thomas in his works, and, in fact, the two figures do not always arrive at all the same conclusions.[52] Nevertheless, in Thomas's work, we may ask whether we may find something analogous or akin to Balthasar's thoroughgoing Trinitarian outlook. In St. Thomas's work as a whole, there is indeed the overarching theme that God is the *end* (and the beginning) of all things, which is also sometimes considered in its Trinitarian depths: "Just as we have been created by the Son and the Holy Spirit, so are we united by them to our final end."[53] In his extended treatments related to eschatology, this accounting for the final end of human salvation as a moment within a larger, embracing Trinitarian procession and return is not always explicit. However, if one asks whether Thomas's work is extensively and explicitly *Christological* in its account of salvation (including its account of the final end of man), then the answer is undoubtedly affirmative.[54] It will be illustrative to consider just a few of the many theological aspects under which Thomas offers a particularly Christological reading of eschatology.

In St. Thomas, one can notice a kind of all-embracing finality brought by Christ in several ways. There is a new age brought by Christ, which is now understood to be the *final* age before the end. There is no additional age to

---

The Eschatology of Hans Urs von Balthasar: Being as Communion (Oxford: Oxford University Press, 2005), 16: "the most characteristic feature of Balthasar's writing on the *eschaton*" is that, for him, "the traditional themes of eschatology such as death, judgement, resurrection, purgatory, heaven, hell, etc. are all considered first as christological and trinitarian events . . . [which] are considered as occurring *within* the person and mission of Christ, and ultimately *within* the Trinity. . . . Eschatology is the revelation of the origin and destiny of the whole created cosmos precisely in so far as it is the revelation of the trinitarian life through Jesus' eucharistic return to the Father in the Spirit [emphasis Healy's]."

52. There will be no attempt here to compare Aquinas and Balthasar on matters of eschatology, although differences regarding at least two different subjects may be mentioned: (1) the interpretation of Christ's *descensus* into hell, including the important question of whether there is any significant and concrete possibility of final damnation, and (2) the time of the resurrection of the dead. On the first, see a recent attempt to explain St. Thomas's position on damnation via aesthetic categories: Francis J. Caponi, "Beauty, Justice, and Damnation in Thomas Aquinas," *Pro Ecclesia* 19, no. 4 (2010): 389–404; this brief article, while applying a method which Balthasar championed in such a seminal way, curiously omits mention of Balthasar's doubts about whether the universal salvific will of God allows for the real possibility of damnation, for example, in *Dare We Hope "That All Men Be Saved"? With a Short Discourse on Hell*, trans. David Kipp and Lothar Krauth (San Francisco: Ignatius Press, 1988). On the second topic, see Kromholtz, *On the Last Day*, esp. 34–38 (for Balthasar's view).

53. *Super Sent.* 1.14.2.2, cited in Torrell, *Saint Thomas Aquinas*, 2:53–79, esp. 60.

54. See, for example, the reflections in Torrell, *Saint Thomas Aquinas,* 2:101–24.

be awaited until the end of the world.[55] In this way, the world, and the church in particular, is inserted in a kind of Christ-marked, final time of grace, though the degree to which one participates in this age varies considerably. In addition, Thomas also suggests that the reason that there is currently a period of time between Christ's Resurrection and the general resurrection is that we must somehow live out, in the current age, suffering and death, just as Christ suffered and then died for a time before rising. In this way, by being conformed to his suffering and death, we may attain to "a participation in the likeness of his resurrection."[56] Thus, we are currently inserted into the suffering and death of Christ that we may share in his life.

This participatory way of conceiving of Christ's life is seen also in the way Thomas treats Christ's Resurrection as a cause of our resurrection. Christ's Resurrection is the efficient cause of the future resurrection of all but also its exemplar cause—that members may be conformed to their head.[57] The Ascension of Christ causes our salvation, preparing the way for our ascent into heaven and efficiently causing it.[58] And the judiciary power he enjoys will, in the Final Judgment, be a power that he shares with his saints.[59] In all these ways, the Christian is finally to share in who Christ is and in what he does.

All this is not to say that there is an absence of consideration of the mission of the Holy Spirit. With respect to the realm of creation in general, Thomas teaches that there is a "trace" of the Persons of the Trinity in each creature. While the creature's subsistence represents the Father and its form represents the Son, its "relation of order" represents the Holy Spirit, insofar as he is "love." Thus, that order or directedness toward the end—the desire of each creature for God's goodness—is the trace of the Holy Spirit in each creature.[60] Regarding the divine work of salvation, in particular, Thomas can speak of the Holy Spirit's role as particularly eschatological. In one place, he considers St. Paul's mention of the Spirit as "pledge" (in Eph 1:14), which speaks of "the holy Spirit of promise, Who is the pledge of our inheritance." He notes that, with the support of an alternate reading, it might be better rendered as "down payment," because the grace by which the Holy Spirit is received in this life is a kind of partial, but real, portion of

---

55. *ST* 1–2.106.4; *Super Sent.* 4.43.1, 4.43.3.2; and *ST* 3.1.6 ad 1, 3.53.2 co.

56. *ST* 3.56.1 ad 1; Kromholtz, *On the Last Day*, 292–95; see also *SCG* 4.55.28; *ST* 1–2.85.5 ad 2, 3.49.3 ad 3, and 3.69.3 co.

57. *ST* 3.56.1 co. and ad 4; *Super Sent.* 4.43.1.3.1 ad 2.

58. *ST* 3.57.6 co. and ad 3.

59. *ST* 3.58.4 ad 3, 3.59.6 s.c.; *SCG* 4.96.4.

60. *ST* 1.45.7 co.; see Bryan Kromholtz, "Eschatology and the Doctrine of God in St. Thomas Aquinas," *Nova et Vetera* (English edition) 12, no. 4 (2014): 1215–231.

that full reception of the Holy Spirit that will be granted to the just in the glorious life to come.[61]

We see, then, that there are some significant ways in which Thomas's theology, and his eschatology in particular, has its own Trinitarian shape, even if this shape is not always made explicit. It is possible that as more of today's theologians search for the traces of the life of the Trinity in the promise of eternal life, more of these traces will become evident.

Conclusion

We have shown the importance of "finality" in Thomas's work; the centrality of beatitude as the goal of humanity, offering some account of its plausibility; and the resurrection as a fitting perfection of the whole person. In addition, we also noted the explicitly Christological form that Thomas's eschatology takes, where the end is portrayed as a participation in divine life, thereby showing forth, at least implicitly and occasionally explicitly, a form that is Trinitarian as well.

Regarding the latter subject, we should point out that, after all, it stands to reason that there is not a particularly massive *amount* of attention, quantitatively speaking, to the Trinitarian dimension of Thomas's eschatological thought, and even the properly Christological dimension is not always prominent. The reason for this is that Thomas's entire project retained a significant focus on trying to offer explanations for what faith holds—normally, explanations of fittingness, supported by what reason can discover.[62] For him, this was not a matter of translating the faith into whatever philosophical systems happened to be in vogue but rather one of painstakingly employing the God-given intellect he had been given, respecting it in others, and considering what it could really grasp, the better to unfold the mystery of God and his saving work. In this, he was always seeking points of contact, as far as possible, with what man could accept by natural means. This approach helps explain his systematic recourse to the notion of beatitude as the orienting goal of each and every person. Who, after all, doesn't want to be happy? Yet our chronic dis-

---

61. *Super Eph.* 1.5 (*Mar.*, para. 43), translation in Thomas Aquinas, *Commentary on Ephesians*, trans. and introd. by Matthew L. Lamb (Albany, NY: Magi Books, 1966), 67; see also *Super II Cor.* 1.5 (*Mar.*, para. 45); *Super II Cor.* 5.2 (*Mar.*, para. 161).

62. On arguments from fittingness in Thomas's theology, and in his Christology in particular, see Jean-Pierre Torrell, *Le Christ en ses mystères: La vie et l'oeuvre de Jésus selon saint Thomas d'Aquin*, vol. 1, Jésus et Jésus-Christ 78 (Paris: Desclée, 1999), 34–37; Torrell, *Saint Thomas Aquinas*, 1:153–56, esp. 156. For a comparison of Aquinas and Balthasar on this matter (and others), see Gilbert Narcisse, *Les raisons de Dieu: Argument de convenance et esthétique théologique selon saint Thomas d'Aquin et Hans Urs von Balthasar* (Fribourg: Éditions Universitaires, 1997).

appointment with whatever in this world promises happiness points us toward something—some One—beyond our experience. Thus, with Thomas's way of proceeding, the doctrine of the Trinity suggests itself not as the primary vehicle by which to explain what is believed but as that revealed mystery toward which more accessible conclusions may point.

It should be mentioned that there are certain important issues related to the end that we have *not* covered, or have mentioned only in passing, issues that also have a significant place in Thomas's teaching. They include the communal dimension of the end; the renewal of heaven and earth; and the Last Judgment, to name just a few. However, what we *have* made clear, we hope, is that for St. Thomas, the end—the goal—of all things is crucial for understanding their meaning now. We have an end—life with God—that answers to our own desire to be happy forever. And, indeed, we are the ones who have that end: we who are spiritual-bodily creatures, who are not merely souls. This brief chapter does not claim to offer any comprehensive understanding of St. Thomas's project, let alone of the great mysteries of the Incarnation and the Trinity that were the subject of his work. However, it does claim that for getting just a little closer to such an understanding, a consideration of the end makes for a good beginning.[63]

BIBLIOGRAPHY

Berger, David. "'. . . de fine immortalis vitae ad quem per ipsum resurgendo pervenimus' – Zur Eschatologie des Thomas von Aquin." *Angelicum* 83 (2006): 727–46.

Burrell, David, and Isabelle Moulin. "Albert, Aquinas, and Dionysius." In *Rethinking Dionysius the Areopagite*, edited by S. Coakley and C. M. Stang, 103–19. Chichester: Wiley-Blackwell, 2009.

Caponi, Francis J. "Beauty, Justice, and Damnation in Thomas Aquinas." *Pro Ecclesia* 19, no. 4 (2010): 389–404.

Chenu, Marie-Dominique. "Le plan de la Somme théologique de saint Thomas." *Revue Thomiste* 47 (1939): 93–107.

Cullmann, Oscar. *Immortality of the Soul or Resurrection of the Dead? The Witness of the New Testament*. London: Epworth Press, 1958.

De Lubac, Henri. *Surnaturel: Études historiques*, ed. M. Sales. Mesnil-sur-l'Estrée: Lethielleux/Groupe DDB, 2010 [orig.: 1945].

Emery, Gilles, and Matthew Levering, eds. *Aristotle in Aquinas's Theology*. Oxford: Oxford University Press, 2015.

Gaine, Simon Francis. *Will There Be Free Will in Heaven? Freedom, Impeccability and Beatitude*. London: T&T Clark, 2003.

---

63. Portions of this paper were presented by the author at the UCLA student chapter of the Thomistic Institute in January 2018.

Gondreau, Paul. "The Passions and the Moral Life: Appreciating the Originality of Aquinas." *The Thomist* 71 (2007): 419–50.

Grisez, Germain. "The True Ultimate End of Human Beings: The Kingdom, Not God Alone." *Theological Studies* 69, no. 1 (2008): 38–61.

Healy, Nicholas J. *The Eschatology of Hans Urs von Balthasar: Being as Communion.* Oxford: Oxford University Press, 2005.

Johnstone, Brian V. "The Debate on the Structure of the *Summa Theologiae* of St. Thomas Aquinas: From Chenu (1939) to Metz (1998)." In *Aquinas as Authority: A Collection of Studies Presented at the Second Conference of the Thomas Instituut te Utrecht, December 14–16, 2000*, edited by P. v. Geest, H. Goris, and C. Leget, 187–200. Publications of the Thomas Instituut te Utrecht, New Series 7. Leuven: Peeters, 2002.

Kromholtz, Bryan. "Eschatology and the Doctrine of God in St. Thomas Aquinas." *Nova et Vetera* (English edition) 12, no. 4 (2014): 1215–231.

———. *On the Last Day: The Time of the Resurrection of the Dead according to Thomas Aquinas.* Studia Friburgensia 110. Fribourg: Academic Press Fribourg, 2010.

Lamb, Matthew L. "The Eschatology of St Thomas Aquinas." In *Aquinas on Doctrine: A Critical Introduction*, edited by T. G. Weinandy, D. A. Keating, and J. P. Yocum, 225–40. London: T&T Clark, 2004.

———. "Wisdom Eschatology in Augustine and Aquinas." In *Aquinas the Augustinian*, edited by M. Dauphinais, B. David, and M. Levering, 258–75. Washington, DC: The Catholic University of America Press, 2007.

Leget, Carlo. "Eschatology." In *The Theology of Thomas Aquinas*, edited by R. V. Nieuwenhove and J. Wawrykow, 365–85. Notre Dame, IN: University of Notre Dame Press, 2005.

———. *Living with God: Thomas Aquinas on the Relation between Life on Earth and "Life" after Death.* Publications of the Thomas Instituut te Utrecht, New Series 5. Leuven: Peeters, 1997.

Lombardo, Nicholas E. *The Logic of Desire: Aquinas on Emotion.* Washington, DC: The Catholic University of America Press, 2011.

Mondin, Battista. "Risurrezione finale." In *Dizionario Enciclopedico del pensiero di San Tommaso d'Aquino*, 530–33. Bologna: Edizioni Studio Domenicano, 1991.

Morales, Isaac Augustine. "'With My Body I Thee Worship': New Creation, Beatific Vision, and the Liturgical Consummation of All Things." *Pro Ecclesia* 25, no. 3 (2016): 337–56.

Narcisse, Gilbert. *Les raisons de Dieu: Argument de convenance et esthétique théologique selon saint Thomas d'Aquin et Hans Urs von Balthasar.* Fribourg: Éditions Universitaires, 1997.

Nevitt, Turner C. "Aquinas on the Death of Christ: A New Argument for Corruptionism." *American Catholic Philosophical Quarterly* 90, no. 1 (2016): 77–99.

———. "Survivalism, Corruptionism, and Intermittent Existence in Aquinas." *History of Philosophy Quarterly* 31, no. 1 (2014): 1–19.

O'Rourke, Fran. *Pseudo-Dionysius and the Metaphysics of Aquinas*. Studien und Texte zur Geistesgeschichte des Mittelalters, 32. Leiden: E. J. Brill, 1992.

Pesch, Otto Hermann. *Thomas von Aquin: Grenze und Größe mittelalterlicher Theologie; Eine Einführung*. Mainz: Matthias-Grünewald, 1988.

Ratzinger, Joseph. *Eschatology: Death and Eternal Life*. 2nd ed. Translated by Michael Waldstein. Washington, DC: The Catholic University of America Press, 2006.

Schenk, Richard. "And Jesus Wept: Notes toward a Theology of Mourning." In *Soundings in the History of a Hope: New Studies on Thomas Aquinas*, 102–30. Ave Maria, FL: Sapientia Press, 2016.

Stump, Eleonore. "Resurrection and the Separated Soul." In *The Oxford Handbook of Aquinas*, edited by B. Davies and E. Stump, 458–66. Reprint ed. Oxford: Oxford University Press, 2014 [orig.: 2012].

Sullivan, Ezra. "Seek First the Kingdom: A Reply to Germain Grisez's Account of Man's Ultimate End." *Nova et Vetera* (English edition) 8, no. 4 (2010): 959–95.

Taylor, Richard C. "Arabic/Islamic Philosophy in Thomas Aquinas's Conception of the Beatific Vision *Super Sent*. 4., D. 49, Q. 2, A. 1." *The Thomist* 76 (2012): 509–50.

Toner, Patrick. "Personhood and Death in St. Thomas Aquinas." *History of Philosophy Quarterly* 26, no. 2 (2009): 121–38.

———. St. Thomas Aquinas on Death and the Separated Soul." *Pacific Philosophical Quarterly* 91, no. 4 (2010): 587–99.

Torrell, Jean-Pierre. *Le Christ en ses mystères: La vie et l'oeuvre de Jésus selon saint Thomas d'Aquin*. Vol. 1, *Jésus et Jésus-Christ*. Paris: Desclée, 1999.

———. *Saint Thomas Aquinas*. Vol. 1, *The Person and His Work*. 3rd ed. Translated by Matthew K. Minerd and Robert Royal. Washington, DC: The Catholic University of America Press, 2023.

———. *Saint Thomas Aquinas*. Vol. 2, *Spiritual Master*. Translated by Robert Royal. Washington, DC: The Catholic University of America Press, 2003.

Trottmann, Christian. *La vision béatifique: Des disputes scolastiques à sa définition par Benoît XII*. Bibliothèque des écoles françaises d'Athènes et de Rome, fascicule 289. Rome: École Française de Rome, 1995.

Urigüen, Rafael Hernández. "Hacia la vision beatifica: Sugerencias para una estética teológica desde la escatología." *Scripta Theologica* 38, no. 2 (2006): 855–79.

White, Thomas Joseph. "Imperfect Happiness and the Final End of Man: Thomas Aquinas and the Paradigm of Nature-Grace Orthodoxy." *The Thomist* 78 (2014): 247–89.

Wood, Jacob W. "The Study of Theology as a Foretaste of Heaven: The Influence of Albert the Great on Aquinas's Understanding of *Beatitudo Imperfecta*." *Nova et Vetera* (English edition) 16, no. 4 (2018): 1103–134.

CHAPTER 14

The Last Act
Balthasar's Eschatology

PATRICK X. GARDNER

INTRODUCTION: ESCHATOLOGY AS STORM CENTER

IN HIS LECTURES DELIVERED AT HEIDELBERG between 1912 and 1913, Ernst Troeltsch famously claimed that "the bureau of eschatology is usually closed these days."[1] Later, in the 1960s, Hans Urs von Balthasar noted that for most of the twentieth century, "the office has been working overtime."[2] Over those fifty-plus years, it seems that the business of eschatology began to boom: expanding its operation from the margins of Christian dogma to the very center of intellectual life.[3] This trend could be seen in the scholarly enthusiasm for the Dead Sea Scrolls; in the renewal of interest in Jewish apocalypticism led by Ernst Käsemann; and in the "theologies of hope" touted by Jürgen Moltmann and Johann Baptist Metz.[4] In secular scholarship, eschatology found a home in the "religious" Marxism of Ernst Bloch and in Karl Löwith's theories of historical progress.[5] Balthasar had reason, then, to see eschatology as a new focus of interest, imagination, and controversy. It had become, he said, the "storm center of the theology of our day."[6]

It certainly proved to be something of a storm center in Balthasar's own thought. As he defines it, eschatology is the study of what governs the

---

1. Ernst Troeltsch, *The Christian Faith* (Minneapolis, MN: Fortress Press, 1991), 38.

2. "Some Points of Eschatology," *ET* 1, 255.

3. Cf. Johann Baptist Metz, *Theology of the World* (New York: Seabury, 1969), 90.

4. Jürgen Moltmann, *Theology of Hope: On the Ground and Implications of a Christian Eschatology*, trans. James W. Leitch (New York: Harper and Row, 1967); Johann Baptist Metz, *Faith in History and Society: Toward a Practical Fundamental Theology*, trans. J. Matthew Ashley (New York: Crossroad, 2007).

5. Ernst Bloch, *The Principle of Hope*, trans. N. and S. Plaice and P. Knight (Oxford: Blackwell, 1986); Karl Löwith, *Meaning in History: The Theological Implications of the Philosophy of History* (Chicago: University of Chicago Press, 1949).

6. *ET* 1, 255.

293

relationship between the soul and its fate in eternity.[7] His earliest writings—
his dissertation and its three-volume expansion, *Apokalypse der Deutschen
Seele* (1937–1939)—examine how this relationship shaped German
literature and culture. His "theology of Holy Saturday" and his ongoing
fascination with universal salvation (*apokatastasis*) provoked the strongest
and most persistent challenges to his orthodoxy,[8] and the mystical
experiences of his spiritual directee, Adrienne von Speyr, had their greatest
influence on this area of his thinking.[9] Indeed, it is no exaggeration to say
that eschatology gave rise to some of Balthasar's most characteristic and
controversial insights. It is the key, he says, to understanding not only what
is distinctive about his theology but what is distinctive about creation as a
whole. It "brings the whole course" of history "to light precisely in its
termination," and it clarifies "the meaning that was intended from the very
beginning."[10]

Yet it is important to note that Balthasar developed many of these insights
as the fruits of his innovative approach to theological sources. As he gained
sympathy for the *ressourcement* movement during his time in Lyon (1932–
1936), Balthasar clarified how his methodological sensibilities diverged from
the neoscholasticism of his day.[11] As early as 1939, he even clarified his sense
of the shortcomings of medieval scholastics like St. Thomas—even as he was

---

7. *A*, 4.

8. *MP*; *TD* 5; and *DWH*. For the most comprehensive critique of Balthasar's
position, see Alyssa Lyra Pitstick, *Light in Darkness: Hans Urs von Balthasar and the Catholic
Doctrine of Christ's Descent into Hell* (Grand Rapids, MI: Eerdmans, 2007).

9. See Henry C. Anthony Karlson III, *The Eschatological Judgment of Christ: The
Hope of Universal Salvation and the Fear of Eternal Perdition in the Theology of Hans Urs
von Balthasar* (Eugene, OR: Wipf and Stock, 2017), 8–16. The influence that Speyr
(1902–1967) had on Balthasar is difficult to exaggerate. Her mystical experiences
allegedly gave her direct insight into Christ's passion and his experience of abandonment
in hell—experiences which Balthasar recorded and interpreted as revelations (with
important implications for his understanding of the last things). See also Johann Roten,
SM, "The Two Halves of the Moon: Marian Anthropological Dimensions in the
Common Mission of Adrienne von Speyr and Hans Urs von Balthasar," in *Hans Urs
Von Balthasar: His Life and Work*, ed. David L. Schindler (San Francisco: Ignatius,
1991), 65–86.

10. "Eschatology in Outline," *ET* 4, 423.

11. Balthasar was deeply influenced in this regard by his contact with Henri de Lubac
(189–1991) and Jean Daniélou (1905–1974), especially when Balthasar began his first
major studies of the church fathers. He was also introduced to more constructive
interpretations of scholasticism by his mentor, Erich Przywara (1889–1972), during his
time in Munich. However, it is arguably his friendship and dialogue with Karl Barth (1886–
1968) throughout the 1940s that most informed his sense of what is lacking in the
scholastic method.

consciously basing his reasoning upon theirs.[12] Like many in his generation, Balthasar was convinced that the virtue of the scholastic age lay in its coherence and systematic rigor.[13] But he was also convinced that retrieving figures like St. Thomas in the modern age required making their ideas more responsive to "the concrete, the unique, and the historical," to a more symphonic understanding of the tradition.[14] The conclusions that Balthasar draws for eschatology are no exception to this conviction. They showcase his creative fidelity to—and departure from—the legacy of thinkers like St. Thomas.

In the remainder of this chapter, I present the contours of Balthasar's eschatology with an eye to how it can clarify the relationship between Balthasar and St. Thomas. I begin with one insight about creation that Balthasar attributes to the scholastics, examining how he interprets it in a new and "dramatic" theological context. I note how his interpretation of this insight explains the other guiding principles that structure his eschatology, as well as how these guiding principles determine his position on more specific eschatological topics: the four "last things" (death, judgment, hell, and heaven).

Guiding Principles of Balthasar's Eschatology

Above all else, Balthasar's eschatology is Trinitarian. This means that for Balthasar, creation's ultimate destiny is God himself: not merely God in his oneness but God as he exists in himself—as eternal and dynamic relationships within a single divine essence. Balthasar bases this claim on an insight from St. Thomas, what he calls the "Scholastic axiom."[15] It states that the entire Trinity is involved in the act of creation, and thus the eternal processions within God are what cause the generation of creatures "outside" of God. As Thomas puts it:

> If, according to our faith, we assume the procession of the Divine Persons, . . . this perfect procession must be the cause and ground of the procession of creatures. However, just as we trace the procession of creatures, representing the perfection of the divine nature in an imperfect manner, back to the perfect prototype [the Son] . . . this same procession of creatures, since it results from the generosity of the divine will, must

---

12. Hans Urs von Balthasar, "The Fathers, the Scholastics, and Ourselves," *Communio* 24 (1997): 347–6. For Balthasar's more direct engagement with St. Thomas as a source for theological aesthetics, see *TD* 4, 393–412.

13. Balthasar, "The Fathers, the Schoastics, and Ourselves," 380–83.

14. Balthasar, "The Fathers, the Schoastics, and Ourselves," 386. Cf. *TS*.

15. *TD* 5, 61.

be traced back to a principle that, as it were, provides the foundation for this whole, freely given communication [i.e., the Holy Spirit].[16]

These eternal processions within the Trinity, therefore, are the "foundation" and "inalienable precondition" for creation. They contain in themselves, and to an infinite degree, the reality that creatures possess, and all creatures proceed from and imitate these eternal processions the way a replica imitates a prototype. The world, therefore, has a "fundamental Trinitarian constitution."[17] Every creature is an *imago trinitatis*—expressing something of God's triune nature by imitating his eternal distinctions.[18]

The relevance this has for Balthasar's eschatology is not difficult to see. If the Trinity is creation's origin, then the Trinity must be its destiny as well. If the divine processions contain the fullness of whatever reality is in creatures, then they embody the perfection that creatures inherently seek. The world, therefore, is understood only when it is seen not only as coming forth from the Trinity but as finally "returning" to it as well. "The triune life of God," Balthasar says, is "the real 'last thing,'" the "true eschaton," and the "last horizon" of God's relationship with the world.[19] And since the divine processions are creation's origin and end, it is meaningful to say that the world is never really "outside" of God. Its final destiny is to be "in" God in a fuller and deeper sense. As "the world's becoming has its origin in the sublime transactions between the persons of the Trinity," the world cannot have any final end or fulfillment apart from them:

> The idea of the world is from God and in God. Accordingly its whole (non-divine) reality cannot be located anywhere else but in him. . . . "its being has its foundation in God, and it is oriented toward eternity. It comes from God and goes to God, and, even when it distances itself from him, it is not outside God."[20]

Balthasar distinguishes himself from his scholastic forbearers, however, by drawing two conclusions that they do not. First, he argues that the Trinitarian character of creation requires us to expand what we can say about the Trinity. For Thomas, beyond the term "procession," there is rather little

---

16. Cf. *TD* 5, 62. Balthasar is quoting a passage from Thomas's commentary on Lombard's *Sentences* (*Scriptum super libros sententiarum magistri Petri Lombardi Episcopi Parisiensis*: I, d.10, q.1, a.1, *solutio*).

17. *TD* 5, 73.

18. *TD* 5, 57.

19. *TD* 5, 56–57.

20. *TD* 5, 100. Balthasar is partially quoting from Adrienne von Speyr, *John*, vol. 2, *The Discourses of Controversy*, trans. Brian McNeil (San Francisco: Ignatius, 1993).

that we can know and say about the divine persons based on our knowledge of creatures and their differences. It is certainly the case that any differences involving imperfection cannot correspond to a reality within the Trinity, so the language we use for such differences can never apply literally and analogously to God.[21] Yet for Balthasar, the world being "in" God means that *all* differences in creation have as their prototypes the distinctions between the divine persons.[22] Even the difference between creatures and God is made possible by the infinitely greater distinctions between Father, Son, and Spirit. For Balthasar, then, it follows that if all our differences have their foundation in God's processions, our language about these differences can be applied analogically to the Trinity. If, for instance, God's being is the ground of our becoming, then it must contain what is real about our becoming in an infinite manner. The Trinity, therefore, can be called an "eternal happening" rather than merely a substance or being.[23]

The same logic applies to other phenomena that we encounter as creatures. Insofar as the processions make possible our self-giving, they can be spoken of as forms of "ultimate self-giving." Insofar as they make possible the ways in which we "lose" ourselves, they can be spoken of as the "self-emptying" (*kenosis*) of one divine person to another.[24] The relation between them can be called a "distance" and even a kind of death ("super-death") that makes possible the change we undergo in death.[25] This more expansive understanding of analogy is what most determines the shape of Balthasar's eschatology: there is more for eschatology to say, since there is more within creation—even its privative aspects—that corresponds to something within the Trinity, as origin and end.

Secondly, he argues that this reasoning also means that our words, when applied to the Trinity, express what always already fulfills these created differences. Even if it is true in some way to say that the Son exists at a "distance" from the Father, or that the divine persons "empty" themselves into one another, what these terms signify still coincide with God's perfect unity and perfection. They are, after all, relationships *of God*, who is not

---

21. *ST* I, Q.4, a.3; Q.13; Q.27, a.1; and Q.32, a.1.

22. See Nicholas Healy, *The Eschatology of Hans Urs von Balthasar: Being as Communion* (Oxford: Oxford University Press, 2005). For more on Balthasar's engagement with Thomas's account of divine naming, especially regarding the Trinity, see Bernhard Blankenhorn, OP, "Balthasar's Method of Divine Naming," *Nova et Vetera* 1 (2003): 245–68; Angela Franz Franks, "Trinitarian *Analogia Entis* in Hans Urs von Balthasar," *The Thomist* 62 (1998): 533–59. See also Karen Kilby, *Balthasar: A (Very) Critical Introduction* (Grand Rapids, MI: Eerdmans, 2012), esp. chap. 5.

23. *TD* 5, 68–69.

24. *TD* 5, 73–78.

25. *TD* 3, 94, 84.

subject to any created shortcoming. For Balthasar, then, even words that seem to imply imperfection, when used to describe the divine processions, express something eschatological: a reality that contains the positive fulfillment and even the resolution of these differences found within creation.

Another structural feature of Balthasar's eschatology is its dramatic character. The bulk of Balthasar's eschatology is presented in the "last act" of his five-volume *Theo-Drama*, which reflects a methodology uniquely his own.[26] Balthasar focuses on drama because the world of created difference is not merely a world of isolated substances. The world that comes from and subsists "in" God is a world made up of actions, events, and relations, of free agents collaborating and competing to influence the way things are. The "form" of drama is what structures the interactions of free agents—the "action" of the *dramatis personae*. And "theo-drama" refers to the form that structures the interactions between God's infinite freedom and the finite freedom of intelligent creatures.[27] According to Balthasar, any retrieval of scholasticism needs to be adapted to an approach to theology that is more attentive to this. It is the creation of free creatures that makes possible a deeper way of being "in" God—"the possibility of involving a non-divine world in the Trinity's love."[28] And this is God's ultimate intention for the world. "This is what the essential eschatology of man consists in," for finite freedom "to be drawn into divine freedom" and share in the divine nature itself.[29] But finite freedom also means the real possibility of rejecting this destiny—a new and wholly negative kind of difference for creatures, that is, sin. for Balthasar, therefore, the drama of eschatology follows from the possibilities opened up by our freedom and by God's desire to give that freedom a fuller participation in his triune life.

Yet to fulfill this purpose, God must find a way of overcoming the negative difference of sin without simply imposing his will upon it. Balthasar's solution to this puzzle is a "Christological eschatology."[30] The mission of Christ (God the Son) is at the "center" of eschatology because it is how God draws created freedom more deeply into union with him. Balthasar argues that Christ fills this role because the mission of the Son is nothing other than the extension of his eternal procession into the world. For Balthasar, the Incarnation is like the "translation" of the Son's eternal relationship with the

---

26. *TD* 5, 13.

27. *TD* 1, 17; cf. Aidan Nichols, OP, *No Bloodless Myth: A Guide Through Balthasar's Dramatics* (Washington, DC: The Catholic University of America Press, 2000), 11, 18; *ET* 4, 435.

28. *TD* 5, 510, 509.

29. *ET* 4, 434; *TD* 5, 509.

30. *TD* 5, 506.

Father into the language of human life, and thus this "translation" occurs when the Son takes on created freedom as a new way or "modality" of how he exists eternally.[31] Once this earthly form becomes a modality of the Son's being, it is then possible for us to imitate it through grace. It opens the way for our adoption as "sons of God" and our sharing in the triune life.[32] Christ is thus the center of eschatology because this "last act" of the drama is about his taking the entire content of world history to himself and exalting creatures beyond what they are naturally capable of achieving.[33]

But Christ's mission is not only to bring the world "into" God but to overcome the world's sinful refusal of God. On Balthasar's view, if all created difference is made possible by the "distance" between the divine persons, then sin, too, is made possible by this divine "distance." Yet by the same reasoning, this "distance" in the Trinity already contains sin's resolution because although it is "distance," it is at the same time perfect communion with God (and communion with God is the overcoming of sin). Since this resolution cannot be imposed upon free creatures without violating their freedom, the Son must enter into our condition and work within the structures that our freedom allows. The mission of the Son, then, is to transform all the structures of finite freedom—even its sinful refusal of God—into new modes or forms that his eternal relationship can take. This, then, is the central pattern of Balthasar's Christology. Christ atones for sin not by destroying it but by "enveloping" it: by entering into this kind of God-abandonment and "absorbing" it as a new expression of the eternal love between the Father and the Son (in the Holy Spirit).[34] Only when this absorbing is complete—after it has encompassed all expressions of our freedom—can we attain our eschaton. Only then can the Son lead even this most distant part of his creation back to the Father with him.

These guiding principles about the Trinity and Christ have an additional implication. Insofar as it has Christ at its center, eschatology for Balthasar is *realized* eschatology. First, it is realized in the sense that the "last things" (*eschata*) are what Christ himself has already undergone. Christ serves as the means of bringing creation to its destiny only by first accomplishing this destiny within his own humanity. His life, death, and Resurrection are how he "takes up" or envelops the world's history and unites it with eternity. It is thus a "personal eschatology" for Jesus that embraces the eschatology of everything else—drawing everything into himself and reorienting everything around him. "Christological eschatology is therefore a primary law of universal

---

31. *TD* 5, 121.
32. *TD* 5, 120; *ET* 4, 432–33.
33. *ET* 4, 260–61: Christ is the "whole essence of the last things."
34. *ET* 4, 435–36.

application."[35] This personal dimension even constitutes a sense of time uniquely Christ's own: a "time" that mediates between God's time and worldly time, integrating and comprehending the latter while revealing the former.[36] So for Balthasar, it is true to say that the eschaton is already fully realized in the "time" that Christ experiences.

Eschatology is also realized because what Christ reveals and unites us with is God's triune life, which, as I've noted, already contains the perfection of every creature and the resolution of all sin. If Jesus' personal eschatology is merely the playing out in time of his eternal relationship with the Father, then the Incarnation is literally the union of humanity with its final end. The Christ-event is, therefore, "the vertical irruption of fulfillment into horizontal time, and it doesn't leave its past, present, or future unchanged: it draws it into itself, giving it a new character."[37] It can be understood only as the encounter between the world and something eternal, something that does not need to "become" anything in the future but always *has been* the fulfillment of created beings. The final act of the great drama, therefore, begins with Christ's eschatology since it is here that the "horizontal" theo-drama (the unfolding of history) is transformed into a "vertical" theo-drama, where history is united with what is realized in Christ from all eternity.[38] Thus, Christianity for Balthasar involves a realized eschatology in the strongest sense. The eschaton is not a yet-to-be-realized future but something real in principle from time immemorial (*as* the divine processions of the Trinity).

Balthasar finds this realized eschatology most clearly in the Gospel of John. The fourth Gospel, he says, best distinguishes Christian eschatology from its Jewish and pagan alternatives. While pagan hope is only a hope for the soul's immortality and Jewish hope is focused exclusively on an unrealized future, for John, the coming eschaton is present already in what Christ undergoes.[39] It is an "actually initiated supernatural order within creation," which Christ's second coming will merely conclude rather than begin. It is something "already hidden or openly present to the old world as the 'New Eon.'"[40] The future expectations of Judaism have been definitively fulfilled by Jesus, so that no further realization beyond the Christ-event is conceivable; only its ongoing interpretations and applications are.[41] Balthasar thus believes that John offers the most faithful picture of Christian hope, and from the

---

35. *TD* 5, 22.
36. *TD* 5, 30, 57.
37. *TD* 5, 25.
38. *TD* 5, 30.
39. *TD* 5, 148.
40. *ET* 4, 423.
41. *TD* 5, 49.

Johannine perspective, the "end times" are happening now as a result of Jesus' death and Resurrection.[42]

This privileging of the Johannine view also explains the sense in which Balthasar's eschatology is apocalyptic. It is apocalyptic primarily in the sense of "unveiling" since it is a matter of Christ revealing something already fulfilled from eternity.[43] Apocalypse consists, then, in an eternal reality (the triune life) taking on new historical expression. There is also for Balthasar a sense in which the introduction of this eschaton into history gives rise to a "crisis" (a moment of decision) and an intensifying resistance to God that results in judgment, both themes characteristic of apocalyptic literature.

However, Balthasar's eschatology is not apocalyptic in the traditional sense of Jewish apocalypticism. He is critical of what he calls Jewish "futurist" eschatology and says that a certain degree of "de-apocalypticizing" occurs in the transition from Old Testament to New. This follows because the Trinity, which breaks into history through Christ, is not technically a *futurum* (a future possibility of created history). It is, instead, something entirely apart from worldly time that draws the messianic dimensions of Jewish apocalypticism into itself, assimilating them and making them converge upon Christ.[44]

In sum, then, the main features of Balthasar's eschatology follow from an "axiom" he finds in scholastic theology, which he nonetheless interprets in innovative ways. He shares with thinkers like Thomas the view that creation is grounded in the Trinity, and the Trinity, therefore, is the world's eschaton. Yet Balthasar explicitly connects the analogy of being (*analogia entis*) with the Trinity in ways Thomas does not. Balthasar concludes that in light of revelation, the Christian is justified in saying that the eternal distinctions in the divine nature are the basis for the real distinction in creatures between essence and existence (and thus for the differences among creatures that follow from this).[45] Compared to Thomas, this connection inspires in Balthasar a greater confidence about what can be said positively about the Trinity. In other words, Balthasar argues that if the Trinitarian relations both enable and contain the perfection of creaturely differences, then theologians are justified in describing those relations using words and concepts original to creatures. Indeed, Balthasar is at his boldest—and perhaps his furthest from Thomas—when he argues that this principle applies even when those creaturely differences involve negation, limitation, and privation. The divine

---

42. *TD* 5, 46.

43. For a fuller account of the sense in which Balthasar's eschatology is apocalyptic, see Cyril O'Regan, *Theology and the Spaces of Apocalyptic* (Milwaukee: Marquette University Press, 2009), 44–53.

44. *TD* 5, 36, 39.

45. See Healy, *The Eschatology of Hans Urs von Balthasar*, 83.

processions involve "super time," "distance," "super-death," self-emptying, and sacrifice, among others,[46] and eschatology is intelligible for Balthasar only as long as it can articulate how Trinitarian realities correspond to these created differences as their origin and end.

This holds especially for expressions of finite freedom, which create both deeper ways of being united with the Trinity and new obstacles to reaching this end. Eschatology is, therefore, dramatic, and Christ, once more, is the key to accomplishing this union and overcoming the obstacles. Eschatology is Christological because Christ envelops our freedom in all its forms, transforming them into new expressions of his eternal relationship with the Father. This is the pattern that both makes Christ the center of eschatology and explains how it is realized and apocalyptic in nature.

These guiding principles are important not only because they begin to clarify Balthasar's dependence on—and departure from—scholastic eschatology but also because they determine the position he takes on more specific eschatological questions. If, for instance, the Trinity is our true end, then in order to understand how this destiny shapes our lives, we must understand these themes in light of the one "last end" of God disclosed in Christ. The traditional topics of eschatology, then—what he calls the "anthropological eschata" of Catholic doctrine: death, judgment, hell, and heaven—are only a matter of applying these structural principles to our situation within the "last act" of the theo-drama.

DEATH AND JUDGMENT

As with the general structure of his eschatology, Balthasar's accounts of death and judgment both appropriate and deviate from scholastic treatments of these topics. Thomas, for instance, defines death as the separation of the rational soul from the matter that constitutes its body. Death is thus a state of privation for humans and certainly one that distinguishes mortal creatures from the living God.[47] According to Thomas, immediately after death, the separated soul (*anima separata*) undergoes a particular judgment by Christ corresponding to the value of its deeds in life and the sanctifying grace it possesses. In this sense, its eschatological status is determined before the end of temporal history. There is, nevertheless, an intermediate state of existence for the soul prior to the general resurrection and final judgment.[48] Christ's

---

46. *TD* 5, 310, 84.

47. Carlo Leget, "Eschatology," in *The Theology of Thomas Aquinas*, ed. Rik Van Nieuwenhove and Joseph Wawrykow (Notre Dame, IN: University of Notre Dame Press, 2005), 368.

48. *ST* III (*Supplementum*), Q.69, a.1–2; Q.70, a.1–3.

role as the one who enacts these judgments is connected with his suffering for us on the cross: the fact that Christ stood in our place is what makes his judgment of us a manifestation of God's mercy and justice.[49]

Yet for Balthasar, eschatology treats death as something essential for realizing our end in God. Death is an effect of sin and thus a kind of created difference that first separates us from God, but Balthasar argues that even death has its "original image" in God, as it corresponds to something real in the Trinitarian processions, which he describes as "super-death." "Super-death" for Balthasar refers to the sense in which the Father can be said to "give away" his life in eternally generating the Son, and the Son can be said to "give away" his life in an eternal act of gratitude to the Father.[50] This means that this eternal sacrifice of life flowing between Father and Son is not only what makes our death possible but what makes it possible for us to overcome it. It is what allows the Son to integrate our creaturely death into his mission, enveloping it as a mode that expresses this "super-death" within the Trinity. Christ is, therefore, sent to take "sinful death" up into his "death" of self-surrender and thereby receive "human death into eternal life."[51] And because Christ assimilates human death in this way—making it part of his personal eschatology—our dying can be given a new meaning, when it is configured to his.[52]

The same dynamic explains why Christ plays the role of eschatological judge. In taking up our death on the cross, he embodies God's final judgment upon our sin: he is *judged* ("God's final judgment is pronounced upon this sin, which the Son now embodies").[53] This judgment occurs when our limited, distorted judgment of God comes into direct confrontation with God's truth, that is, his eternal love. On God's side, then, this judgment is nothing other than the love between the divine persons, and because he unites our distortion with divine love, Christ embodies this confrontation for us: "the judgment is completely present in the judge himself."[54] Balthasar argues that Christ is able to embody this judgment because his eternal obedience to and "distance" from the Father serves as the condition for it.[55] Once more, according to Balthasar, we see the same pattern: what Christ does as judge is

---

49. *ST* III, Q.10, a.2; Q.14, a.2; and Q.59, a.2–3; cf. Matthew Lamb, "The Eschatology of St. Thomas Aquinas," in *Aquinas on Doctrine: A Critical Introduction*, ed. Thomas G. Weinandy, Daniel A. Keating, and John P. Yocum (London: T&T Clark, 2004), 235.

50. *TD* 5, 84–85.

51. *TD* 5, 251–55.

52. *ET* 4, 438.

53. *TD* 5, 261.

54. *ET* 4, 448.

55. *TD* 5, 283.

assimilate the judgment on our sin into an expression or mode of his eternal obedience to the Father. In this sense, judgment has always already taken place as that Trinitarian relationship; the Lamb has been slain "from the foundation of the world" (Rev 13:18).[56] When we look upon Christ crucified, we are merely presented with this judgment in a new form.

An implication of this is that God's judgment on us as individuals is realized already in the judgment that Christ undergoes on the cross. Drawing on the insights of Adrienne von Speyr, Balthasar reasons that when Christ unites our judgment with Trinitarian love, the pay-off is that all individual sins are expiated in principle.[57] He has taken our position of sin and abandonment, and so he has a unique "competence" for judging humanity on the last day. He knows what he is judging from the inside,[58] even though it is true that Christ came to save and not to judge (Jn 3:17; 12:47). He conducts the final judgment in himself, so it is as if he has "already borne the guilt of the person he is judging."[59] Whatever else follows for us "can only be an effect and consequence of this event, already inherent in it."[60] For Balthasar, then, all that remains for the last day is the full revelation of the judgment's result. It follows that there is really only one judgment for all of us, but how it is applied to each of us remains hidden within the judge himself until that final day.

What does this mean for the intermediate state of souls after death? The realized nature of the judgment means that it is difficult for Balthasar to make sense of any intermediate state for disembodied souls between a particular and final judgment. He notes that the New Testament does not engage in speculation about such an intermediate state, and for the drama of eschatology, it is not a question "of great moment."[61] He rejects what he calls the "Protestant view" that the body and soul are both destroyed in death, but he thinks that positing two distinct judgments is merely strained theological conjecture.[62] Balthasar argues instead that we should not think about the judgment in chronological terms. Because it is already realized in Christ and within the Trinity, it is better to think of the judgment as occurring apart from and alongside history, such that every moment of history can, in principle, be related to it. So at some level, the fact that the judgment is first

---

56. *ET* 4, 449.

57. *TD* 5, 260. Balthasar is here citing Speyr's *Die katholischen Briefe*, vol. 1, *Der Jakobusbrief. Die Petrusbriefe* (Einsiedeln: Johannesverlag, 1961), 333.

58. *ET* 4, 449.

59. *ET* 4, 450; *TD* 5, 271.

60. *TD* 5, 277.

61. *TD* 5, 356.

62. *TD* 5 133, 356.

and foremost a Christological and Trinitarian reality means that we cannot meaningfully distinguish it into two judgments separated by time.

Balthasar's point is that if we needn't distinguish the particular and final judgments chronologically, then we needn't think of the soul's state after death in chronological terms. What he calls the "heavenly super-time" of God does not coincide with historical time.[63] So if our final status is determined already in Christ, then our condition after bodily death is only "intermediate" from our perspective within time.[64] The question of when our disembodied souls will be reunited with our bodies is for Balthasar "insoluble" as long as we remain within earthly history. If our destiny has been determined and exists alongside this history, however, then it is even possible to speculate that those destined for resurrection with Christ in some sense already have been resurrected. It is, in other words, unimportant whether we imagine a temporal hiatus between our death and our rising to new life.[65] Balthasar seems to draw the conclusion that a realized eschatology allows us to imagine a communion of saints without positing any disembodied souls at all.

There are similar consequences for Balthasar's interpretation of purgatory, which must be seen, he says, as "one aspect of judgment" and thus must be understood from within the encounter between the sinner and Christ, who is our eschaton. As with the judgment, then, Balthasar argues that it is not proper to think of purgatory in terms of historical time or an intermediate state. It is "beyond the earthly calculation of time."[66] He even says it is pointless to distinguish the "fires" of purification from the eschatological fire of judgment.[67] Purgatory results more directly from the cross. It is the application to us, or our share in, the "fire" of judgment that Christ has already undergone in the crucifixion. Balthasar retains the traditional sense of purgatory as a state of "isolation" and "temporal" suffering, therefore, but argues that it cannot be directly correlated with history. Any meaningful sense of its duration remains, like our final status, hidden with God.

Hell and Descent

The most controversial aspects of Balthasar's eschatology concern his interpretation of hell and Christ's descent to the dead. On the traditional

---

63. *TD* 5, 358–59.

64. See Andrew Hofer, "Balthasar's Eschatology on the Intermediate State: The Question of Knowability," *Logos* 12, no. 3 (2009): 158–59.

65. *TD* 5, 360, 353.

66. *TD* 5, 360–61. Here Balthasar is quoting Joseph Ratzinger, *Eschatologie-Tod und ewiges Leben* (Regensburg: Friedrich Pustet Verlag, 1977), 187–88.

67. *TD* 5, 360, n.1; *ET* 4, 455.

Thomist view, the existence of hell is necessitated by God's justice. Justice requires that human sins not expiated in this life must be punished in the next, so damnation is an essential part of Christ's office as eschatological judge. For Thomas, if God is our final end and supreme good, and mortal sin is our free choice to deprive ourselves of this good, then hell results when death makes this freely chosen deprivation immutable. This deprivation itself has the character of punishment: to be perpetually deprived of one's final end is a great pain for the soul, and Thomas holds that this state even merits pain for the senses as well.[68] Given this understanding of damnation, Thomists traditionally interpret the words "he descended into hell" in the Apostle's Creed to mean that Christ's soul descends in glory to manifest his power among the dead. This descent, however, does not extend to the hell of the damned. Christ descends only to what tradition refers to as the bosom of Abraham: the state of the patriarchs and the righteous dead from before the time of Christ.

In contrast, Balthasar's "theology of Holy Saturday" departs from this understanding by arguing that Christ *does* descend to the hell of the damned. Indeed, Balthasar even holds that the nature of this descent requires Christ to suffer the effects of hell and to experience damnation. He reasons that if Christ atones for sins by taking up the position of sinners, then this must include taking upon himself the most extreme consequences of sin: freely chosen isolation from God. This leads Balthasar to interpret Christ's descent into Sheol or Hades as encompassing more than the hell of the patriarchs, and it leads him to conclude that this is not a descent in glory, with the appearance of Christ's victorious soul. Rather, in line with the mystical experiences of von Speyr, Balthasar sees Christ going down to the deepest depths of God-abandonment. This is the terminal point of the Son's mission, and it makes his descent a continuation of his experience on the Cross. If Christ is truly in solidarity with sinners, then he must truly be in solidarity with the dead. He must experience the powerlessness, isolation, and passivity of death. If he is to redeem it, he must endure the full consequences of created freedom gone astray.

According to Balthasar, then, more than the pains of damnation, what Christ undergoes in hell as the real consequence of human freedom is abandonment by God the Father. Balthasar describes the Father as "loading" sin upon the Son, such that in a way he "becomes sin" for us (2 Cor 5:21).[69]

---

68. *ST* (*Supplementum*), Q.70, a.3; I-II, Q.87, a.4; and III, Q.1, a.2; cf. Reginald Garrigou-Lagrange, OP, *Life Everlasting and the Immensity of the Soul: A Theological Treatise on the Four Last Things: Death, Judgment, Heaven, Hell*, trans. Patrick Cummins, OSB (Rockford, IL: Tan Books and Publishers, 1991), 109.

69. *GL* 7, 208. See also Pitstick, *Light in Darkness*, 117.

Sin is a rejection of God because it turns us inwards and closes us in upon ourselves, and because this isolation results in God-abandonment, Christ must experience abandonment by the Father in order to expiate our sin. Balthasar holds that Christ even experiences the Father's "wrath" (his "No" to sin). He is thus forced to conclude quite radically that "The Son's 'God-forsakenness' on the Cross cannot be interpreted one-sidedly as something felt solely by the dying Jesus. If God is objectively forsaken here, then we must say that God is forsaken by God."[70]

But why must Christ endure hell to redeem us? The purpose of Christ experiencing damnation is "to embrace fallen creaturely freedom in the Trinitarian love by outstripping it in its most extreme form."[71] Even hell—the greatest and most negative distance from God we can manage—is somehow conditioned by the eternal "distance" between Father and Son. Once more, this "distance" between the Father and Son is always already infinitely greater and more positive than hell. It is a higher form of "God-abandonment" in the sense that the divine persons "abandon" themselves to one another in eternal acts of love. The overcoming of sin is made possible by the Son entering into created freedom's dereliction, "outstripping" it and rendering even this perverse expression of freedom a modality of Trinitarian love, a form expressing something real in God's being. The goal is thus to "make possible fallen freedom's union with infinite freedom in the same Trinitarian life."[72]

Even hell, then, is a Trinitarian and Christological reality for Balthasar. In his Resurrection, "Christ leaves behind him Hades . . . but by virtue of his deepest Trinitarian experience, he takes 'Hell' with him, as the expression of his power to dispose, as judge, the everlasting salvation or the everlasting loss of man."[73] The hell of the damned, in other words, becomes a real possibility only *after* Christ's death, descent, and Resurrection. It is "a product of the redemption."[74] This follows from the fact that Christ's descent renders the God-abandonment of Sheol into an expression of and way of participating in the God-abandoning love of the Trinity.

Yet Christ's redemption can never force this solution upon the sinner. Once more, Balthasar takes it as a governing law of the theo-drama that the corruption of created freedom cannot be redeemed by compulsion.[75] Rather,

---

70. *TD* 3, 530; Pitstick, *Light in Darkness*, 119.

71. Pitstick, *Light in Darkness*, 257.

72. Pitstick, *Light in Darkness*, 144.

73. *MP*, 177; Karlson, *The Eschatological Judgment of Christ*, 107; see also Edward T. Oakes, "The Internal Logic of Holy Saturday in the Theology of Hans Urs von Balthasar," *International Journal of Systematic Theology* 9, no. 2 (2007): 184–99.

74. *MP*, 174; *TD* 5, 362–64.

75. Cf. *TD* 5, 287.

God must enter into the space of that freedom and outmaneuver its corrupted possibilities. This means that for Balthasar it is still possible to reject what Christ's descent accomplishes and to choose oneself as one's final end: freely closing oneself off from participation in the Trinitarian love now opened up to the sinner. There is a way in which hell for Balthasar exists "in" the damned person (a private hell), as if he freely chooses to cling to or reclaim the sin that Christ separated from him on the cross. And there is also a sense in which hell "is located in God." The "fire" of hell *just is* the fire of God's love for Balthasar, but it is experienced as his wrath, exactly proportionate to the love offered through Christ and subsequently scorned.[76]

So while damnation remains a real possibility of self-isolation, it is equally possible on Balthasar's view that hell is empty. The power of Christ's descent—his transforming the depths of God-abandonment into a mode expressing and uniting us with God's love—means that it is possible none have freely chosen to endure in their rejection of this love.[77] Christ has accomplished what is objectively necessary for all human freedom (even sinful human freedom) to be taken into God. There is even a sense in which this is the outcome God has desired all along; his aim for the whole theo-drama. Yet the outcome of that judgment, and thus whether any *actually have* exercised their freedom to reject Christ, is not known to us. Once more, it is among the data of eschatology not yet revealed. Balthasar is clear, therefore, that we cannot know whether hell is populated or, if it is, by whom. We can only "dare" to hope for the salvation of all, motivated by God's universal salvific will for his creation.

Heaven and Hope

What, then, is Balthasar's view of heaven? Here, too, Balthasar both presupposes a number of points found within Thomist eschatology and draws distinctive conclusions from them. For Thomas, heaven signifies the final end for human beings and thus our attainment of God himself. He describes it as a higher degree of participation in the divine life, a participation we are not capable of realizing on our own. It is an end, moreover, that is opened to us only by what Christ accomplishes in his Incarnation. What Thomas means by this participation in God's life is a sharing in the very beatitude that God experiences: the eternal act by which he rejoices in knowing and loving himself for all eternity.[78] This union with and possession of God is thus realized in the beatific vision (seeing God's essence directly, "face-to-face"). Heaven is

---

76. *TD* 5, 301.

77. Karlson, *The Eschatological Judgment of Christ*, 139.

78. *ST* I-II, Q.3, a.4; Garrigou-Lagrange, *Life Everlasting*, 217.

thus a supernatural fulfillment of our wills and intellects and derivatively, a fulfillment for our glorified bodies, once more united with the souls possessed of sanctifying grace and the merits of Christ.[79]

Alternatively, Balthasar begins by defining heaven explicitly in terms of the divine processions. Heaven just is the Trinity itself: "God is the 'last thing' of the creature: gained, he is heaven; lost, he is hell."[80] Balthasar cites John 17:1–23 here as his guiding text: "so that all may be one as you, Father, are in me and I in you, that they too may be in us."[81] So heaven is primarily about creatures being "in" God in that more intimate sense that God intends throughout the theo-drama. Eternal life is, therefore, not merely a beholding of God but our fuller participation in the processions of the Trinity from which we originate. We share in "the very surging life of God himself" and it is as though we become "an internal gift from each Divine Person to the Other."[82] Balthasar thus suggests that the image of a beatific vision is not rich enough to capture the sense of union with God that the heavenly state involves.

This Trinitarian view implies for Balthasar that heaven begins during our earthly life. We find our place "in" the divine processions through our encounter with the missions of the divine persons. The ultimate goal of the Son's mission, after all, is not just to redeem created freedom but to introduce us "into" God in a new way. Moreover, heaven can be considered already realized in Balthasar's eschatology since Christ's Resurrection and return to the Father reveals—and proleptically enacts—heaven on our behalf. Because the mission of the Son is simply the unfolding within history of what has always already been fulfilled in God, it follows that we encounter heaven when we encounter Christ. In a way, then, it is our relationship with Christ that determines heaven for us. His Resurrection encompasses our decision for or against him, which constitutes heaven or hell for us. Then because of this, the presence of the Spirit that we receive when we are baptized "into Christ" makes possible our indwelling by the divine persons even now (in faith, hope, and love).[83]

Yet a major question that looms over Balthasar's account is the question of universal salvation. Does his interpretation of Christ's redemptive work commit Balthasar to universalism about the heavenly state? As I've noted, it is certainly true that Balthasar's position supports a strong *hope* that heaven will be the final state for all human beings. He wrote on many occasions about

---

79. *ST* I, Q.82, a.3; I-II, Q.1; and Garrigou-Lagrange, *Life Everlasting*, 218, 223–30.

80. *ET* 1, 260; cf. Geoffrey Wainwright, "Eschatology," in *The Cambridge Companion to Hans Urs von Balthasar*, ed. Edward T. Oakes, SJ, and David Moss (Cambridge: Cambridge University Press, 2004), 120.

81. *ET* 4, 442.

82. *ET* 4, 442; *TD* 5, 507.

83. Nichols, *No Bloodless Myth*, 224–27, 229.

the prospect of universalism (*apokatastasis*) in works like *Dare We Hope, Theo-Drama V*, and his final lecture at the University of Trier in 1988.[84] And Geoffrey Wainwright is correct to note that Balthasar acknowledges the presence of traditions in the New Testament that imply the possibility of souls being eternally lost.[85] As I've noted, Balthasar's reasoning requires that he affirm the enduring possibility of some—perhaps perpetually—refusing heaven. He even notes that too confident an affirmation of universal salvation "seems to empty God's involvement in the world of every last trace of tragedy."[86] So, in fact, what Balthasar counsels is a prudent agnosticism. We must resist the urge to synthesize the strands of revealed truth in a way that would warrant us to claim a knowledge we cannot have in this life.

Even so, it is undeniable that the thrust of Balthasar's reasoning errs on the side of the hope that all will reach their final destiny "in" God's triune life. There is a sense in which Balthasar thinks the merit of Christ so outweighs the power of human sin because it precedes and conditions all free refusal of God: "indeed, the cross of Christ . . . must stand beyond all hell, where the Son is forsaken by the Father in a way that only he can know."[87] Balthasar suggests, then, that we ought to take seriously the very manner in which God accomplishes salvation in Christ—never imposing or destroying but outmaneuvering sin—as a strong motive for our hope. The aim of the Son's descent makes heaven possible for all, even those in the state of furthest abandonment. And this itself is confirmation of God's will for the salvation of all: "God's purpose must be fulfilled even against all opposing obstacles."[88]

Conclusion

Balthasar's eschatology provides a fitting example of how he receives traditional sources and develops constructive positions from them. His approach begins with a basic principle about creation rooted in scholastic theology but draws seemingly radical conclusions from it. Consistent with what he calls the "Scholastic Axiom," Balthasar understands creation as coming forth from and imitating the divine processions, so it must return to them (having their end "in" the Trinity). Creation is thus theocentric and Trinitarian in nature.

The key for Balthasar is how he interprets this point in the context of his "theodramatic theory." He more directly relates creation to the divine

---

84. Cf. Wainwright, "Eschatology," 113.
85. Wainwright, "Eschatology," 122; *DWH*, 29.
86. *TD* 5, 269.
87. *TD* 5, 193.
88. *DWH*, 237; cf. Wainwright, "Eschatology," 123.

processions because he argues that a wider range of differences within creation correspond to something real about the Trinity—even differences that imply imperfection. If eschatology is about articulating the correspondence between creatures and their divine prototypes, then eschatology can speak more boldly and directly about the Trinity on the basis of this correspondence. This is especially true for the dramatic dimension of creation, that is, finite freedom and its negative expressions. These ingredients together clarify why Balthasar's eschatology is Christological, realized, and apocalyptic. Christ brings together our finite freedom with its eschaton in God, assimilating the former into a mode or expression of the latter. He does this for us by first accomplishing it in his own humanity, meaning that our eschaton is not an unfulfilled future event. It is already realized as the Trinity, revealed and applied to us through the "apocalypse" of Christ's life, death, and Resurrection.

These structural features also make sense of how Balthasar's position on the "anthropological eschata" diverge from the Thomist position. Death for Thomas is a privative state, a created difference that cannot directly correspond to anything in the Trinity. But for Balthasar, our death does correspond to the eternal giving of life between the divine persons ("super-death"), meaning that it is a dimension of our existence that can ultimately unite us with our eschaton when Christ envelops and undergoes our death himself. Similarly, for Thomists, separated souls undergo a particular judgment by Christ upon death, in an intermediate state prior to the Resurrection and final judgment. For Balthasar, however, our judgment also corresponds to something real in God, which Christ unites us with when he takes our place and enacts our judgment within himself. Because this judgment is in principle realized already in Christ, Balthasar is more skeptical about the soul's intermediate state. There is one judgment in Christ, but how we appropriate it from our place within history gives the impression of two judgments separated in time.

Once more, as hell for Thomas is a state of self-chosen privation, and thus something that does not correspond to any reality in the divine processions, Christ's descent is a descent in victory to the dead but not to those in the hell of the damned. Alternatively, for Balthasar, even hell is somehow made possible by the relation ("distance") between the Father and the Son. So once again, hell signifies an expression of our freedom that Christ can absorb and transform into a means of reaching that eternal "distance," meaning that Christ must descend to the utmost depths of hell to truly redeem that freedom. Finally, heaven for Thomas is primarily our beatific vision of the divine essence: the fulfillment of the soul's faculties (intellect and will) and secondarily of our glorified bodies, in a manner that exceeds our innate capacities. For Balthasar, however, heaven is more explicitly about the Trinitarian relations. It is the state of being "in" the divine processions that all creation seeks, somehow partaking of those relations in a deeper way than we share in them simply as creatures. Christ accomplishes heaven first in his Resurrection and Ascension, introducing our humanity into his eternal relationships with the Father and Spirit, and as a result of this experience, we are introduced into the divine processions even in this life (through the indwelling of the Son and Spirit that grace enables).

The end, once more, makes sense of the whole for Balthasar. It is the "central mystery of the theo-drama" precisely because it gives meaning to everything that precedes it.[89] Yet in spite of his intellectual boldness, Balthasar does exercise a degree of caution in his eschatological judgments. This area of his thought, after all, is the most speculative and the least defined. Its subject matter includes mysteries that, by his own account, remain hidden with Christ (seated now at the Father's right hand). We relate to them with an attitude of hope, and Balthasar insists that hope is not knowledge. On this side of paradise, we cannot perfectly synthesize our judgments about them, so Balthasar suggests that we ought to interpret his conclusions as expressions of what it is proper for Christians to hope for. When weighing his indebtedness to and divergence from scholastic theology, we ought to read Balthasar as offering significant and often passionate speculations to the mind of the church—his own "reasons for the hope" that is in us (1 Pet 3:15).

Bibliography

Aquinas, Thomas. *Summa theologiae.* Translated by the Fathers of the English Dominican Province. Allen: Christian Classics, 1981.Balthasar, Hans Urs von. "The Fathers, the Scholastics, and Ourselves." *Communio* 24 (1997): 347–96.

Blankenhorn, Bernhard, OP. "Balthasar's Method of Divine Naming." *Nova et Vetera* 1 (2003): 245–68.

Bloch, Ernst. *The Principle of Hope.* Translated by N. and S. Plaice and P. Knight. Oxford: Blackwell, 1986.

Franks, Angela Franz. "Trinitarian *Analogia Entis* in Hans Urs von Balthasar." *The Thomist* 62 (1998): 533–59.

Garrigou-Lagrange, Reginald, OP. *Life Everlasting and the Immensity of the Soul: A Theological Treatise on the Four Last Things: Death, Judgment, Heaven, Hell.* Translated by Patrick Cummins, OSB. Rockford, IL: Tan Books and Publishers, 1991.

Healy, Nicholas. *The Eschatology of Hans Urs von Balthasar: Being as Communion.* Oxford: Oxford University Press, 2005.

Hofer, Andrew. "Balthasar's Eschatology on the Intermediate State: The Question of Knowability." *Logos* 12, no. 3 (2009): 148–72.

---

89. *TD* 5, 285.

Karlson, Henry C. Anthony III. *The Eschatological Judgment of Christ: The Hope of Universal Salvation and the Fear of Eternal Perdition in the Theology of Hans Urs von Balthasar.* Eugene, OR: Wipf and Stock, 2017.

Kilby, Karen. *Balthasar: A (Very) Critical Introduction.* Grand Rapids, MI: Eerdmans, 2012.

Lamb, Matthew. "The Eschatology of St. Thomas Aquinas." In *Aquinas on Doctrine: A Critical Introduction,* edited by Thomas G. Weinandy, OFM, Cap, Daniel A. Keating, and John P. Yocum, 225–40. London: T&T Clark, 2004.

Leget, Carlo. "Eschatology." In *The Theology of Thomas Aquinas,* edited by Rik Van Nieuwenhove and Joseph Wawrykow, 365–85. Notre Dame, IN: University of Notre Dame Press, 2005.

Löwith, Karl. *Meaning in History: The Theological Implications of the Philosophy of History.* Chicago: University of Chicago Press, 1949.

Metz, Johann Baptist. *Faith in History and Society: Toward a Practical Fundamental Theology.* Translated by J. Matthew Ashley. New York: Crossroad, 2007.

———. *Theology of the World.* New York: Seabury, 1969.

Moltmann, Jürgen. *Theology of Hope: On the Ground and Implications of a Christian Eschatology.* Translated by James W. Leitch. New York: Harper and Row, 1967.

Nichols, Aidan, OP. *No Bloodless Myth: A Guide Through Balthasar's Dramatics.* Washington, DC: The Catholic University of America Press, 2000.

Oakes, Edward T. "The Internal Logic of Holy Saturday in the Theology of Hans Urs von Balthasar." *International Journal of Systematic Theology* 9, no. 2 (2007): 184–99.

O'Regan, Cyril. *Theology and the Spaces of Apocalyptic.* Milwaukee: Marquette University Press, 2009.

Pitstick, Alyssa Lyra. *Light in Darkness: Hans Urs von Balthasar and the Catholic Doctrine of Christ's Descent into Hell.* Grand Rapids, MI: Eerdmans, 2007.

Ratzinger, Joseph. *Eschatologie-Tod und ewiges Leben.* Regensburg: Friedrich Pustet Verlag, 1977.

Roten, Johann, SM. "The Two Halves of the Moon: Marian Anthropological Dimensions in the Common Mission of Adrienne von Speyr and Hans Urs von Balthasar." In *Hans Urs Von Balthasar: His Life and Work,* edited by David L. Schindler, 65–86. San Francisco: Ignatius, 1991.

von Speyr, Adrienne. *John.* Vol. 2, *The Discourses of Controversy.* Translated by Brian McNeil. San Francisco: Ignatius, 1993.

———. *Die katholischen Briefe.* Vol. I, *Der Jakobusbrief. Die Petrusbriefe.* Einsiedeln: Johannesverlag, 1961.

Troeltsch, Ernst. *The Christian Faith.* Minneapolis, MN: Fortress Press, 1991.

Wainwright, Geoffrey. "Eschatology." In *The Cambridge Companion to Hans Urs von Balthasar,* edited by Edward T. Oakes, SJ, and David Moss, 113–30. Cambridge: Cambridge University Press, 2004.

Polyphonic Harmony
Beyond Polemical Opposition

MICHAEL WALDSTEIN

ST. THOMAS AQUINAS LISTENED ATTENTIVELY to the distinct voices of the theological tradition. He listened to scripture with its two testaments, each holding many different writings within itself. He listened to "the Saints," as he often calls the fathers of the church, and to the *Magistri* up to his own time. He disagrees on important points with some of them, even with St. Augustine. As a rule, however, he hears the many voices as standing in harmony. Polyphonic harmony rather than polemical opposition is the normal way in which the voices of the Catholic theological tradition can be heard together.

It is thus surprising that Thomas and Balthasar are often placed in polemical opposition to each other. The purpose of this epilogue is to suggest that one should hear them as related in the normal pattern of voices in Catholic theology, polyphonic harmony.

My immersion in Thomas and Balthasar began before polemical opposition became a pattern expected by many. Taken together, they are parts of a great synthesis of the Catholic tradition, which opens into prayer and the liturgy as a single movement toward the Father. I experienced the solidity of this synthesis in contrast to the liberal Protestant scripture scholarship (Bultmann school) that surrounded me as a doctoral student at Harvard Divinity School.

In a lecture at Catholic University in Washington, D.C., Balthasar located himself in the landscape of European theology, not with theologians who take the human desire for God as their point of departure (Blondel, Marechal, Rahner) but with two exegetes, Heinrich Schlier and Heinz Schürmann, as well as Louis Bouyer. He describes these theologians as

> overwhelmed by the Word of God in the way the beloved is overwhelmed by the declaration of the lover: "I love you because you are you"; or as one is overwhelmed by a great work of art—of Bach or Mozart, of Poussin or Dante—by something that is unmistakably unique and bears the imprint of grace. This approach cannot be described as "extrinsicist," to use an expression of the modernists.

God can reveal and give himself as he is: in the glorious radiance of his love right up to the folly of the cross. This love needs no other proof than itself. It is unique and cannot be invented by man. It was not invented by the early church, and it cannot be surpassed by any human effort.[1]

SALZBURG (1971–1973)

My parents were members of a lay religious community (the *Gemeinschaft*) inspired by the Benedictine order. Dietrich von Hildebrand (1889–1977) helped in the founding and was an active member until his death.[2] He lived in New York but often spent summers in Europe. He regularly visited my family, and we went on trips with him. True to its Benedictine inspiration, one characteristic of the *Gemeinschaft* was wakeful openness and love for beauty in all its forms. As we Waldstein children grew up (I am the second of six), Hildebrand organized meetings in which he opened our ears more fully to Bach, Mozart, Beethoven, Schubert, Wagner—and our eyes to Michelangelo, Giorgione, and Titian. On trips to Florence, Venice, and Rome, he helped us to see the beauty of landscapes, architecture, and cities. He also gave talks about love between man and woman and about marriage and family life, in many ways close to John Paul II's *Theology of the Body*.

In 1971, my junior year in high school, I became friends with a Swiss seminarian, Erich Häring, who was studying theology in Salzburg. He had just discovered the writings of Hans Urs von Balthasar. Full of fresh enthusiasm, he introduced me to the first volume of *Glory: A Theological Aesthetics*. I had been reading Nietzsche and felt the fascinating seductive power of his writings. Balthasar, so it seemed to me, was able to respond to Nietzsche on the same level, eye to eye, in German prose of similar wealth and pith. Reading English translations of Balthasar, including my own, is—in sharp contrast—like riding a bicycle on a street of cobblestones.

What struck me increasingly about Balthasar was his astonishing openness and breadth of vision:

This man is perhaps the most cultivated of his time. If there is a Christian culture, then here it is! Classical antiquity, the great European literatures, the metaphysical tradition, the history of religions, the diverse

---

1. Hans Urs von Balthasar, "Current Trends in Catholic Theology and the Responsibility of the Christian," *Communio* 5 (1978): 77–85, at 80, 81–82.

2. Wolfgang Waldstein, "Der Weg der Herz Jesu Gemeinschaft, in *Herz Jesu Gemeinschaft: Auswahl aus frühen Schriften,* ed. Wolfgang Waldstein (Salzburg: Herz Jesu Gemeinschaft, 2006), 13–29.

exploratory adventures of contemporary man and, above all, the sacred sciences, St. Thomas, St. Bonaventure, patrology (all of it)—not to speak just now of the Bible—none of them that is not welcomed and made vital by this great mind.[3]

I experienced Balthasar's writings as a confirmation of the faith I had received as a child, as a deepening of that faith in a new key. For Christmas in 1971, my parents gave me the first volume of Balthasar's theological aesthetics. In the summer of 1972, I worked in the packaging department of a pharmaceutical plant in Switzerland to earn enough money to buy the remaining six volumes of that work and others by Balthasar. With Erich Häring's help, I made my way through a good part of volume 1 of the aesthetics, the introductory account of the perception of glory. A little later, I began the voyage through volume 4, which discusses glory in the ancient world, beginning with Homer. In my high school Greek class, we had been reading Homer's Iliad, painfully laboring with the Greek grammar, mostly blind to the beauty of the text, but Balthasar helped me see the greatness of Homer.

Most important, I was fascinated by Balthasar's particular love for the Gospel of John and by the depth of his reading of that Gospel. I decided then and there that I would study scripture, especially the Gospel of John, and that decision has stood the test of time.

Through members of the *Gemeinschaft* living in New York, my parents heard about Thomas Aquinas College (TAC) and its great books program. The breadth of readings and the format of tutorial discussion attracted me. It seemed in many ways like Balthasar's openness in familiarizing himself with all the great authors of the literary, philosophical, and theological tradition. This likeness was one of the reasons why I decided to attend TAC.

When Hildebrand heard that I was going to attend TAC, he took me aside for an extended conversation to warn me earnestly against Thomas's main errors. I still remember the seven items in the syllabus of errors.

ERROR 1: Knowledge of necessary truths is reached through the senses. TRUTH: What we sense is always contingent, not necessary. There must be direct independent contact with necessary essences—ultimately ideal essences in the divine mind.

ERROR 2: Matter is the principle of individuation. TRUTH: Persons have a higher form of individuality than that of matter.

ERROR 3: The human person is a single substantial whole. TRUTH: The human person is composed of body and soul.

---

3. Henri de Lubac, "A Witness of Christ in the Church: Hans Urs von Balthasar," in Henri de Lubac, *The Church: Paradox and Mystery* (New York: Ecclesia Press, 1969), 103–21, at 105.

Error 4: Happiness is the end of human life. Truth: The inner objective goodness of things, above all the infinite goodness of God, is not a mere means for producing an affective state of happiness in oneself.

Error 5: The essence of goodness is desirability. Truth: Desirability is a result of intrinsic goodness, not constitutive of it.

Error 6: Virtue is a habit of acting according to the mean. Truth: Habit makes acts mindlessly automatic while virtue increases awareness of the good.

Error 7: The primary meaning of marriage is procreation. Truth: The primary inner meaning of marriage is the union of love between man and woman. Procreation is its primary external end.

Thomas Aquinas College (1973–1977)

In loyalty to Hildebrand's corrections, I fought against the seven errors during my years at TAC. Mark Berquist, the outstanding tutor at TAC, whose brilliance and patience I came to respect highly, discussed the issues with me often and for hours. I resisted as best I could, which often was not very good at all. Still, my attachment to Hildebrand was strong. On many other questions, Aristotle and Thomas began to make much sense.

As a steady companion of the texts assigned at TAC, I studied what Balthasar has to say about them. He comments on almost all of them, often in much detail. Even when he disagrees with them, he does not encapsulate himself against them and keep them at arm's length, but rather is able to enter them with a loving and supple regard. A characteristic example is his treatment of his main opponent, Hegel.[4]

The track of reading Balthasar ran peacefully next to my other studies, although I became aware of differences and tensions. Controversy focused on the issues in Hildebrand's syllabus of errors. Few of Balthasar's works had been translated into English. He was not a subject of conversation at TAC, and I was alone in reading him.

In the summer between junior and senior years, my family vacationed as usual with our Swiss cousins on a farm in the Swiss Jura Mountains. Balthasar lived not far from there in Basel. I wrote to him, asking him to help me understand some difficult passages in the aesthetics. He invited me to visit him and was generous with his time. I was struck by how tall he was and what strength he radiated. I felt quite shy and remembered the imperative "Do not be afraid!" that often shields the appearing of supernatural powers in scripture. Shyness gave way to joy about Balthasar's lucid and gentle explanations. At

---

4. A brilliant analysis of Balthasar's treatment of Hegel can be found in Cyril O'Regan, *The Anatomy of Misremembering: Von Balthasar's Response to Philosophical Modernity*, vol. 1, *Hegel* (New York: Crossroad, 2014).

the end of our meeting, he wrote a short dedication into my copy of volume 1 of *Glory*, here translated into English.

> Cordially dedicated to Mr. Michael Waldstein
> Hans Balthasar.
> When the house becomes transparent, the stars belong to the feast as well.
> Hofmannsthal

Balthasar's decided option for Aristotle against Plato in the opening paragraphs of his aesthetics made me ready to learn about the unity of human nature from "the Philosopher." I came to doubt Hildebrand's objections against sensation as the basis of knowledge and his Platonic/Cartesian understanding of the distinction between body and soul. Berquist's arguments on this issue increasingly rang true. The following passage of the aesthetics impressed itself on me like a hot seal:

> Plato went back behind the primal phenomenon by conceiving of a soul that fell into matter only at a secondary point in time later in its existence, understandably, because he thought he could save the unity of what dissolved in death only by locating that unity in a separated (abstract, absolute) spiritual mode of being. For the sake of the spirit's freedom and dignity, he turned the primordial into something derivative and became the father of all those who replace the "symbol" (truth-sign) by "allegory" (otherwise-speech) and of all those who ask in a wholly superfluous and only apparently scientific mindset how (psychologically) and by what supposed "conclusions" the soul can get out of its inwardness to reach the so-called outside world. Aristotle remained loyal to the phenomenon: man and the world showed themselves in their *Gestalt*,[5] but the limit became clear as well: the impossibility of interpreting or constructing a promise of human wholeness beyond earthly life. Greek tragedy had been the cry of transient existence at this limit. Only the gift of God from the new earth and the flesh that rises into eternal life can give true rest to this question and prevent falling back into heightened Platonism, which has done so much damage even to Christian theology.[6]

The phrase *but the limit became clear as well* is translated differently in Erasmo Leiva's usually excellent translation. It reads: *Aristotle's limitations*

---

5. The usual translation of *Gestalt* by *form* is confusing if one understands *form* along the lines of Aristotle's *morphe*. Balthasar follows Goethe's use of *Gestalt*. Definition: *Gestalt* is a being in its sensible appearance or this sensible appearance itself inasmuch as it is united from within by an expression of its inner life and nature.

6. Hans Urs von Balthasar, *Herrlichkeit: Eine theologische Ästhetik*, vol. 1, *Schau der Gestalt* (Einsiedeln: Johannes Verlag, 1961) 18–19.

also became clear.[7] The German has no reference to Aristotle in this phrase. It is not one of Aristotle's limitations but one of his strengths, he affirms the bodily nature of human beings so clearly and firmly that an objective limit becomes clear, namely, the impossibility of answering the question of human wholeness after death.

UNIVERSITY OF DALLAS (1977–1981)

I planned to begin scripture studies right away after TAC, but my father advised me to study philosophy first. As a historian of Roman law, he had come to see that conflicting interpretations of texts are usually due to conflicting philosophical starting points. He suggested that I enter the PhD program at the University of Dallas, where three Hildebrand students were teaching: Josef Seifert, John Crosby, and Damian Fedoryka.

I followed his advice, still hoping to find an intellectual home in Hildebrand's phenomenology. As the discussions unfolded in Dallas, I was surprised to realize that I was turning into a Thomist, or rather, that I had already become one, especially on the unity of human nature. Memories of the discussions with Mark Berquist returned. My attitude had changed, and the eyes of my mind were open to see the strength of his arguments.

In the last four points of his syllabus of errors, Hildebrand uses the key terms with a different meaning. In ERROR 4, Aristotle's word *eudaimonia* and Thomas's *felicitas/beatitudo* do not, as Hildebrand assumes, refer to an affective state of joy. They refer to a life about which one can say "it is good," good not only in some respects but completely and finally good.[8] The affective state of joy (the predominant meaning of happiness in modern languages) is one of the fruits of a life that is finally good, "a *per se* accident of it" (*ST* I-II, q. 3, a. 4, corp.).

IN ERROR 5: According to Thomas, *good* is one of the first notions, like *being*. It cannot be grasped by anything before it. The only way to grasp it more distinctly is to look at characteristic effects of the good, such as love and desire: The definition, "The good is what all desire" is the definition of a cause in light of its effect.[9]

IN ERROR 6: in contrast to the usual meaning of English *habit*, Greek *hexis*, and Latin *habitus* do not signify a semiconscious automatic pattern of acting but instead any lasting disposition to act (see *ST* I-II, qq. 49–55). As for the mean, it is not a mere average but found *by conformity to reason* (*ST* I-II, q. 64, a. 1, ad 2).

---

7. *GL*, 21.

8. Michael Waldstein, "Dietrich von Hildebrand and St. Thomas Aquinas on Goodness and Happiness," *Nova et Vetera* 1 (2003): 403–64, at 449–51.

9. Waldstein, "Hildebrand and St. Thomas on Goodness and Happiness," 414–29.

In Error 7: Hildebrand assumes that *primary* and *secondary end* express a hierarchy of importance or preference among the ends of marriage, that the union of love between husband and wife is downplayed as of secondary importance. In the context of answering the question, *What is marriage? primary* and *secondary* do not have this meaning. In this context, an end is called *primary* if it is the end that gives to a being or an act *what that being or act is* in its specific nature. For example, when one asks, *What are eyes?* one turns to the act of seeing. *Seeing* is the end that gives to eyes *what they are.* Eyes can have other ends, and these ends can be primary in the sense of being more important in some circumstances, such as "You have ravished my heart, my sister, my bride; you have ravished my heart with a glance of your eyes" (Song of Songs 4:9).[10] If one takes *primary* and *secondary* as Hildebrand does, then among the traditional list of three ends, "*fides, proles, saramentum* (faithful union, children, and sacrament," sacrament is the best and thus primary good of marriage.[11]

Balthasar's aesthetics convinced me of the importance of maintaining the unity of human nature as bodily, sensory, and intellectual together. Berquist's arguments had done their part, yet, I found it difficult to work out a detailed account. [12] I read and re-read relevant texts in Aristotle's *Physics* and *De anima* with Thomas's commentary and corresponding passages in the *Summa, Contra gentiles,* the disputed questions *De anima,* and other works. I found help in new discussions with Berquist and also found answers to some of my questions in John of St. Thomas's, *Cursus Philosophicus Thomisticus.*[13]

Most illuminating is a passage in Thomas's disputed questions *De spiritualibus creaturis* (a. 3, corp.), which gives an account of the root difference between Plato and Aristotle:

> The difference between these two views comes from the following: in searching for the truth about the nature of things, some began from intelligible accounts (*ex rationibus intelligibilibus*), which was characteristic of the Platonists, others from sensible things, which was characteristic of Aristotle's philosophy.

---

10. For a discussion of Hildebrand's understanding of marriage and his critique of the Thomistic account, see Waldstein, *Glory of the Logos in the Flesh,* 174–200, 287–95.

11. Thomas, *IV Sent.,* d. 31, q. 1, a. 3 = *Supplementum,* q. 49, a. 3.

12. See the chapter "The Logos of Nature in Aristotle's Physics," in Michael Waldstein, *Glory of the Logos in the Flesh: St. John Paul's Theology of the Body* (Ave Maria, FL: Sapientia Press, 2021), 258–300.

13. John of St. Thomas, *Cursus Philosophicus Thomisticus: Natural philosophy Part One: On mobile being in general* (Turin: Marietti, 1933), esp. q. 3, *On materia prima,* 55–83; *Part Four: On ensouled mobile being* (Turin: Marietti, 1937), esp. q. 1, *On the soul in general and its definitions,* 12–38; and q. 9, *On the rational soul in itself,*" 278–95.

Hildebrand's phenomenological starting point in *the given* closely resembles the Platonic starting point in *intelligible accounts* since sensible things are received and thus given to the human mind according to the mode of the recipient. Due to this starting point, Hildebrand tends not to focus on aspects of the given that arise from the mode of the recipient, from the human way of knowing, as opposed to aspects that belong to sensible things in themselves. In the order of logic, the genus *body* and the specific differences *living, sentient*, and *rational* lie outside each other. Not all bodies are alive, not every living being is sentient, and not every sentient being is rational. In the human person, by contrast, they are not outside each other. They are aspects of one single *What it is*.[14] Among the many bodies that make up our world, some bodies are somebody.

This unity of one essence is reflected in the dependence of understanding on sensation. "For the understanding to understand its own object in act it must turn to sensible appearances (*phantasmata*), in order to watch the universal nature as it exists in the particular" (*ST* I, q. 84, a. 7, c). Balthasar's comment on this text is "*verissimum!*" Balthasar's aesthetics can be understood as unfolding the encounter with real beings made possible by the power Thomas calls *vis cogitativa* or *ratio particularis*. This power and its achievement are often neglected. Many tend to jump immediately from the five senses and their objects (color and shape) to the intellect and its universal object. We do not merely reach a universal understanding of color and shape but of the acts and nature of the being whose color and shape they are. How do we recognize that a particular color and shape are those of a human being? There is relatively little reflection on this intermediate step among Thomists, yet without this step, there could be no understanding of human nature. Balthasar, by contrast, gives a detailed account of this transition, most detailed in the first volume of *Theo-Logic*.[15]

There is a close connection between turning to *phantasmata* and the Johannine theme of *remembering* Jesus (Jn 2:17; 2:22; 12:16; 14:26; 15:20; 16:4): "The retrospective remembering and *anamnesis* of what has been seen—the *conversio ad phantasma* (*verissimum!*)—constitutes the basis of understanding anything."[16] For us who live two millennia later and do not immediately see and touch Jesus as the apostles did, the place for such remembrance instituted by Jesus himself and passed on by the apostles is the liturgy, which joins reading about Jesus in the Gospels with the celebration of the Eucharist "in memory (*anamnesis*) of me" (Lk 22:19; cf. 1 Cor 11:24).

---

14. Waldstein, *Glory of the Logos in the Flesh*, 265–87.

15. *TL* 1, esp. 143–200; *Theo-Logic I*, 131.

16. *Herrlichkeit* 1, 27; *GL* 1, 30.

A good preparation for studying the Gospel of John, I thought on these foundations, would be to write a doctoral dissertation on Balthasar's philosophical aesthetics, focusing on the act of perception, with special attention to the unity between the outward perceptible appearance and the expression of the person's inner life in that sensible appearance.[17]

Biblicum, Rome (1981–1984)

Much time and effort at the Biblicum goes into learning the languages needed for biblical studies (Greek, Hebrew, Aramaic, Coptic, Italian, French, Spanish). Still, I continued reading Balthasar and began reading Thomas's scripture commentaries, especially his lectures on John.

The Biblicum's John scholar at that time was Ignace de La Potterie SJ, a man of immense learning and spiritual depth. He esteemed Balthasar and urged me to continue studying his writings, especially his discussions of the Gospel of John. I took all of de La Potterie's courses that I could fit into my schedule: one of them on the Prologue to John for an entire semester; several on other passages or themes in John; the course on biblical hermeneutics, in which he made much use of Balthasar's aesthetics; and a seminar on patristic exegesis, for which I wrote a paper on the agony in the garden according to Maximus the Confessor, relying mainly on Balthasar's monograph on Maximus.[18] De La Potterie's mastery as an interpreter of John is particularly evident in his analysis of literary structure and the theological significance of that structure.[19] I took courses with similarly excellent teachers, among them Albert Vanhoye, SJ (Hebrews, Synoptics) and Luis Alonso Schökel, SJ (Job and Psalms). Alonso, who had a rich literary sensibility in reading scripture, admired the excellent degree of this sensibility in Balthasar.

Before my wife Susie and I moved to Rome in 1981, I wrote to Balthasar, asking him to suggest persons in Rome who knew his work. He sent me contact information for Jacques Servais, SJ, now Rector of the Casa Balthasar in Rome, and Marc Ouellet, now Cardinal Prefect of the Congregation for Bishops. Their friendship became a great gift for me. Jacques Servais took us to

---

17. Michael Waldstein, "Expression and Form: Principles of a Philosophical Aesthetics according to Hans Urs von Balthasar" (PhD diss. in philosophy, University of Dallas, 1981).

18. Hans Urs von Balthasar, *Kosmische Liturgie: Das Weltbild Maximus des Bekenners* (Einsiedeln: Johannes Verlag, 1961); *CL.*

19. The rich fruits of analyzing literary structure are evident in his main work, the two-volume monograph on *truth* in John, *La Vérité dans Saint Jean*, vol. 1, part 1, "Le Christ et la verité," and part 2, "L'Esprit et la verité"; vol. 2, "Le croyant et la verité," 2nd ed. (Rome: Pontifical Biblical Institute, 1999); references to Balthasar are indexed in vol. 2, 1120, middle column.

the Sunday mass of the movement *Communion and Liberation* in the basilica Santa Maria in Trastevere. In the piazza after Mass, we met a young philosopher who knew Balthasar's works well, Massimo Borghesi.[20] His wife, Carmen, and he had a child the same age as our first, and we became friends and spent time together. He told us that a close friendship had sprung up between Balthasar and Luigi Giussani, the founder of *Communion and Liberation*. Susie and I were attracted to the experience of this movement, and we have been members of it ever since.

Through Jacques Servais, I met Fr. Christoph Schönborn, who was teaching at the Angelicum. He was thrilled by the curriculum and pedagogy of Thomas Aquinas College. A renewal of theological education, he said, was urgent, and one could learn from this example. Studying the great masters of theology would sharpen the sense for quality in theology. Balthasar's greatest strength, he said, lay in the reading of scripture, of the fathers, and of key figures of the theological tradition. He was more hesitant about Adrienne von Speyr's teaching about the passion and death of Jesus.

One of my fellow students in the Hebrew class (1981–1982) was Fr. Thomas Herron, Cardinal Ratzinger's American secretary. "The Cardinal likes to meet students," he told me, and suggested setting up an appointment for me. I agreed, but on the bus from Piazza Venezia to the Palazzo del Sant'Uffizio, I became anxious: Why should I waste the Cardinal's time? I had no reason, no issue to discuss with him.

Cardinal Ratzinger came into the room with amazingly gracious and gentle simplicity. He put me at ease right away. He spoke with me as if he had nothing else to do, as if he and I were the only persons in Rome. We discussed John 1:1 (the Logos is God) and 1:14 (the Logos became flesh) and the hymn in Philippians 2:5–11, according to which the one who "was in the form of God emptied himself" to the cross and was glorified. Cardinal Ratzinger had read most of the scholarly literature I was reading and remembered it in detail. I told him about my desire to follow both Thomas and Balthasar as teachers, and he urged me to continue studying both, together with the Greek and Latin fathers.

He explained that one should see different levels of Balthasar's work. One of them is his insistent and searching reading of scripture, the primary level. Another is his rich and deep presentation of the tradition. The third is his own systematic theological vision, much of it received from Adrienne von Speyr rather than developed by himself out of the desire for breaking through to something novel, which governs much of academic life.

---

20. A recent insightful publication is Massimo Borghesi, *The Mind of Pope Francis: Jorge Mario Bergoglio's Intellectual Journey* (Collegeville, MN: Liturgical Press, 2017), which shows, among other factors, the deep roots of Bergoglio's thought in Romano Guardini, one of Pope Benedict's favorite authors.

He added that one needs to avoid Luther's thesis that Jesus suffered the pains of damnation because damnation means fixed and frozen hatred of God. Balthasar himself writes, "The state of sin is experienced by Jesus in a way that cannot be identical with the way in which sinners, who hate God, would have to experience it."[21] "The work of Jesus goes in a direction exactly opposed to that of hell. Hell is hatred . . . while the work of Christ is a work of love and of union. The death it demands is the complete contrary of the one that is eternal death."[22] When Balthasar discusses the "descent to hell" (1 Pet 3:19; cf. Eph 4:9; Col 2:15), he makes clear that God's love is at work in the beginning, middle, and end of this descent.

Cardinal Ratzinger's judgment about Balthasar in our conversation was similar to judgments that have been published. The earliest (1961) is a review article that documents Ratzinger's first encounter with Balthasar's writings:

> Balthasar's work is a true gift to theology in our time. The relentless radicality with which he wholly believes and wholly thinks . . . is a sign inspiring the confidence that also in today's world the faith—the whole faith, not merely a watered down makeshift—can be thought, loved, and lived.[23]

In his 1988 funeral homily for Balthasar, Cardinal Ratzinger explained why Pope John Paul II wanted to create him a Cardinal:

> What the Pope wanted to express with this gesture of recognition, even revering [*Verehrung*], remains valid: not merely individuals and private [persons] but the Church itself in its official responsibility tells us that he was a right teacher [*rechter Lehrer*] of the faith, a sign-post pointing to the sources of living water—a witness of the word from whom we can learn Christ, from whom we can learn life. . . . We ask our Lord to enable us to keep alive the great testimony of this servant of his and to pass it on.[24]

In an interview with Peter Seewald, Pope Benedict describes the first impression he had of Balthasar when he wrote the 1961 review quoted above:

---

21. *Theodramatik III*, 313; *TD* 4, 336.

22. *Theodramatik III*, 313, n. 10; *TD* 4, 336, n. 10. See also the five-point summary "The Main Features of Atonement in the New Testament," *Theodramatik III*, 221–24; *TD* 4, 240–43, in which the love of God is always primary.

23. Karl Ratzinger, "Christlicher Universalismus: Zum Aufsatzwerk Hans Urs v. Balthasars," *Hochland* 54 (1961/62): 68–76, reprinted in Walter Kasper, ed., *Logik der Liebe und Herrlichkeit Gottes. Hans Urs von Balthasar im Gespräch* (Ostfildern: Grünewald Verlag, 2006), 14–24, at 24.

24. Cardinal Ratzinger, "Ein Mann der Kirche in der Welt," in *Hans Urs von Balthasar: Gestalt und Werk*, ed. Karl Lehmann and Walter Kasper (Cologne: Communio, 1989), 349–54, at 353 and 354. The quote is from Augustine, *serm.* 88.5; PL 38:542.

Benedict XVI: He was a true aristocrat, tall, lean, noble, restrained in an aristocratic way. We simply understood each other very well, from the very first moment.

Seewald: What is special about this, after all, very intense relationship.

Benedict XVI: I suddenly became aware of him in 1961 when the journal Hochland asked me to review two recent books of his. . . . Of course, to write a good review this meant I had to read the books carefully and thoroughly. Ever since then, the name Balthasar has been a household name for me. Here was the theology of the Fathers, a spiritual vision of theology that is truly developed from faith and from a contemplation that enters the depth. This is why it is also new. It is not just academic material that in the end one doesn't know what to do with, but the synthesis of learned scholarship, true professionalism, and spiritual depth. This is what convinced me about him. From then on there was a bond between us. . . . Although I cannot keep up with his scholarship, the vision as such was shared.

Seewald: You couldn't keep up with him?

Benedict XVI: No, absolutely not. Truly not. It is unbelievable what this man has written and achieved.[25]

Some years after our first meeting, Cardinal Ratzinger invited me to join a group of usually about ten to twelve theologians who met with him once a year to discuss some theological topic. Particularly memorable was a session in which he spoke about Emmaus (Lk 24:13–35) as a pattern of the church's liturgy: Jesus first quotes and interprets scripture and then gives himself in the breaking of bread. My contribution to the session was an account of the wedding at Cana as a symbolic prepresentation of Golgotha and thus as parallel to the Eucharistic liturgy, which is a real representation of Golgotha.

Pope Benedict asked me to serve as a helper at the 2008 Synod of Bishops on scripture. The task of helpers was to listen to the contributions of the Synod fathers, to study them in their written form, and then to draw up a systematic account of them for Cardinal Marc Ouellet, the relator of the Synod. Different topics were assigned to different helpers, and the topic assigned to me was the truth of scripture, including the question of inerrancy, which was hotly debated at the Synod.[26]

---

25. Benedict XVI, *Letzte Gespräche mit Peter Seewald* (Munich: Droemer, 2016), 172.

26. Based on this experience, I wrote the essay *"Analogia Verbi:* The Truth of Scripture in Rudolf Bultmann and Raymond Brown," *Letter & Spirit* 6 (2010): 93–140.

Harvard (1984–1988)

Harvard was an environment altogether different from the Biblicum. The field of New Testament Studies, I found after arriving at the Divinity School, had come to be defined as "History of Religions from Alexander the Great to Constantine." Helmut Koester, Rudolf Bultmann's last doctoral student, was the dominant figure in the department. I had to sift through what was valid and less valid in this way of reading the New Testament. I became more aware of my vast and lasting ignorance by learning much and asking many questions I had not thought to ask before.

As the topic for my dissertation, I chose a topic dear to Balthasar, "The Obedience of Jesus in the Gospel of John." The written proposal had to be distributed to all students and faculty a week before the seminar that was to evaluate the proposal. Helmut Koester, my thesis director, opened the seminar with a bang. "Obedience is the root of all evil." I was stunned. One of my fellow students laughed, "But you *do* want your students to do what you say, don't you." Koester laughed to shrug it off, but the point was quite true and serious.

I obediently changed my topic from obedience to the mission of Jesus, the other side of the same coin, and included a comparison with Secret John, a Gnostic text preserved in four Coptic manuscripts.[27] After I had written much of the dissertation, Koester sent me a formal letter in which he wrote, "Unless I see that you are willing to hate the Gospel of John and consider it heretical, I cannot accept your work because it will not have the scholarly objectivity demanded by the open academic culture of Harvard." I made the mistake of writing back in anger, stating that I would rather work as a gas station attendant for the rest of my life than be a scripture scholar on these terms. How could I receive communion together with others while inwardly denying communion by committing myself to noncommitment? It was not a prudent way of answering. Disaster was certain, I thought.

But the arrival of a prominent visiting professor, Tjitze Baarda of the University of Utrecht, unexpectedly prevented the disaster. Baarda liked the dissertation, particularly the discussion of Bultmann, and volunteered to serve on the committee. In deference to him, Koester allowed the dissertation to come up for defense, which already implied passing it.[28]

---

27. Frederick Wisse and I produced a critical edition of the four Coptic manuscripts in which this text has come down to us. See Michael Waldstein and Frederik Wisse, *The Apocryphon of John: Synopsis of Nag Hammadi Codices II,1 III,1 and IV,1 with BG 8502,2*, Nag Hammadi Studies 33 (Leiden: Brill, 1995).

28. Michael Waldstein, "The Mission of Jesus in John: Probes into the *Apocryphon of John* and the Gospel of John" (ThD thesis, Harvard Divinity School, 1989).

The pressure that came out openly and explicitly in Koester's letter had been there all along in various ways and had weighed on me painfully. The life of Communion and Liberation (CL) in Cambridge, the web of friendships built up by it, was a source of strength to continue as a Catholic theologian, even under pressure. In these years, Luigi Giussani (Don Gius, as people in CL often call him) often visited the United States to help begin the life of CL in the new American setting. Since I knew Italian and English, I regularly served as his translator. I sat next to him during his talks. He would say a sentence in Italian and I would repeat it in English. It was a good way for me to learn. I came to love him and his charisma dearly.

I found the most substantial intellectual help for standing up under the pressure in two tracks of reading. One was Balthasar's *Theodramatik*. With its focus on the good, it is the true heart of Balthasar's great trilogy of aesthetics, dramatics, and logic. I began reading through it in my study carrel in the Divinity School Library, which was at times rather noisy. Cardinal Law offered me a peaceful place, a desk, and bookshelves at the *John Paul II Center for Christian Anthropology* in Cambridge. Fr. Francis George (later Archbishop of Chicago) was there to work on a book about John Paul II,[29] as was Kenneth Schmitz, also working on a book about John Paul II.[30] It was good to be with them, to have occasional conversations with them, and to read slowly through *Theodramatik*.

The second track of sustained reading was Thomas's commentary on the Gospel of John. On Fridays, I drove out to Worcester to meet with Duane Berquist, Mark Berquist's brother, to study the commentary with him. I found a masterful teacher in him.

Despite tensions between the two tracks, I experienced Balthasar and Thomas together as a source of peace, clarity, and strength.[31]

NOTRE DAME (1988–1996)

In 1985, Cardinal Ratzinger organized a celebration in Rome for Balthasar's 80th birthday. It began with a concert in Castel Sant'Angelo and

---

29. Francis George, *Inculturation and Ecclesial Communion: Culture and Church in the Teaching of Pope John Paul II* (Rome: Urbaniana University Press, 1990).

30. Kenneth L. Schmitz, *At the Center of the Human Drama: The Philosophical Anthropology of Karol Wojtyła / Pope John Paul II* (Washington, DC: The Catholic University of America Press, 1993).

31. I reflected on what I learned on the two tracks in Michael Waldstein, "The Analogy of Mission and Obedience: A Central Point in the Relation between *Theologia* and *Oikonomia* in St. Thomas Aquinas's *Commentary on John*," in *Reading John with St. Thomas Aquinas*, ed. Michael Dauphinais and Matthew Levering (Washington, DC: The Catholic University of America Press, 2005), 92–112.

continued with dinner in the circle of ramparts on top of the castle. The view of Rome from the ramparts is high and open, making it a splendid and joyful event. On the way into the castle, I met David Schindler for the first time in person. We had been in contact when he published an article on Balthasar I had submitted to *Communio*.[32] We became friends immediately, in large measure due to the shared love for Balthasar.

In 1988, when I was still working on the dissertation, Schindler arranged for Notre Dame to offer me a position in the Program of Liberal Studies (PLS), the great books program at Notre Dame in which he himself was a faculty member. The offer was subject to the condition that I would finish the dissertation within the year. I had little hope of doing so until Tjitze Baarda entered the stage of the drama as an unexpected *deus ex machina*. Schindler and I were colleagues in PLS for four years, until his move to the John Paul II Institute. In these years, the friendship with him intensified and our collaboration increased. I came to esteem him, and still esteem him highly, as a man of exceptional intelligence, depth, and charity.

I learned much from Schindler, even something I had no desire to understand, namely, football. Before I went to TAC, I knew football only in the form of soccer. When I first saw American football, it confused me. Why did the players spend much of their time standing on the field doing nothing? Why did they again and again bring the game to a sudden stop, only to stand on the field, again doing nothing? Schindler had played football as a quarterback in high school and knew the game inside out. I learned intricately how intelligent football strategy can be. In addition to Balthasar, football became a love shared between us.

It is a paradox, though an understandable one, that disagreements between friends who share much intellectual ground are likely to cause painful tensions, while much deeper disagreements with people who do not share the same ground are less troubling. Schindler and I organized a seminar on the first volume of Balthasar's theological aesthetics. We worked through the text slowly and carefully, which allowed differences of reading and thinking to show themselves clearly and sharply. In Schindler's judgment, my reading was too objectivist, too little attentive to the subjective dimension of Balthasar's theology, too much in line with, as he put it, "Aristotle's substantialism and essentialism." I did not immediately grasp what this criticism meant and where it came from.

---

32. Michael Waldstein, "Hans Urs von Balthasar's Theological Aesthetics," *Communio* 11 (1984): 13–27. Some years later, I contributed three more articles to *Communio*: "An Introduction to von Balthasar's *The Glory of the Lord*," *Communio* 14 (1987): 12–33; "The Foundations of Bultmann's Work," *Communio* 14 (1987): 115–45; and "The Mission of Jesus and the Disciples in John," *Communio* 17 (1990): 311–33.

Schindler earned a master's degree in philosophy (1972) at Gonzaga University, which familiarized him with the Thomistic tradition, and then studied at Claremont graduate school for a doctorate in religion (1976). Under the leadership of John Cobb, Claremont's religion department was at that time a center of process thought, inspired by John Alfred Whitehead. Schindler aligned himself with Whitehead but criticized aspects of process thought with strength and courage, injecting the voices of Aristotle and Thomas into the debate, voices not always welcome in process thought circles.

In line with process thought, however, Schindler criticized Aristotle as caught up in "essentialism and substantialism" without sufficient understanding of interiority and of relations that are interior and constitutive.[33] Thomas achieved a partial breakthrough by his understanding of *esse* but failed to free himself completely from Aristotle. By stripping away the Aristotelian layer of essentialism and substantialism from Thomas, Schindler proposed, one can bring Thomism into fruitful dialogue with Whiteheadian process thought:

> Gerald Phelan, while pinpointing the metaphysics of *esse* as Aquinas's distinct contribution to philosophy, nonetheless argues that Aquinas couched his insights in the vocabulary of Aristotle, with the result that those insights "still bore the stamp of the essentialism or substantialism of that great Greek thinker." . . . Phelan's article . . . [suggests] an interesting historical situation for the continuing discussion between Thomists and Whiteheadian process philosophers. For is it not the case that much of this discussion has presupposed in Aquinas just the essentialistic, substantialistic, or formalistic horizon of Greek philosophical literature to which Phelan refers? What exactly would result from a Thomism rethought in terms of a metaphysics of *esse* disengaged from such a horizon?[34]

In Aristotle's account, according to Schindler, accidents are added secondarily to substance. They are extrinsic to substance. Substance as such is free of them. This understanding, he argued, makes it impossible to understand intrinsic and constitutive relations, such as the sonship of created persons

---

33. The relevant early writings in chronological order are "Creativity as Ultimate: Reflections on Actuality in Whitehead, Aristotle, Aquinas," *International Philosophical Quarterly* 13 (1973): 161–71; "Knowing as Synthesis: A Metaphysical Prolegomenon to a Critical Christian Philosophy" (PhD diss., Claremont Graduate University, Faculty in Religion, 1976), unpublished; "Whitehead's Challenge to Thomism on God and Creation: The Metaphysical Issues," *International Philosophical Quarterly* 19 (1979): 285–99; "W. Norris Clarke, SJ, *The Philosophical Approach to God*," *Process Studies* 11 (1981): 40–46; and "Whitehead's Inability to Affirm a Universe of Value," *Process Studies* 13 (1983): 117–31.

34. David Schindler, "W. Norris Clarke, SJ, *The Philosophical Approach to God*," 40, quoting Gerald B. Phelan, "The Being of Creatures," *Proceedings of the American Catholic Philosophical Association* 31 (1957): 118–25.

in relation to God. Sonship arises primordially in the depth of created persons when they receive their very being (*esse*) from God. It is not a secondary addition extrinsic to the human person.

I argued in response that seeing accidents as extrinsic to substance runs the danger of understanding them as *beings* in the sense that they themselves have being. The word *substance* seems to be part of the trouble. It suggests something standing under something else, two entities, each of which has being, close to each other but still external to each other. It is less misleading to begin with the Greek word *ousia*, which is conventionally rendered as *substance*. *Ousia* combines the participle of the verb *to be* with the suffix *-ia*, which turns participles into nouns, either into concrete nouns (*being* into *a being*) or abstract nouns (*being* into *beingness*).[35] As an abstract noun, *ousia* can mean *what* a being is, its essence. As a concrete noun, it means *that which has being, a being, a substance*.

How are accidents related to that which has being, to substance?

> To say *a being* (*ens*) is equivalent to saying *that which has being*. This, however, is only substance, which subsists. Accidents, by contrast, are called *beings*, not because they are, but rather because by them themselves something is (*non quia sunt, sed quia magis ipsis aliquid est*), as whiteness is said to be because its subject is white. And therefore he [Aristotle] says that they are not simply called beings, but beings of a being (*entis entia*).[36]

According to this text, only substance has being and is a being. Accidents are called beings not because they are. They do not have being. This cannot mean that they are nothing. How, then, should one understand them?

Thomas's answer is packed into the ablative case of *ipsis*, translated above as *by them themselves* or *in their very own ways*. Accidents are ways of being by which or in which a being (= a substance) has not only its substantial being (its being at all rather than not at all) but also further ways of being that presuppose being at all rather than constituting it. To be a substance is to subsist, that is, *to have being*, taking that phrase absolutely, as *being at all* rather than *not at all*. For a substance to have accidents is for that very same substance *to be*, not absolutely or simply speaking, but in some respect. For example, when I am in the living room, being in the living room is a way in which I have being. It is not my being at all rather than not at all. It presupposes this absolute form of being. I do not cease to be when I walk out of the living room. I only cease to be there. I cease to be in a certain respect rather than absolutely.

---

35. Smyth, *Greek Grammar*, § 840.
36. Thomas, *Ssuper meta.* 12.1, Marietti no. 2419, emphasis added.

To say that being in the living room is an accident is thus in no way to imply that it is additional or external to me. I myself am there. The accident does not have being but I myself have it as a form of being. There is nothing in me, however internal it may be, that escapes being in the living room. When I am there, I am comprehensively there.

Being in the living room can be called an *accident,* not only to signify that it is an *ens entis* but also to signify that it is not necessarily and always present or to signify that it is not a particularly deep or important way of being among my many ways of being. To call a relation an accident in the sense of *ens entis* does not imply that it is an accident in these other senses.

A created person's sonship vis-à-vis God is always and necessarily present. It is primordially constitutive of the inner order that belongs to a creature. When one calls it an accident in the sense of *ens entis,* one says only that it is not the mode of being by which the creature has being, speaking absolutely, that is, by which it has *being at all* rather than *not at all.* One does not increase the necessary presence, centrality, or importance of a relation by denying that it is an accident in the sense of *ens entis.*

In the whole created order, relation cannot subsist: it cannot have its own being. It can only be an *ens entis,* that is, the *being in some respect* of something that has being, simply speaking. In the unlimited ocean of *ipsum esse subsistens,* by contrast, relations necessarily subsist as divine persons.

Several decades after our discussions at Notre Dame, Schindler raised a similar set of questions about my introduction to the translation of John Paul II's *Theology of the Body* (TOB):

> Waldstein rightly emphasizes John Paul's rejection of a Cartesian in favor of an Aristotelian-Thomistic understanding: "the purpose of TOB as a whole," he says, "is to defend the spousal meaning of the body against the alienation between person and body in the Cartesian vision of nature." My question, however, is whether his argument suffices to give us more than Aristotle's human-organic body: in other words, whether what this line of argument gives us in the end is truly a filial-spousal body or indeed person: a body or person understood as gift or love already in its constitutive order qua body and qua person.
>
> On Waldstein's reading, it seems to me, the human person really becomes a matter of love first via his own enactment of the gift of self (*agere*). On such a reading, however, it is more the case that we make the body into a gift than that we reenact in freedom—to be sure, in a new way—what the body itself already signifies and expresses in its very givenness, or giftedness, qua body.[37]

---

37. David Schindler, "The Embodied Person as Gift and the Cultural Task in America: *Status Quaestionis," Communio* 35 (2008): 397–431, at 417–18 and 421.

In my introduction to TOB, I explicitly say the opposite:

Self-gift and fruitfulness are rooted in the very nature of the body, and therefore in the very nature of the person. . . . God's plan and its renewal by Christ, the redeemer, is *imprinted deeply within the bodily nature* of *the person as a pre-given language* of self-giving and fruitfulness.[38]

Schindler is not a careless reader. He has a reason for understanding me as *really* saying the opposite of what I do say. The reason is that I agree with Aristotle's view that relations are accidents, which therefore means I agree that relations are extrinsic rather than intrinsic and constitutive.

Our Aristotles are not the same—which is a good thing. It explains why I can agree with Schindler on a matter that is much more important to both of us. Sonship in relation to God is an interior and constitutive relation that arises at the very root of our being as creatures before any voluntary act: "We are not our own. Belonging to ourselves at its root is always anteriorly a belonging to God and to others, to the entire community of being."[39]

FROM ITI AUSTRIA (1996–2008) TO THE PRESENT

"When you get tenure," my wife Susie said to me after I accepted the position at Notre Dame, "we will buy a grave plot in the Notre Dame graveyard." It was an eloquent expression of her desire to settle down. I did receive tenure, but we did not buy the grave plot. Instead, we moved to Austria because Cardinal Schönborn (then Auxiliary Bishop of Vienna) invited me to help build up the International Theological Institute (ITI) there as its first president.

Pope John Paul II was the prime force behind the institute. He asked the Austrian bishops to establish a theological institute with special focus on marriage and the family, an international institute with students from the West as well as from the former Soviet Bloc. The Austrian Bishops entrusted the task to Bishop Schönborn.

Several times since we first met in Rome, Fr. Schönborn and I had discussed the renewal of theological studies. Among the lights that guided our discussions, two stand out. One is Balthasar as a reader of scripture, the fathers, and other great theologians of the tradition. The other is the great books pedagogy of Thomas Aquinas College, with Thomas Aquinas's writings in a sapiential role.

---

38. Michael Waldstein, "Introduction," in John Paul II, *Man and Woman He Created Them: A Theology of the Body* (Boston: Pauline Books and Media, 2006), 1–128, at 104–5, emphasis added.

39. Schindler, "The Embodied Person as Gift and the Cultural Task in America," 397.

Guided by these lights, we designed the curriculum and reading list of ITI. The *Summa* is a steady companion in many courses. Much room is given to the Greek fathers, especially the Cappadocians and Maximus; to the Latin fathers, especially Hilary and Augustine; to medieval authors such as Richard of St. Victor and Bonaventure; to Doctors of the church, such as Thérèse of Lisieux; and, finally, to more recent theologians such as Scheeben, Guardini, Balthasar, John Paul II, and Ratzinger.

Already in the first year, a set of questions about Trinitarian theology emerged in the life of ITI, and they have remained central in my teaching and writing after the move to Ave Maria (2008–2018) and then Franciscan University. What is the exact status of Augustine's and Thomas's account of the Trinity based on the likeness of the inner word that proceeds in the human mind from knowledge? How is this account related to approaches based on communion between human persons?

> *BALTHASAR:* "One can understand the uncreated person as pure relation to a *you* because the divine Being is pure act" (Leo Scheffczyk). And in the order of creation, the full unfolding of the immanent acts of a person is in the first place the consequence of an interpersonal address and surrender. . . . The relation between persons thus takes first place among the images and likenesses of God's being.[40]

> *JOHN PAUL II: Man became the "image and likeness" of God not only through his own humanity but also through the communion of persons,* which man and woman form from the very beginning. . . . Man becomes an image of God not so much in the act of solitude as in the act of communion. He is, in fact, "from the beginning" an image in which not only the solitude of one Person, who rules the world, mirrors itself but also the inscrutable, essentially divine communion of Persons. (John Paul II, TOB 9:3; emphasis in original)

A learned Thomist who took much interest in the development of ITI earnestly warned me as a friend against the thesis that man and woman are an image of the Trinity:

> Don't go down that path. It leads nowhere. Augustine (*De trinitate* 12.2.5–6) and Thomas (*ST* I, q. 93, a. 6, ad 2) refuted this supposed image of the Trinity. Follow their account of the image of the Trinity in the procession of the inner word. The analogy of the inner word, not the analogy of mutual love, is the heart of Trinitarian theology. It is the most proper theological expression of the church's faith in the Trinity.

---

40. Hans Urs von Balthasar, "Pneuma und Institution," in *Pneuma und Institution: Skizzen zur Theologie IV* (Einsiedeln: Johannes Verlag, 1975), 201–35, at 204n1; Balthasar, "Spirit and Institution," *ET* 4, 210–43, at 211, introductory note.

When I discussed this warning with Bishop Schönborn, he responded that there had been many requests to include the analogy of the inner word in the Catechism. In agreement with Thomas's own understanding of this analogy as an argument from natural reason (*ST* I, q. 32, a. 1, ad 2), the committee for the Catechism chaired by Cardinal Ratzinger decided not to include it. The church's faith in the Trinity, Schönborn added, is expressed by the names *Father, Son, and Holy Spirit*, one God, three persons. God is one but not alone. Thomas, of course, affirms this point:

> Never was the Father alone (*solitarius*) without the Son or Word but always this one, namely the Word, was with God (*Super Ioannem*, ch. 1, lect. 2, Marietti no. 61).
> Alone (*solus*) . . . can in no way be accepted in the divine because one person always has the fellowship of the society of another person, *consortium societatis alterius personae.* (I *Sent.*, d. 21, q. 1, a. 1, qc. 1, c)
> Against being alone, we confess the harmony and bond of love *consonantiam et connexionem amoris.* (*De potentiae*, q. 9, a. 8, c)
> The word alone must be avoided so that one does not take away the fellowship of the three persons (*consortium trium personarum*). (*ST* I, q. 31, a. 2, c)

The image of the Trinity resisted by Augustine and Thomas in *ST* I, q. 93, a. 6, ad 2 posits a specific pattern of relations of origin between Adam, Eve, and their child. Adam is an image of the Father. Adam and Eve's son Seth is an image of the Son. Eve is an image of the Holy Spirit because she comes from Adam without being his daughter. Thomas points out, among other difficulties, that Eve is Seth's mother, but the Holy Spirit is not the origin of the Son. Neither Balthasar nor John Paul II posit the pattern resisted by Thomas.

The overall issue addressed by q. 93, a. 6 is whether the image of God is in man according to the mind alone or also according to the body. The response makes clear that the phrase *according to* focuses on what *first accounts for* the specific likeness required for an image. Man is an image of God while irrational animals are not. The image of God is therefore *seen first* according to what distinguishes man from irrational animals, namely, the rational mind.

Article three of the same question focuses not only on where the image of God is seen *first* but also on where it is seen *secondarily*. The overall issue addressed by the article is whether angels are more to the image of God than man:

> We can speak about the image of God in two ways. In one way with respect to that in which the account of image is *seen first*, which is the intellectual nature. And in this way the image of God is more in angels than in men, because the intellectual nature is more perfect in them.

In a second way, we can consider the image of God in man with respect to that in which it is *seen secondarily*, inasmuch as in man one finds a certain imitation of God, for example, man is from man as God is from God. . . . In these and similar [respects] the image of God is more perfect in man than in an angel.

But in this respect the account of the divine image is not found *per se* in man, except if the first imitation is presupposed, which is according to the intellectual nature. (*ST* I, q. 93, a. 3, c)

The Blackfriars edition of the *ST* translates *secondarily* (*secundario*) as *accidental qualities*: "Secondly, we may consider the image of God in man as regards its accidental qualities." This translation appears to be the root of a widespread misreading of the text according to which Thomas says that the image of God is not found *per se* but only *per accidens* in *man from man*. The negation *not found per se in man from man* in the last sentence quoted above may look like a confirmation of this reading. The negation, however, must be read together with "*except if*," which converts the negation into an affirmation. The divine image "*is found per se* in *man from man* if the first imitation is presupposed." Human generation takes place in a bodily manner similar to generation among animals, but man from man is person from person, somebody from somebody, and, therefore, is *per se* an image of the Trinity. According to Thomas, then, man and woman as origins of a child are *per se* an image of the Trinity.[41]

Two questions were raised above: What is the exact status of Augustine's and Thomas's account of the Trinity based on the likeness of the inner word that proceeds in the human mind from knowledge? How is it related to approaches based on the likeness of the communion of human persons? *ST* I, q. 32, a. 1, ad 2 answers the first of these questions by explaining that the analogy of the inner word is an argument from natural reason. It is a verisimilar argument comparable to the hypotheses about epicycles and eccentrics in Ptolemy's astronomy. It is not a proof either of the existence of processions in God or of their character as processions according to intellect and according to love:[42]

Just as we can know about God that he is but not what he is, so we can know about God that he understands but not how he understands. Conceiving a word in understanding belongs to how God understands. Hence this argument [based on wherever there is knowledge there must be a word] cannot sufficiently prove, but from what is in us it can conjecture in some way by likeness, *ex eo quod est in nobis aliqualiter per simile coniecturare.* (*De potentia*, q. 8, a. 1, ad 12)

---

41. For more detail, see Waldstein, *Glory of the Logos in the Flesh*, 597–605.
42. See Waldstein, *Glory of the Logos in the Flesh*, 619–53.

Despite the limits of the analogy of the word just pointed out, Balthasar sees it as needed for balance in Trinitarian theology, which answers the second question raised above: How is it related to approaches based on the likeness of the communion of human persons? The analogy of the inner word is incomplete because in us, the faculties and acts belong only to one person. The analogy of interpersonal love is likewise incomplete because in God the three persons are one substance.[43] In this way, they complement each other:

> The image of the Trinity in the spiritual realm of creatures . . . can only be unfolded in two series in the order of being and of thought that are related to each other as an antinomy. One is the inner structure of the created spirit. . . . [The other is] the encounter in which the I becomes truly itself by giving itself to a you and both realize themselves in a we in which both overcome any preoccupation with themselves alone. It is only in such transcendence that the first image, the image interior to the spirit, becomes an event. . . . It is thus inappropriate to exclude all use of the second schema out of strict adherence to the first, where likeness with God lies above all in the unity of the spirit, or to declare that a divine you is impossible [within the Trinity]. Conversely, a naïve construction of the divine mystery from relationships between human beings . . . must not take itself to be absolute, because it overlooks the crude anthropomorphism of a plurality of substances. The creaturely image must resign itself to look at one and the same time from its two points of departure in the direction of the mystery of God.[44]

Conclusion: Polyphonic Harmony

The journey sketched above, which began before polemics between Thomists and Balthasarians flared up, convinces me that a nonpolemical way of hearing the voices of Thomas and Balthasar is both possible and desirable. Dismissing one in favor of the other diminishes one's access to the wealth of the Catholic tradition. To follow Thomas, it is not enough to read him. One needs to follow him by doing what he did. He listened to the many voices present in the tradition up to his own time and heard their polyphonic harmony. Placing particular disagreements in the foreground to the point of blinding oneself to the large areas of agreement and complementarity impoverishes theology. Genuine polyphony repays patient listening by the riches it communicates.

---

43. Cf. Maurice Nedoncelle, "L'intersubjectivité humaine est-elle pour saint Augustin une image de la Trinité?" in *Augustinus Magister*, 3 vols. (Paris: Études Augustiniennes, 1954), 1:595–602, at 600.

44. Balthasar, *Theodramatik*, 2/2, 480–82; *TD* 3, 525–26.

BIBLIOGRAPHY

Balthasar, Hans Urs von. "Current Trends in Catholic Theology and the Responsibility of the Christian." *Communio* 5 (1978): 77–85.

Benedict XVI. *Letzte Gespräche mit Peter Seewald*. Munich: Droemer, 2016.

Borghesi, Massimo. *The Mind of Pope Francis: Jorge Mario Bergoglio's Intellectual Journey*. Collegeville, MN: Liturgical Press, 2017.

De La Potterie, Ignace. *La Vérité dans Saint Jean*. Vol. 1, pt. 1: "Le Christ et la verité"; pt. 2: "L'Esprit et la verité." Vol. 2: "Le croyant et la verité." 2nd ed. Rome: Pontifical Biblical Institute, 1999.

De Lubac, Henri. "A Witness of Christ in the Church: Hans Urs von Balthasar." In *The Church: Paradox and Mystery*, 103–21. New York: Ecclesia Press, 1969.

George, Francis. *Inculturation and Ecclesial Communion: Culture and Church in the Teaching of Pope John Paul II*. Rome: Urbaniana University Press, 1990.

John of St. Thomas. *Cursus Philosophicus Thomisticus*. Vol. 2, *Naturalis philosophiae*, pt. 1: *De ente mobile in communi*. Turin: Marietti, 1933.

Nedoncelle, Maurice. "L'intersubjectivité humaine est-elle pour saint Augustin une image de la Trinité?" In *Augustinus Magister*, vol. 1, 595–602. Paris: Études Augustiniennes, 1954.

O'Regan, Cyril. *The Anatomy of Misremembering: Von Balthasar's Response to Philosophical Modernity*. Vol. 1, *Hegel*. New York: Crossroad, 2014.

Ratzinger, Joseph. "Christlicher Universalismus: Zum Aufsatzwerk Hans Urs v. Balthasars." *Hochland* 54 (1961/62): 68–76. Reprinted in Walter Kasper, ed., *Logik der Liebe und Herrlichkeit Gottes. Hans Urs von Balthasar im Gespräch*. Ostfildern: Grünewald Verlag, 2006.

———. "Ein Mann der Kirche in der Welt." In *Hans Urs von Balthasar: Gestalt und Werk*, edited by K. Lehmann and W. Kasper, 349–54. Cologne: Communio, 1989.

Schindler, David L. "Creativity as Ultimate: Reflections on Actuality in Whitehead, Aristotle, Aquinas." *International Philosophical Quarterly* 13 (1973): 161–71.

———. "The Embodied Person as Gift and the Cultural Task in America: Status Quaestionis." *Communio* 35 (2008): 397–431, at 417–18 and 421.

———. "Knowing as Synthesis: A Metaphysical Prolegomenon to a Critical Christian Philosophy." PhD diss., Claremont Graduate University, 1976.

———. "Whitehead's Challenge to Thomism on God and Creation: The Metaphysical Issues." *International Philosophical Quarterly* 19 (1979): 285–99.

———. "Whitehead's Inability to Affirm a Universe of Value." *Process Studies* 13 (1983): 117–31.

———. "W. Norris Clarke, SJ. *The Philosophical Approach to God*." *Process Studies* 11 (1981): 40–46.

Schmitz, Kenneth L. *At the Center of the Human Drama: The Philosophical Anthropology of Karol Wojtyła / Pope John Paul II*. Washington, DC: The Catholic University of America Press, 1993.

Waldstein, Michael. "The Analogy of Mission and Obedience: A Central Point in the Relation between *Theologia* and *Oikonomia* in St. Thomas Aquinas's *Commentary on John*." In *Reading John with St. Thomas Aquinas*, edited by M. Dauphinais and M. Levering, 92–112. Washington, DC: The Catholic University of America Press, 2005.

———. *Analogia Verbi:* The Truth of Scripture in Rudolf Bultmann and Raymond Brown." *Letter & Spirit* 6 (2010): 93–140.

———. "Dietrich von Hildebrand and St. Thomas Aquinas on Goodness and Happiness." *Nova et Vetera* (English edition) 1 (2003): 403–64.

———. "Expression and Form: Principles of a Philosophical Aesthetics according to Hans Urs von Balthasar." PhD diss., University of Dallas, 1981.

———. *Glory of the Logos in the Flesh: St. John Paul's Theology of the Body.* Ave Maria, FL: Sapientia Press of Ave Maria University, 2021.

———. "Hans Urs von Balthasar's Theological Aesthetics." *Communio* 11 (1984): 13–27.

———. "Introduction." In John Paul II, *Man and Woman He Created Them: A Theology of the Body*, 1–128. Boston: Pauline Books and Media, 2006.

———. "The Mission of Jesus in John: Probes into the *Apocryphon of John* and the Gospel of John." ThD thesis, Harvard Divinity School, 1989.

Waldstein, Michael, and Frederik Wisse. *The Apocryphon of John: Synopsis of Nag Hammadi Codices II,1 III,1 and IV,1 with BG 8502,2.* Nag Hammadi Studies 33. Leiden: Brill, 1995.

Waldstein, Wolfgang. "Der Weg der Herz Jesu Gemeinschaft." In *Herz Jesu Gemeinschaft: Auswahl aus frühen Schriften*, edited by W. Waldstein, 13–29. Salzburg: Herz Jesu Gemeinschaft, 2006.

Index

Contributors

Michael Altenburger is an independent scholar who received his BA from Loyola University Maryland in 2007 and his MTS and PhD from the University of Notre Dame in 2013 and 2019, respectively. He specializes in modern Catholic theology, political theology, and apocalyptic theology.

Brian Carl is Associate Professor of Philosophy and the Director of Center for Thomistic Studies at the University of St. Thomas in Houston. He received his BA in Classical Humanities (2005) and MA in Philosophy (2008) from Saint Louis University, and his Ph.D. in Philosophy from the Catholic University of America in 2015. His research focuses particularly on the metaphysics and moral psychology of Thomas Aquinas, with a particular emphasis on the divine attributes, and he has published and lectured widely both in these areas as well as natural philosophy, cognitive theory, and philosophy of religion.

Anne Carpenter holds the Danforth Chair of Theological Studies at St. Louis University. She received her BA from the University of Steubenville in 2006. She received her MTS in 2008 and her PhD in 2012, both from Marquette University. She is author of *Nothing Gained Is Eternal: A Theology of Tradition* (Fortress Press, 2022) and *Theo-Poetics: Hans Urs von Balthasar and the Risk of Art and Being* (University of Notre Dame Press, 2015). Prof. Carpenter's work focuses on the intersection between the symbolic worlds of art, especially poetry, and the rigors of philosophy, especially Thomistic metaphysics. Her work can be found in *Religion & Literature*, *Nova et Vetera*, and *Modern Theology*.

Jonathan Martin Ciraulo received his BA from George Fox University in 2010 and his MTS and PhD from the University of Notre Dame in 2012 and 2018, respectively. Having previously taught at Saint Meinrad Seminary, Jonathan joined The Catholic University of America's School of Theology and Religious Studies as an Associate Professor in 2024. He is author of *The Eucharistic Form of God: Hans Urs von Balthasar's Sacramental Theology* (University of Notre Dame Press, 2022) and the translator of Xavier Tilliette, SJ, *The Eucharist in Modern Philosophy* (The Catholic University of America Press, 2023). He is editor of the journal *The New Ressourcement*.

Kristen Drahos is Assistant Professor of Great Texts and Theology at Baylor University. She received her BA (2009), MTS (2011), and PhD (2016) from the University of Notre Dame. Before joining Baylor, she held the Sisters of Saint Francis Endowed Chair of Theology at Briar Cliff University. She also held a postdoctoral teaching fellowship at Carthage College and spent several years there as a visiting Assistant Professor in Religion. Prof. Drahos has specialties in systematic theology and modern and postmodern continental philosophy. Her work explores various cruciform dimensions of Catholic thought, philosophy, and literature. She is particularly interested in questions related to beauty, doubt, death, and suffering. She is also part of a cohort dedicated to emerging ethical questions related to transhumanism, AI, and the body. Her work can be found in *Religion & Literature*, *Scottish Journal of Theology*, *Irish Theological Quarterly*, *Horizons*, the *Church Life Journal* and *Practical Matters*.

Rev. Emmanuel Durand, OP, is Professor of Theology at the University of Fribourg (Switzerland). A specialist in Trinitarian theology and the author of numerous books and articles, his recent publications include *Divine Speech in Human Words: Thomistic Engagements with Scripture* (The Catholic University of America Press, 2023), *Théologie de l'espérance* (Cerf, 2024).

Patrick X. Gardner is Assistant Professor of Philosophy and Religion at Christopher Newport University. He received his BA in Philosophy and Theology from the University of Notre Dame in 2008, his MTS from Duke University in 2010, and his PhD from the University of Notre Dame in 2016. Dr. Gardner specializes in systematic and fundamental theology, philosophy of religion, and Catholic dialogue with atheists, agnostics, and the non-religious. His articles have appeared in the journals *Modern Theology*, *New Blackfriars*, *Religions*, and *The International Journal of Systematic Theology*.

Rev. Bryan Kromholtz, OP, of the Province of the Most Holy Name of Jesus (western USA), is Professor of Theology at the Dominican School of Philosophy & Theology, Berkeley, California, where he is also a member of the Core Doctoral Faculty at the Graduate Theological Union. He is the author of *On the Last Day: The Time of the Resurrection of the Dead according to Thomas Aquinas* (2010), and of articles in *Nova et Vetera* (English), the *Revue Thomiste*, and *Antiphon*.

Rev. Andrew Liaugminas is a priest of the Archdiocese of Chicago. A specialist in the Christology of Thomas Aquinas and Hans Urs von Balthasar, he holds a Doctorate in Sacred Theology from the Gregorian University in Rome (STD, 2017). In 2021, he was appointed an official of the Congregation for the Doctrine of the Faith.

Francesca Murphy is Professor of Theology at the University of Notre Dame. Prior to that, she was Professor of Christian Philosophy at Aberdeen University in Scotland; Lecturer in Christian Studies at St. Martin's College in Lancaster, England; and Lecturer in Religion at the College of St. Mark & St. John in Plymouth, England. Prof. Murphy is the author of numerous books, including *Christ the Form of Beauty* (T & T Clark), *God is Not a Story* (OUP) and a theological commentary on *I Samuel* (Brazos). She is currently editing a series for Bloomsbury Academic called Illuminating Modernity.

Roger Nutt (STL, STD) is the Provost of Ave Maria University, where he also serves as a Professor of Theology and co-director of the Aquinas Center for Theological Renewal. His research focuses on Christology and Sacramental Theology, and especially the Theology of St. Thomas Aquinas. These interests are reflected in the three books that he has authored: *Thomas Aquinas' 'De Unione Verbi Incarnati'* (Peeters Publishers, 2015); *General Principles of Sacramental Theology* (The Catholic University of America Press, 2017); and *To Die is Gain: A Theological (re-)Introduction to the Sacrament of Anointing of the Sick for Clergy, Laity, Caregivers, and Everyone Else* (Emmaus Academic, 2022). His articles and book chapters have appeared in many publications such as *Nova et Vetera, Gregorianum, Louvain Studies, The Thomist, Harvard Theological Review, Angelicum, Antiphon: A Journal of Liturgical Renewal,* and the *Oxford Handbook of the Reception of Aquinas.* Nutt has also co-edited numerous volumes, including: *Thomas Aquinas as Spiritual Teacher* (Sapientia Press of Ave Maria University, 2023); *Thomas Aquinas and the Crisis of Christology* (Sapientia Press of Ave Maria University, 2021); *Aquinas the Biblical Theologian* (Emmaus Academic, 2021); *Thomas Aquinas and the Greek Fathers* (Sapientia Press of Ave Maria University, 2019); and *Thomism and Predestination: Principles and Disputations* (Sapientia Press of Ave Maria University, 2016).

Michael J. Rubin earned his master's and doctoral degrees in philosophy at The Catholic University of America, where Monsignor John F. Wippel directed his dissertation on whether beauty is a distinct transcendental for St. Thomas Aquinas. His research on beauty and the transcendentals has won multiple awards, including the Karen Laub-Novak Doctoral Fellowship for Studies in Being, Truth, and Beauty, First Place at the 2017 Veritas et Amor Contest in Aquino, Italy, and the Karen Chan Young Scholar Award at the 2020 Meeting of the American Catholic Philosophical Association. Rubin has taught at The Catholic University of America, the University of Mary Washington, and Thomas Aquinas College, and currently teaches Philosophy at Christendom College in Front Royal, Virginia.

Michele M. Schumacher is a wife and mother of four adult children, a doctor in sacred theology (STD), and a private docent (habil.) at the University of Fribourg (Switzerland). In addition to numerous articles and book chapters on feminism, sexual ethics, marriage, spirituality, she is the author of *A Trinitarian Anthropology: Adrienne von Speyr and Hans Urs von Balthasar in Dialogue with St. Thomas Aquinas* (The Catholic University of America Press, 2014); *Metaphysics and Gender: The Normative Art of Nature and Its Human Imitations* (Emmaus Academic, 2023; also coming out in French with Editions Salvator); and *God Acting in Man: Founding Human Freedom in Aquinas's Natural Desire to See God Doctrine* (forthcoming). She is also the editor and contributing author of *Women in Christ: Towards a New Feminism* (Cambridge, UK / Grand Rapids, MI: Eerdmans, 2004).

Jacob W. Wood is Associate Professor of Theology and Director of Master of Theological Science/Master of Art in Theological Studies at Franciscan University of Steubenville, and the Chairman of the Board of the Academy of Catholic Theology. He holds a Masters of Theology (Honours) from the University of Saint Andrews (2007), and a PhD in Systematic Theology from The Catholic University of America (2014). A specialist in the theological anthropology of Thomas Aquinas as well as Aquinas's context and reception, Wood has published widely on Aquinas's understanding of natural desire, sin and grace, as well as knowledge and faith. His most recent book is *To Stir a Restless Heart: Thomas Aquinas and Henri de Lubac on Nature, Grace, and the Desire for God* (The Catholic University of America Press, paperback 2021).